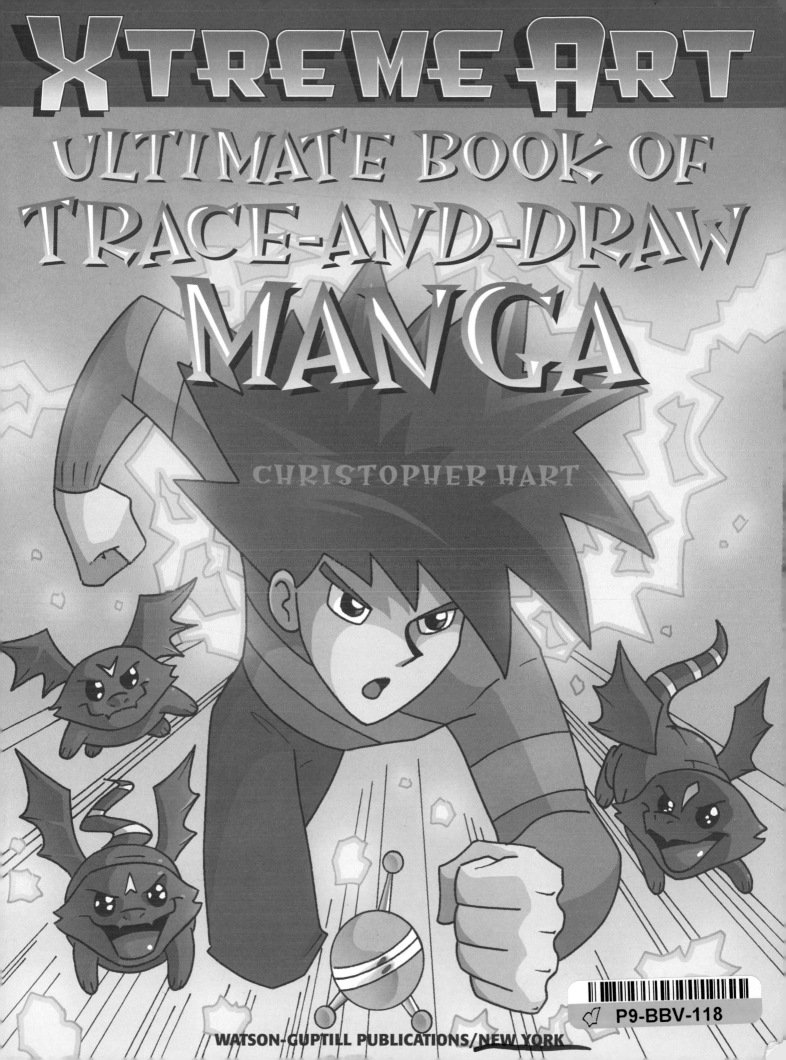

XTREME ART
ULTIMATE BOOK OF TRACE-AND-DRAW MANGA

CHRISTOPHER HART

P9-BBV-118

WATSON-GUPTILL PUBLICATIONS/NEW YORK

My thanks go to all of the people who helped make this book possible:
Julie Mazur, Bob Ferro, Hector Campbell, and Bob Fillie.

I'd also like to thank Francesca Hart for suggesting great names for the characters,
and Isabella Hart, for contributing her artistic judgment.

Senior Acquisitions Editor: Julie Mazur
Production Editor: Sarah McDonough
Designer: Bob Fillie
Production Manager: Alyn Evans
Text set in 12-pt Formata Regular

All drawings by Christopher Hart
Cover art by Christopher Hart

This collection was previously published in separate volumes as:
Xtreme Art Draw Manga! (978-0-8230-0369-3), Copyright © 2003 by Christopher Hart
Xtreme Art Draw Manga Chibi! (978-0-8230-0368-6),
Copyright ©2004 by Christopher Hart
Xtreme Art Draw Manga Monsters! (978-0-8230-0372-3),
Copyright ©2005 by Star Fire, LLC.

The 2009 edition is published by Watson-Guptill Publications,
an imprint of the Crown Publishing Group, a division of Random House, Inc., New York.
www.crownpublishing.com
www.watsonguptill.com

Library of Congress Catalogue-in-Publication Data
The CIP data for this title may be obtained from the Library of Congress
Library of Congress Card Number: 2008048893

ISBN: 978-0-8230-9806-4

Printed in China

First printing, 2009

1 2 3 4 5 6 7 8 9 / 17 16 15 14 13 12 11 10 09

CONTENTS

INTRODUCTION

I've written many books that teach young artists, like yourself, how to draw. But I am especially proud of this series, *Xtreme Art*. These books use a special technique that will help you draw all kinds of cool characters quickly and easily!

Each drawing is broken down into four easy steps. Start by tracing or drawing step 1. Then just add the new lines in steps 2, 3, and 4. Before you know it, you'll have drawn characters that would normally take much longer to create!

You'll find all kinds of characters to draw, starting with easier ones and getting a little harder as you go. A few of the drawings have backgrounds added (just for fun!). You can either draw or trace them if you like.

Manga, the Japanese word for "comics," is an extremely popular style of cartooning, known for the huge eyes of its characters. Manga began in Japan, but it has become a craze that has swept the globe. We'll start by drawing the many different kinds of people you'll find in manga. They are supercool and sometimes even have superpowers.

In the second section, we'll work on Chibi-style characters. They are short, round, hyper-adorable, and irresistably squeezable. You'll find a huge variety of fun chibi characters to draw in this book. They include wizards, ballerinas, sword fighters, and fairies. Everyone loves chibis!

The manga monsters have invaded this book's third section and have lots of fans, too. The fun part about drawing manga monsters is that each one is unique. Some are fluffy, some are clawed, and some are made out of metal, but no manga monster can help being extraordinarily cute! They are usually drawn as friends of human characters, but they can also be enemies. So be careful!

Are you ready to make the world of manga leap off the page? Grab a pencil and some paper, and let's get started!

Tips for Using This Book

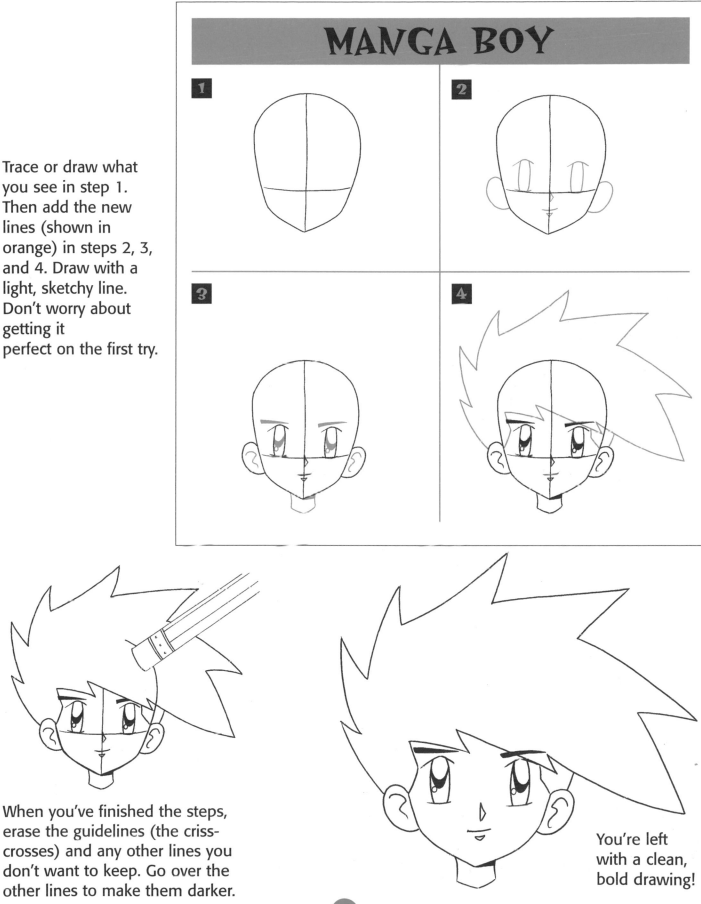

Trace or draw what you see in step 1. Then add the new lines (shown in orange) in steps 2, 3, and 4. Draw with a light, sketchy line. Don't worry about getting it perfect on the first try.

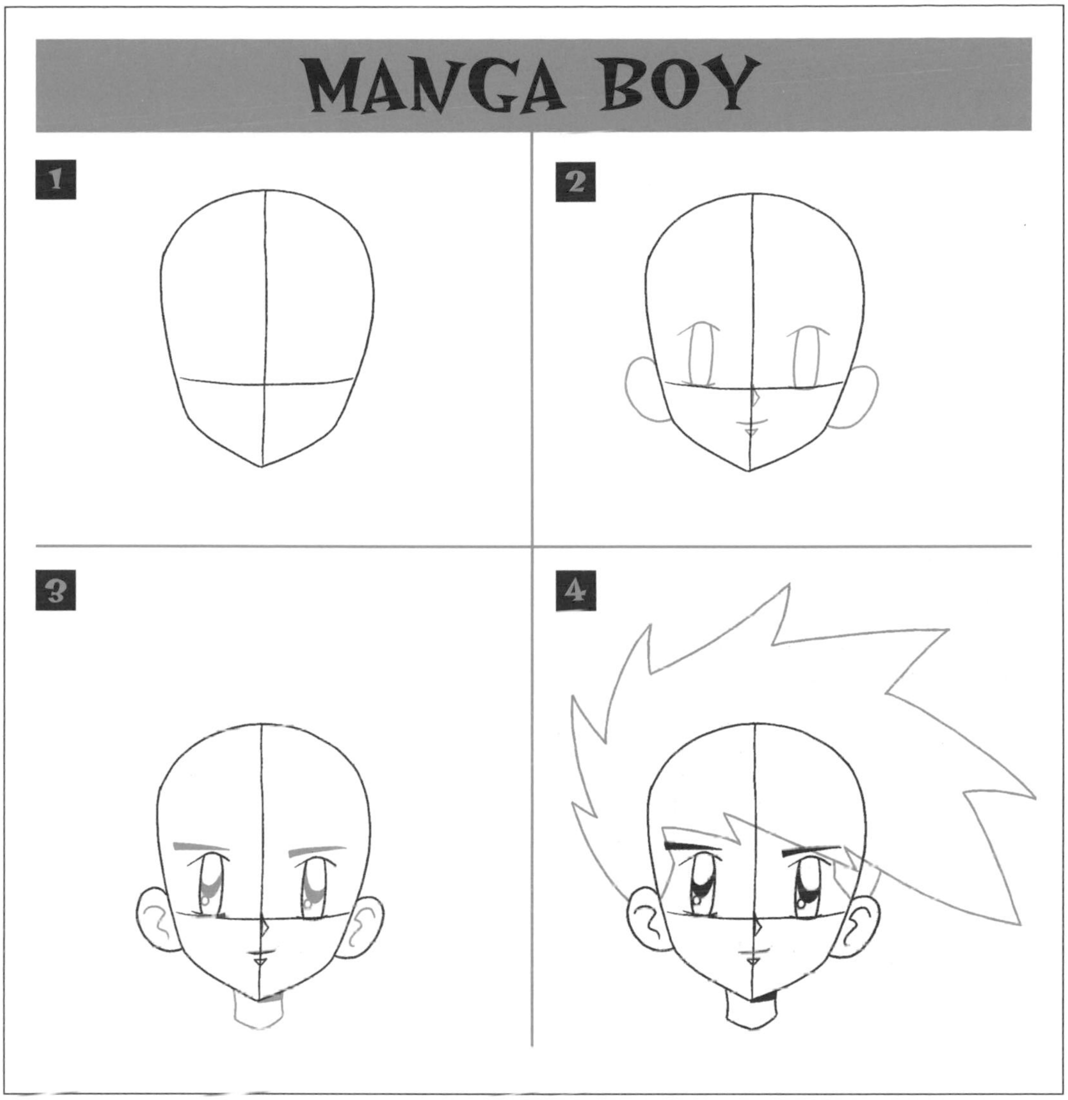
MANGA BOY
1
2
3
4

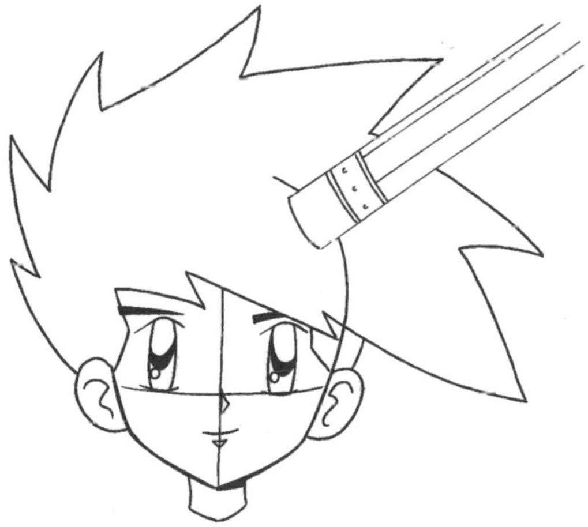

When you've finished the steps, erase the guidelines (the criss-crosses) and any other lines you don't want to keep. Go over the other lines to make them darker.

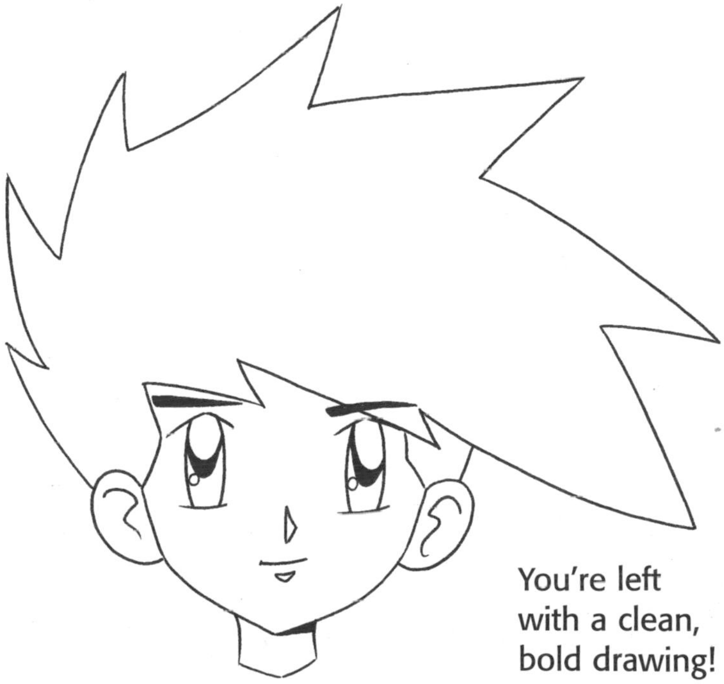

You're left with a clean, bold drawing!

PART 1
DRAW MANGA!

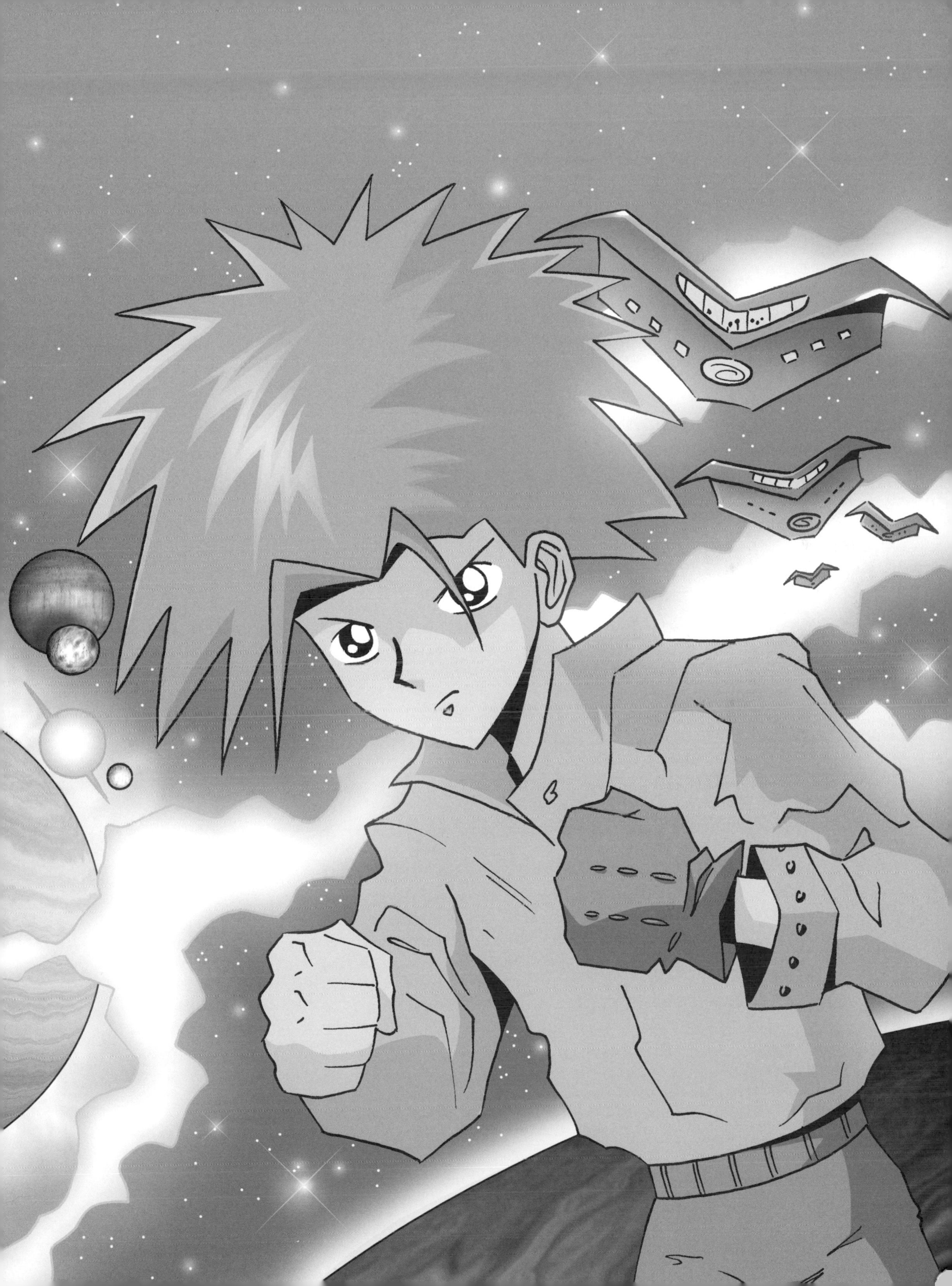

THE BASICS

Let's start by going over some basics.

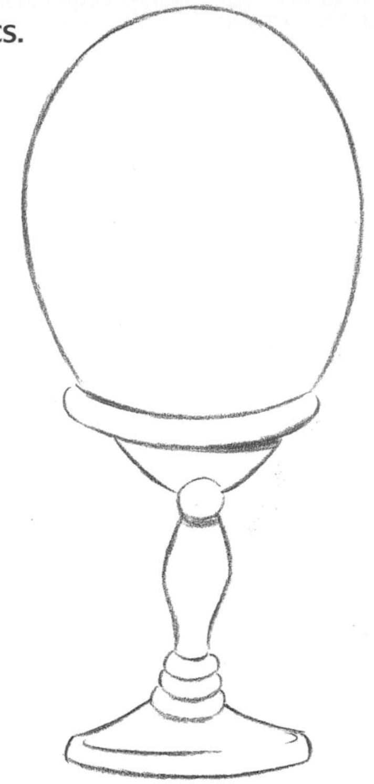

You might think of the head as a circle, but it's really more of an *egg shape.* The narrow end is at the bottom, where your chin is.

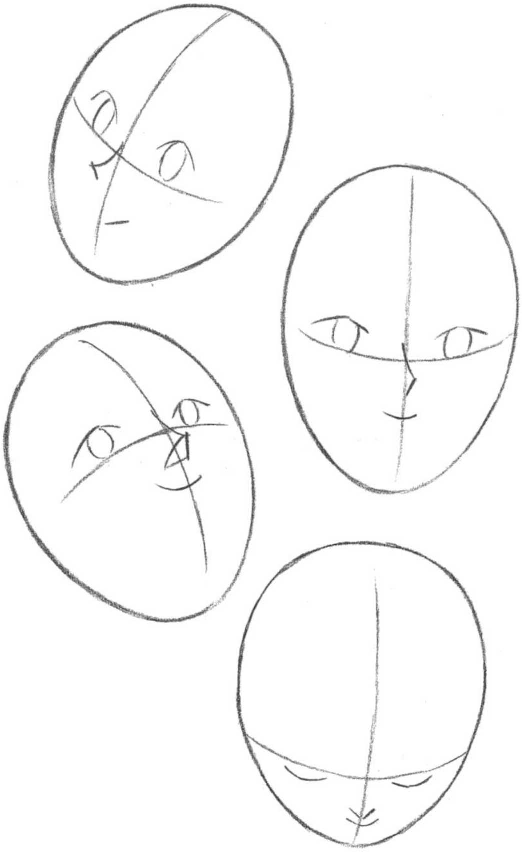

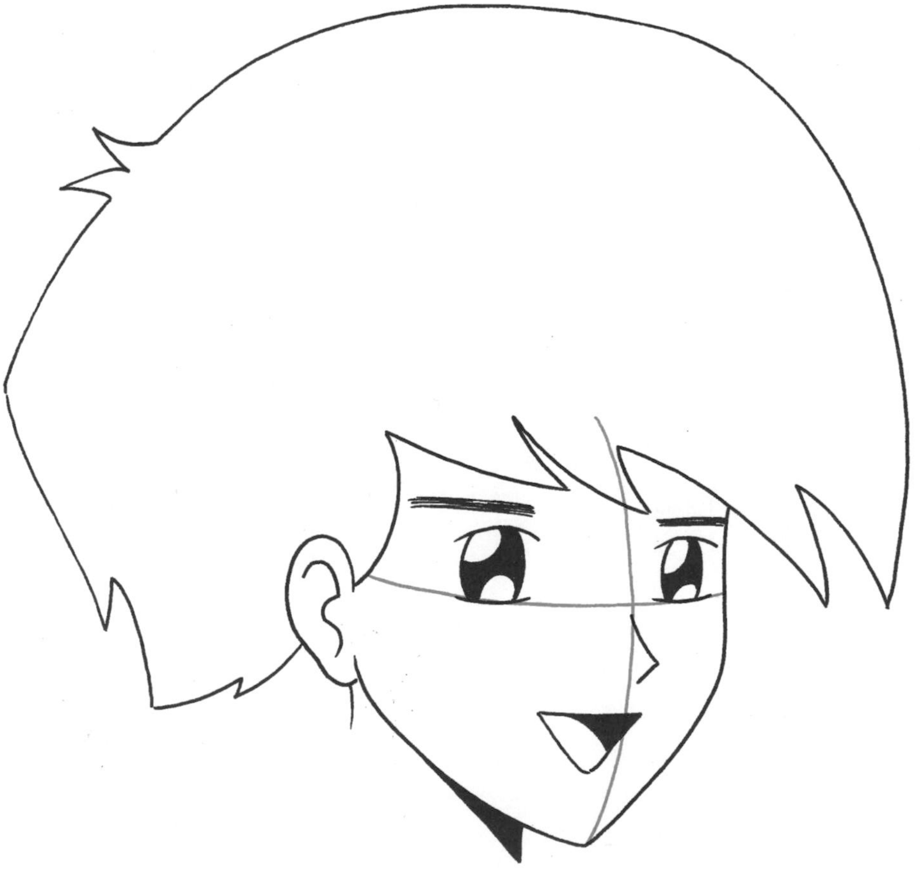

When artists draw faces, they use crisscross lines, like the ones you see here. These are called *guidelines.* Why do artists use guidelines? Well, there are two reasons. First, they show where to place the eyes and the nose. Second, they show which way the head is facing.

Manga characters are famous for their huge, shiny eyes. Now you're going to learn the secret to drawing them. It takes practice, but it's not hard to do. The first thing to remember is that the *shape* of the eyes changes with the *age* of the character.

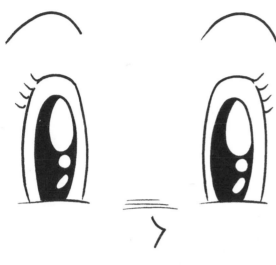

Young characters have very tall eyes.

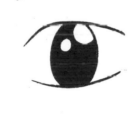

Teenagers' eyes are big, but not as tall as kids' eyes.

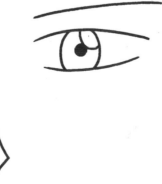

Adults' eyes are the narrowest.

The Basic Shape of Each Eye

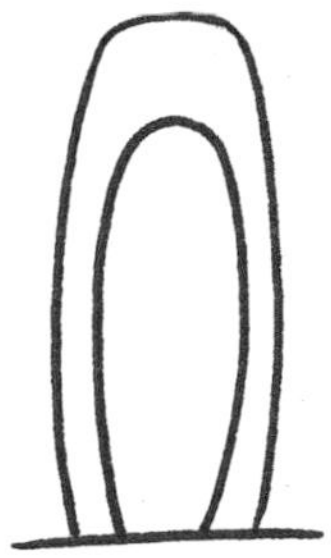

KID

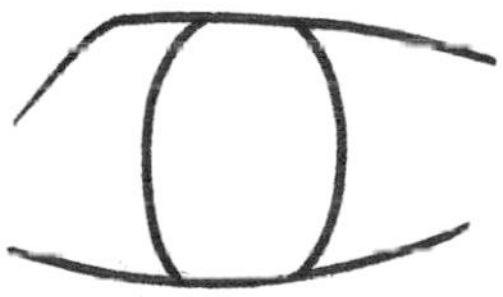

TEENAGER

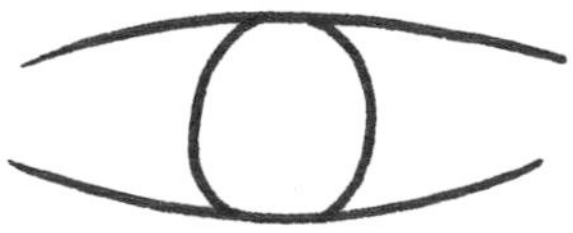

ADULT

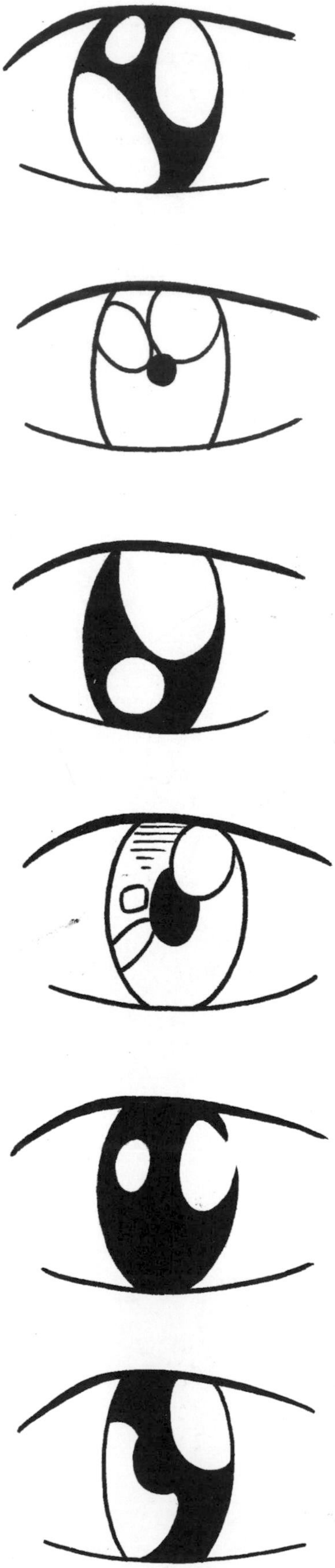

Here are some popular kinds of manga-style eyes. You can trace or draw these, or make up some of your own!

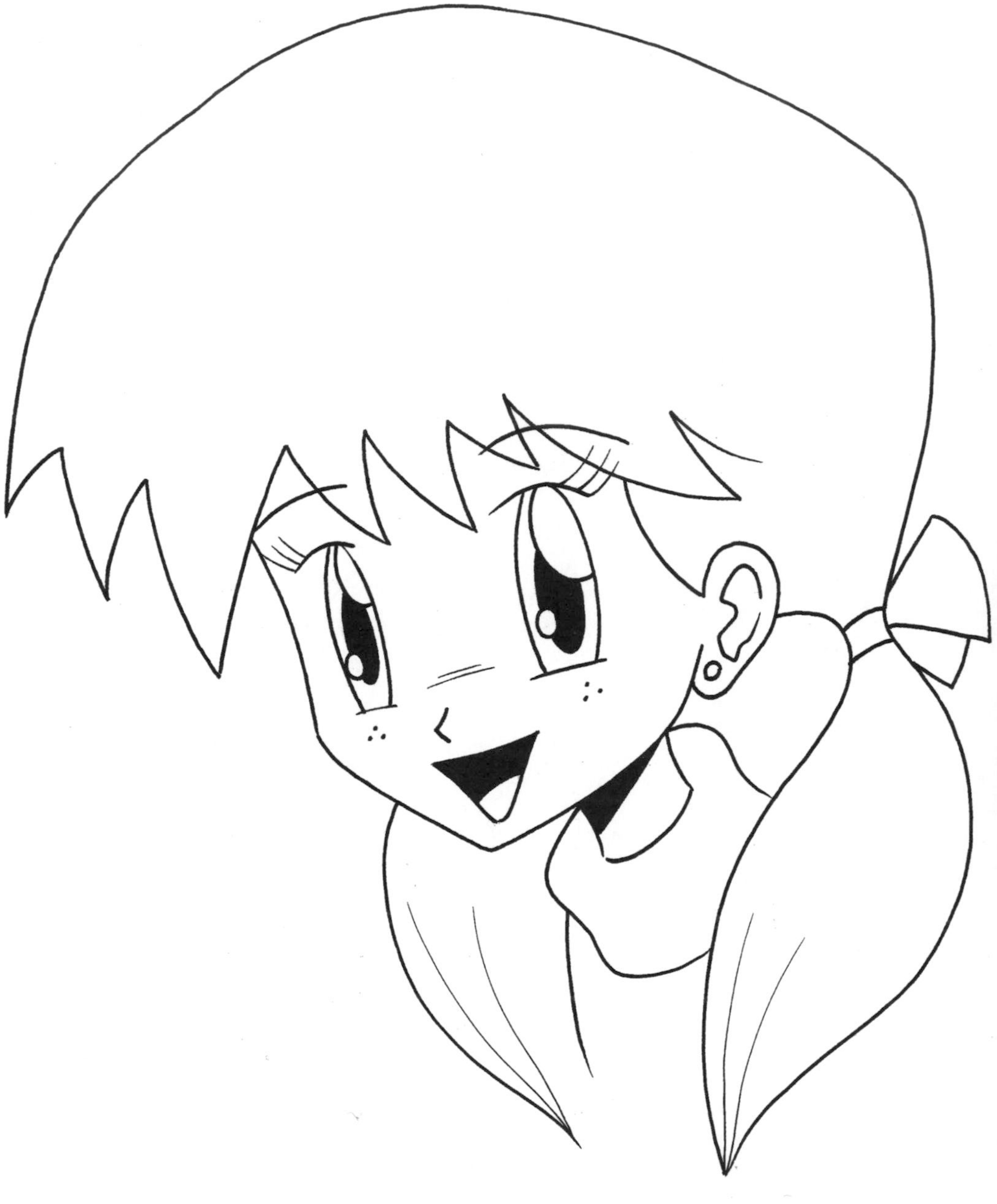

When you draw a character from the front, both eyes have the same shape. But when the head starts to turn, the *far eye* becomes narrower. The more the head turns, the *narrower* it gets.

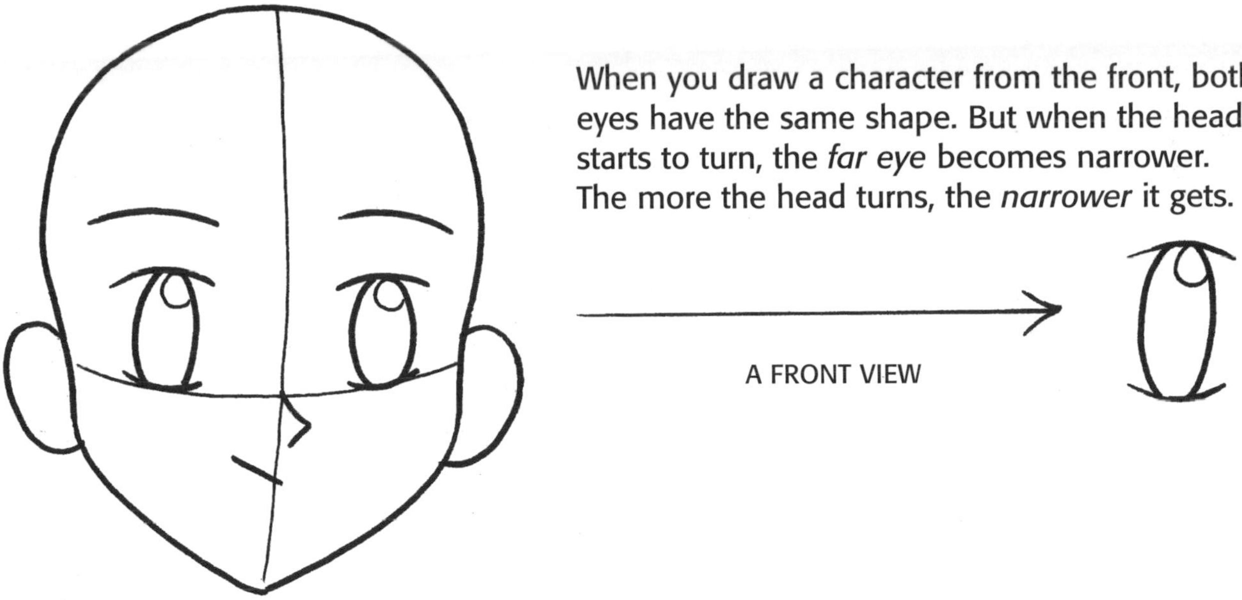
A FRONT VIEW

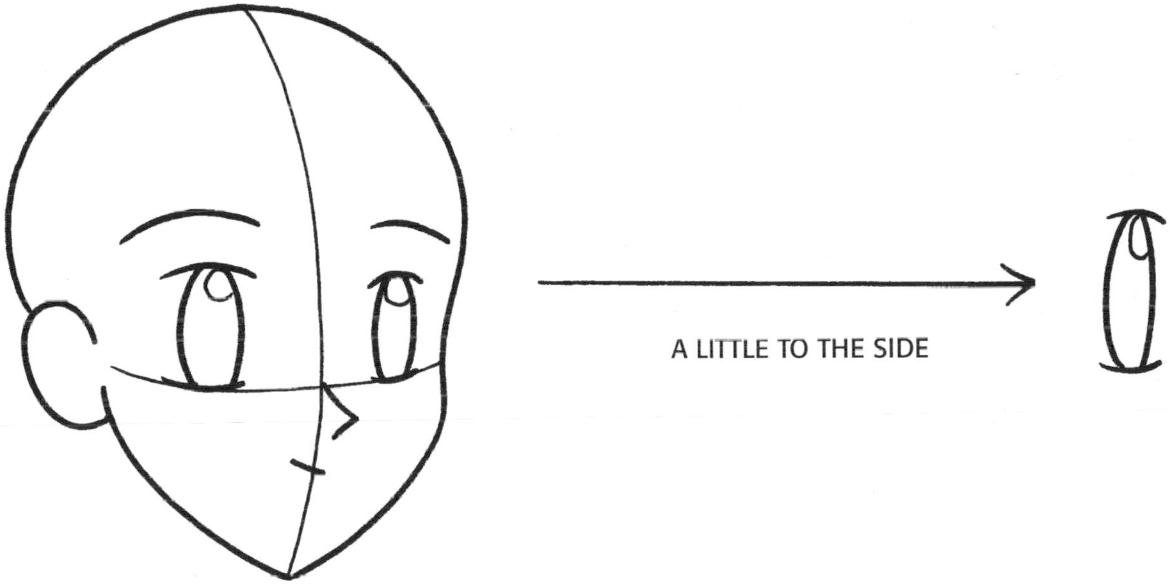
A LITTLE TO THE SIDE

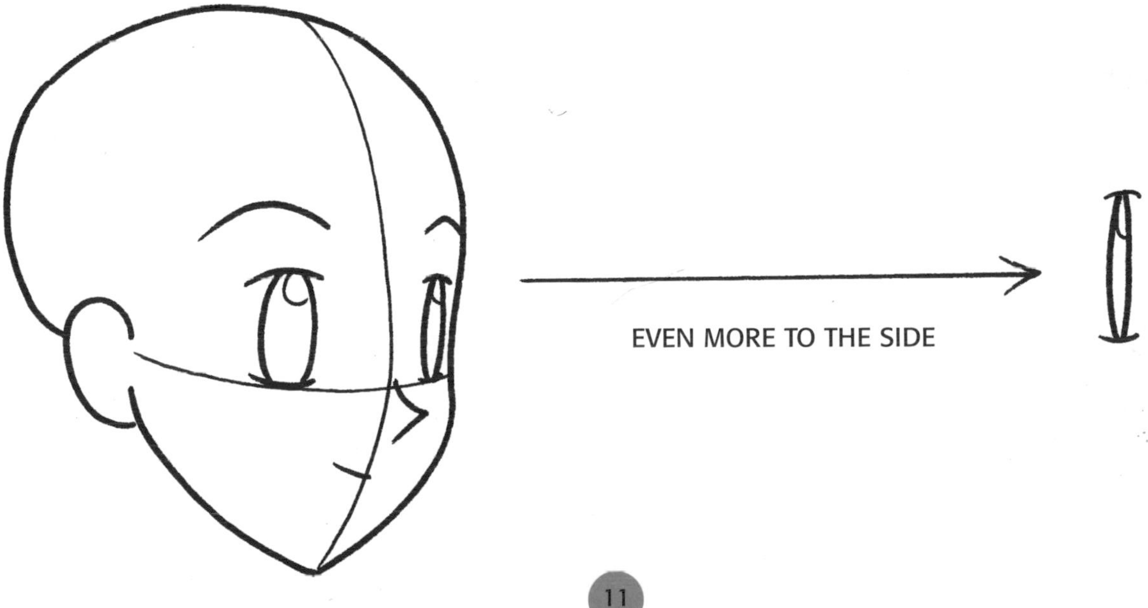
EVEN MORE TO THE SIDE

Hands can be hard to draw, so here are some tips to help you. Let's start with the back of the hand.

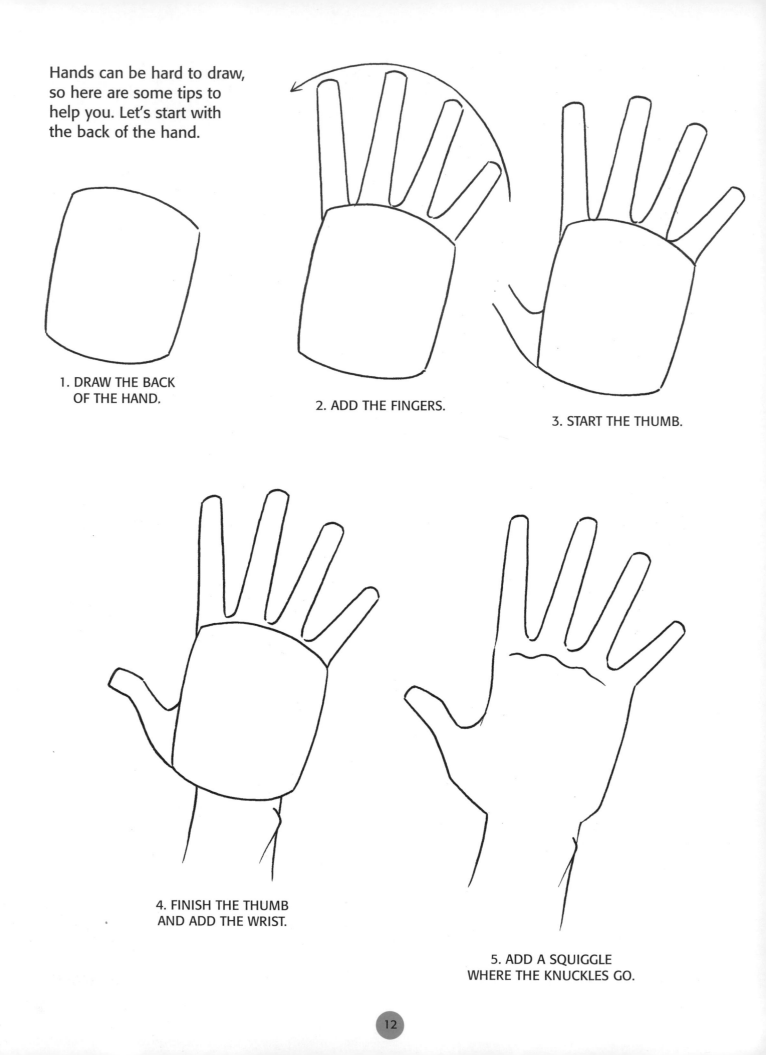

1. DRAW THE BACK OF THE HAND.

2. ADD THE FINGERS.

3. START THE THUMB.

4. FINISH THE THUMB AND ADD THE WRIST.

5. ADD A SQUIGGLE WHERE THE KNUCKLES GO.

Now let's do the front of the hand.

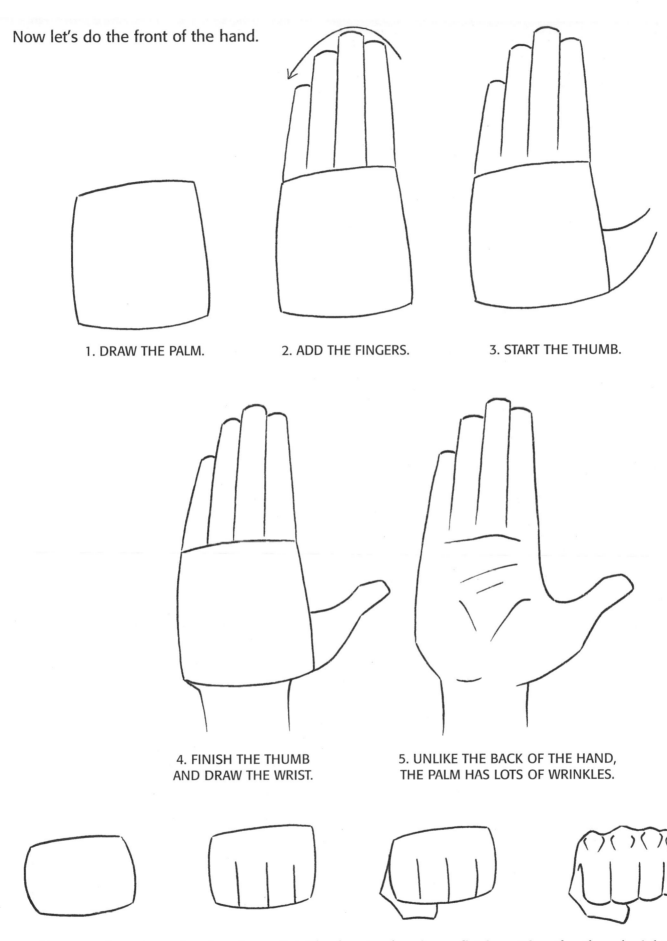

1. DRAW THE PALM.

2. ADD THE FINGERS.

3. START THE THUMB.

4. FINISH THE THUMB
AND DRAW THE WRIST.

5. UNLIKE THE BACK OF THE HAND,
THE PALM HAS LOTS OF WRINKLES.

Here are four steps for drawing a fist. The key to drawing a fist is getting the thumb right.

Hairstyles are very important in manga. They give each character a unique look. See how the same face looks different, just by changing the hairstyle? Remember, you don't have to copy my drawings exactly. It's perfectly okay to change my characters by making up your own manga hairstyles.

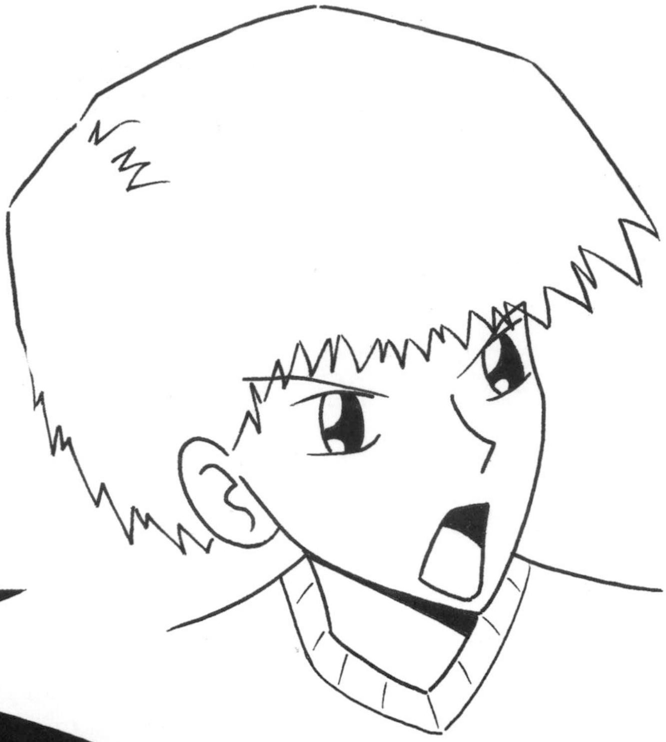

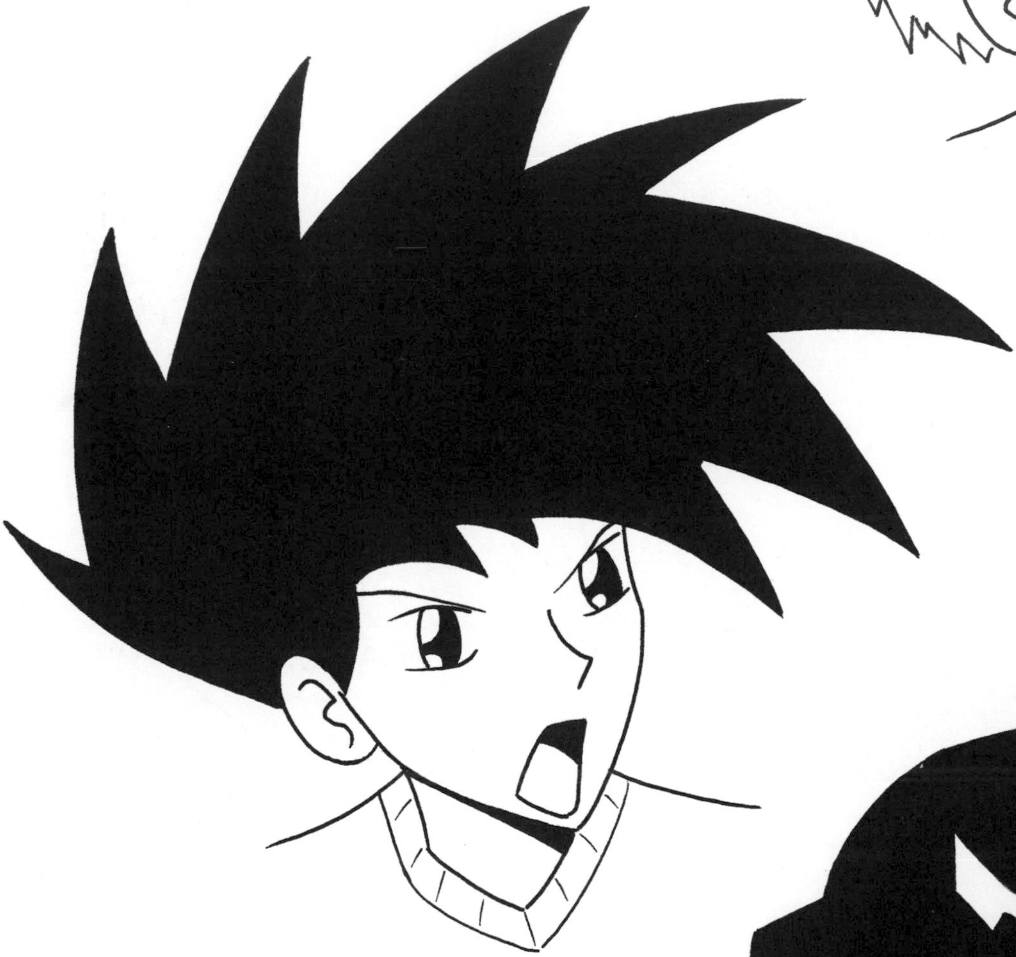

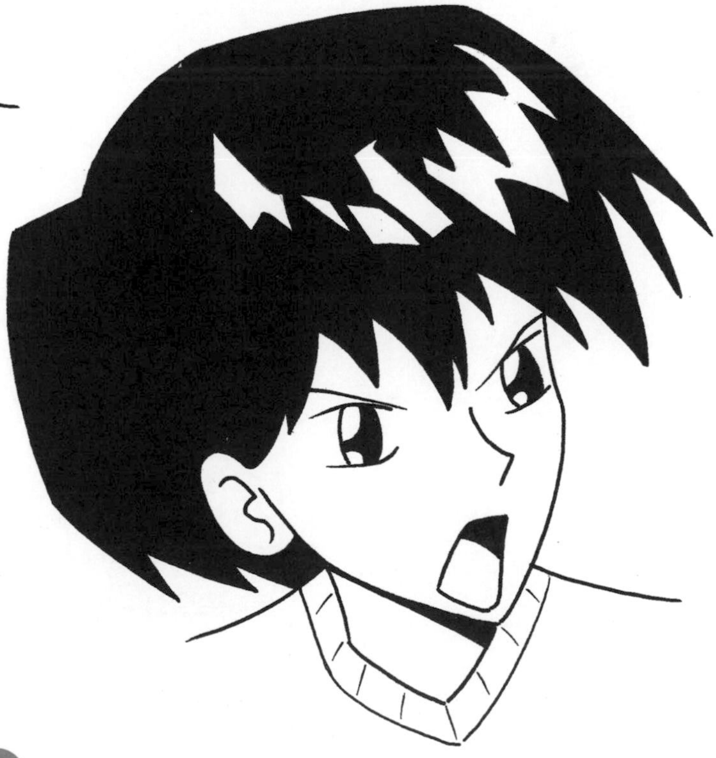

Here are a few more tips to help you. Take a look, then turn the page and start drawing!

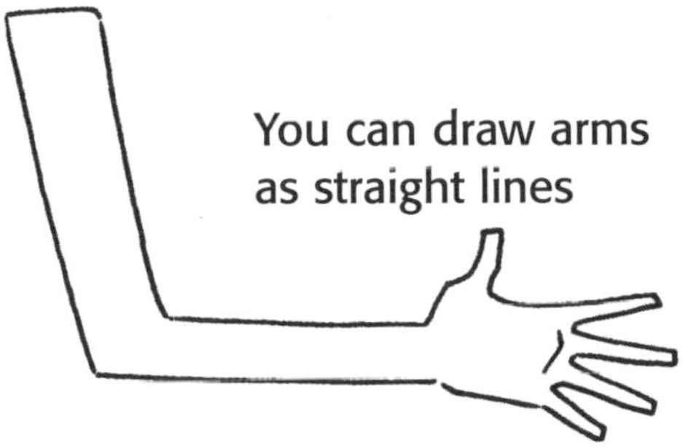

You can draw arms as straight lines

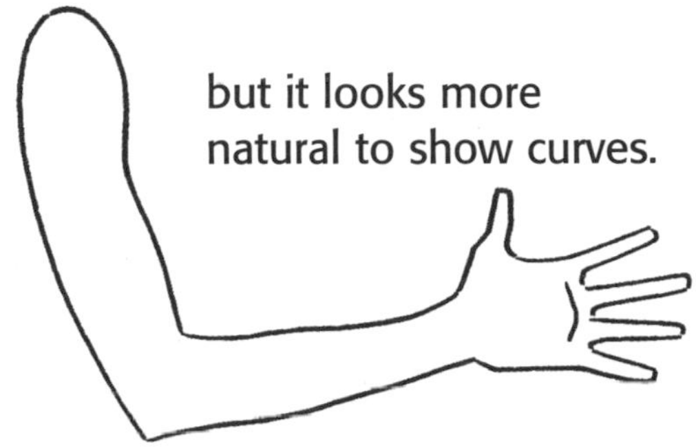

but it looks more natural to show curves.

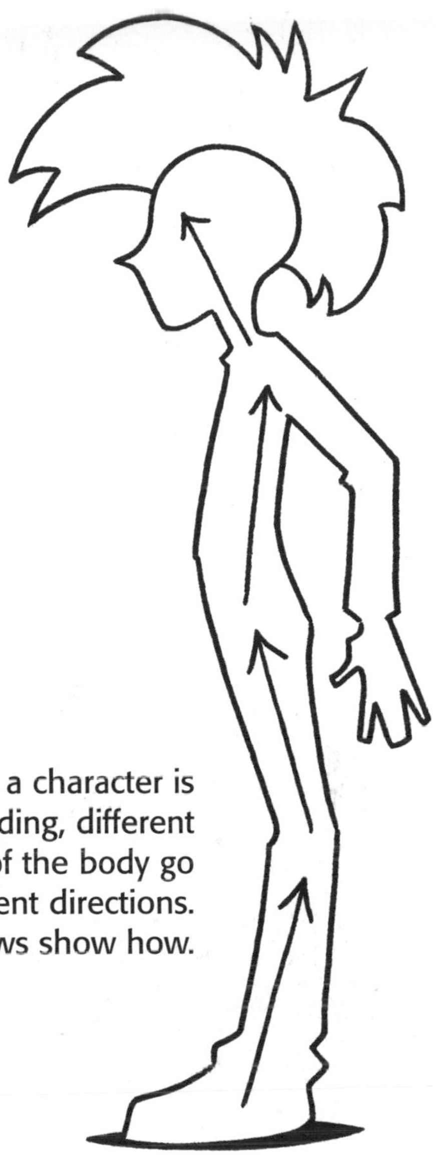

When a character is standing, different parts of the body go in different directions. These arrows show how.

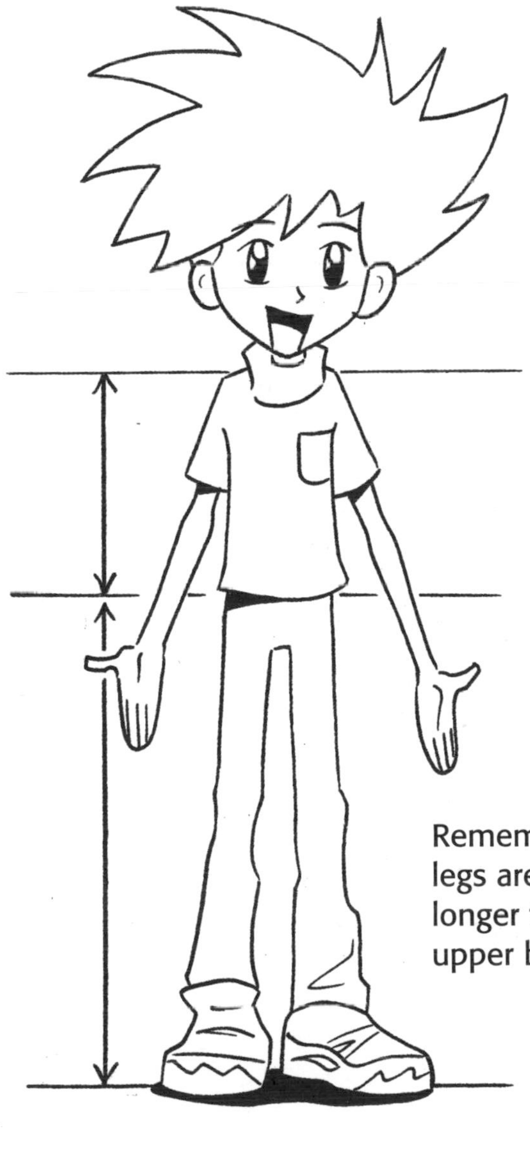

Remember that legs are *always* longer than the upper body.

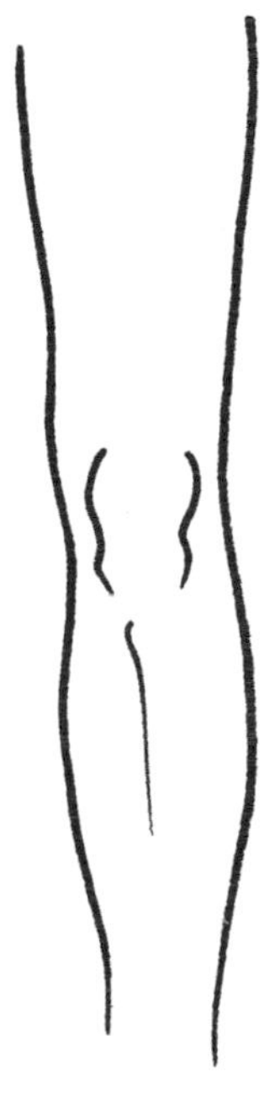

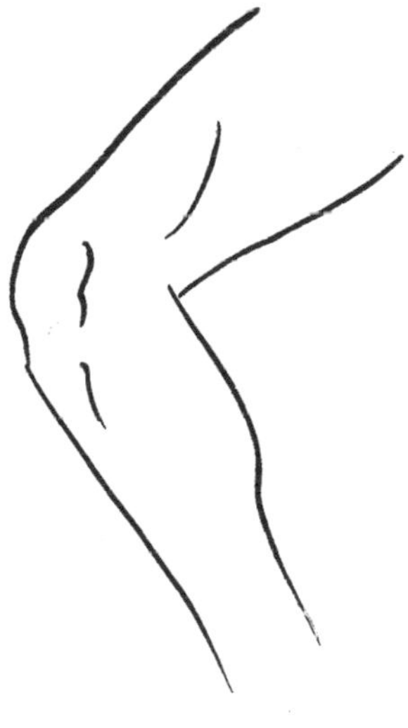

Knees can be tough to draw. Here are two examples to help you.

POPULAR BOY

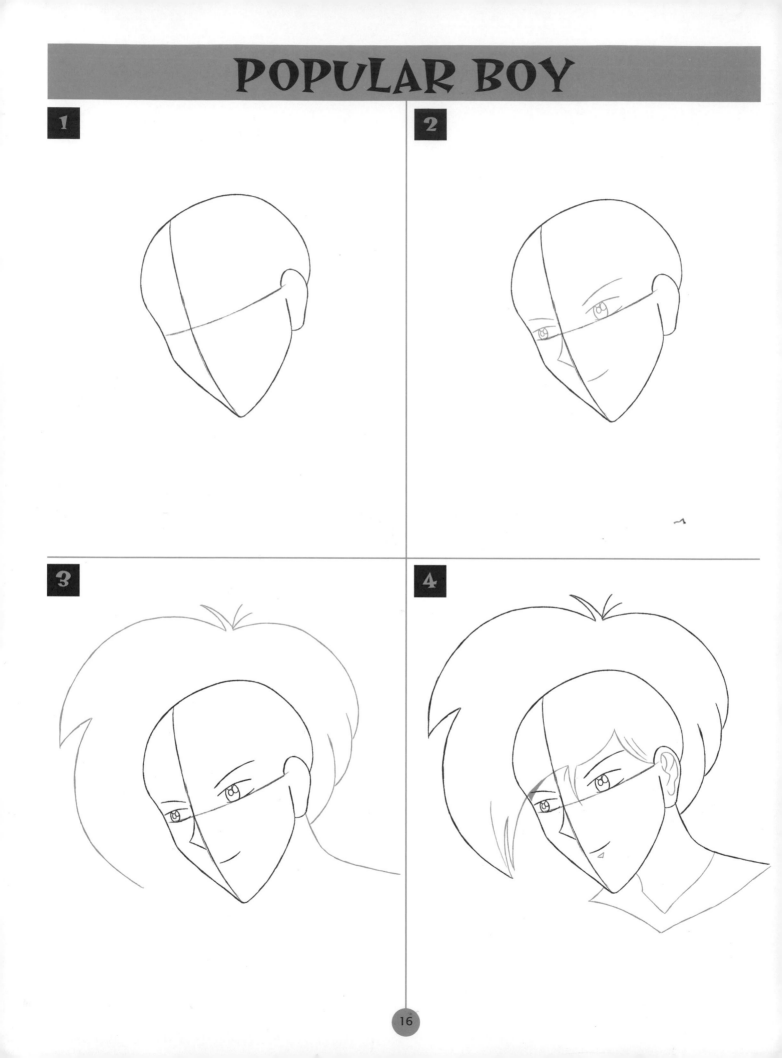

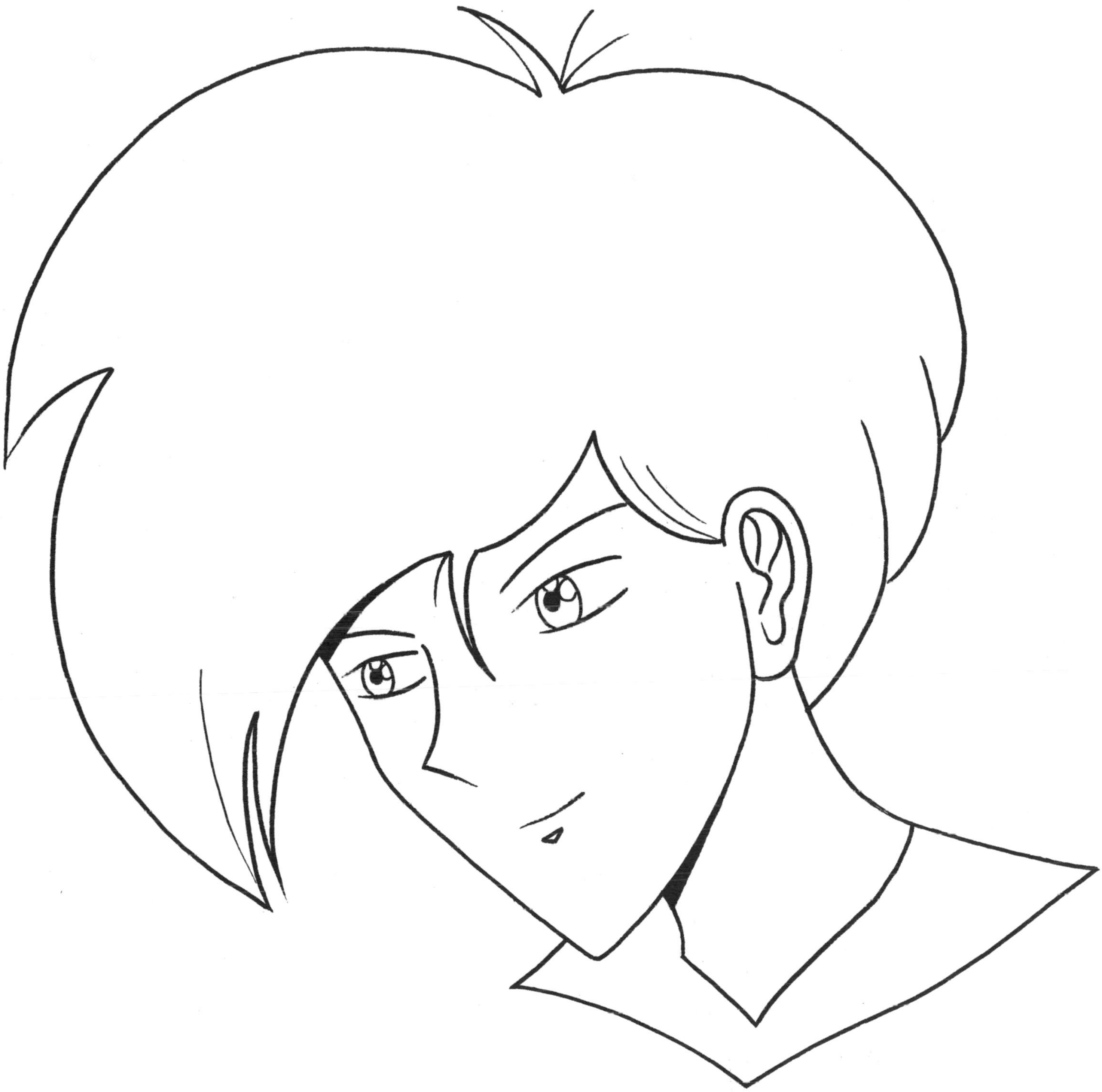

SCHOOLGIRL

1

2

3

4

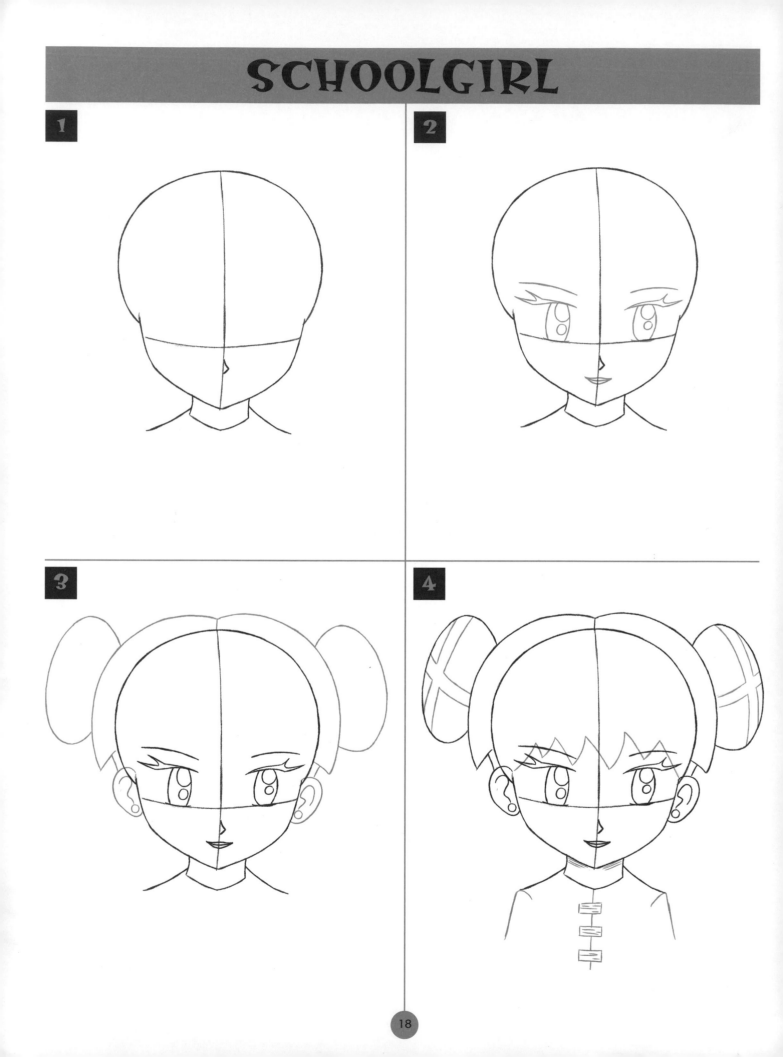

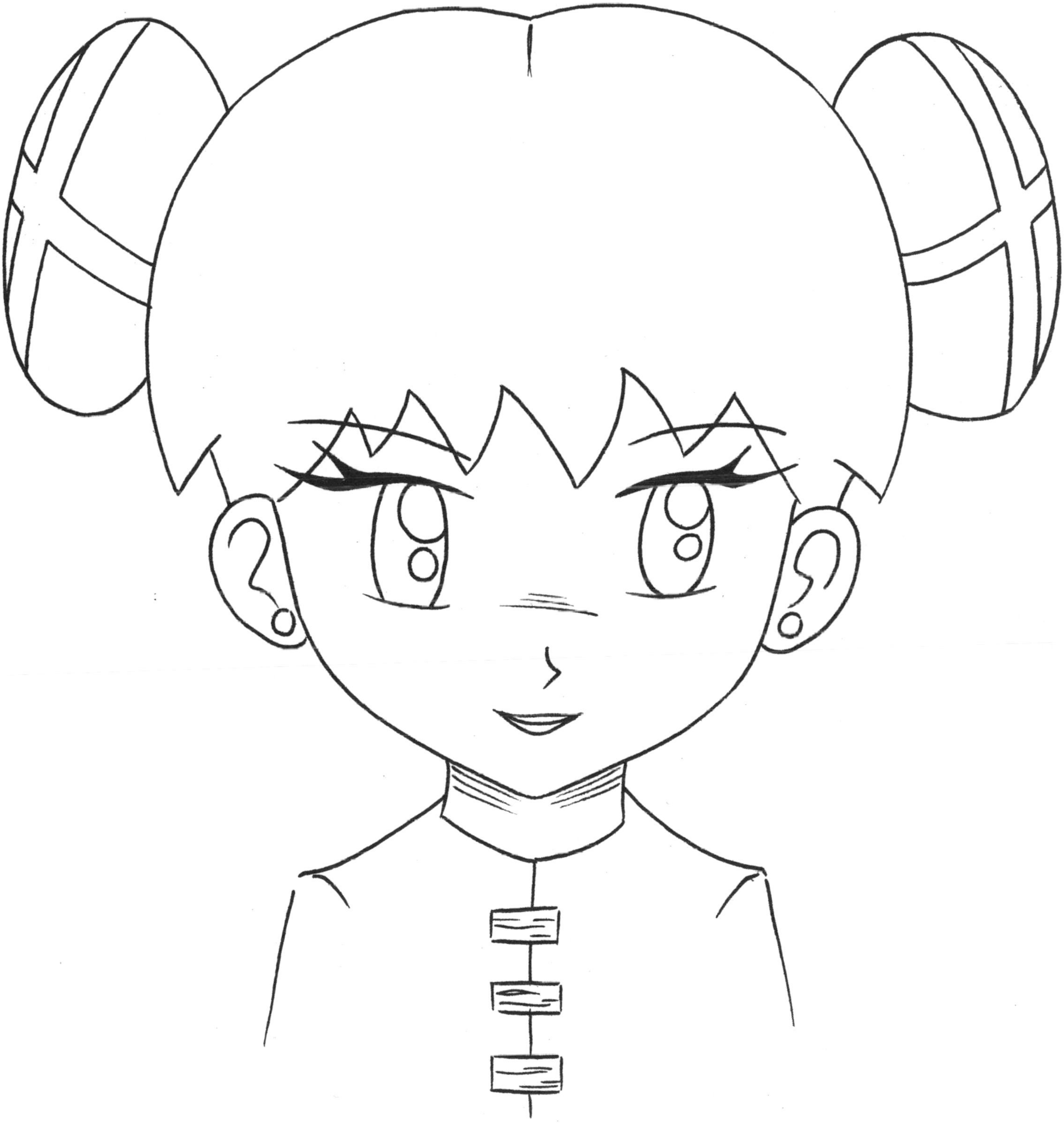

STARSHIP COMMANDER

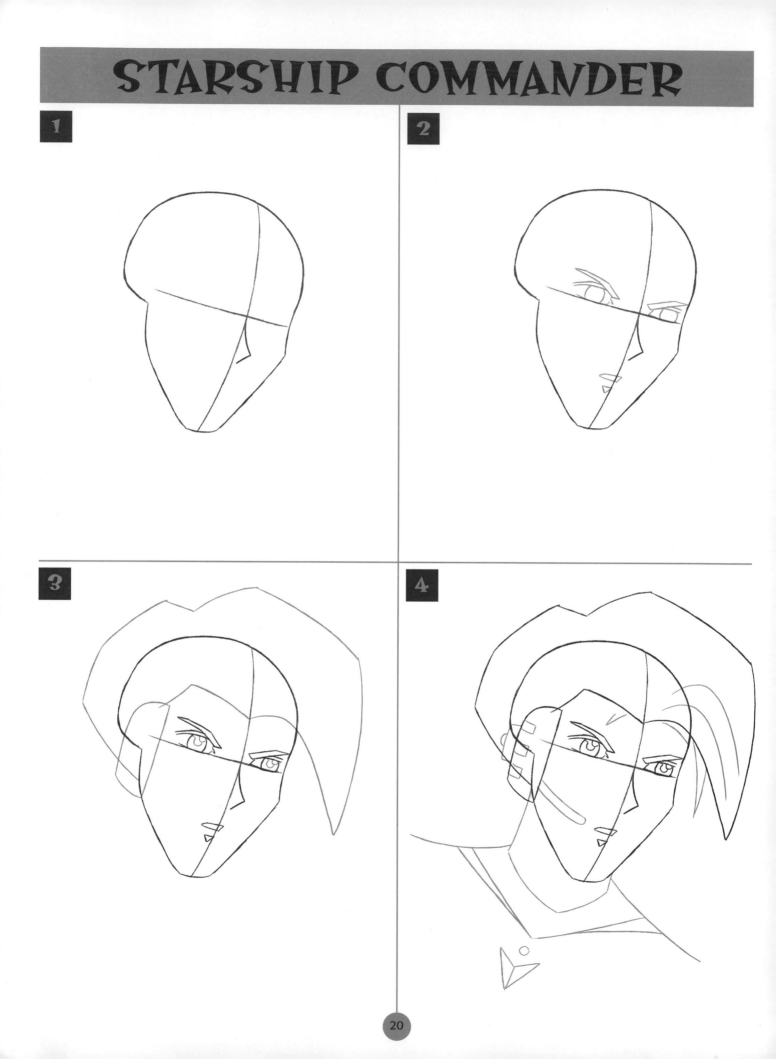

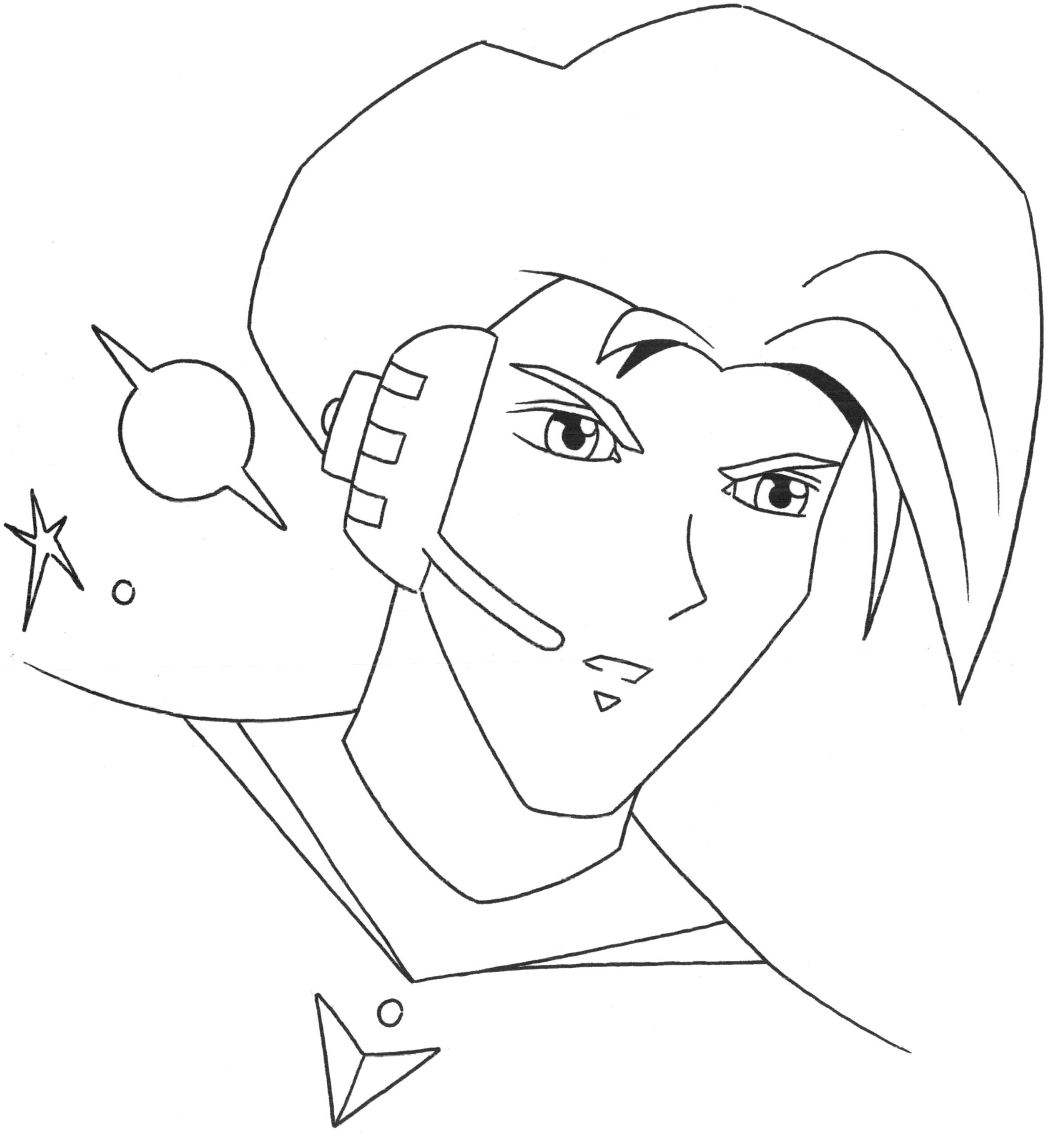

FASHION TEEN

1

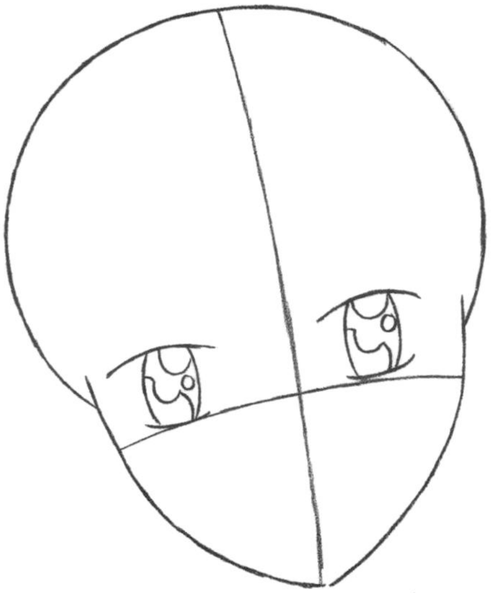

2

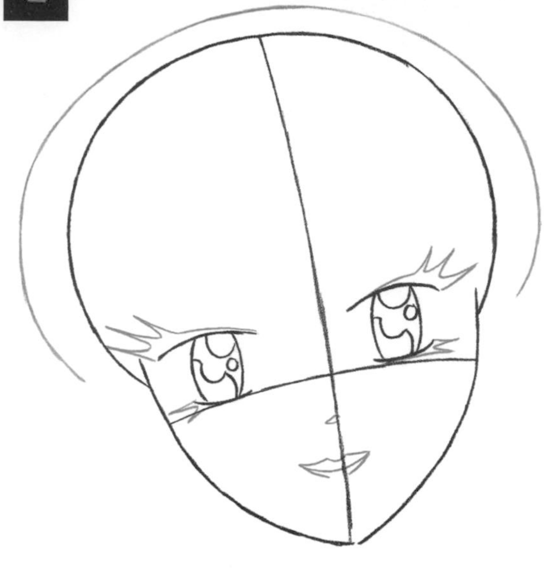

3

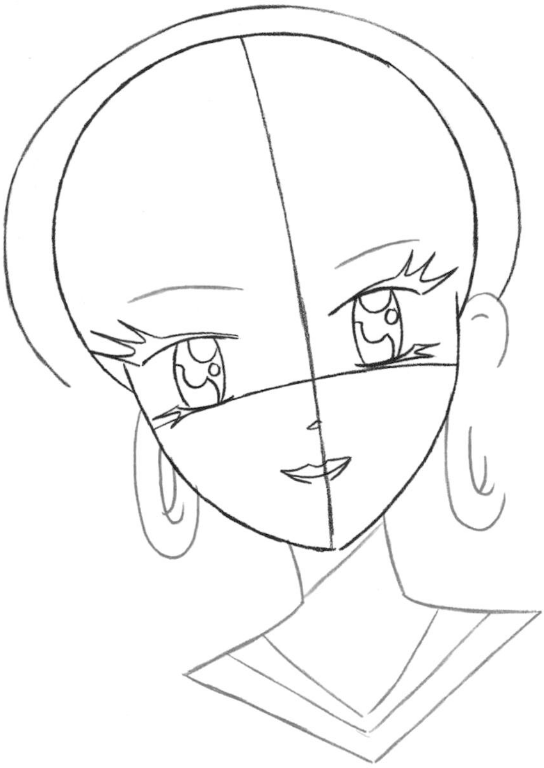

4

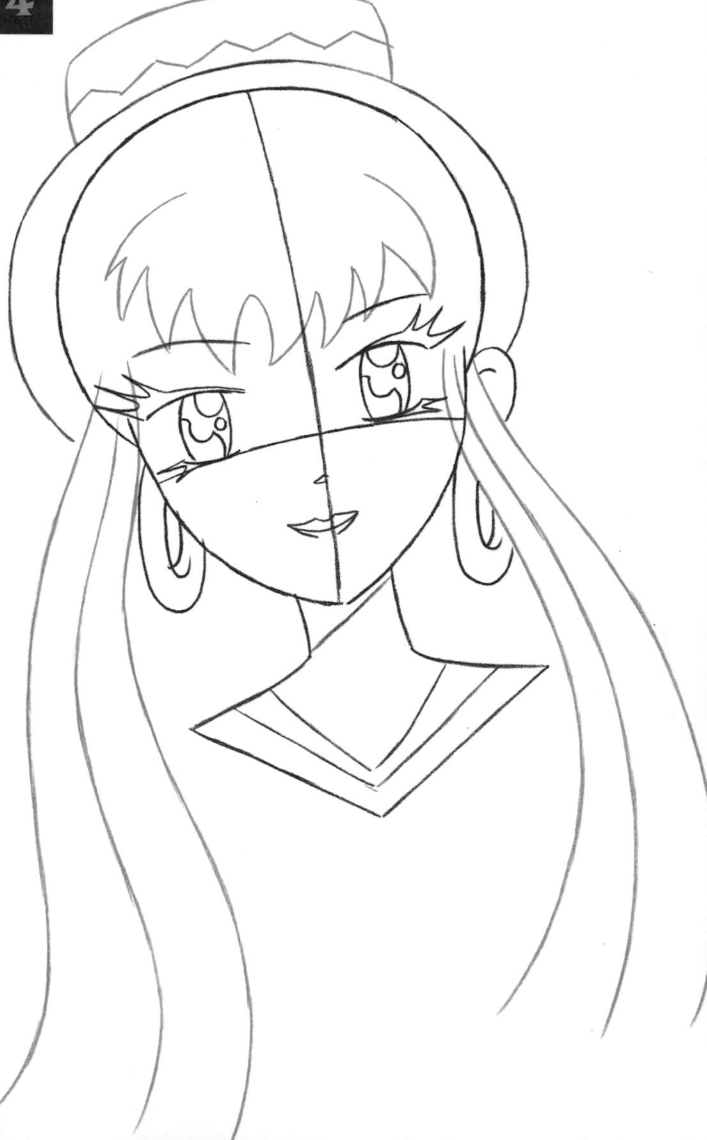

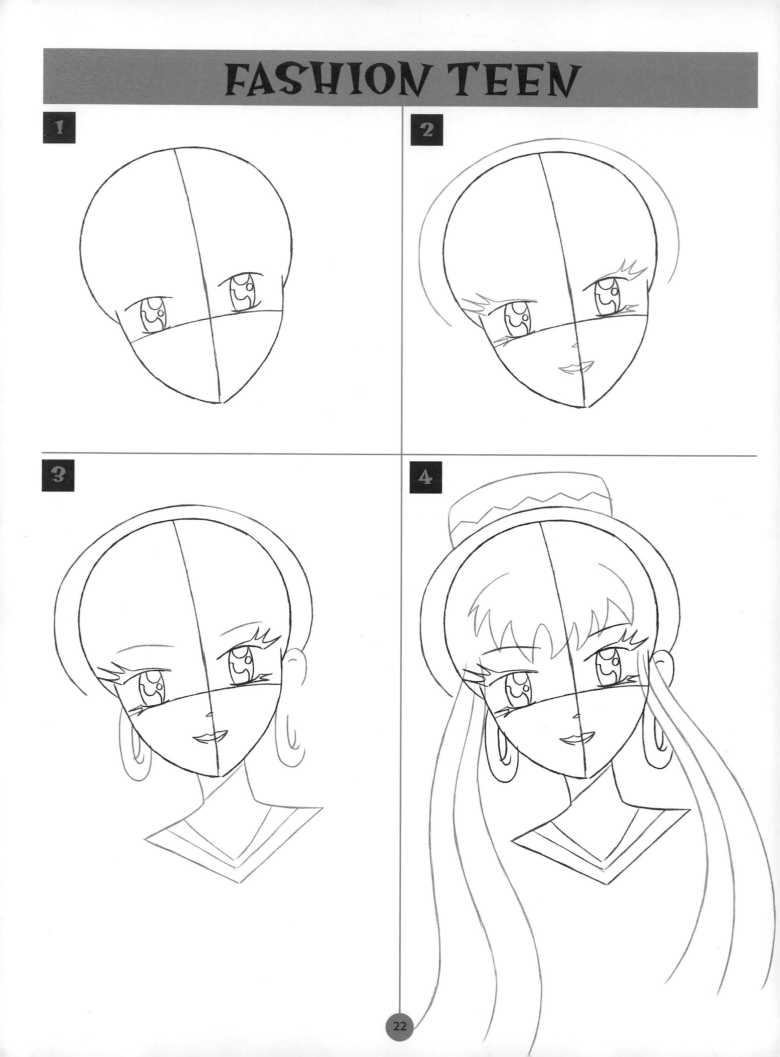

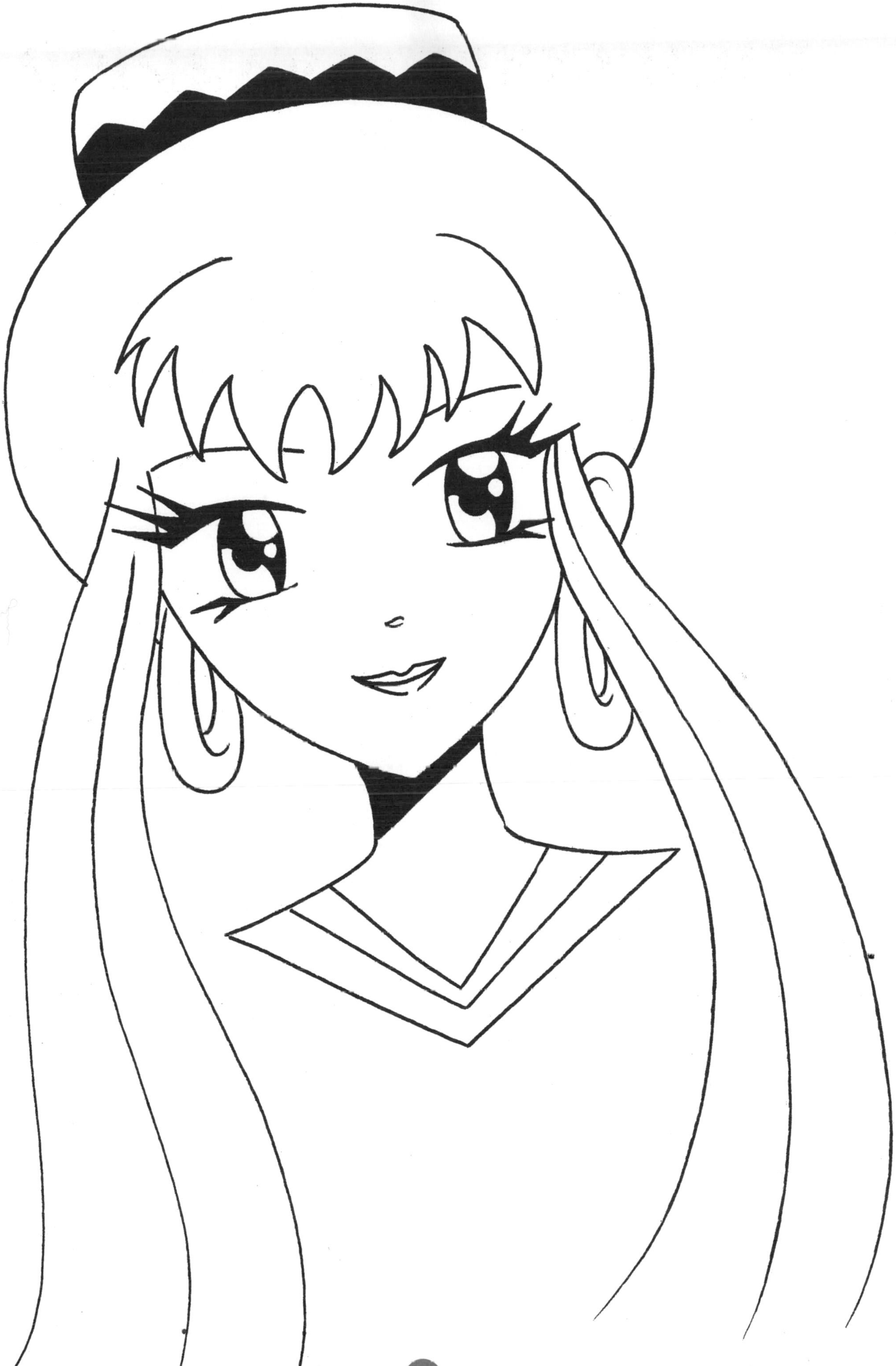

HIGH SCHOOL WARRIOR

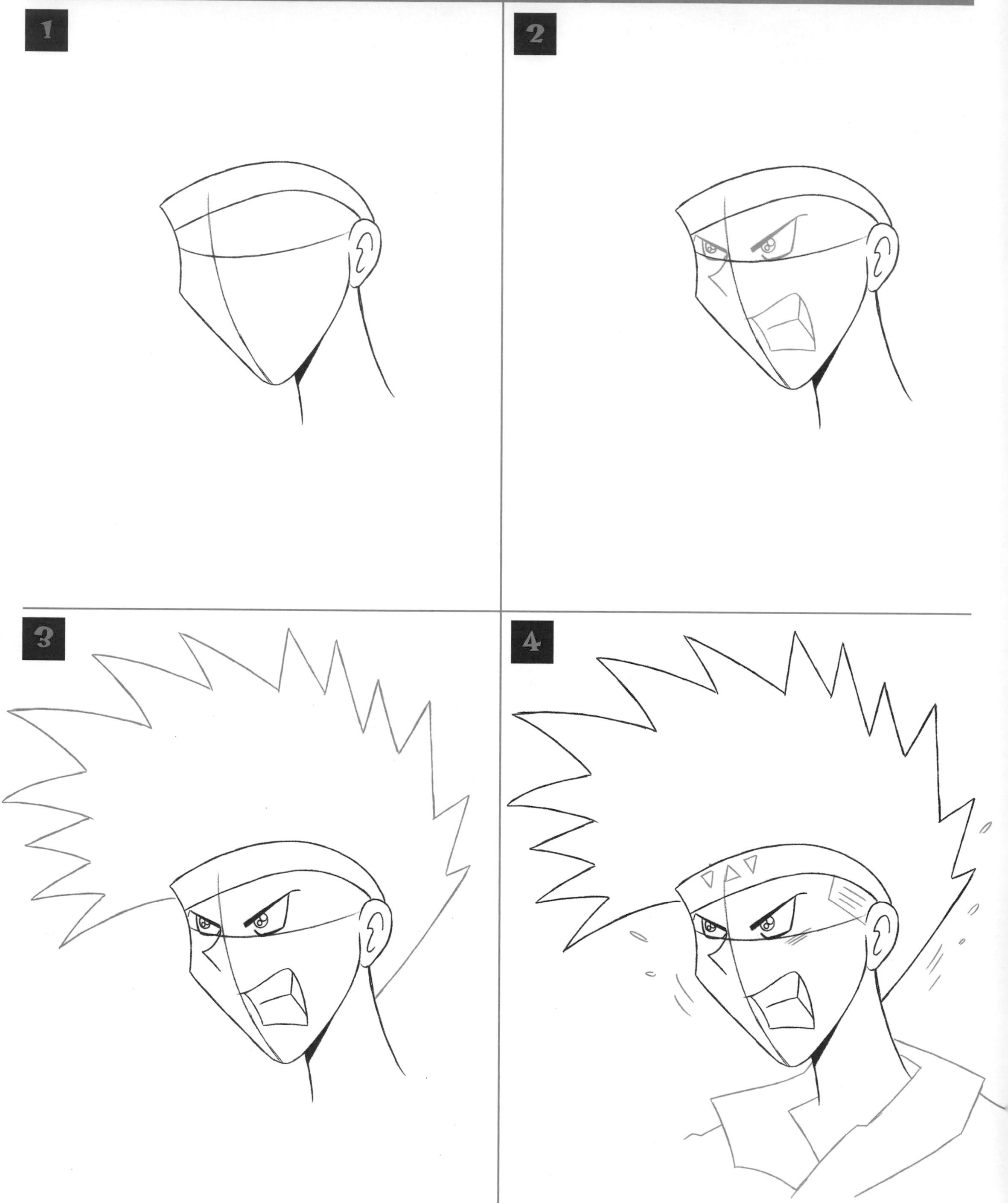

1
2
3
4

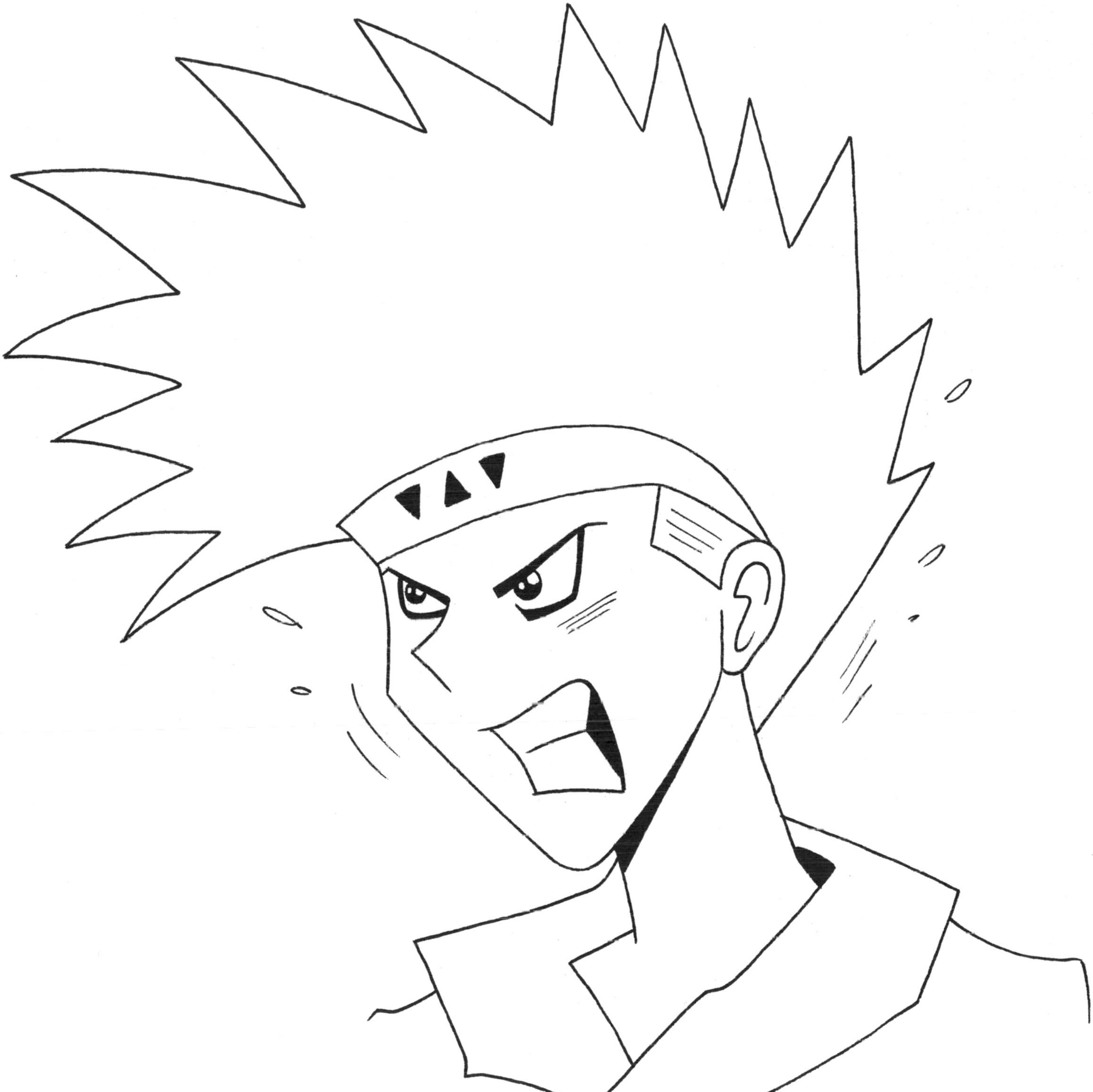

BIG GENERAL

1

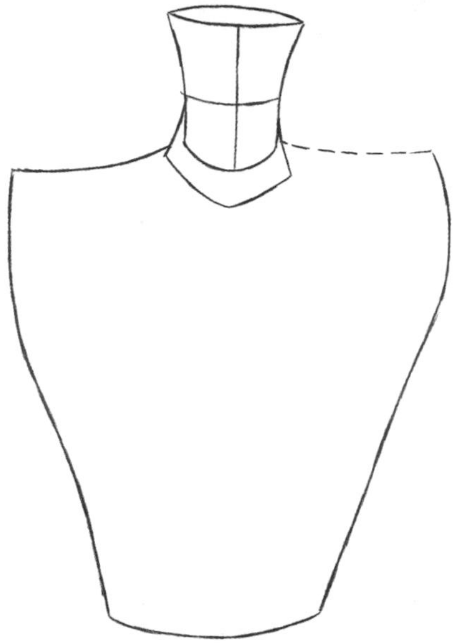

2

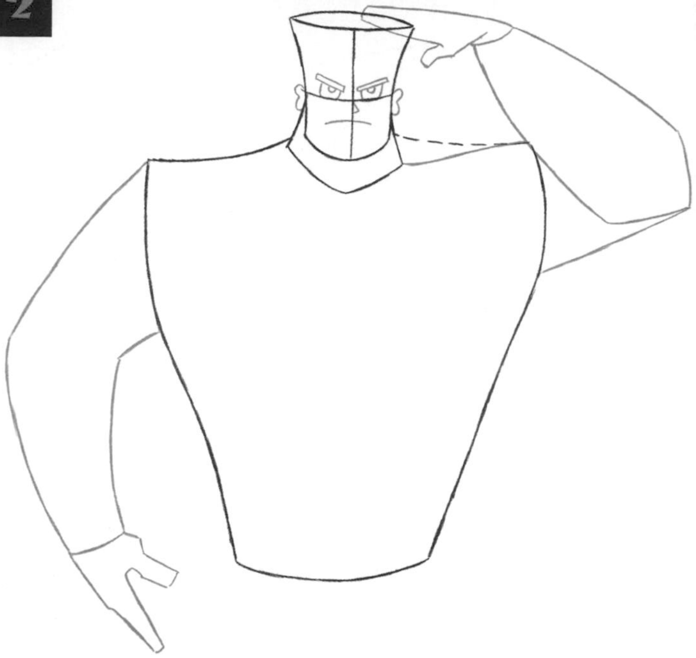

3

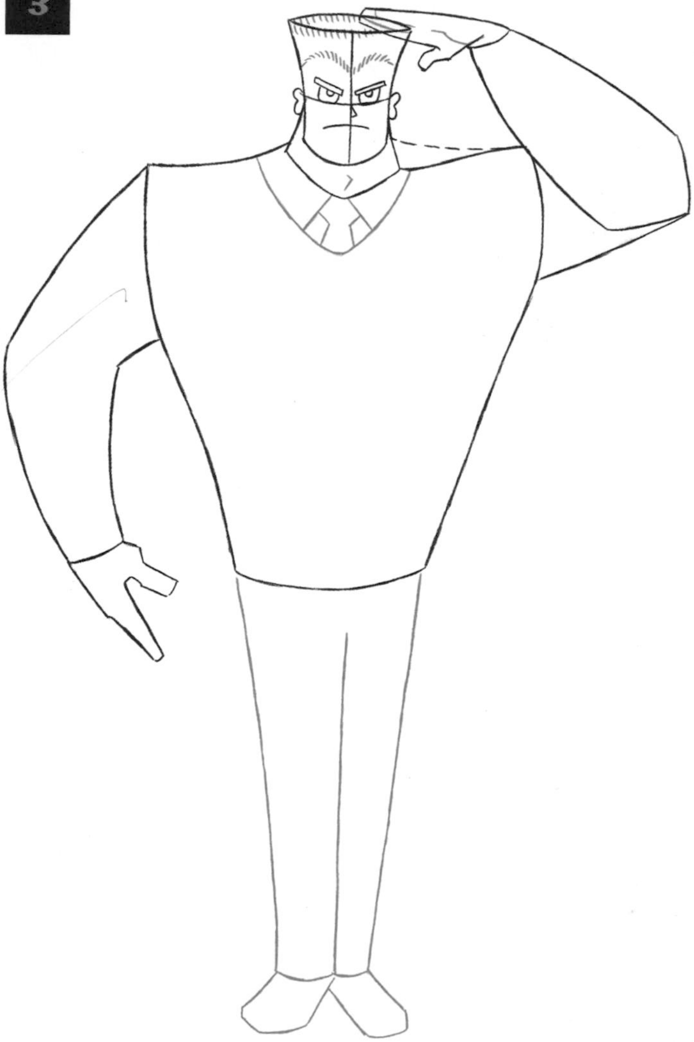

4

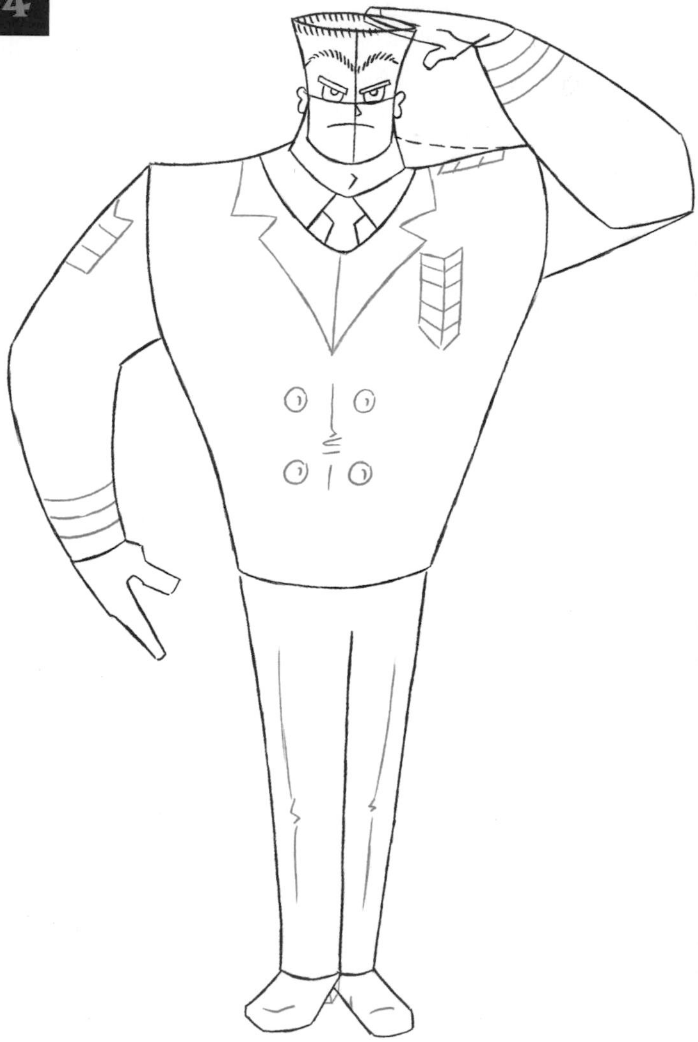

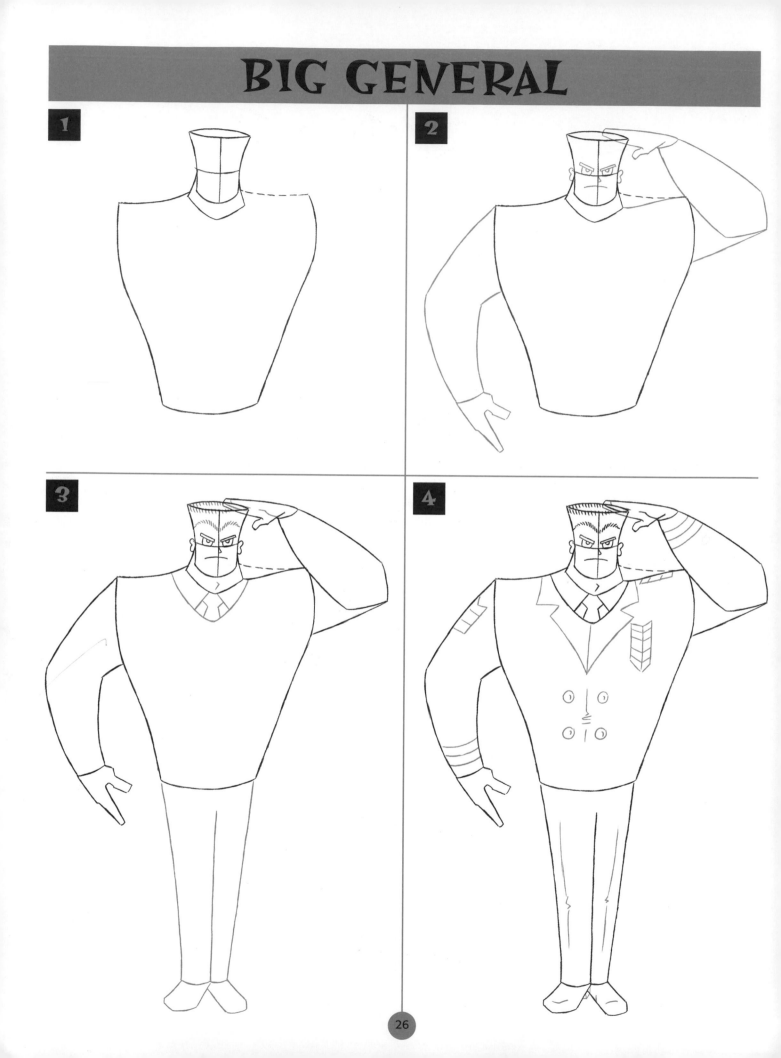

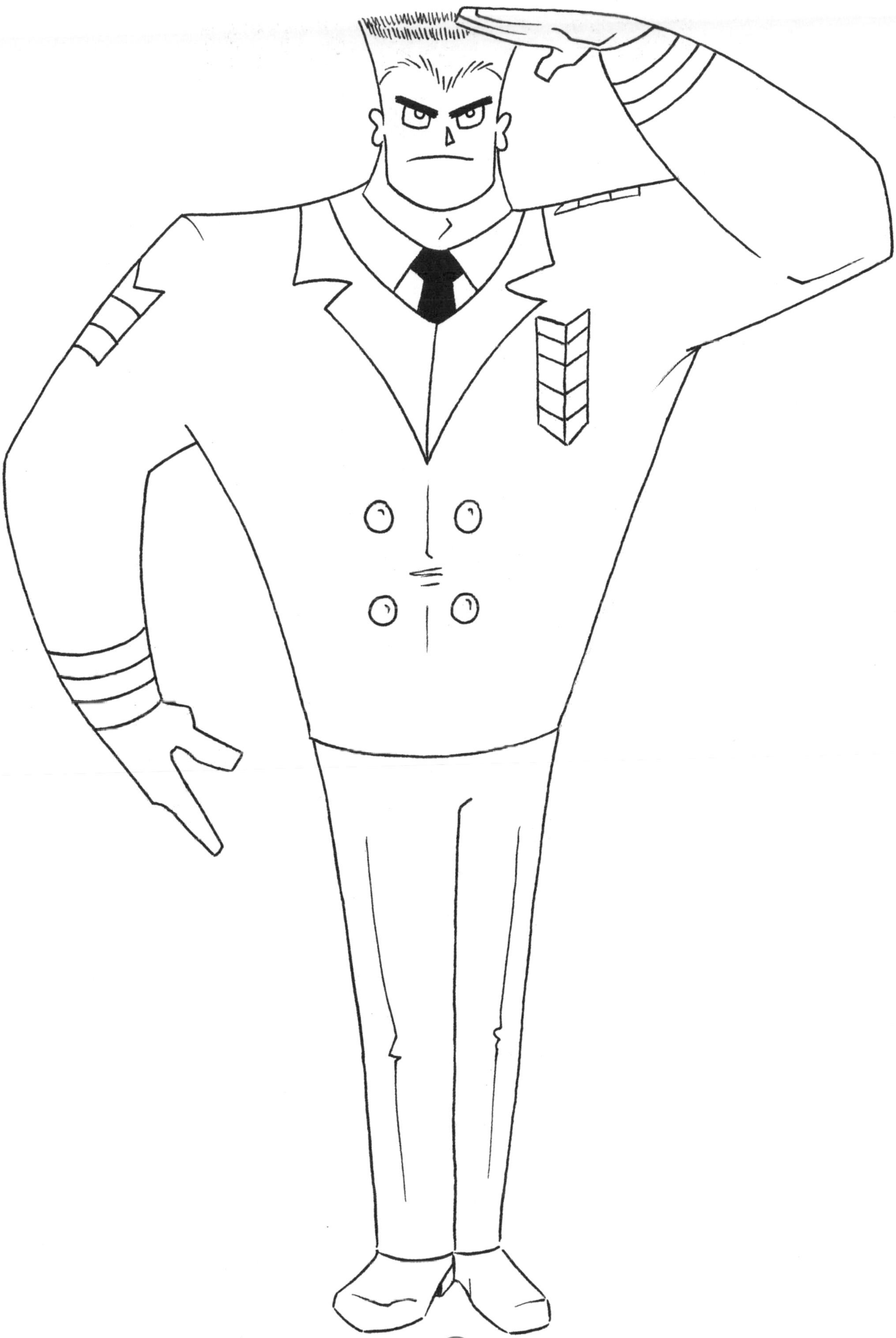

POP-STAR GIRL

1

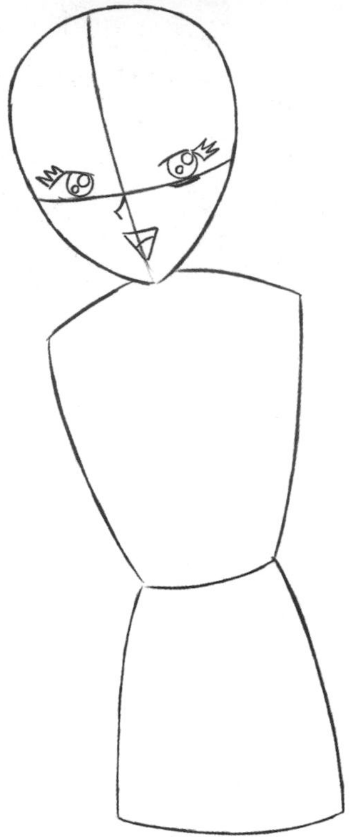

2

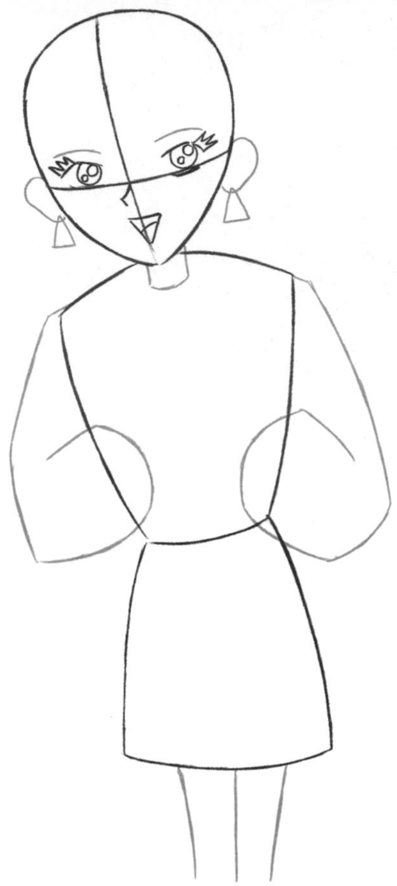

3

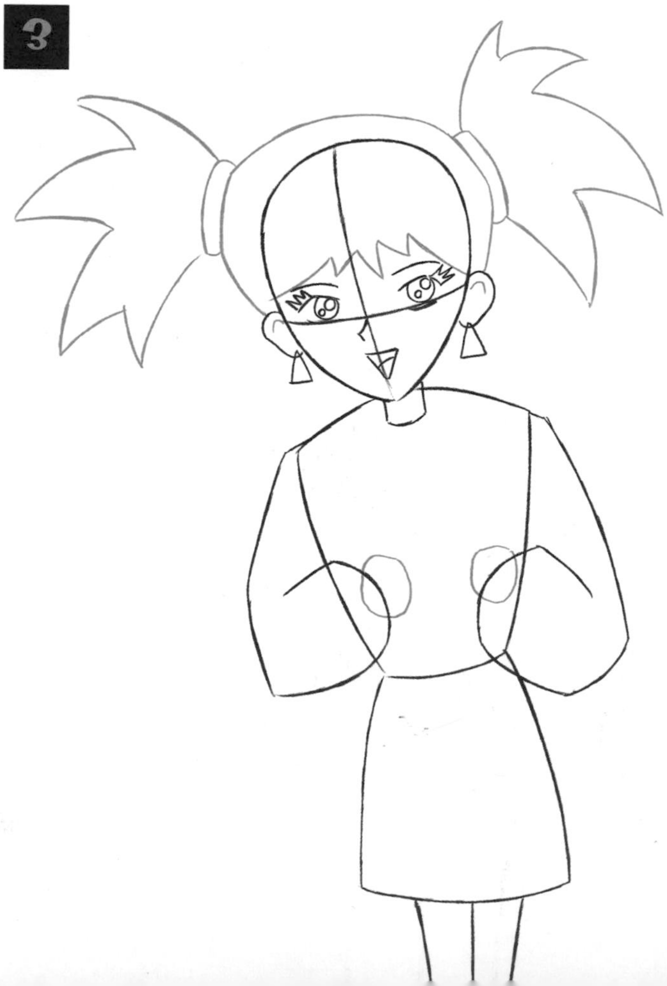

4

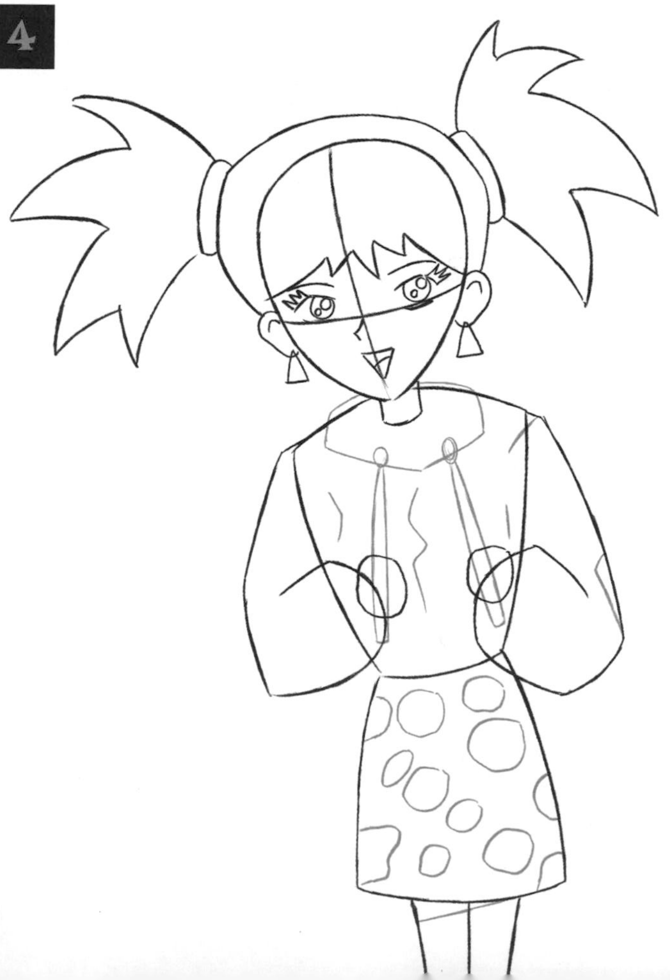

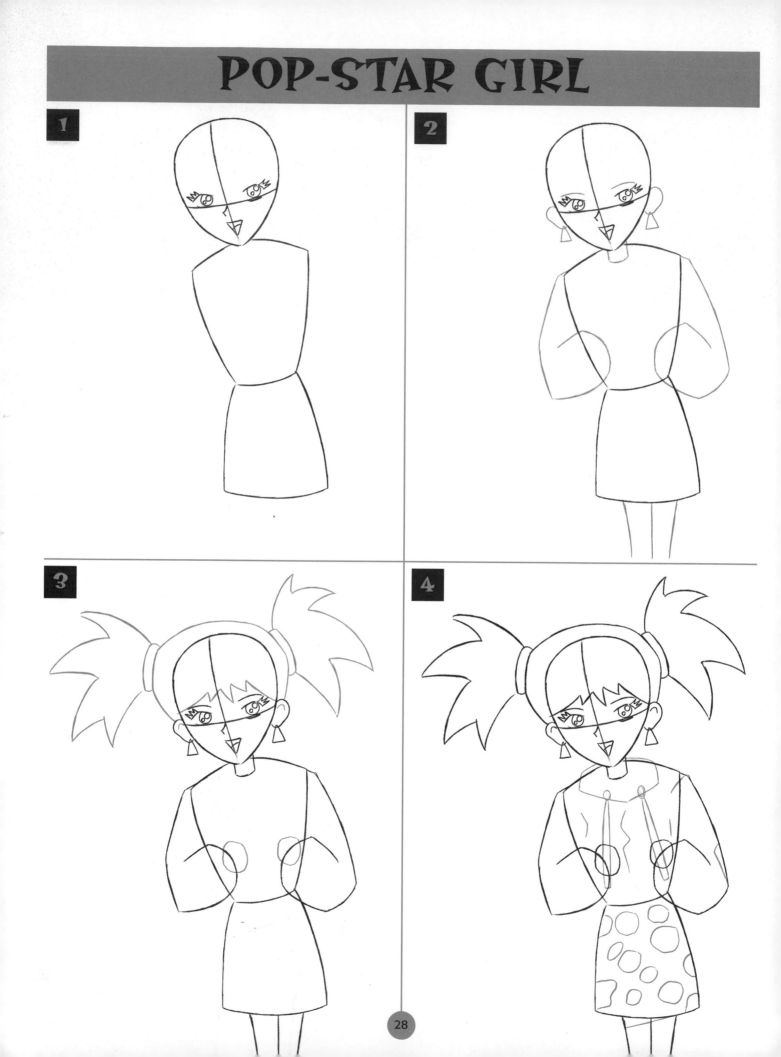

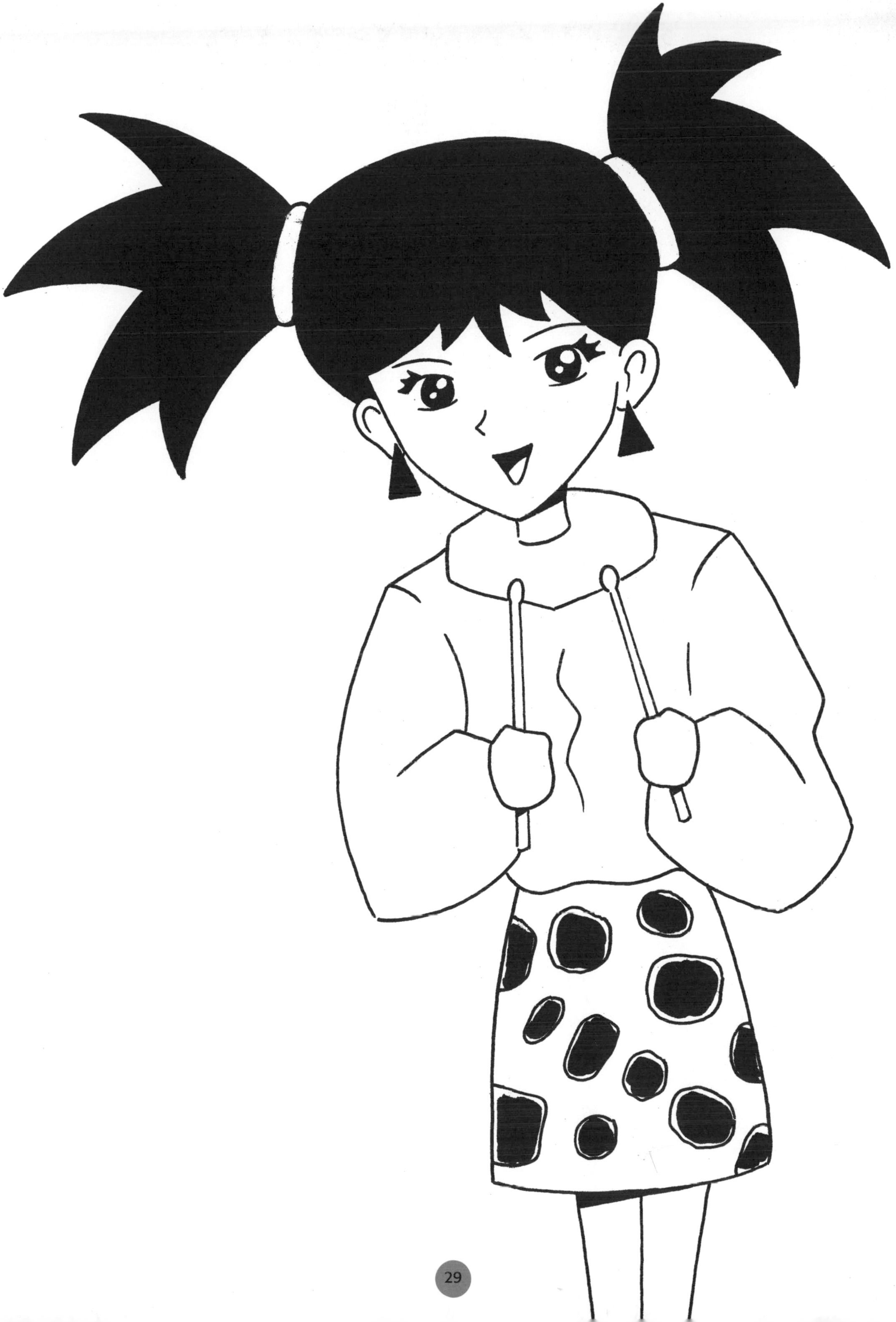

BACKPACK KID

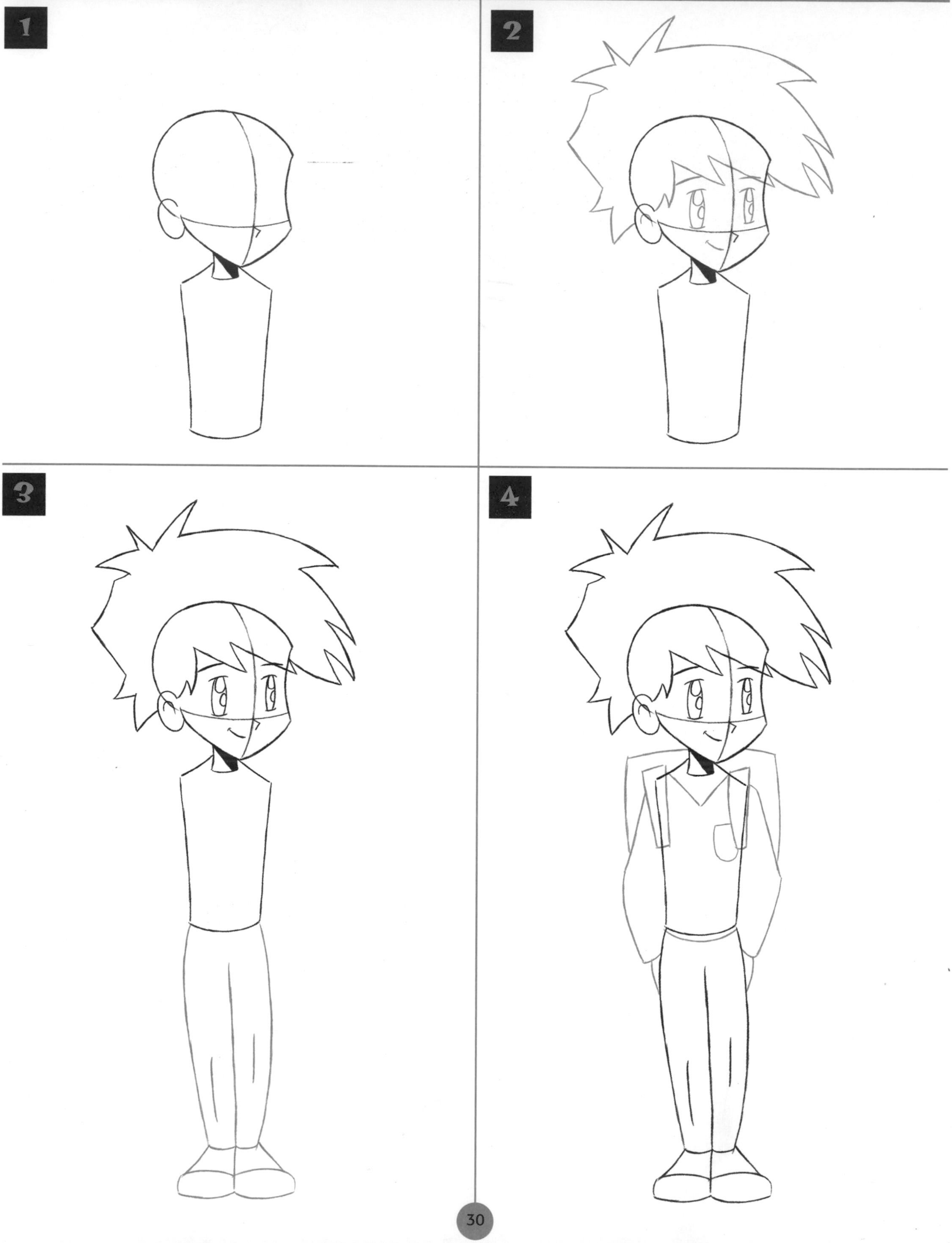
1
2
3
4

RETRO GIRL

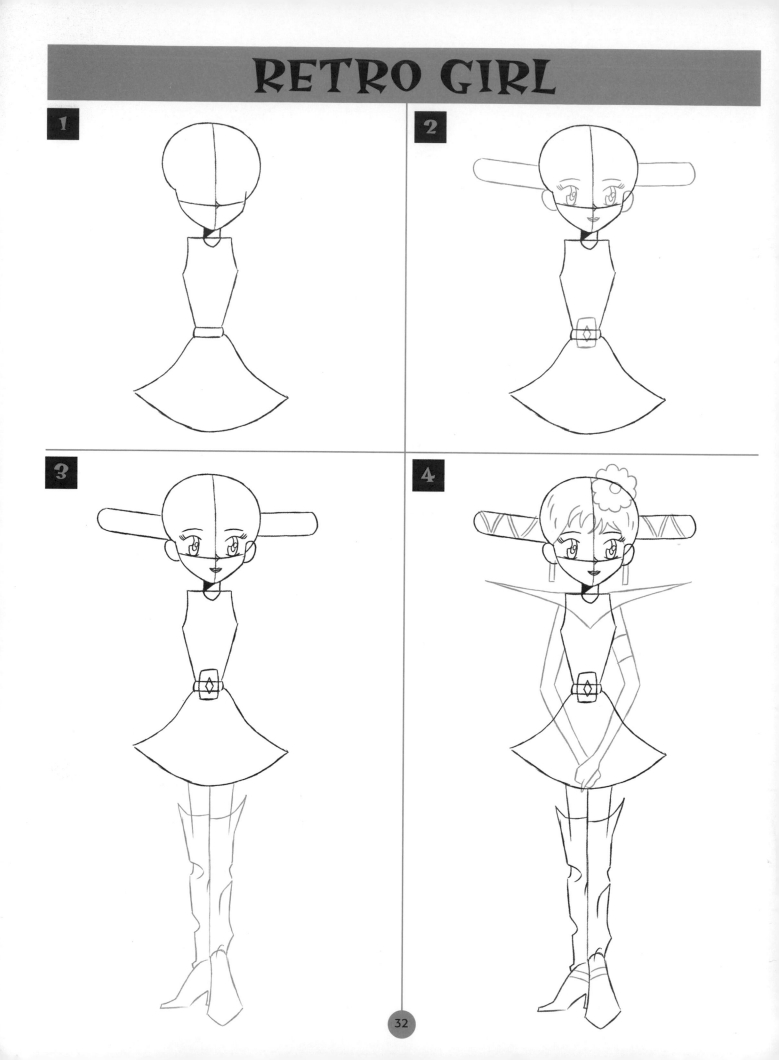

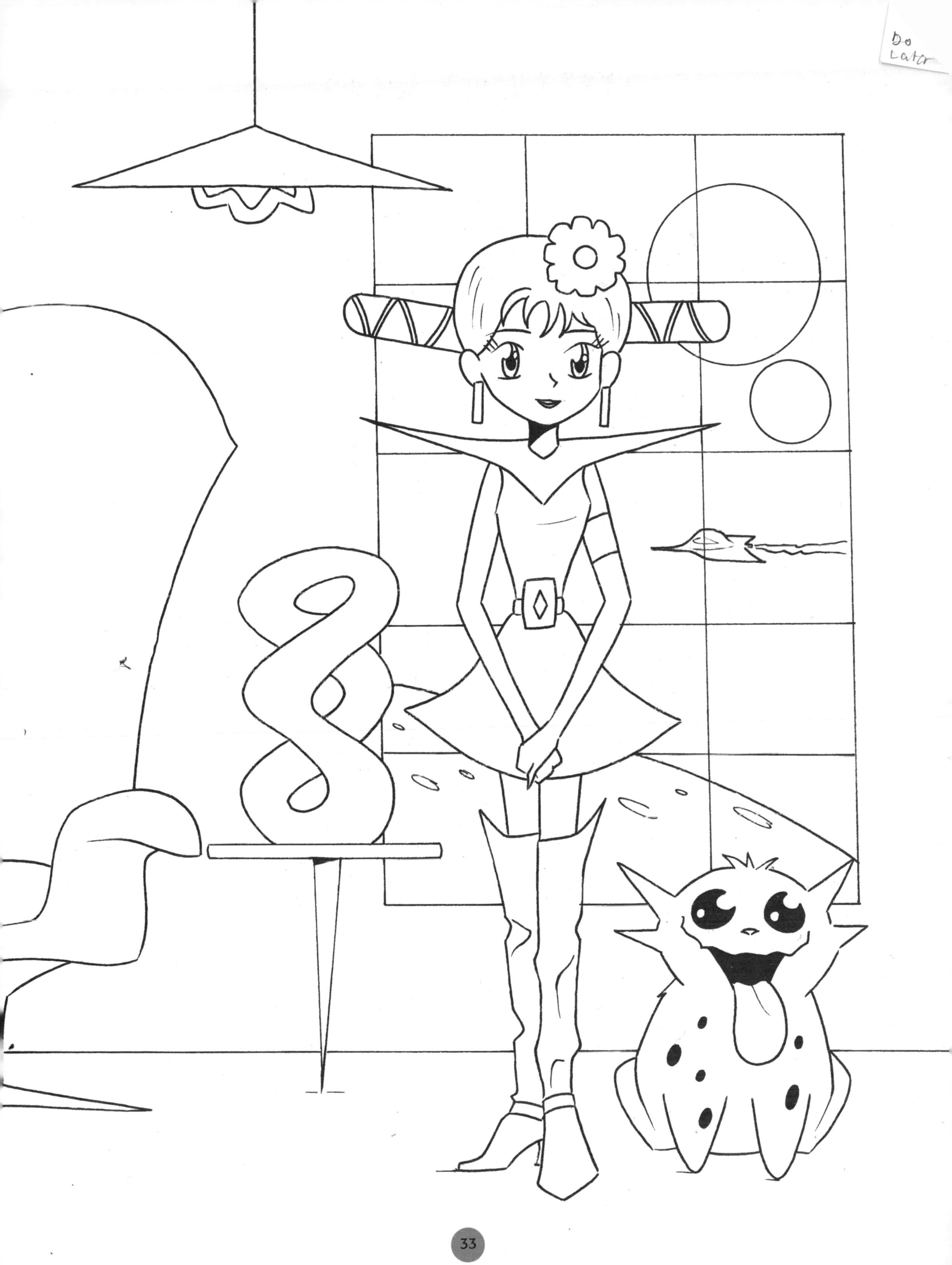

PILOT BOY

1

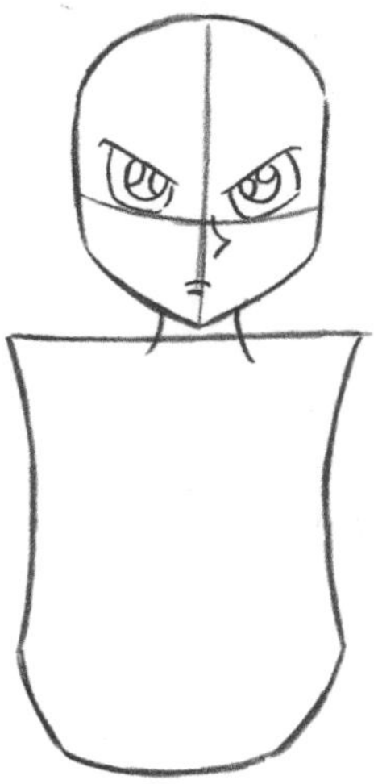

2

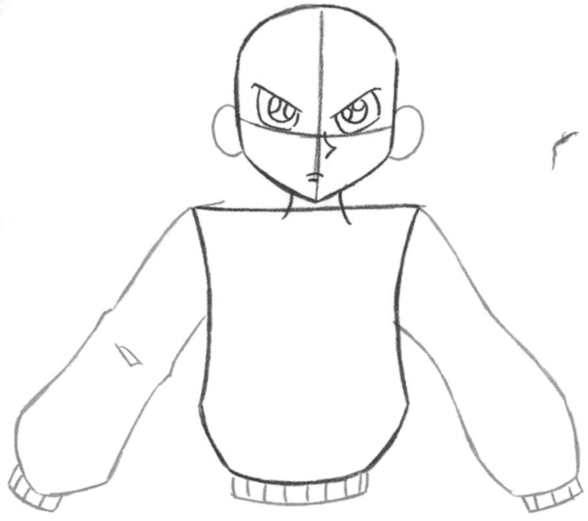

3

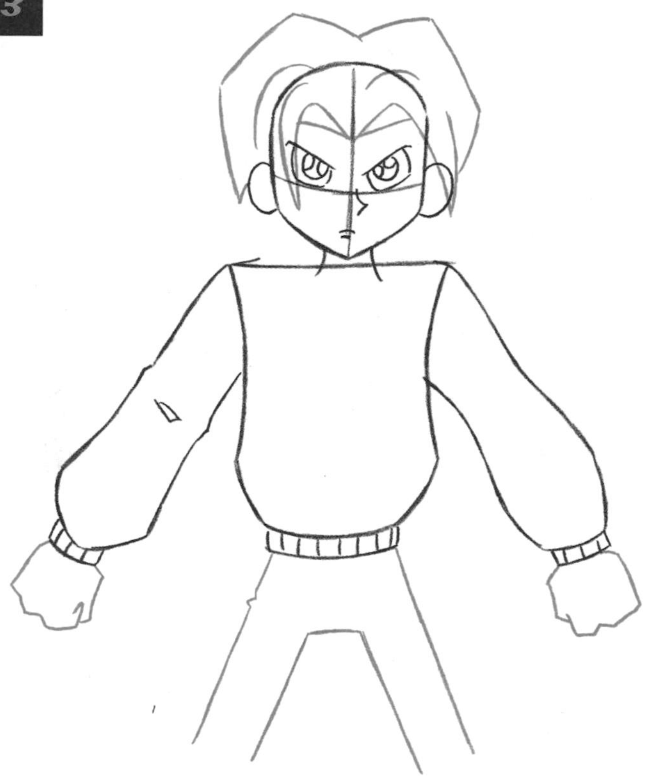

4

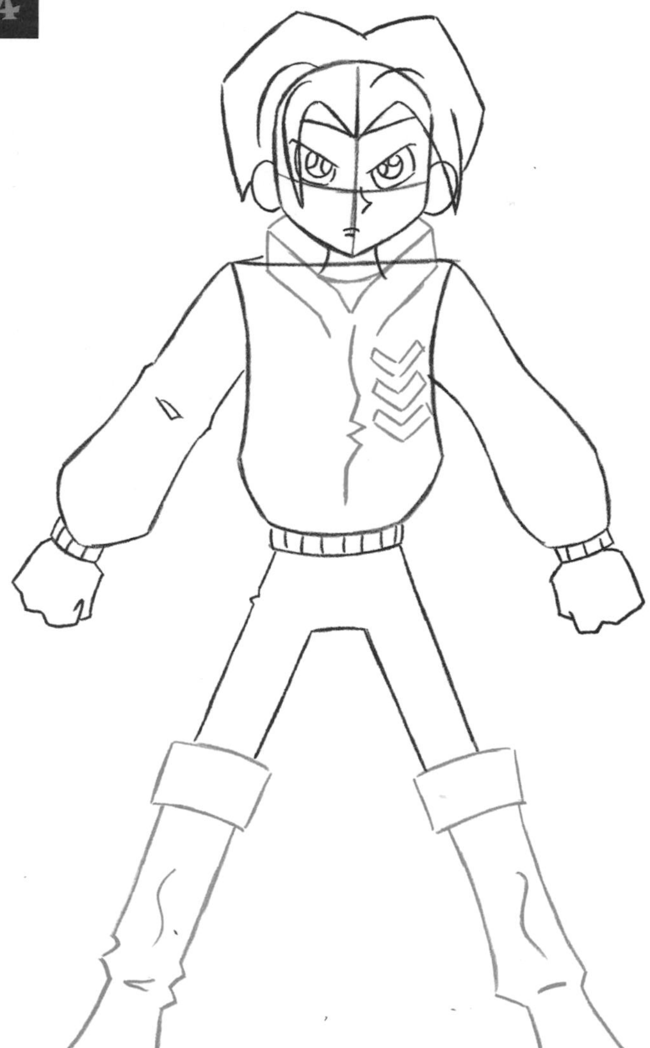

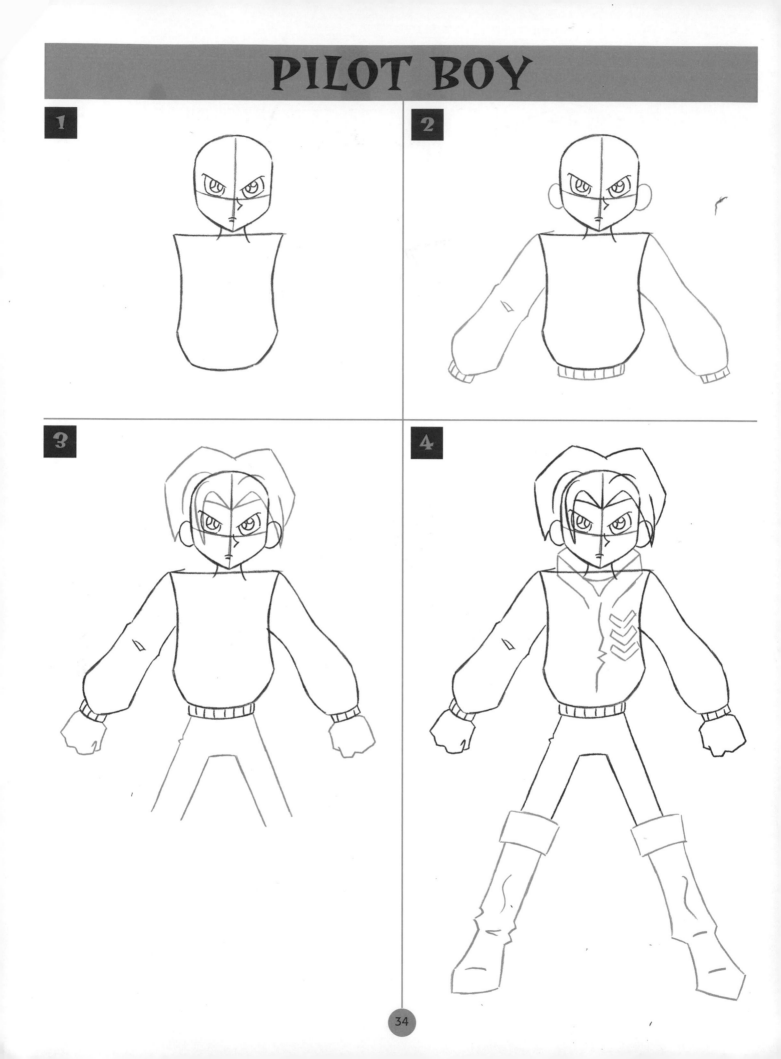

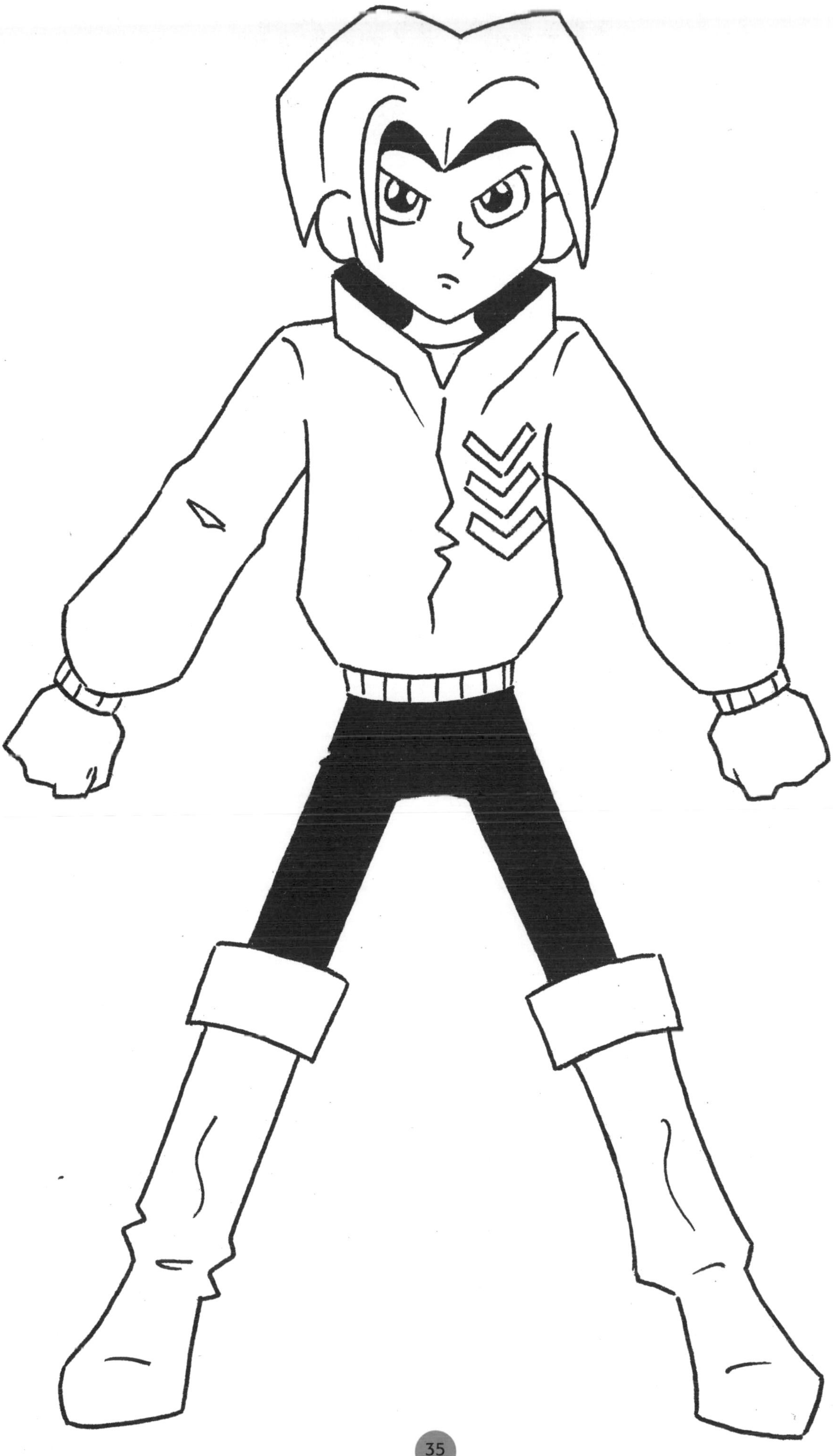

BIG BRAT

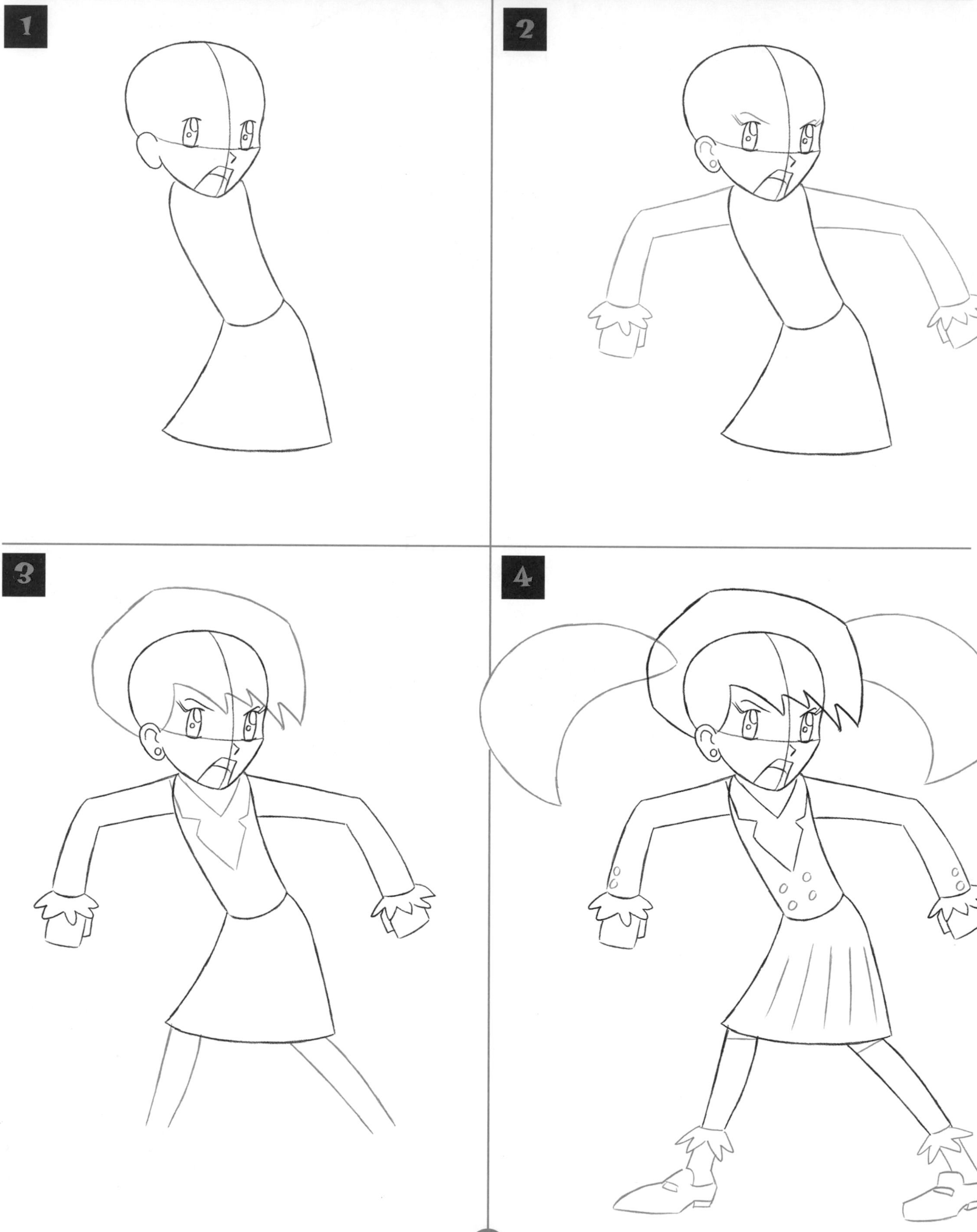
1
2
3
4

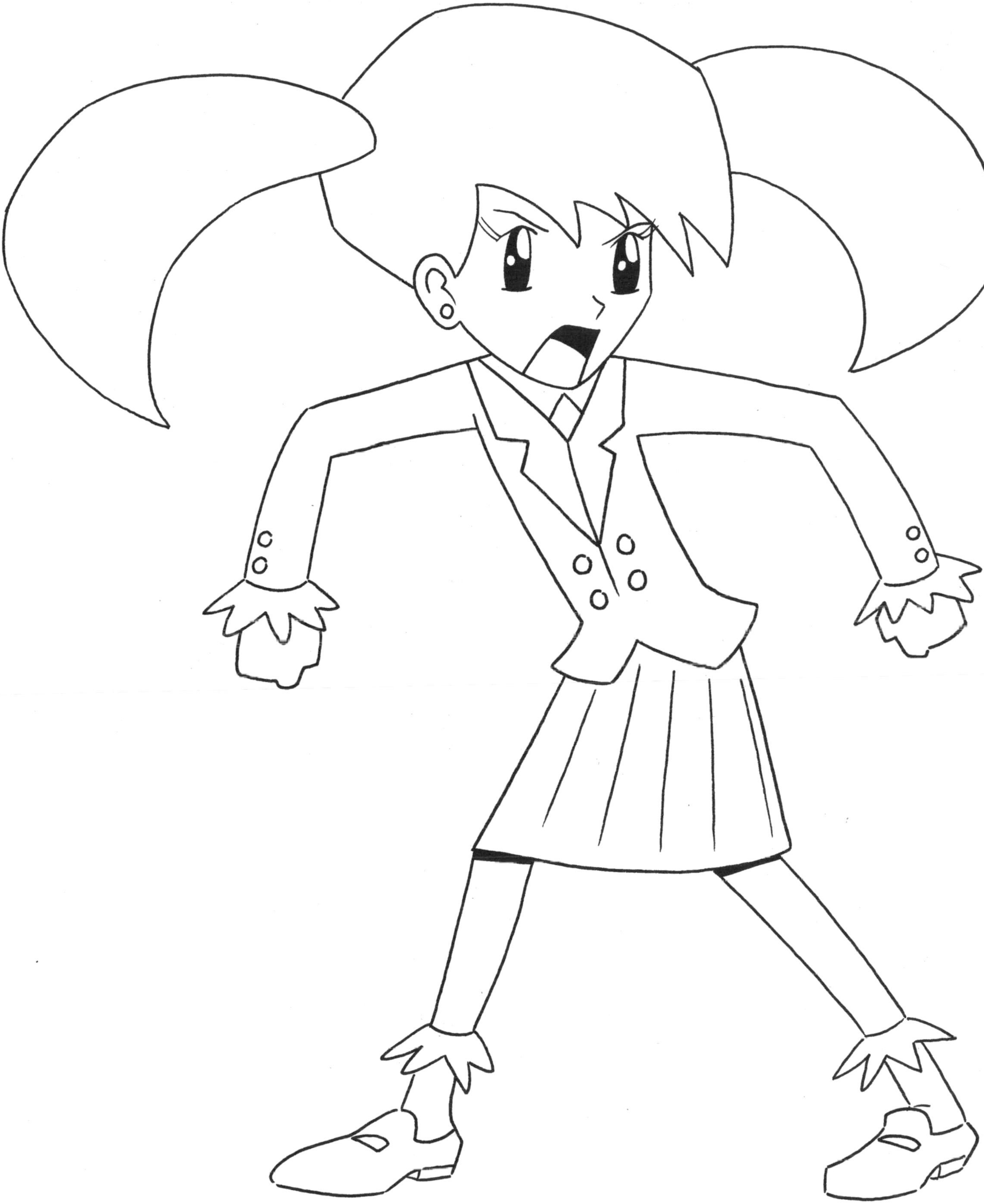

MECHA SOLDIER

1

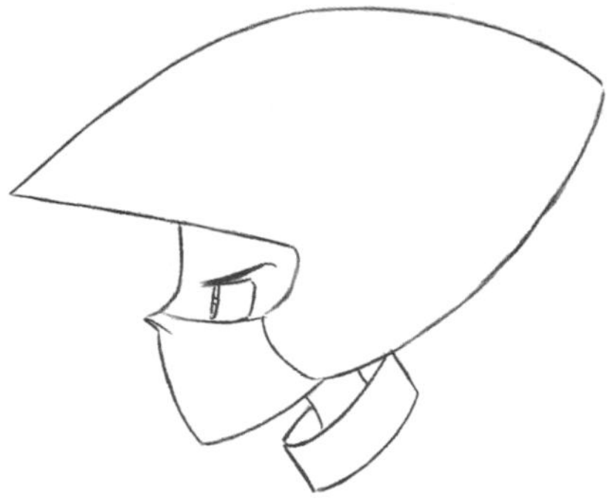

2

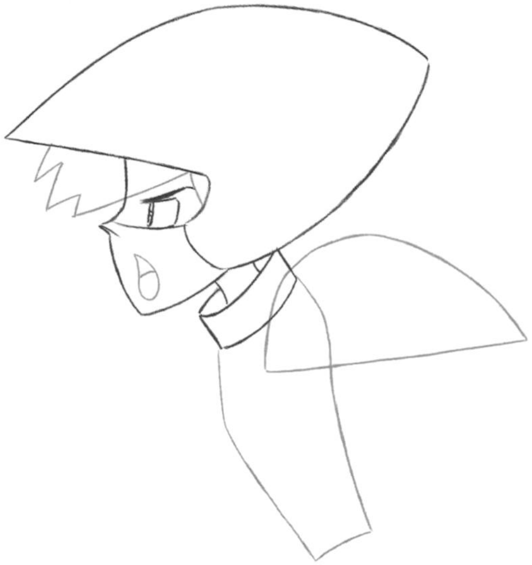

3

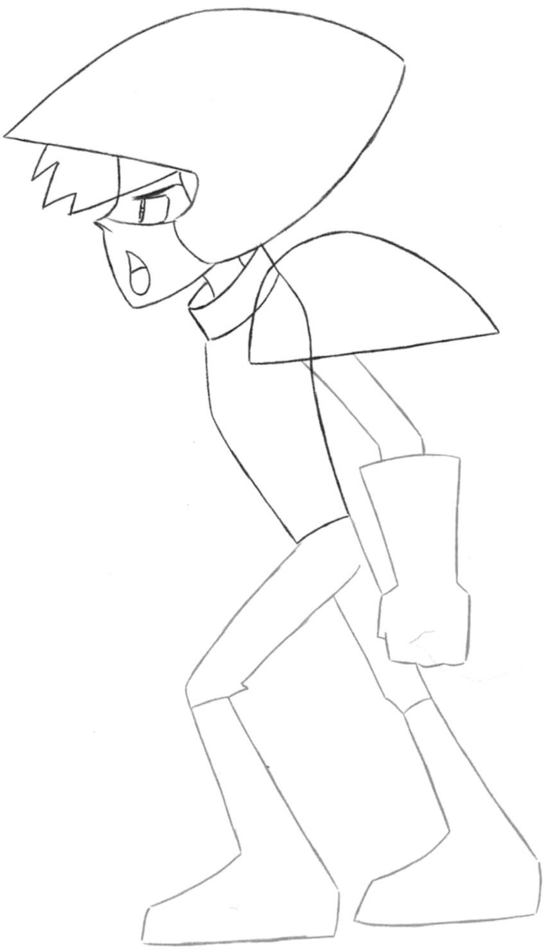

4

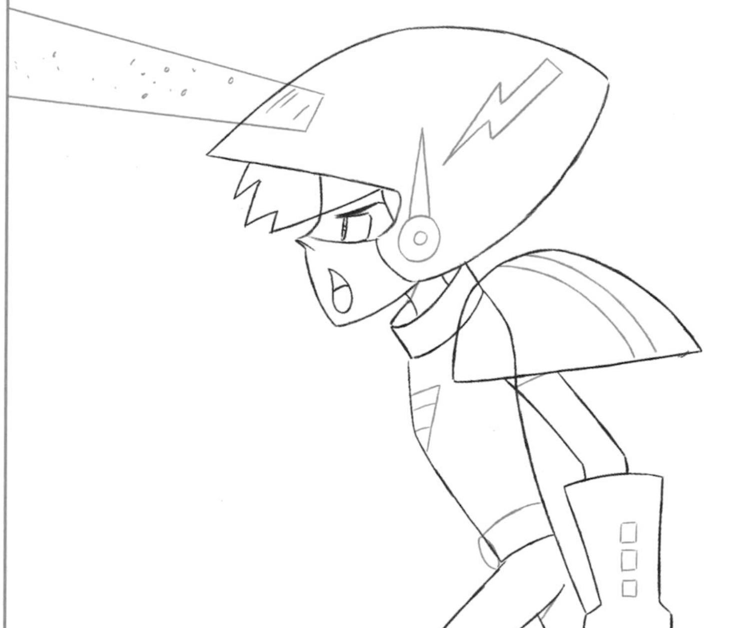

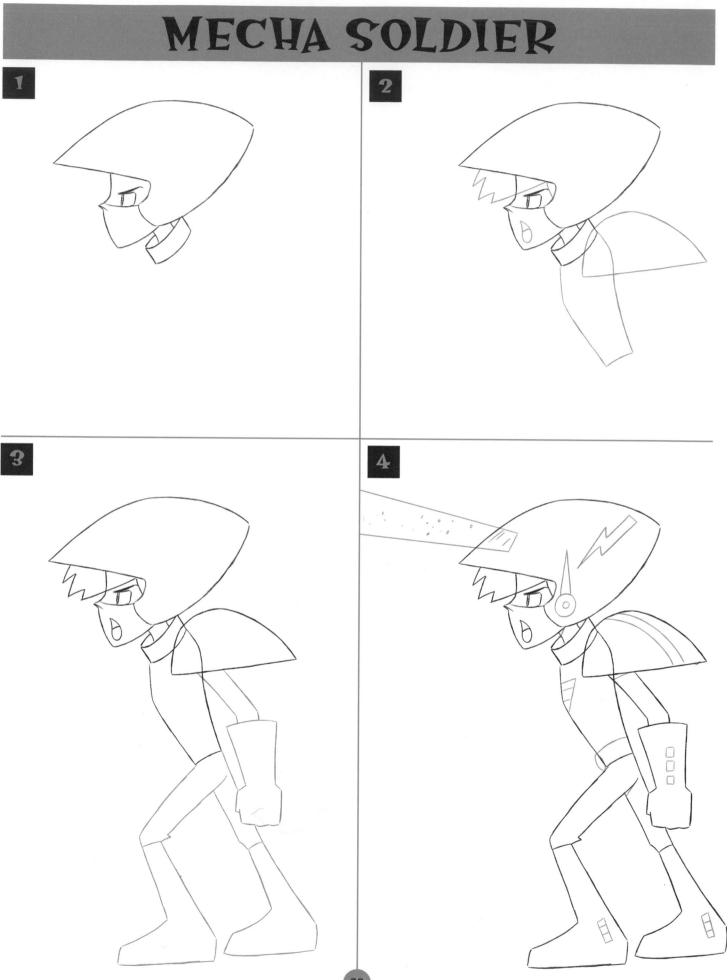

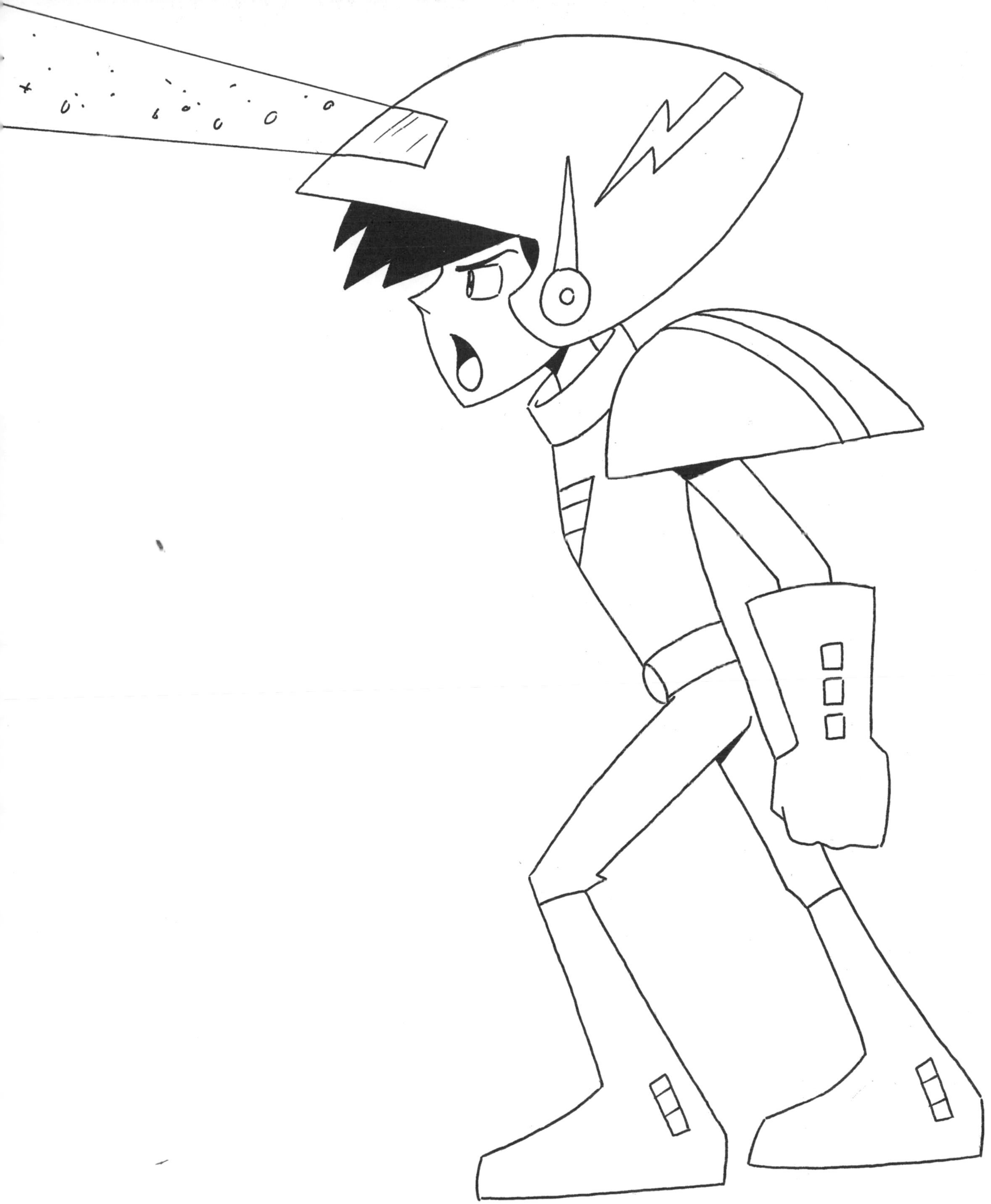

POUNDING PUNCHER

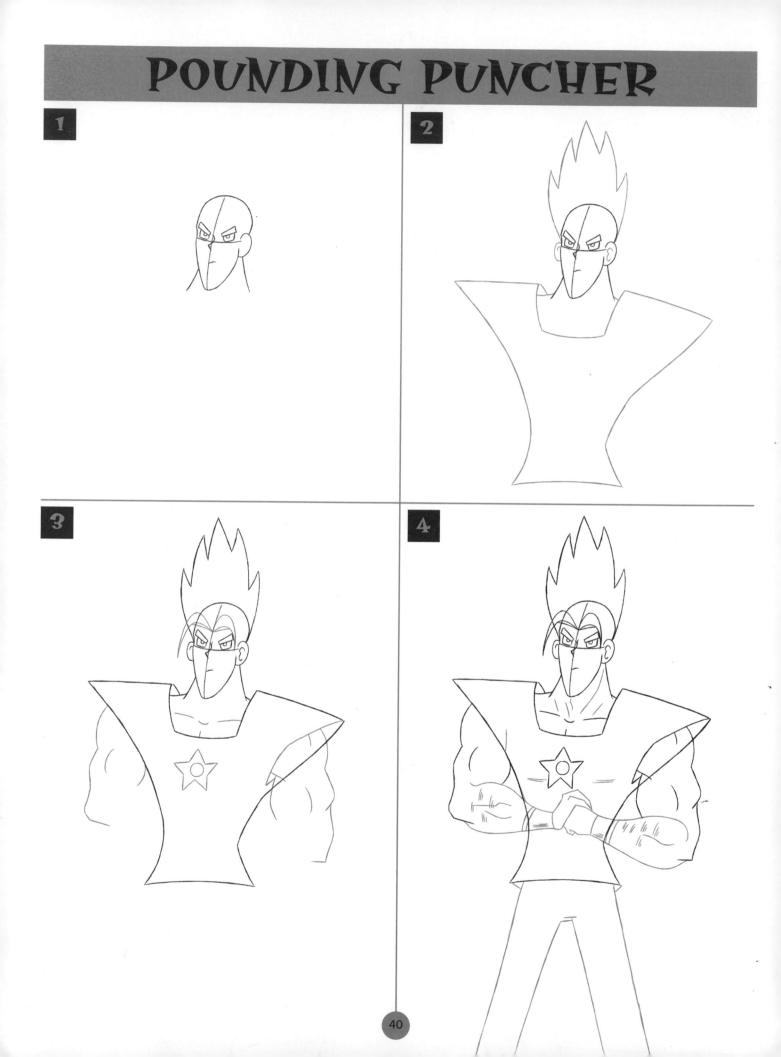

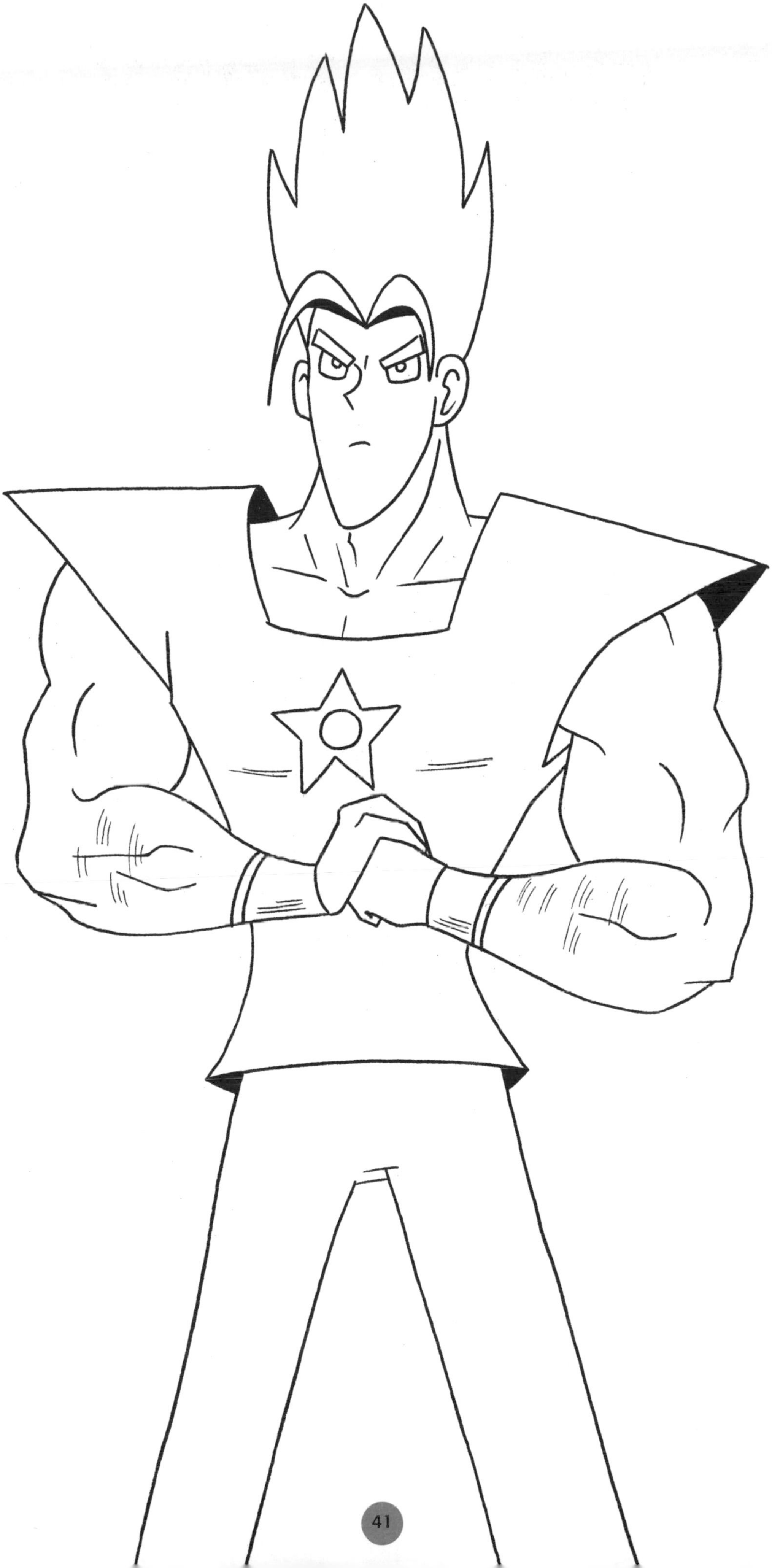

CUDDLY KITTY

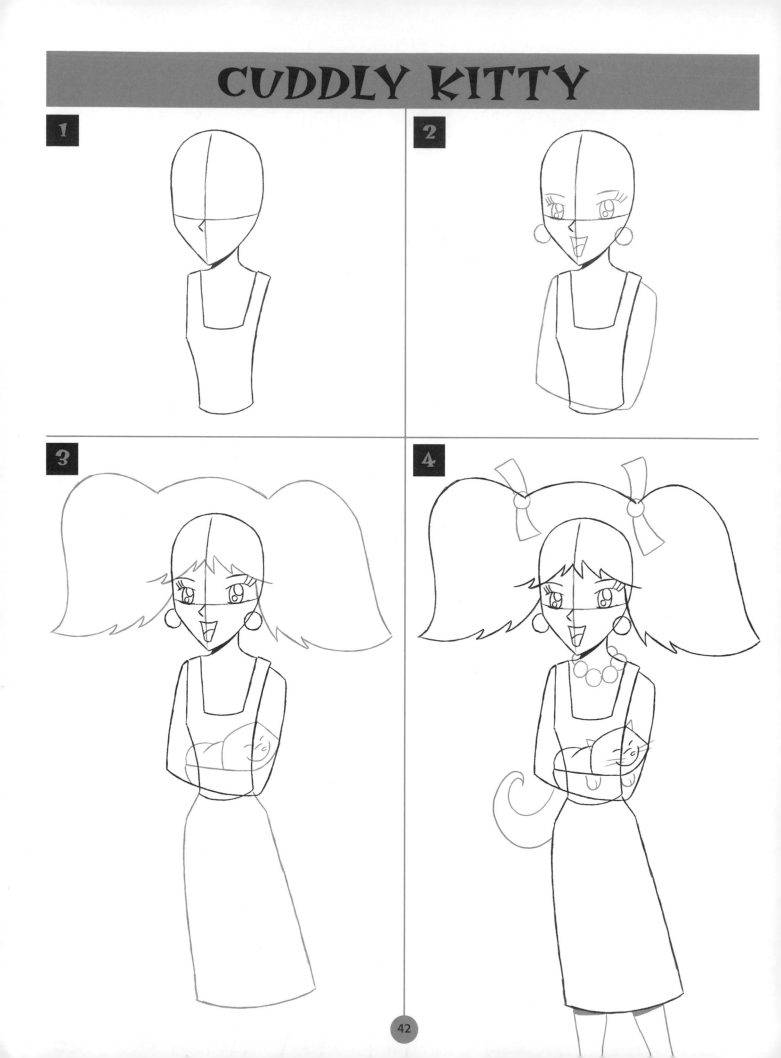

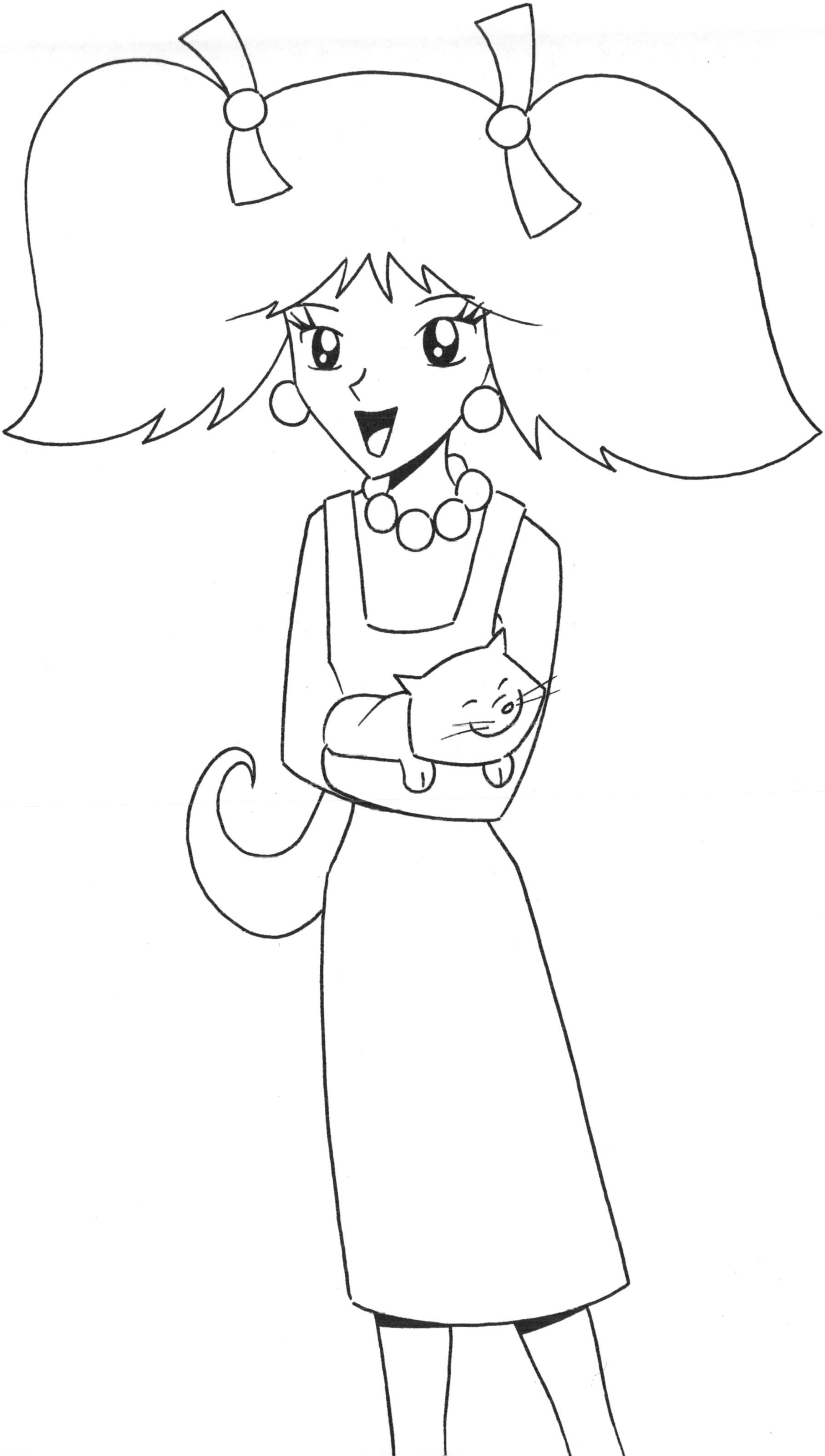

UNDERCOVER AGENT

1

2

3

4

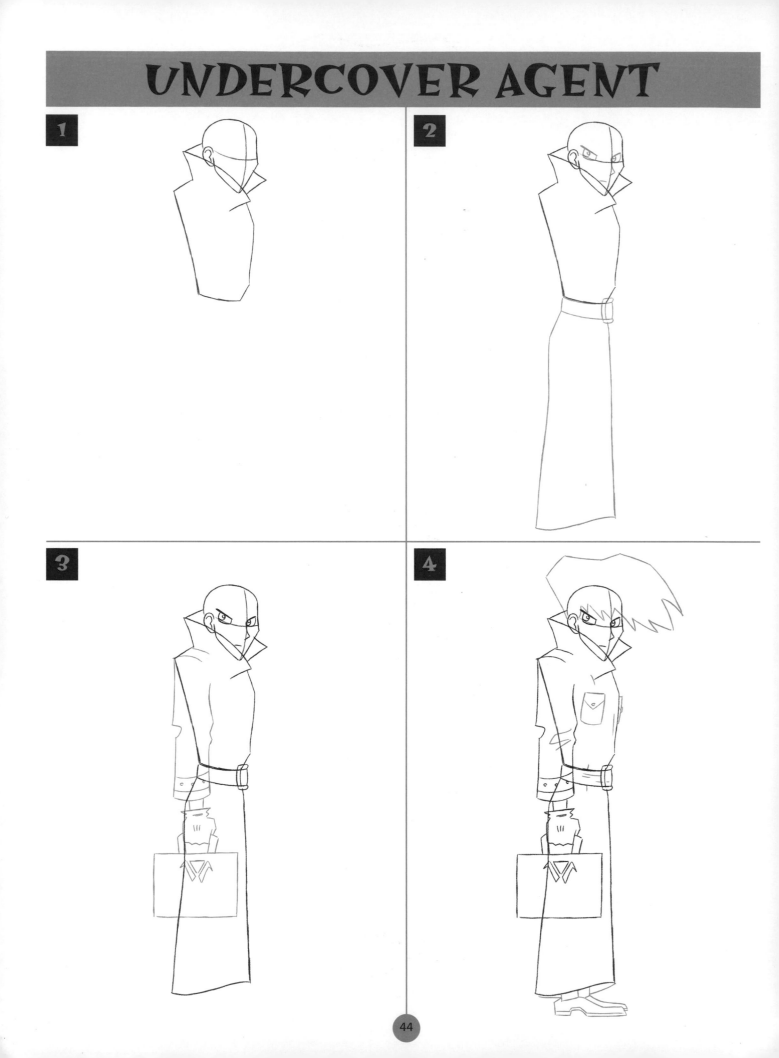

FRIENDLY GIRL

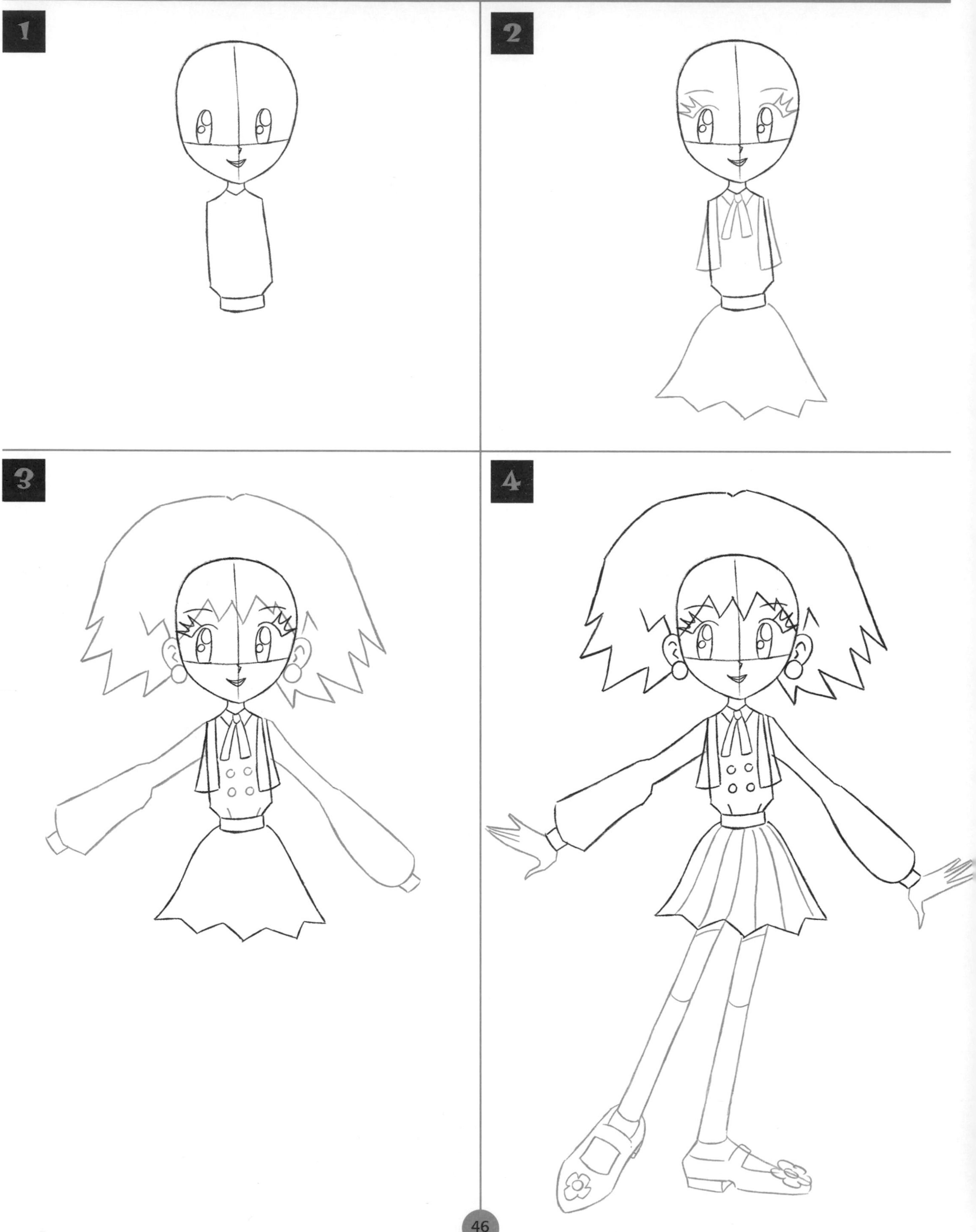
1
2
3
4

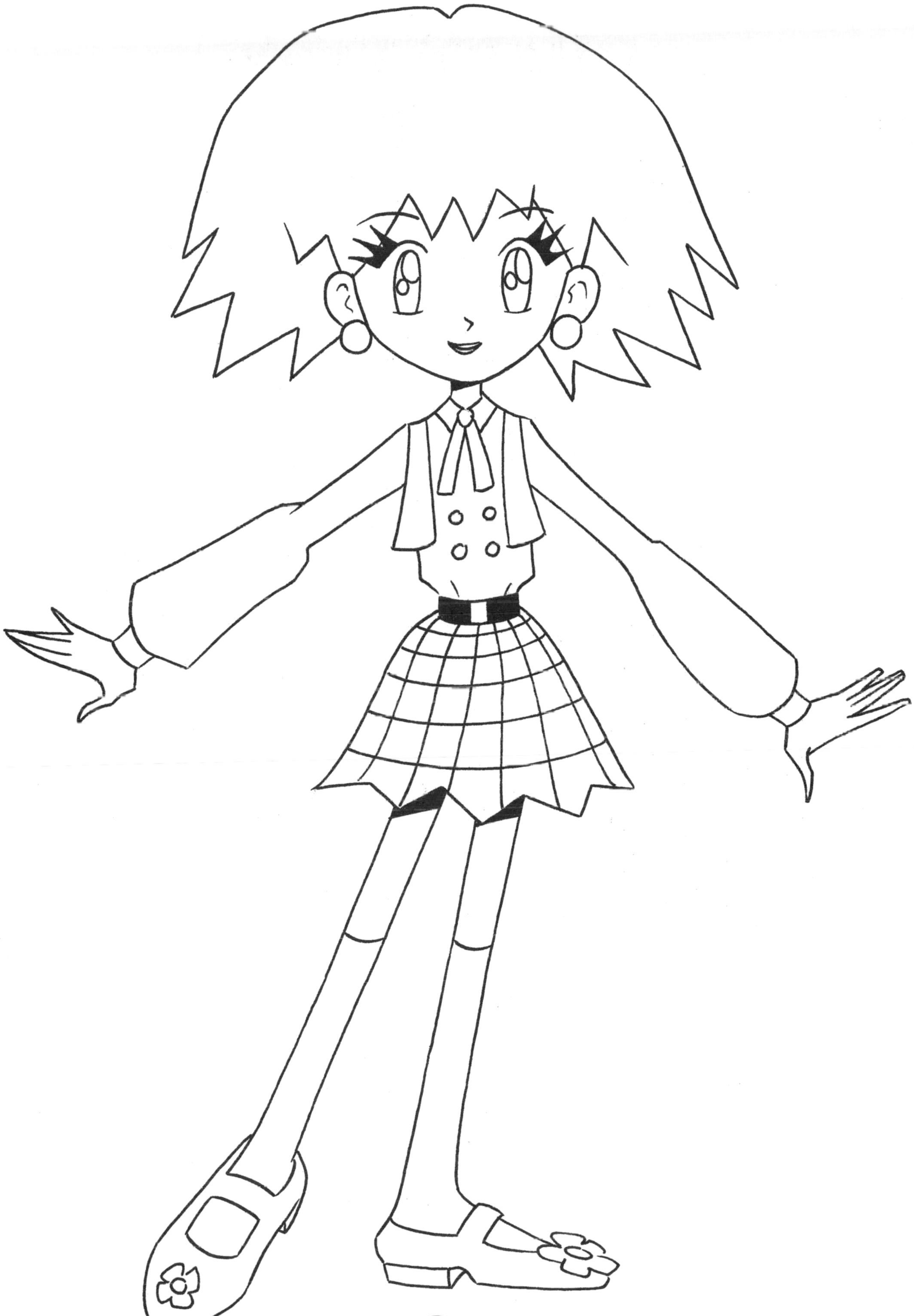

SHADY LADY

1

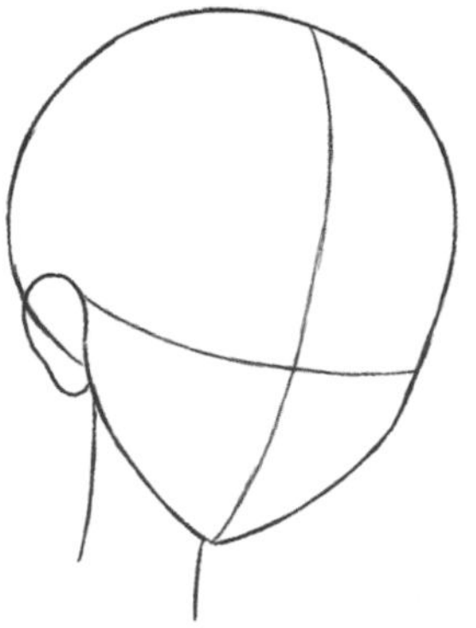

2

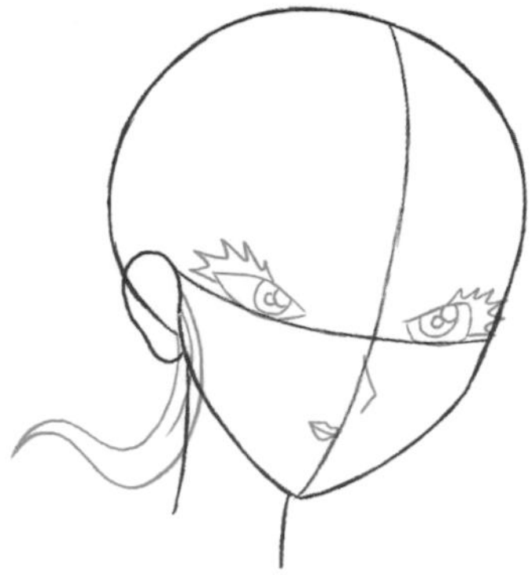

3

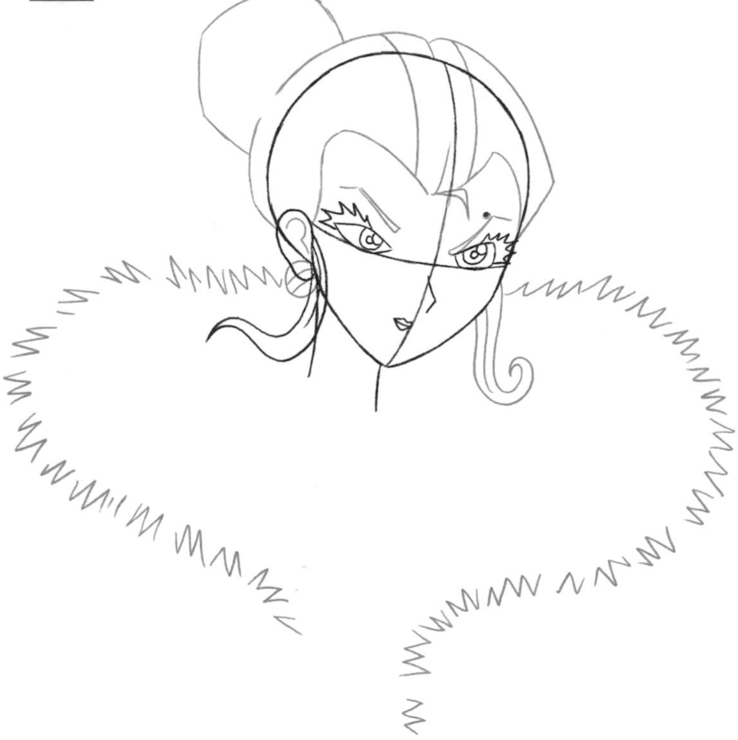

4

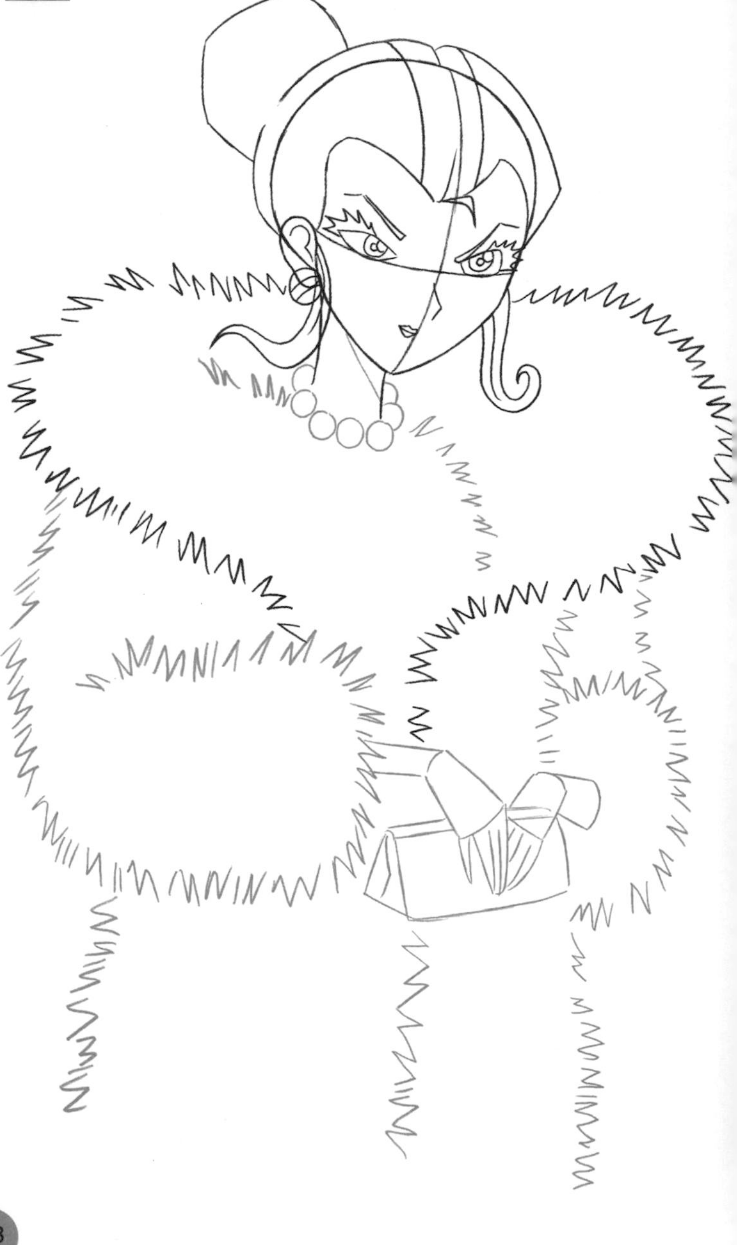

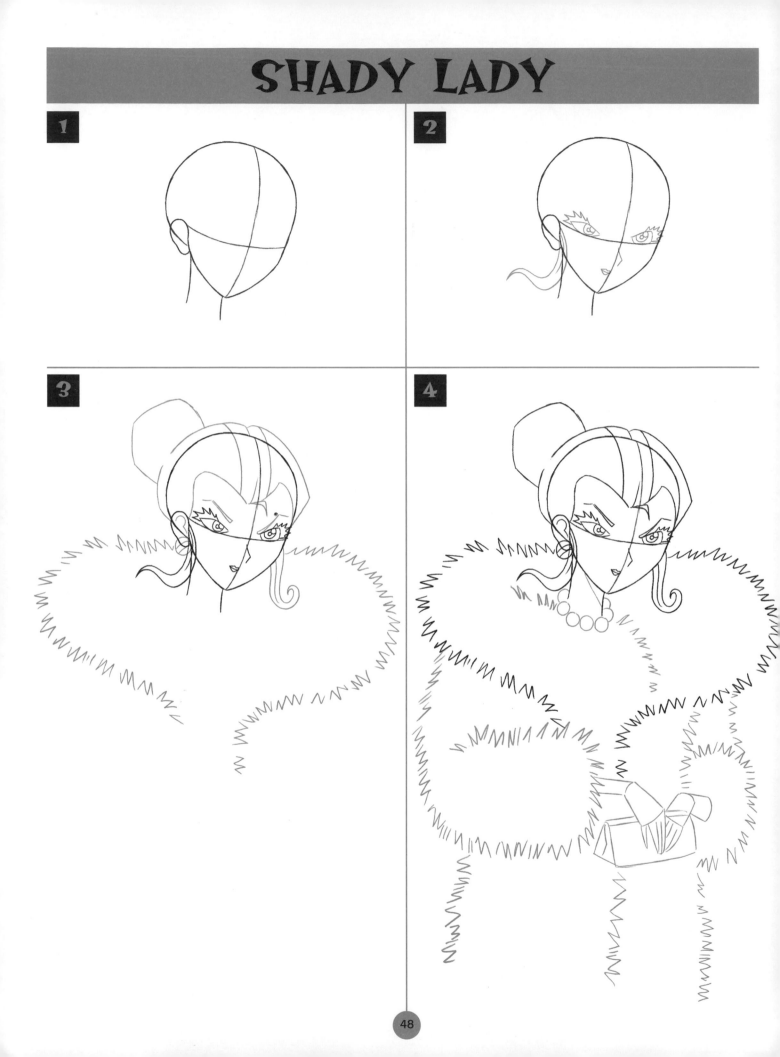

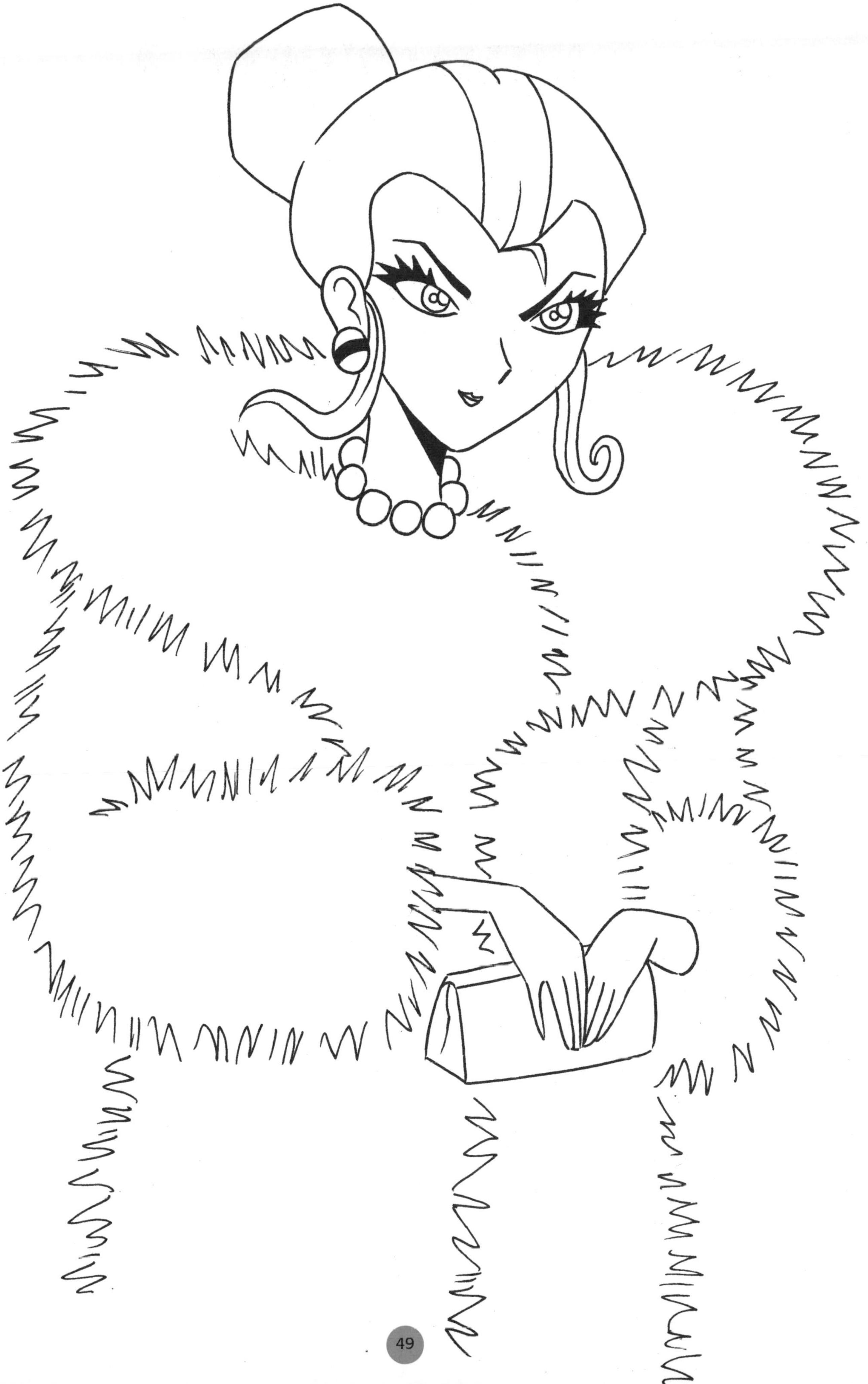

MEAN TEEN

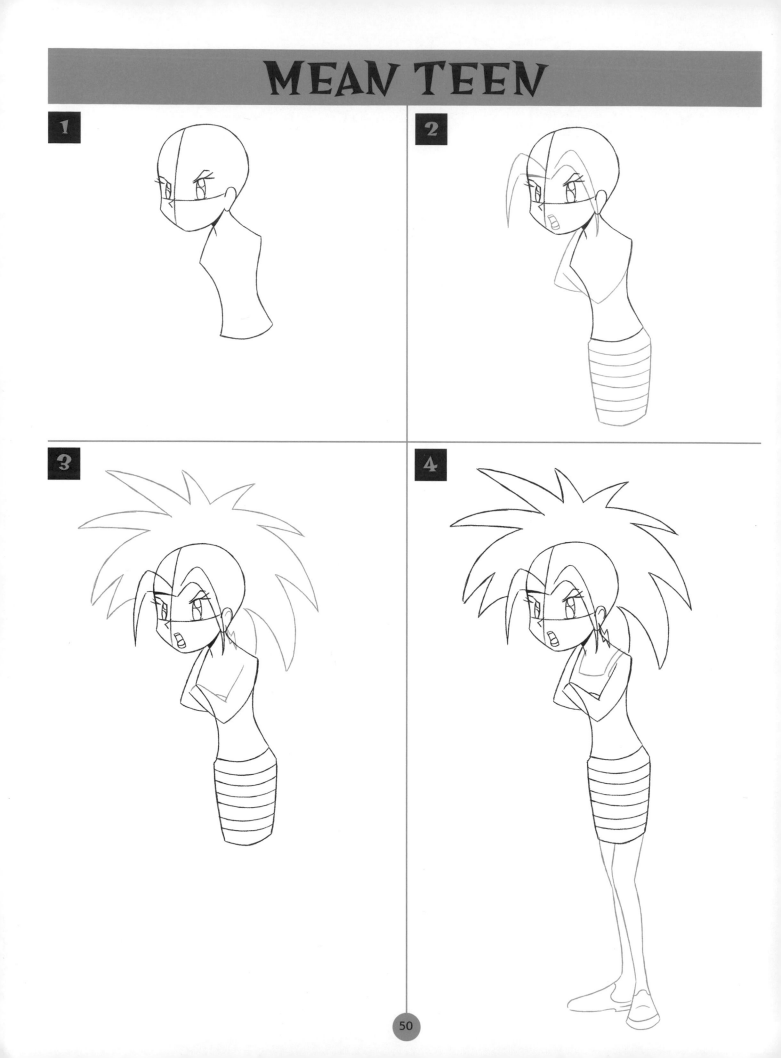

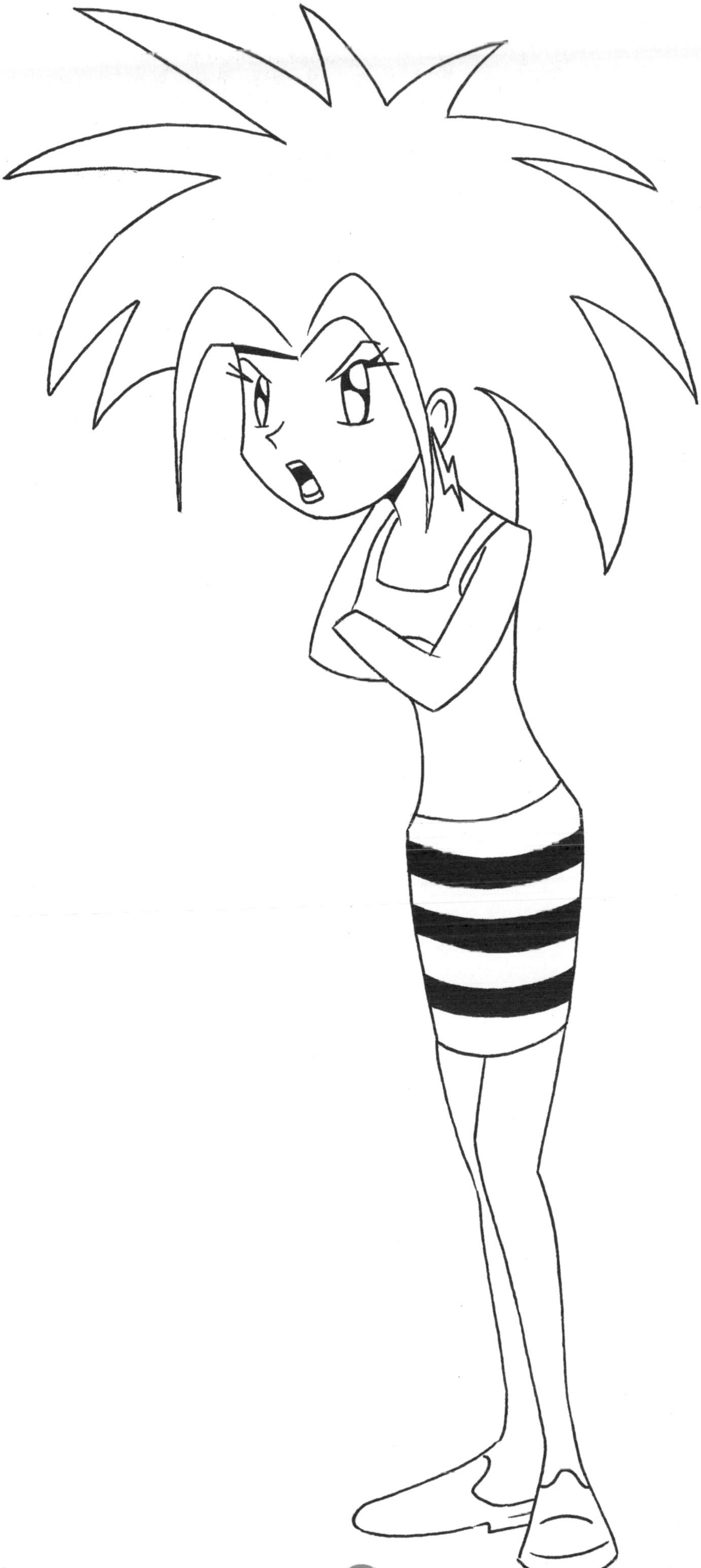

MR. COOL

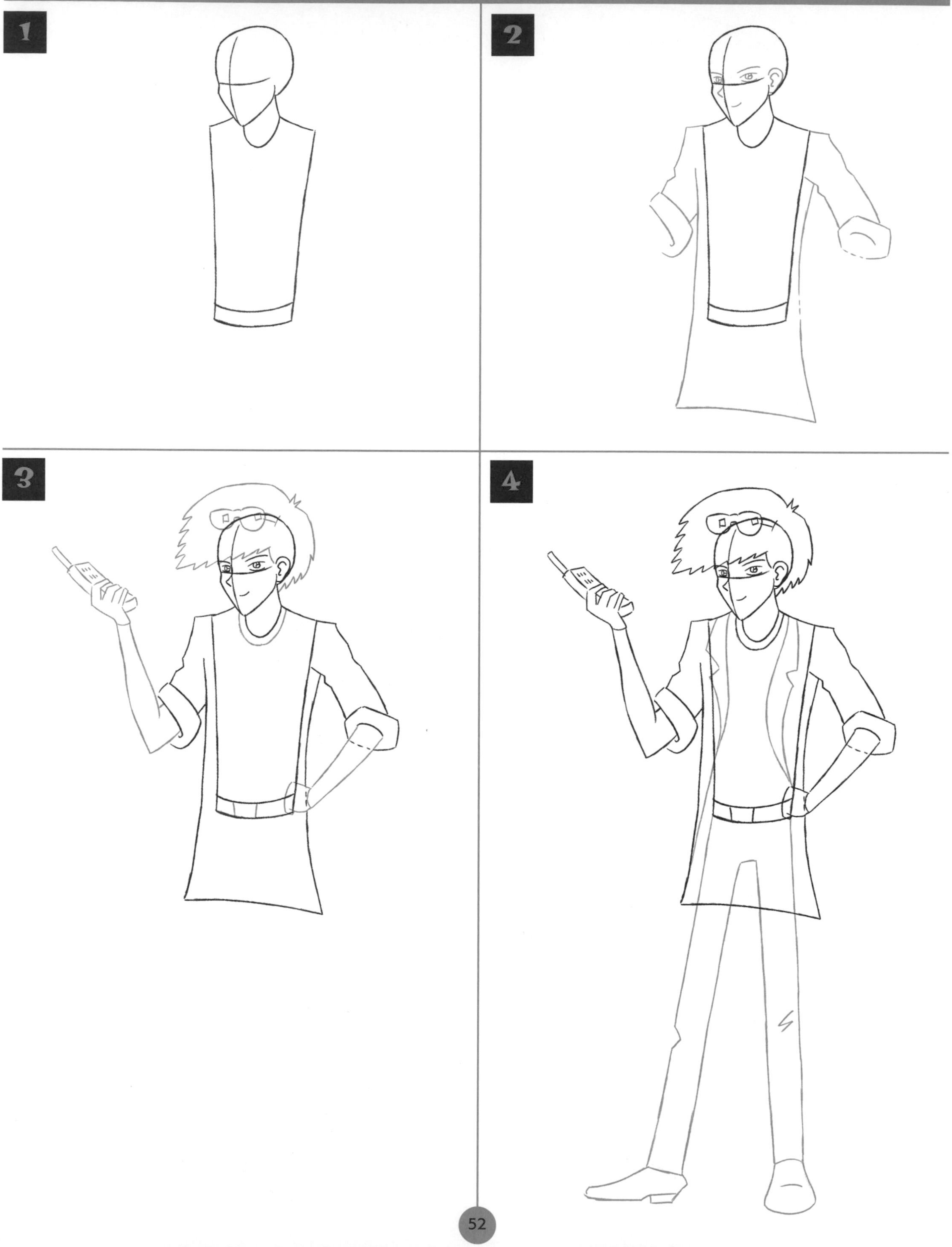

1
2
3
4

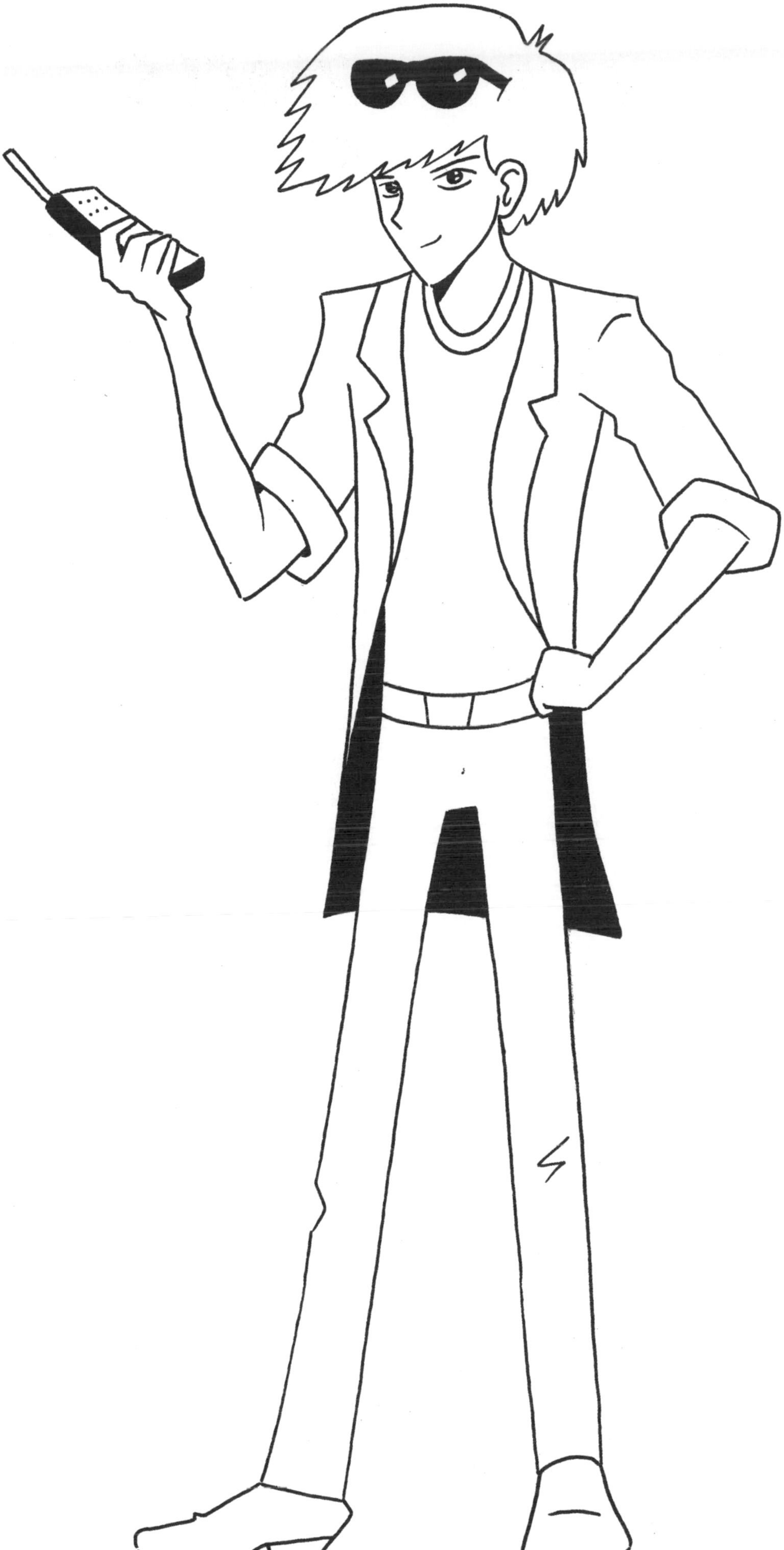

ZEBRA PANTS

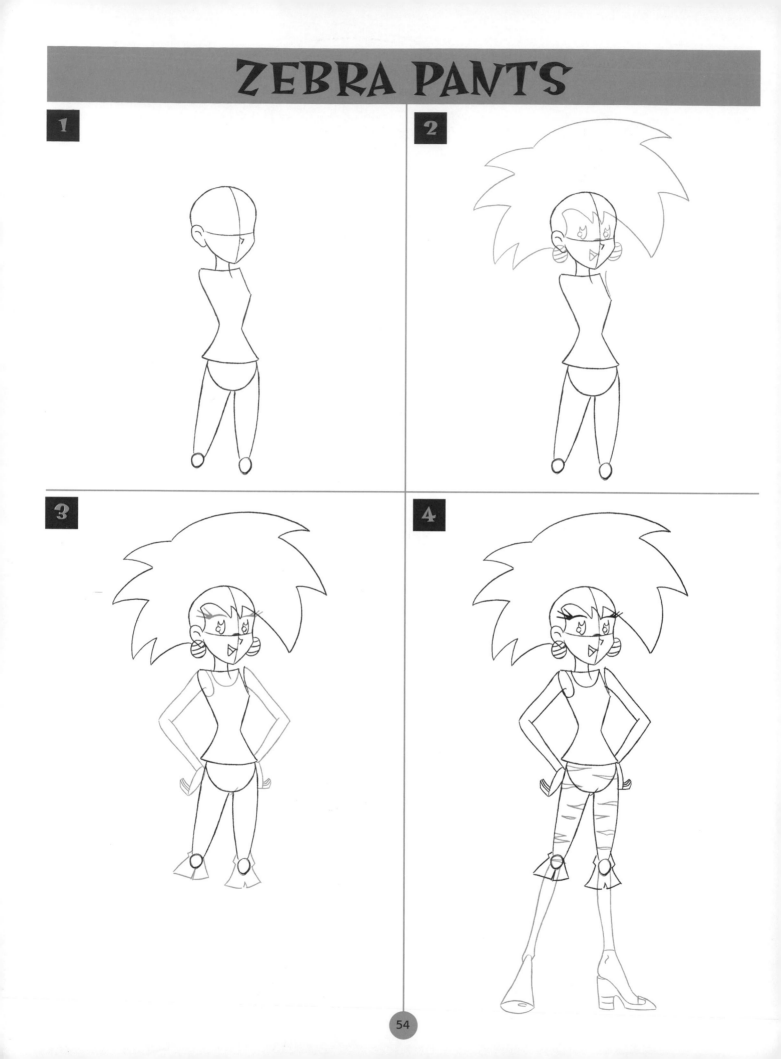

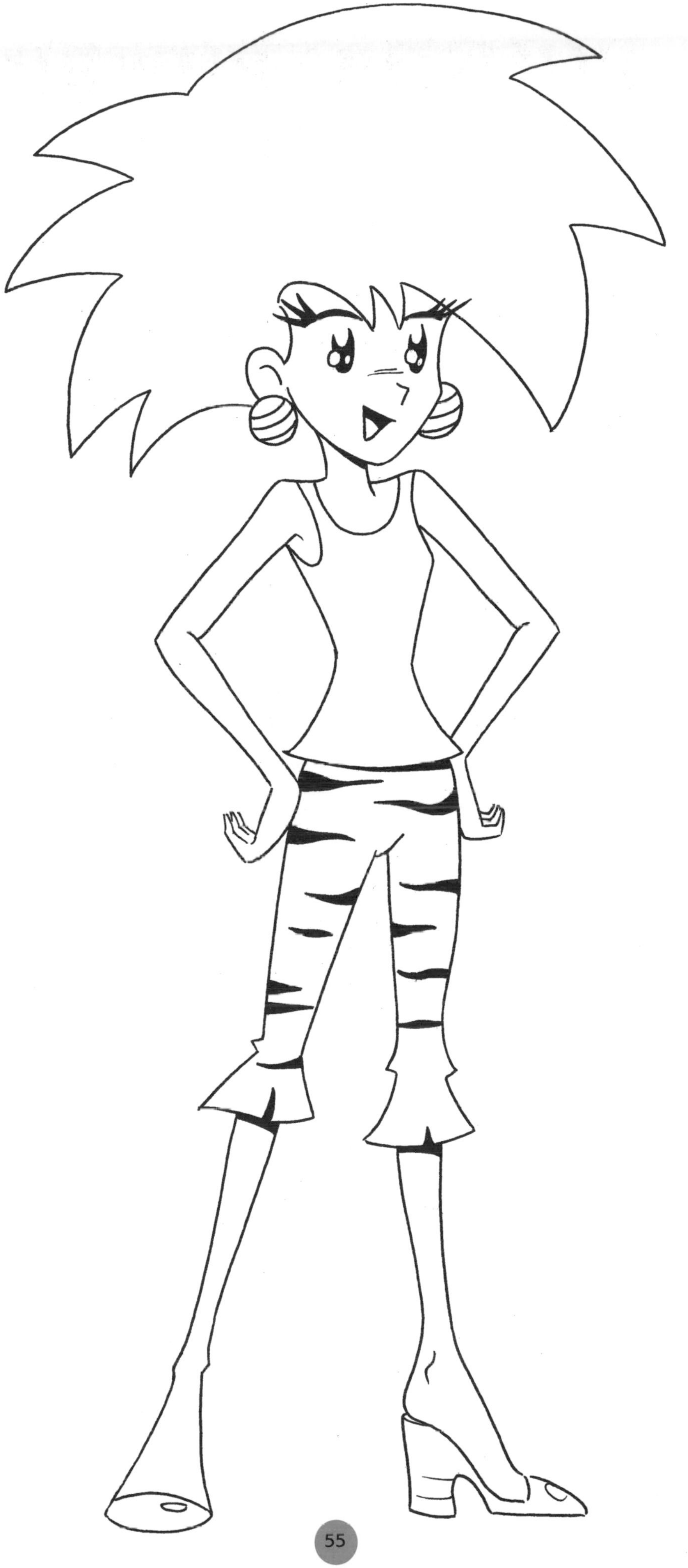

PULSING POWER

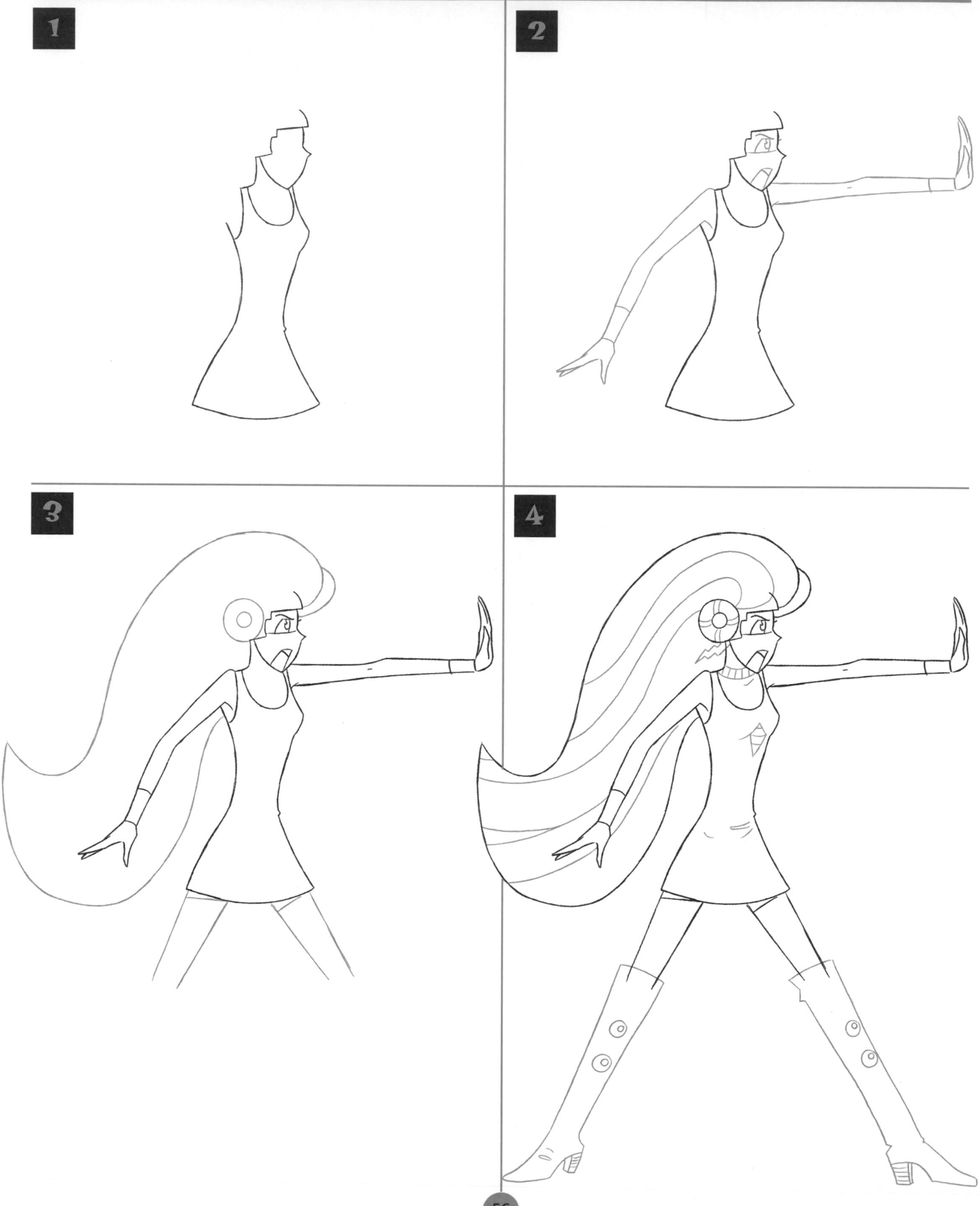
1
2
3
4

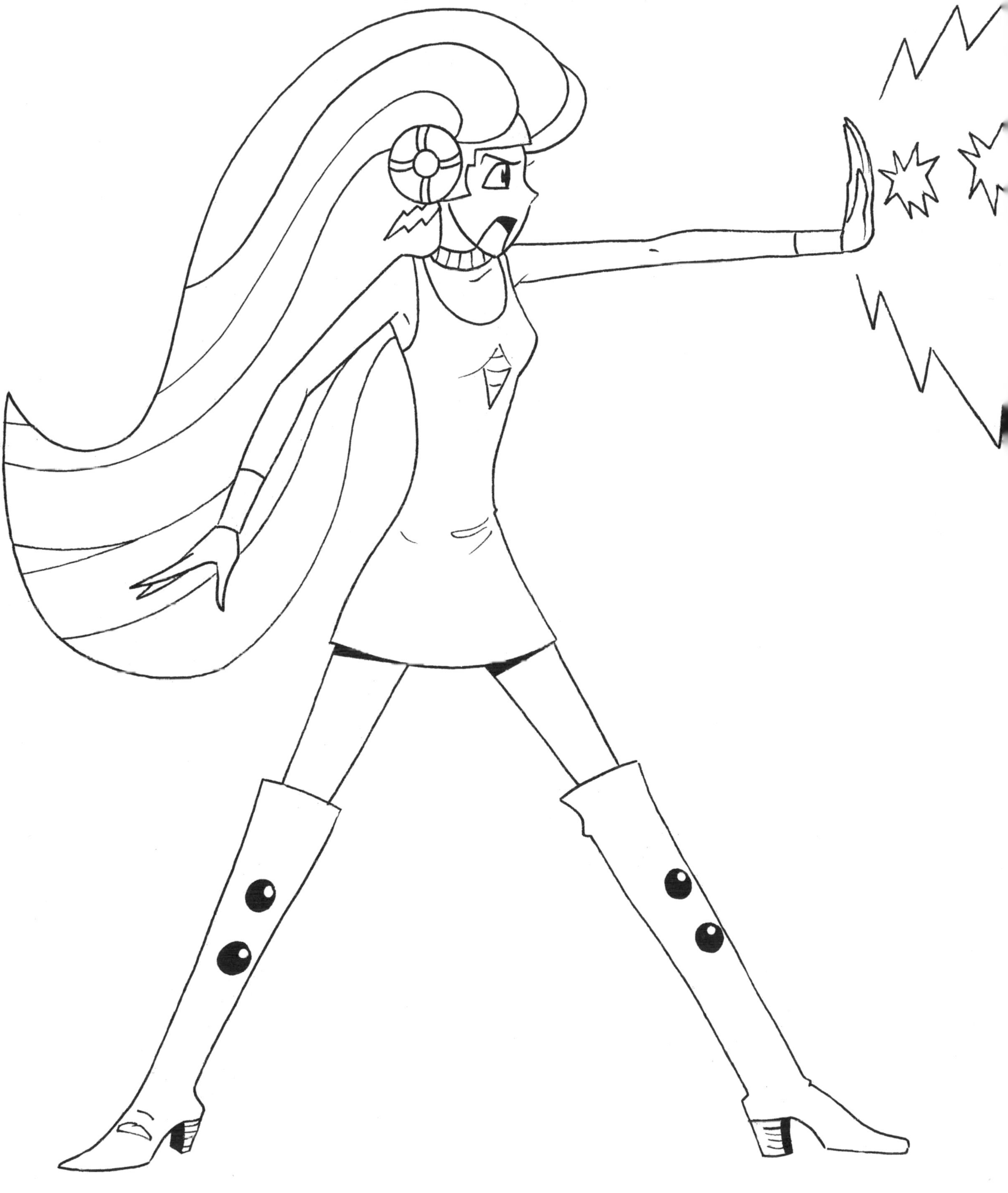

EVIL WARLOCK

1

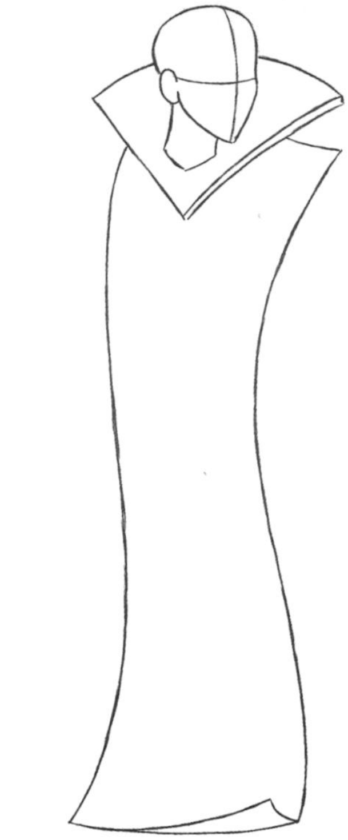

2

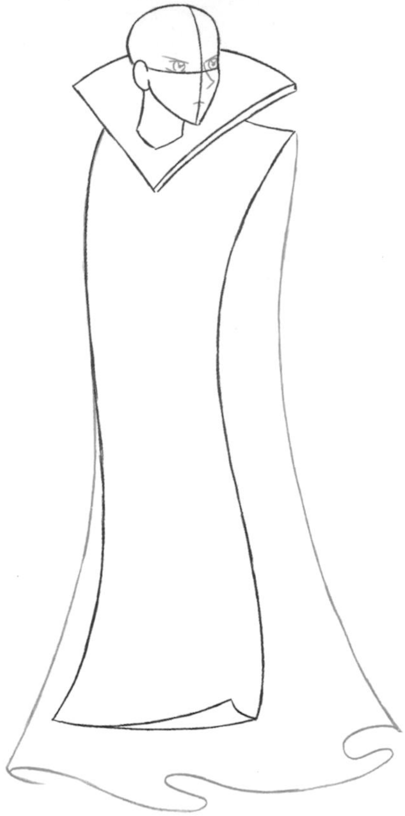

3

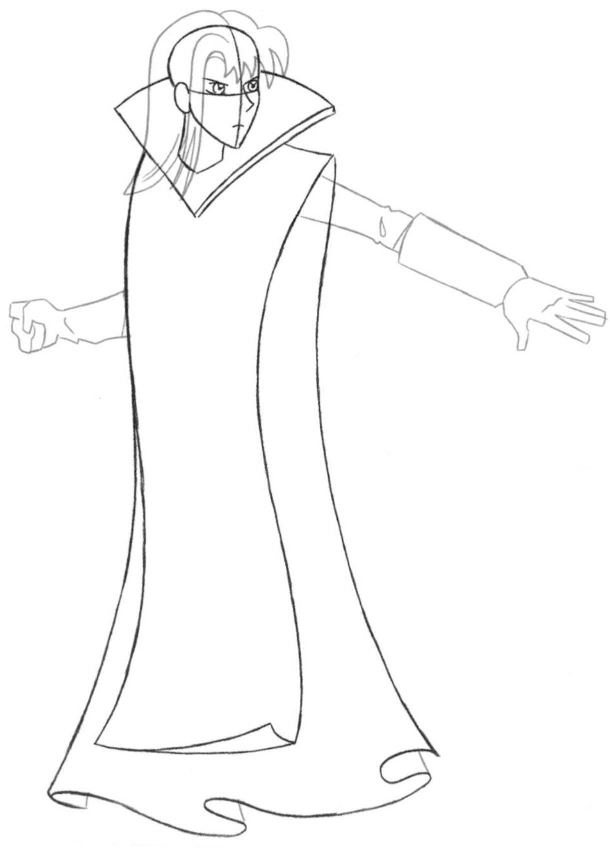

4

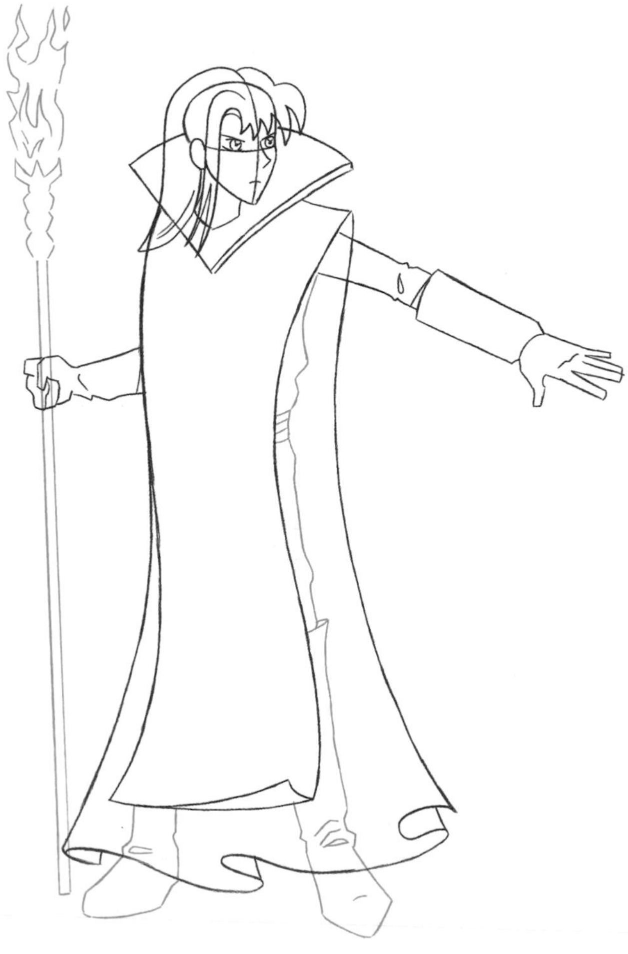

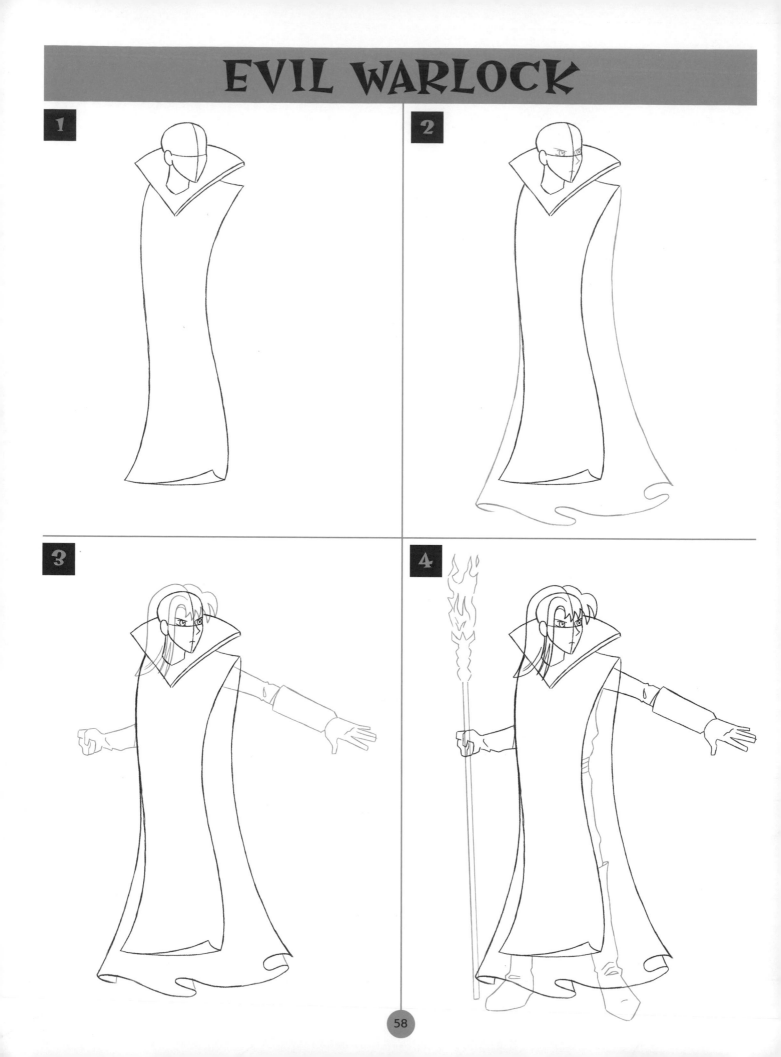

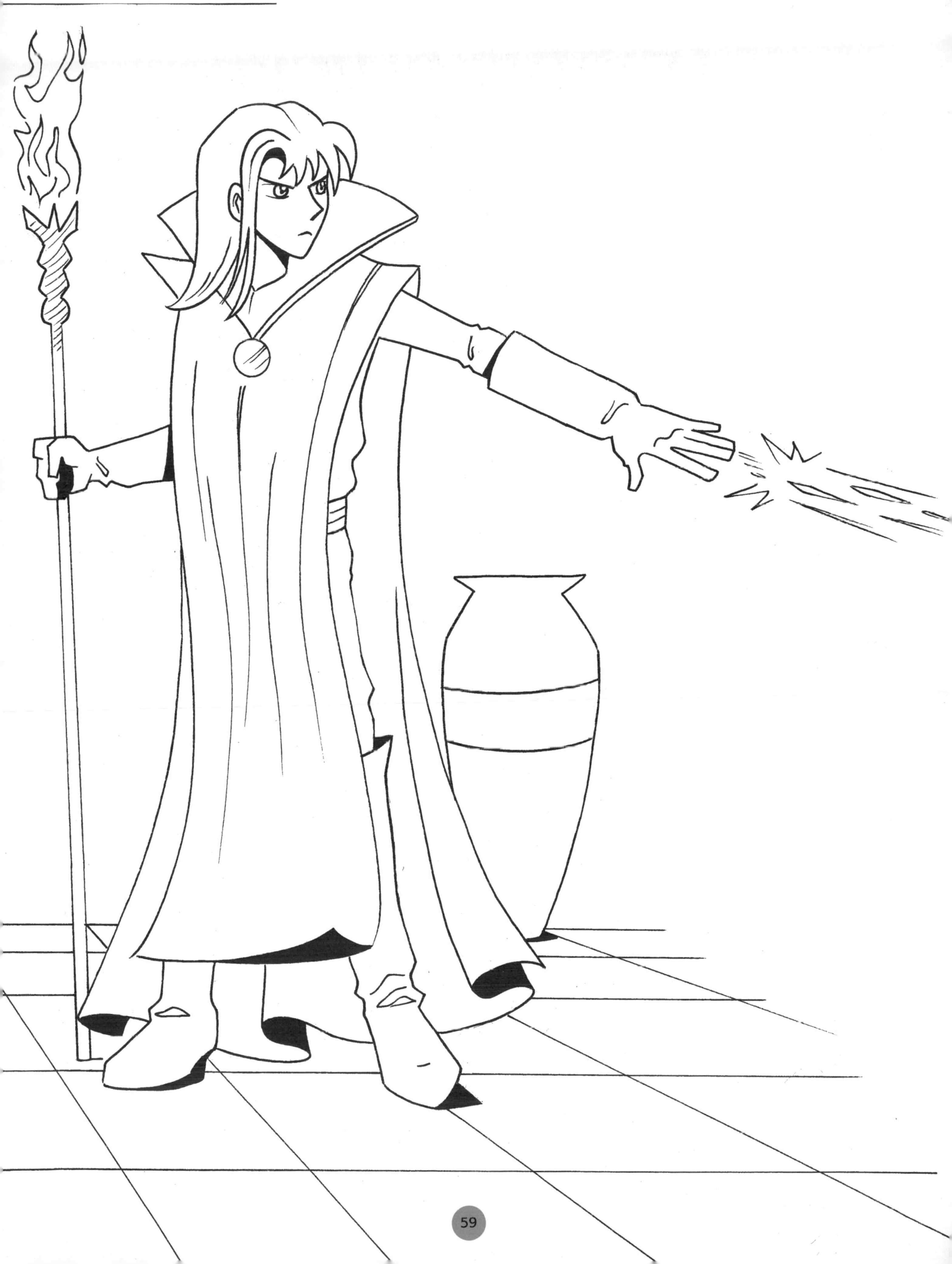

LEAPING DANCER

1

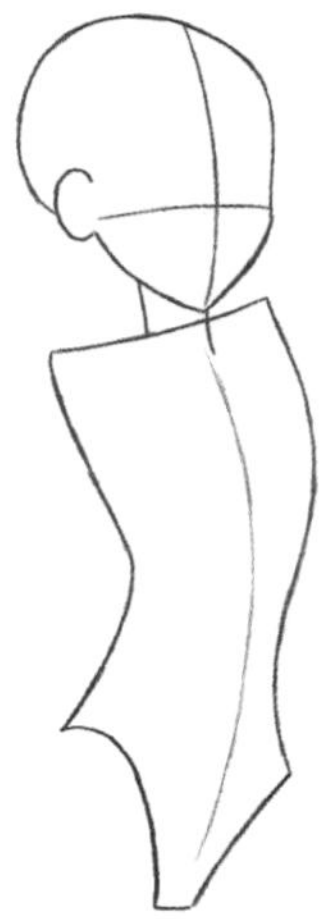

2

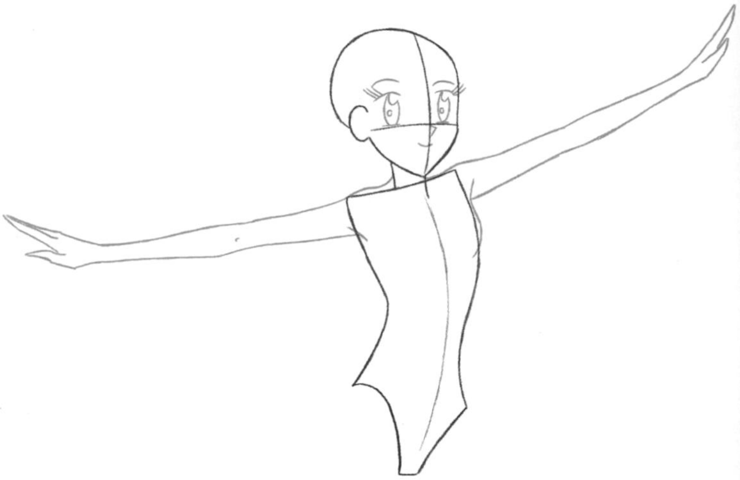

3

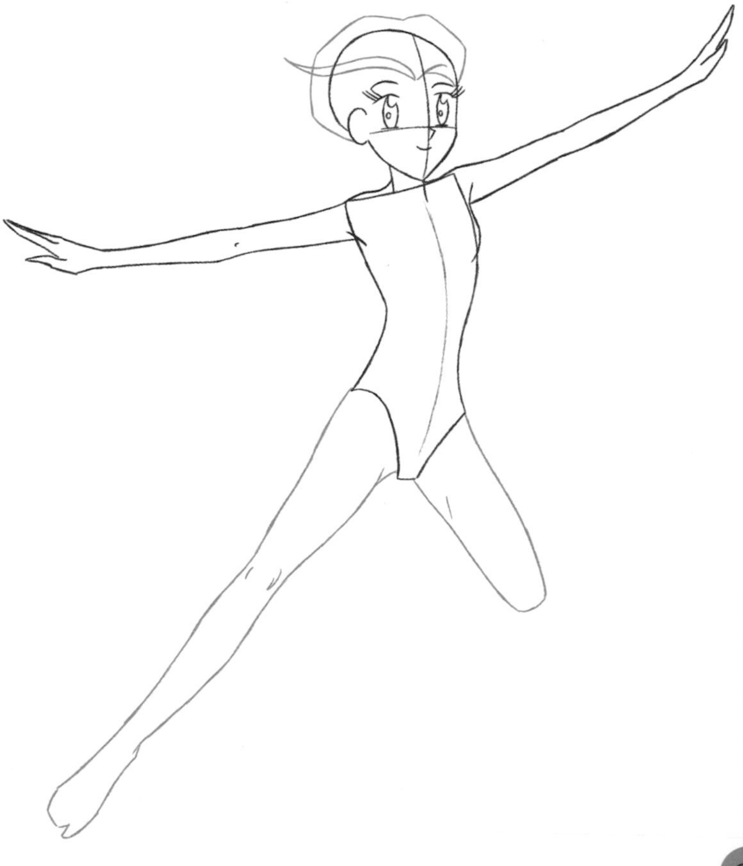

4

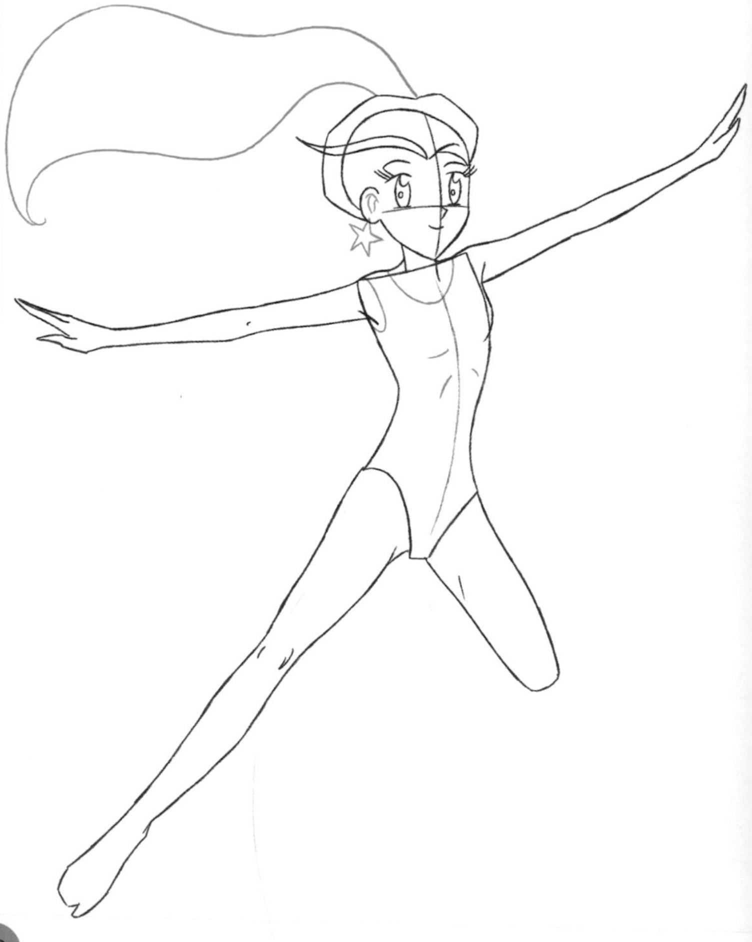

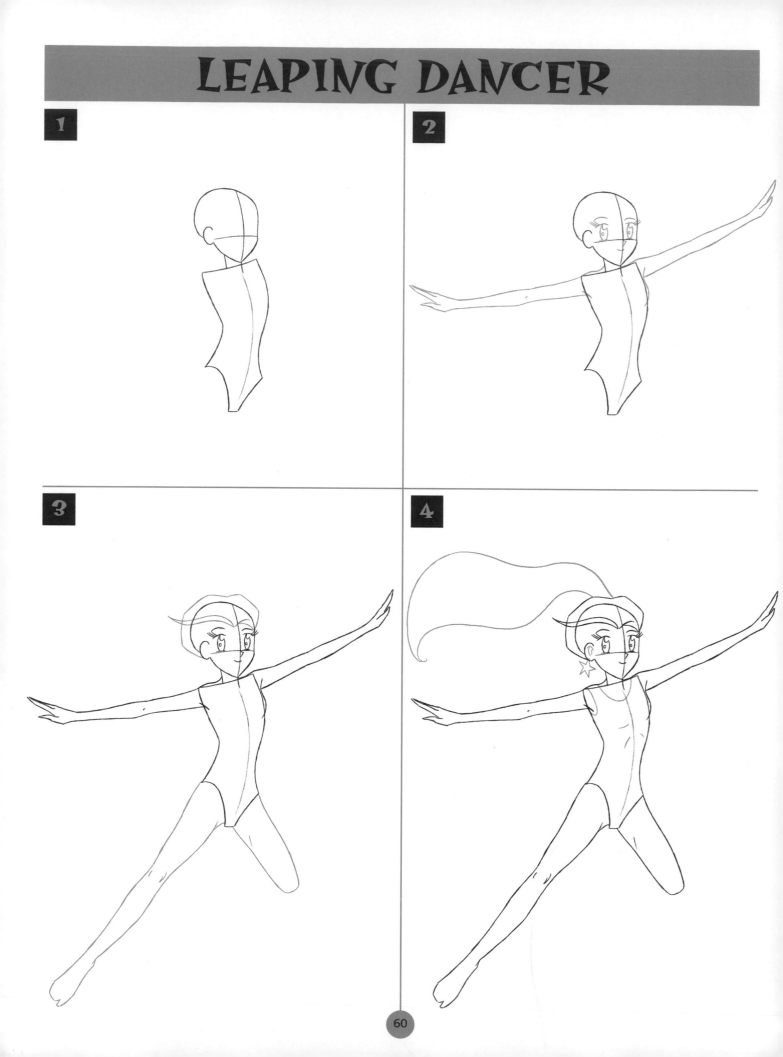

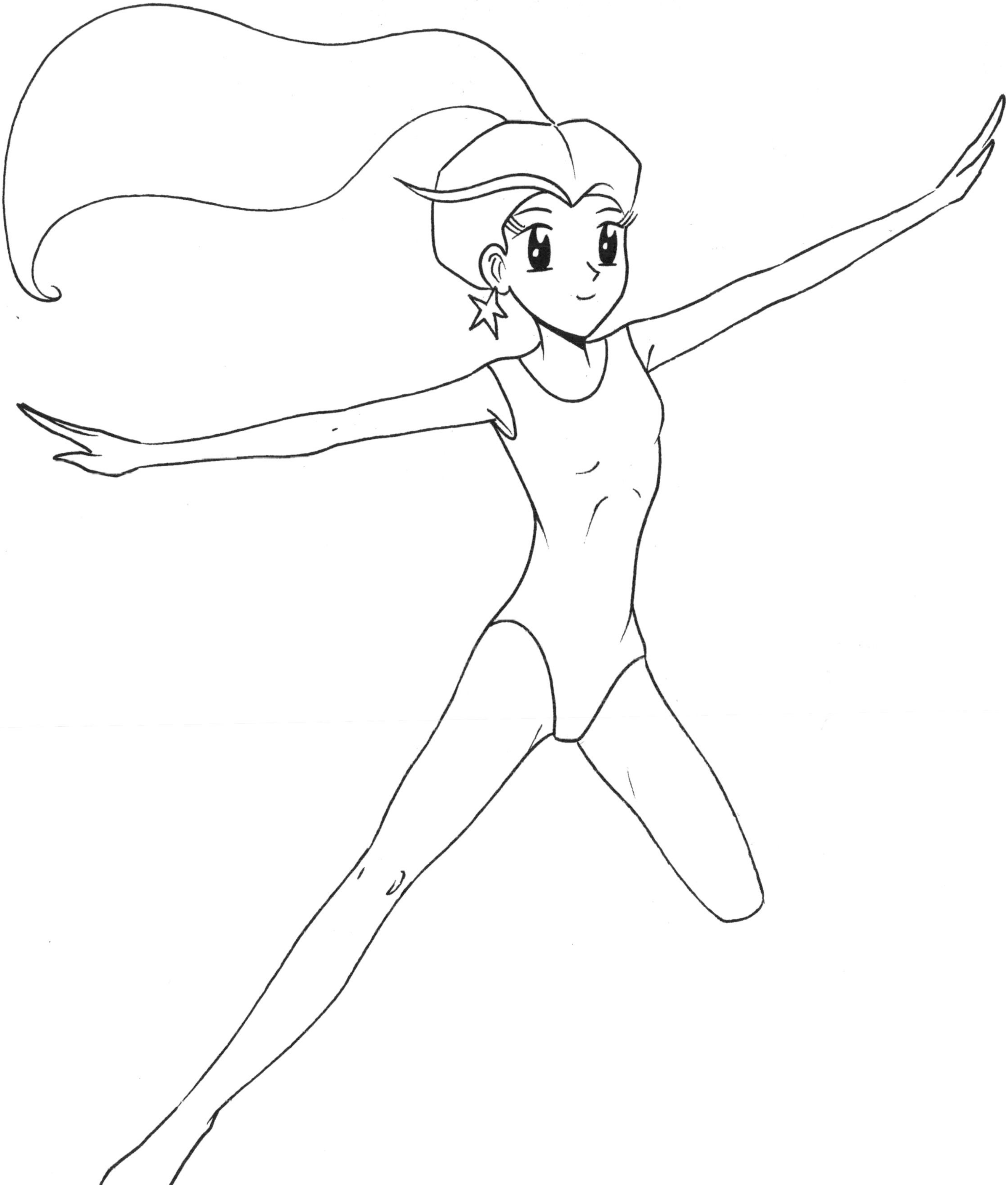

BIG CRUSH

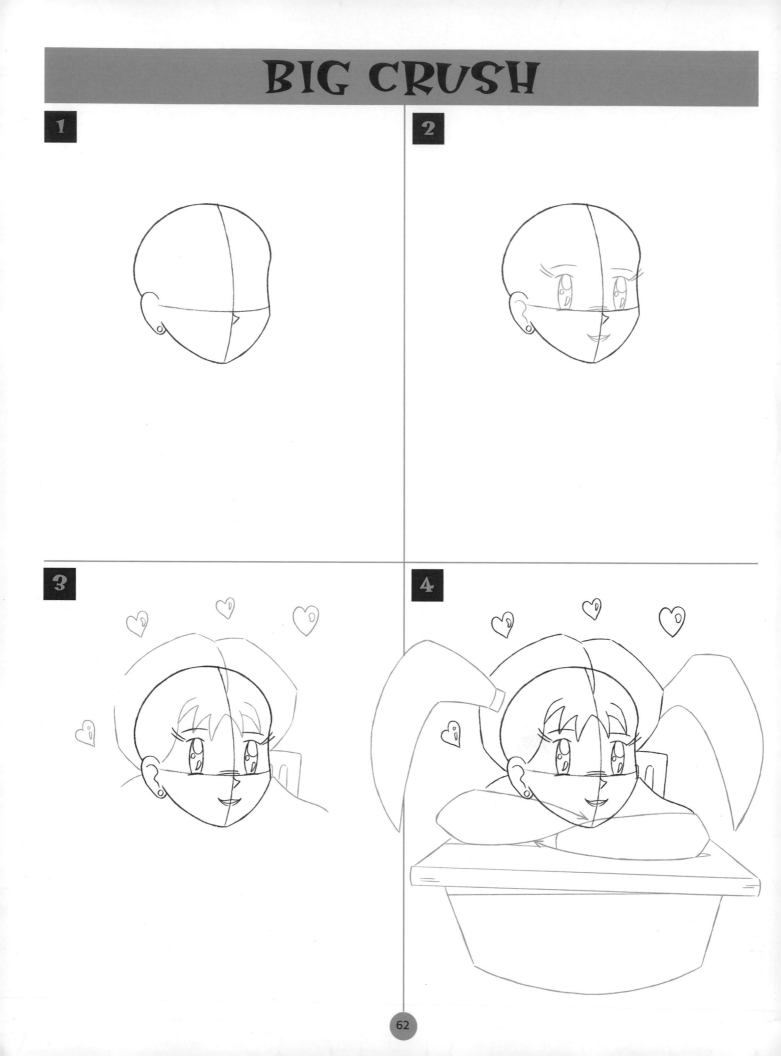

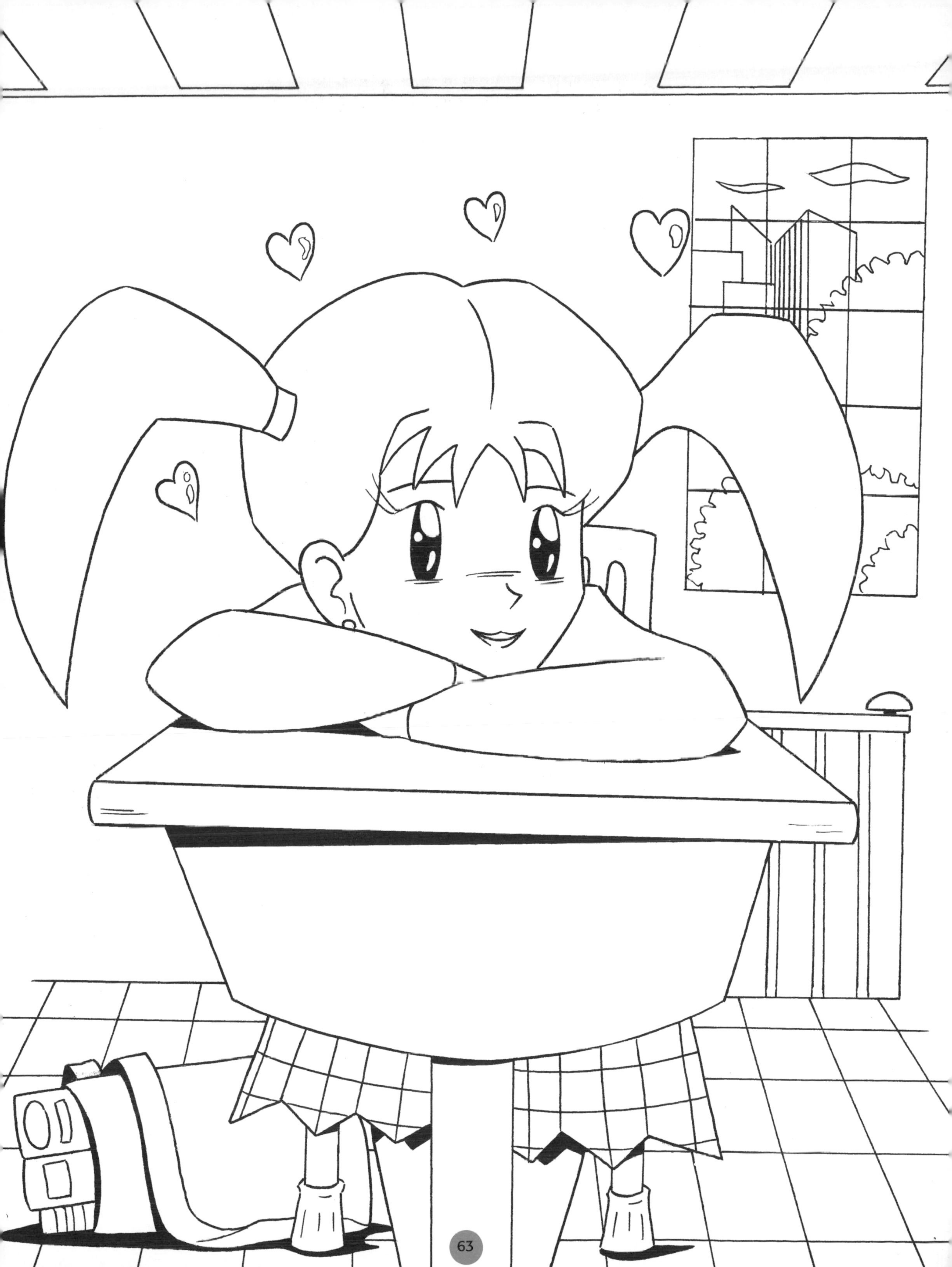

METEOR GIRL

1

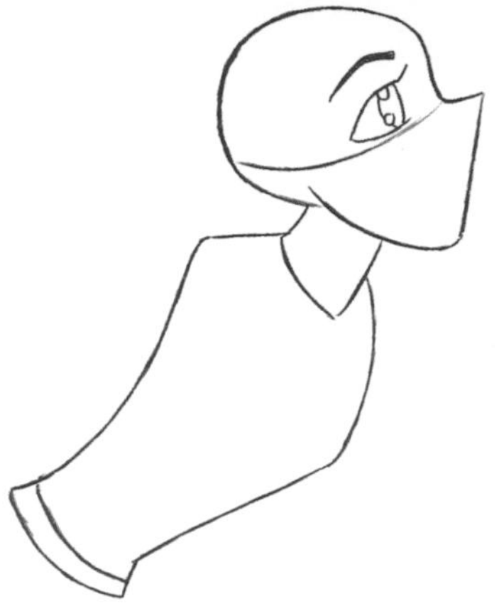

2

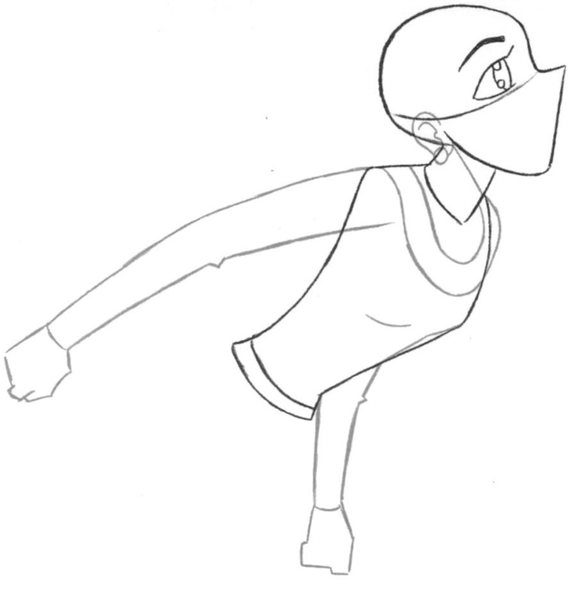

3

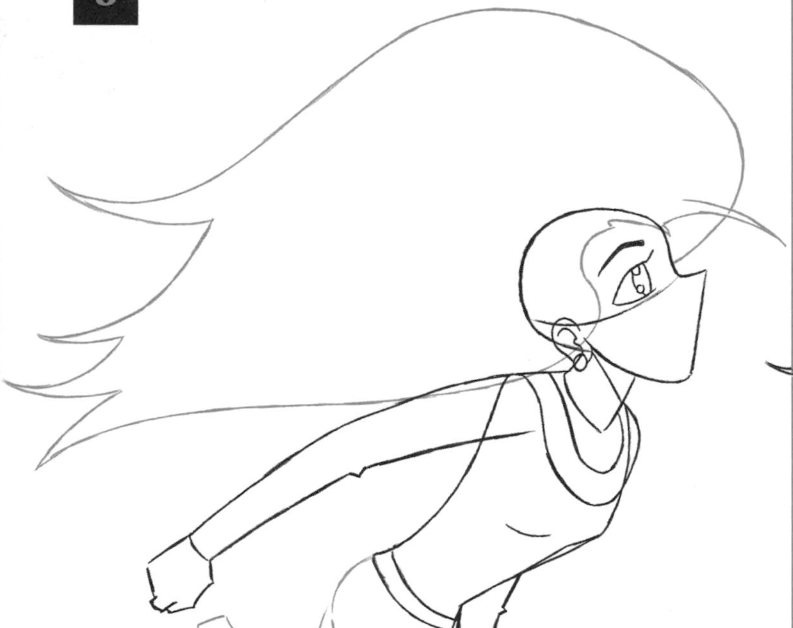

4

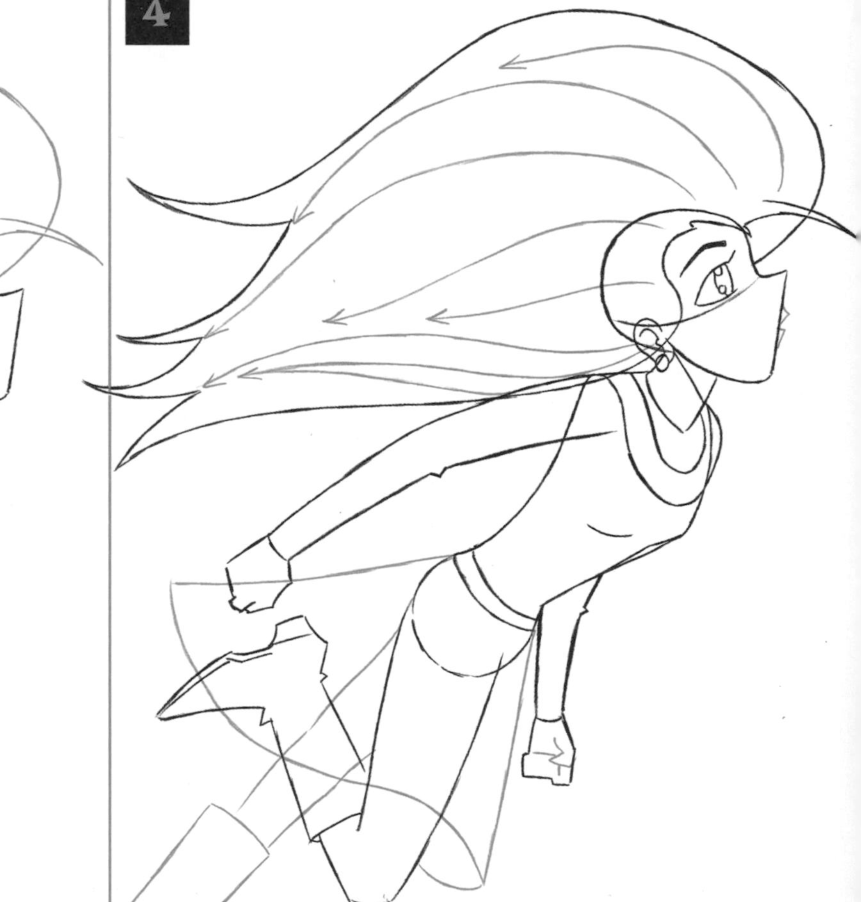

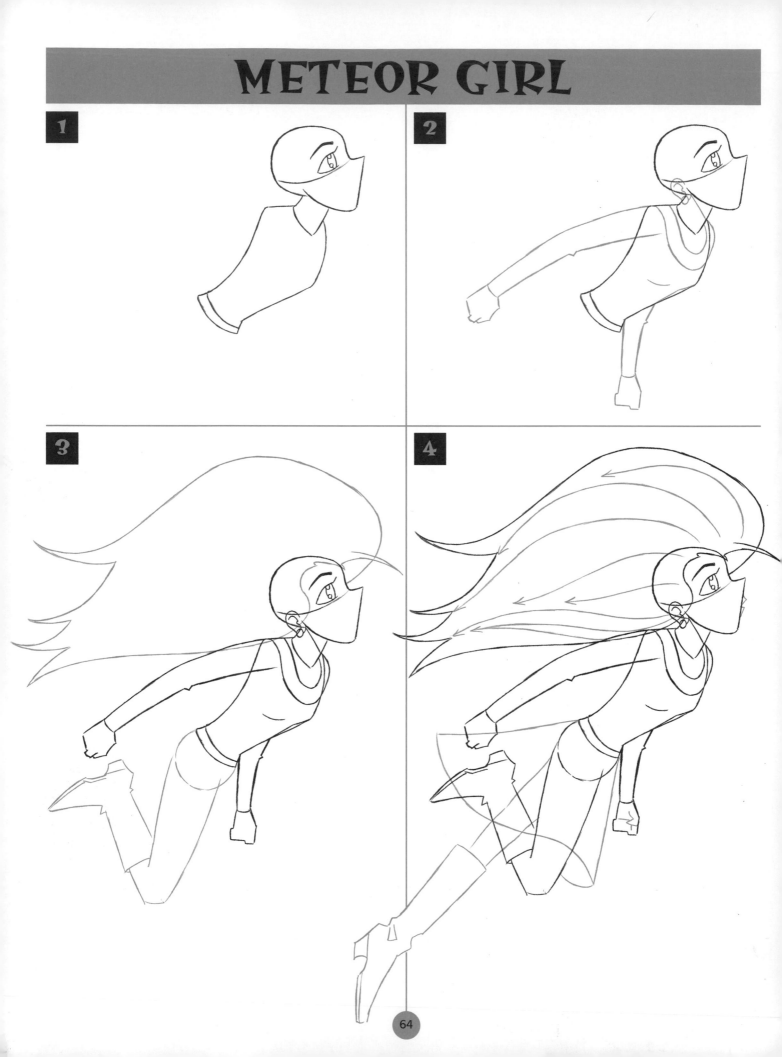

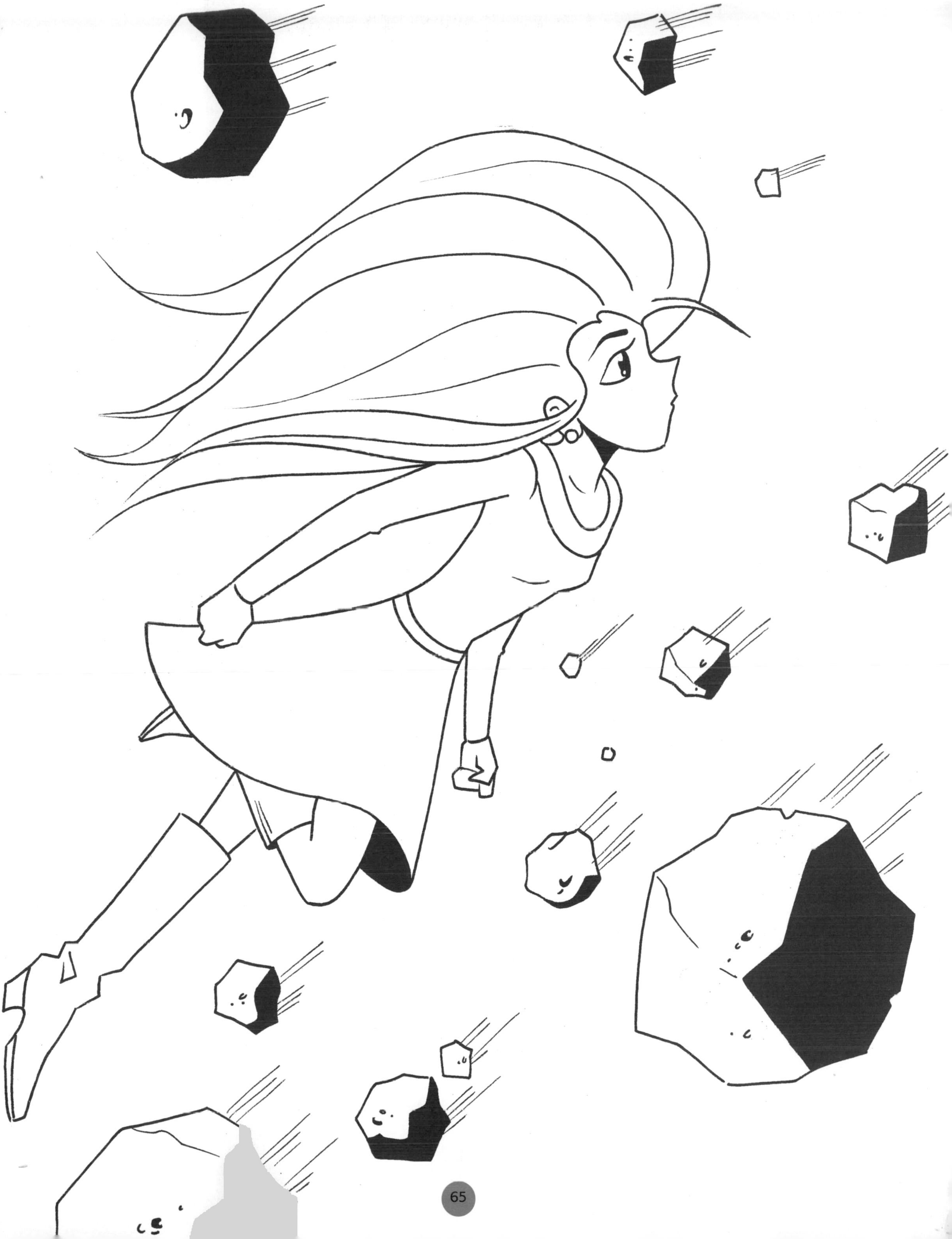

FLYING BOY

1

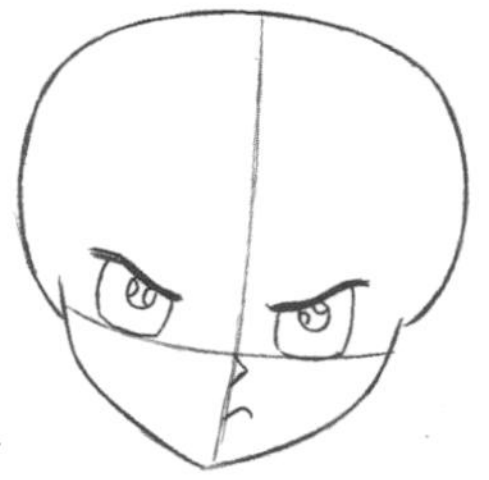

2

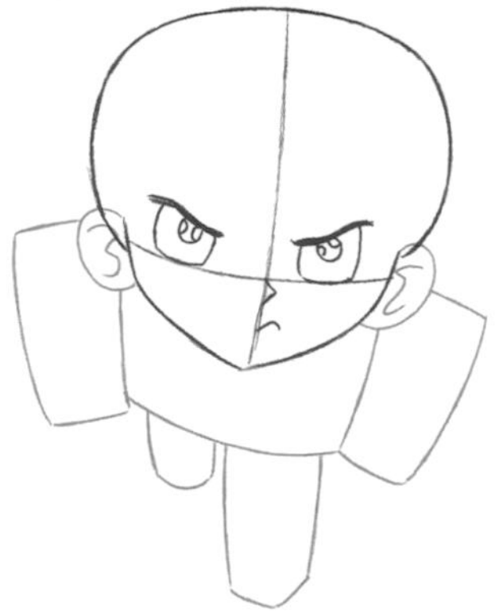

3

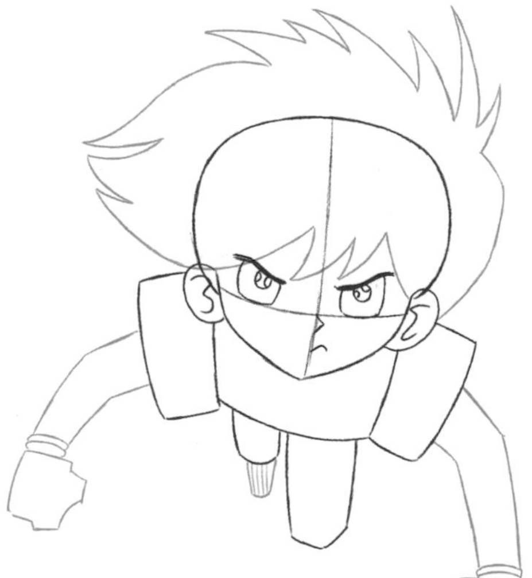

4

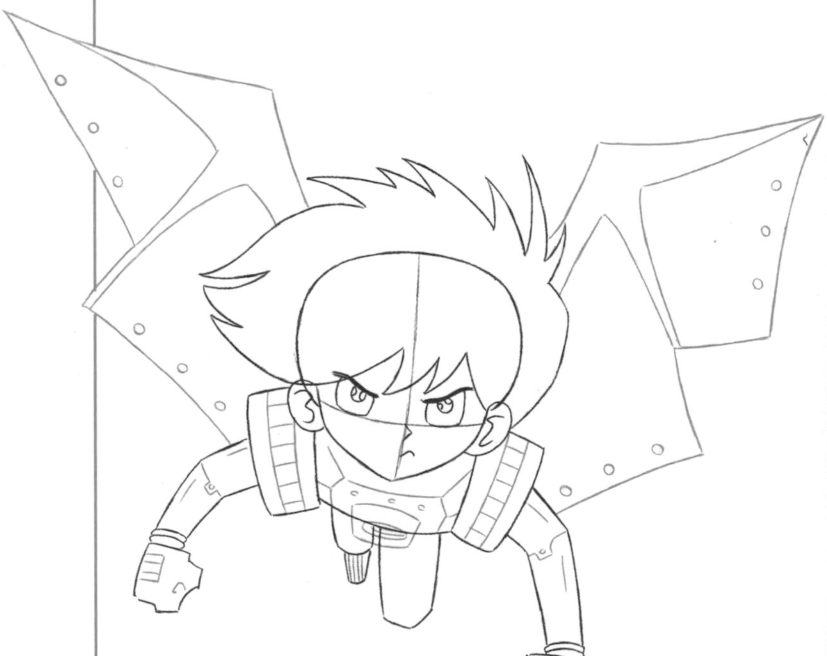

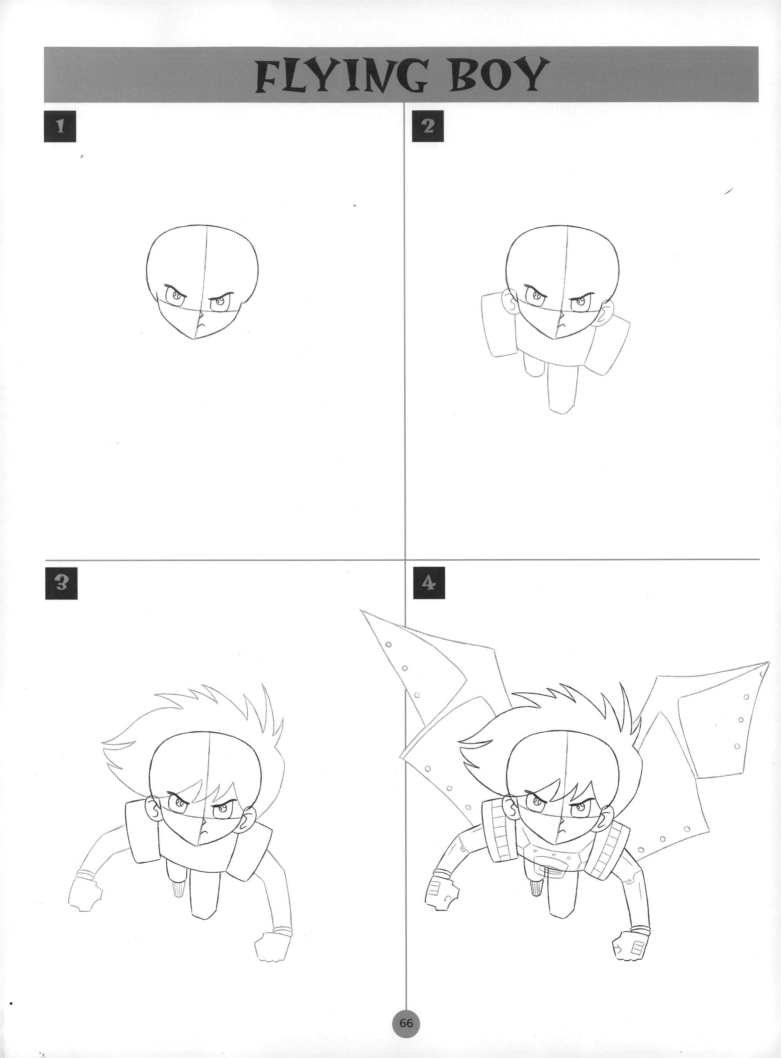

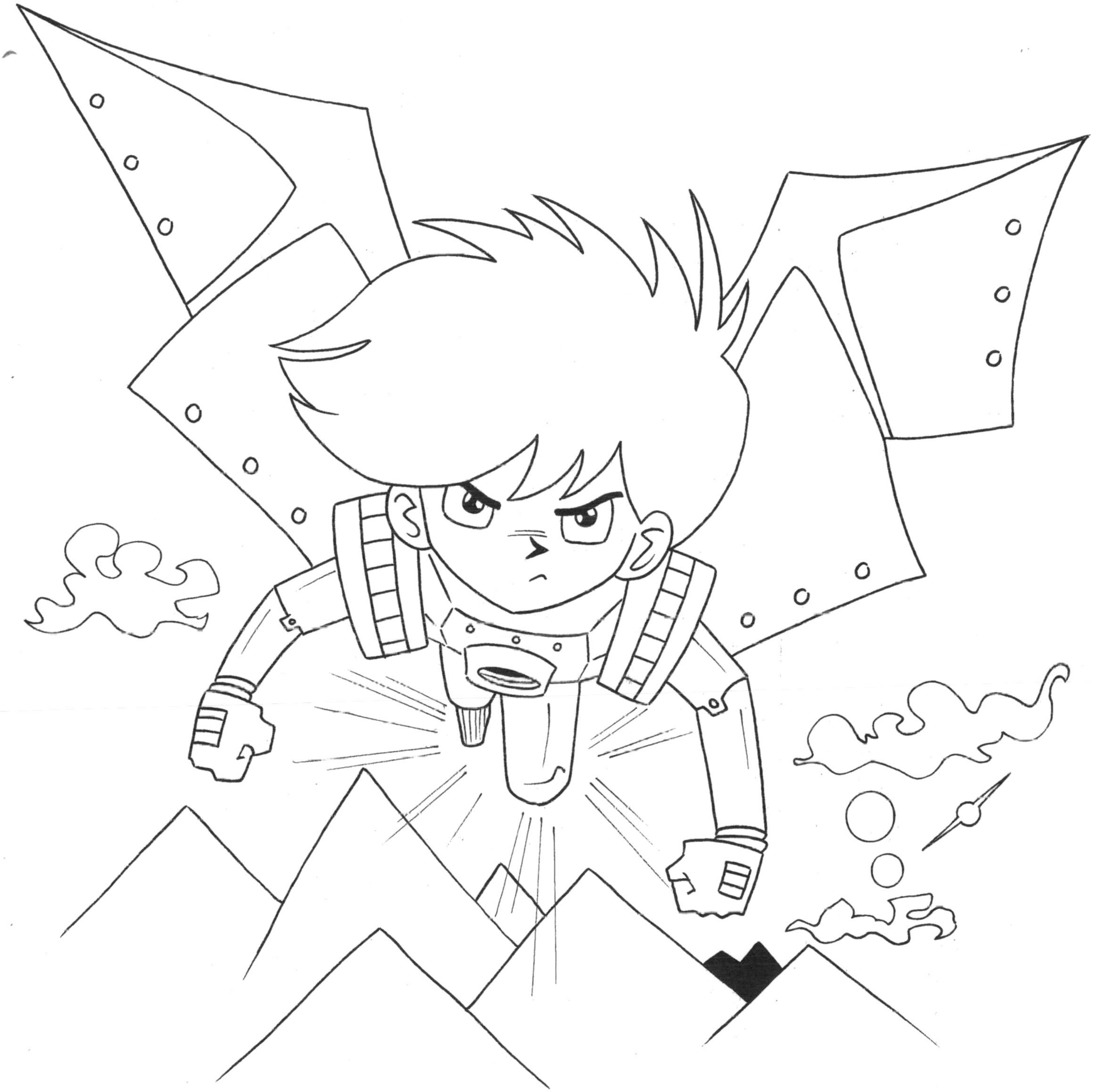

PART 2
DRAW MANGA CHIBI!

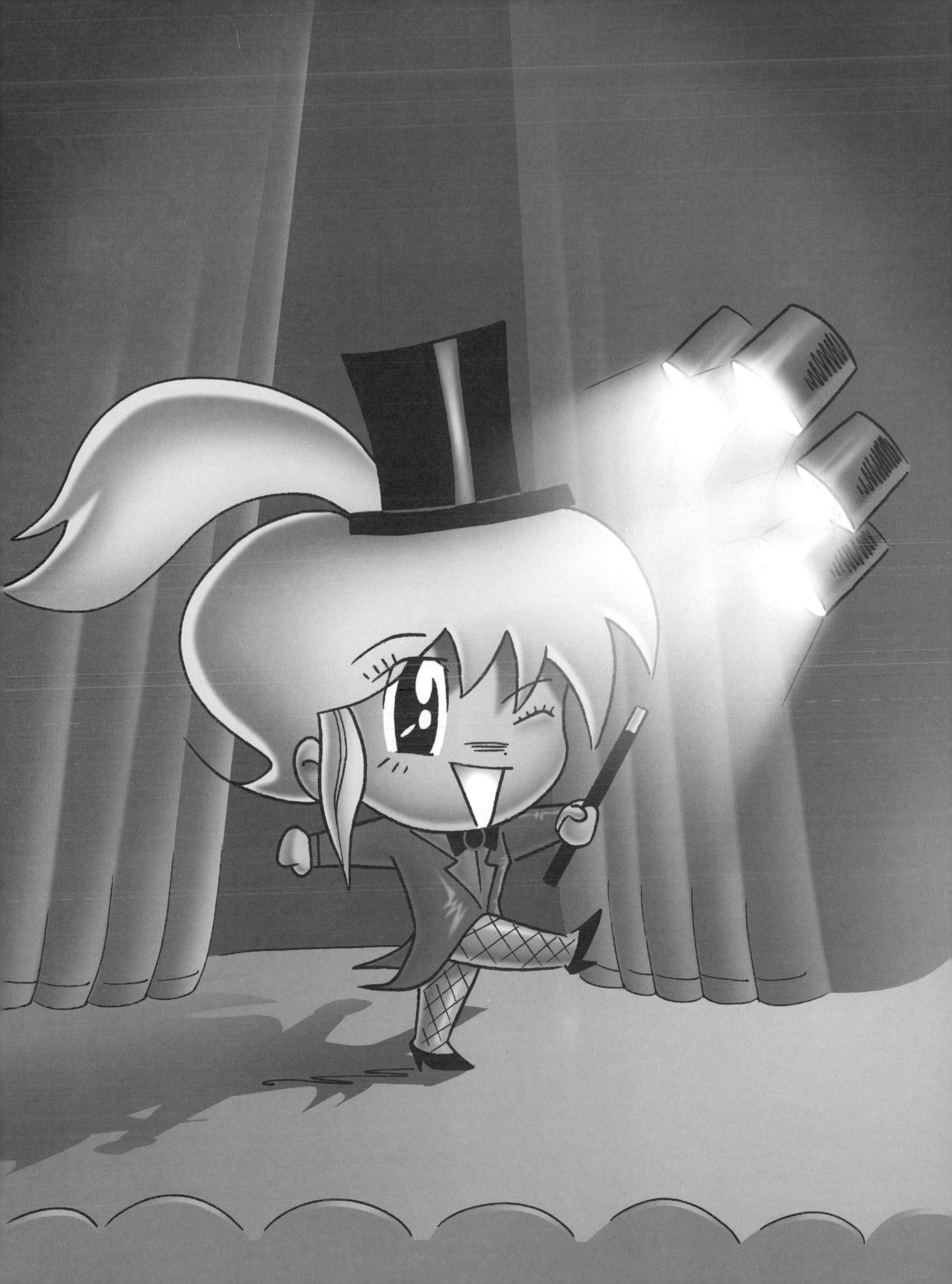

THE BASICS

Let's start with some basics for drawing chibi-style characters.

Chibis are shorter, rounder, and cuter than other manga characters. To help show you the difference, I've drawn the same girl two different ways. Here she is drawn as a regular manga-style cartoon. Below, she's drawn as a chibi.

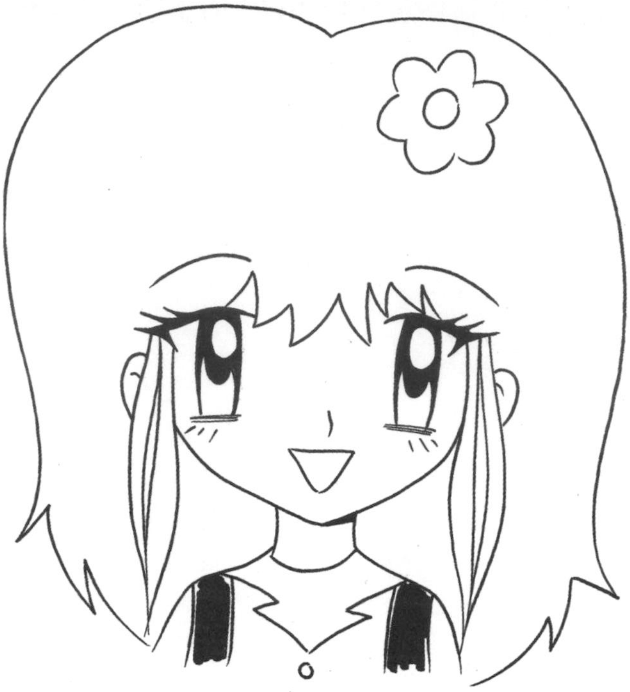

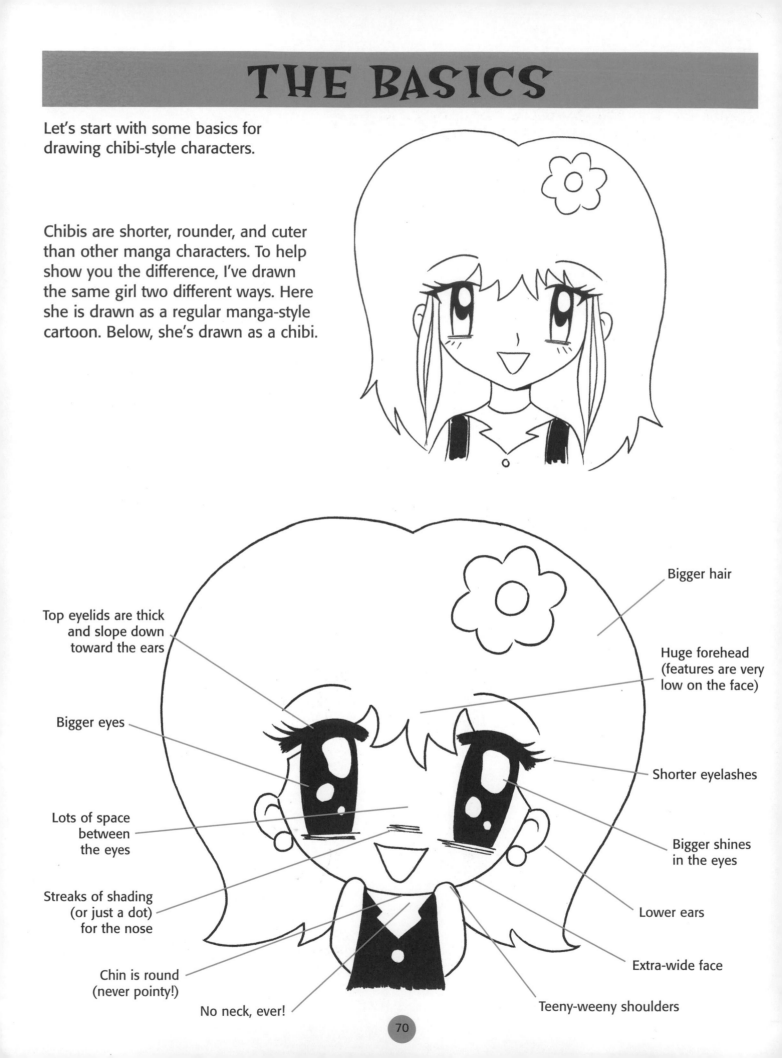

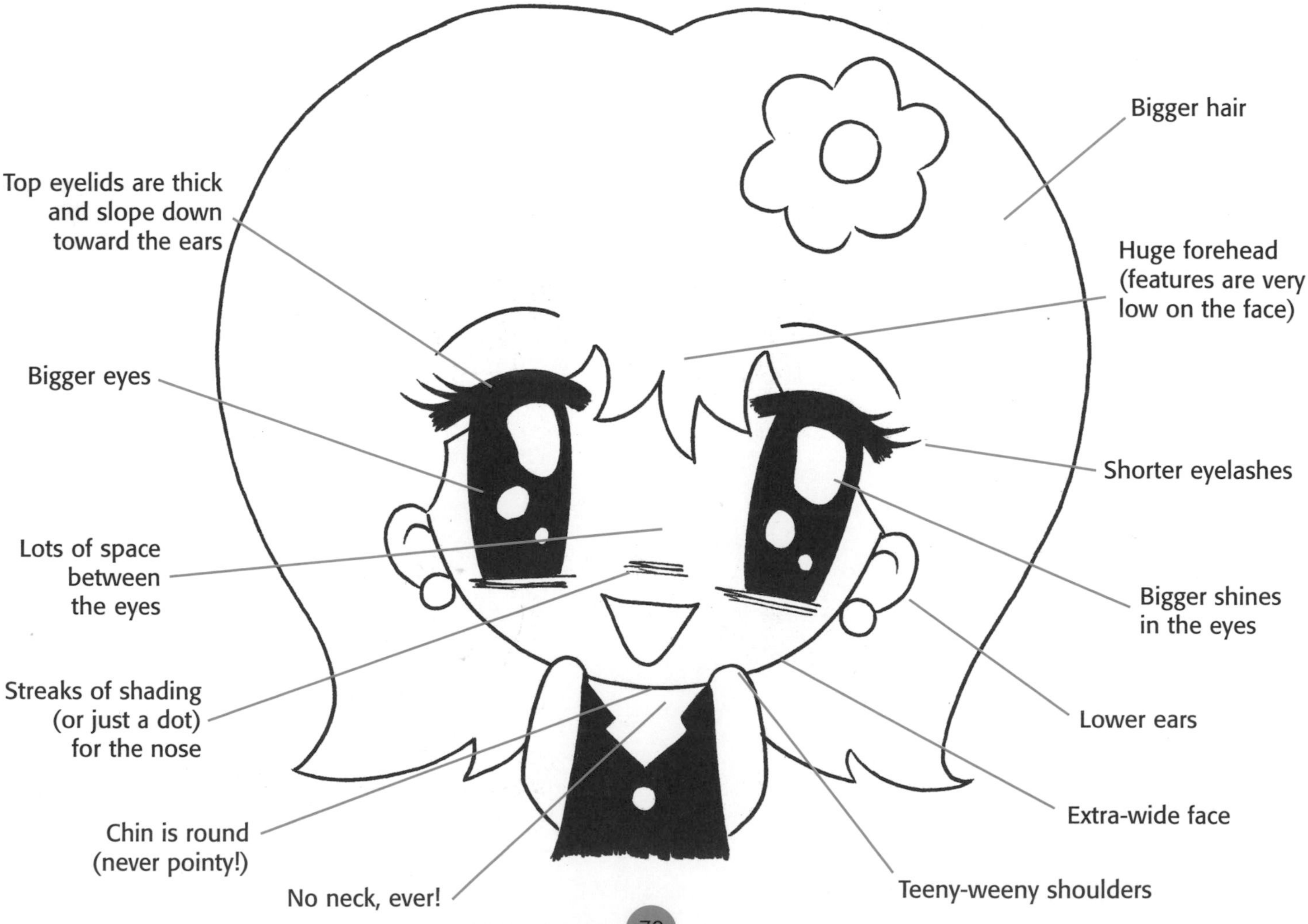
Bigger hair
Top eyelids are thick and slope down toward the ears
Huge forehead (features are very low on the face)
Bigger eyes
Shorter eyelashes
Lots of space between the eyes
Bigger shines in the eyes
Streaks of shading (or just a dot) for the nose
Lower ears
Extra-wide face
Chin is round (never pointy!)
No neck, ever!
Teeny-weeny shoulders

Chibis have eyes that are huge and full of shines. To draw them, start by drawing the overall shape of the eye. Then fill in the details. Just follow these steps and you'll see how simple and fun it is!

The eyelids should tilt down.

1. DRAW "TALL" EYES.

2. MAKE THE TOP EYELIDS REALLY THICK.

The ends of the eyelids should have these points on them.

3. ADD EYELASHES TO THE ENDS, THEN DRAW TWO HUGE SHINES IN EACH EYE.

4. COLOR IT ALL IN (EXCEPT THE SHINES). ADD THE EYEBROWS.

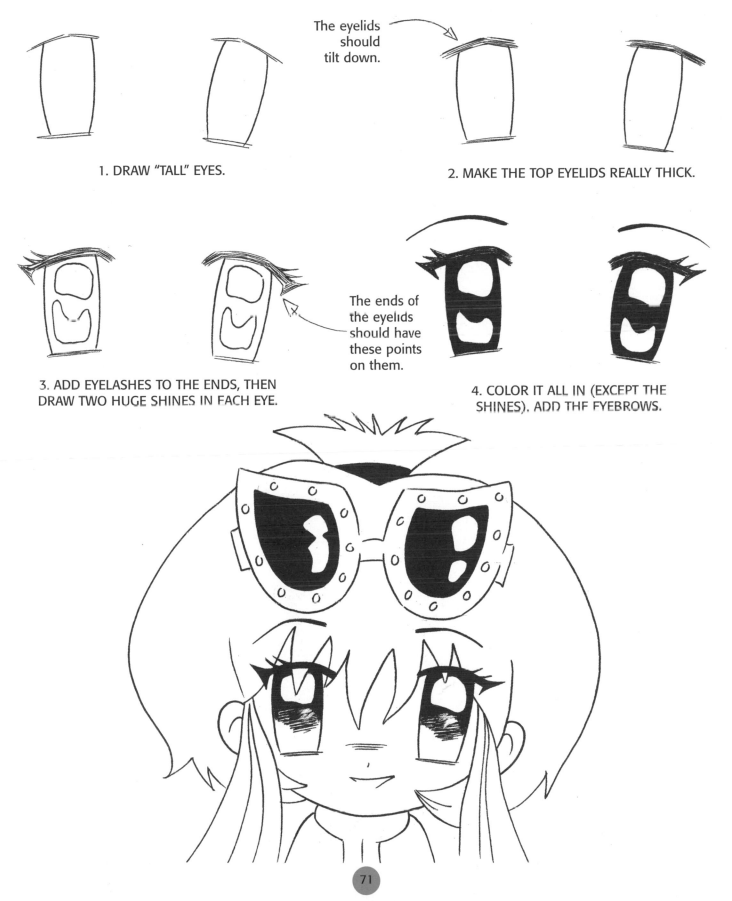

Most real people are about six and a half heads tall. But chibis are only two heads tall. This means that a chibi's head is as big as its body! Chibi legs are short, while the legs of regular-sized characters are long. If you draw a chibi and it doesn't look cute enough, go back and check the proportions. Chances are, you need to make the head bigger.

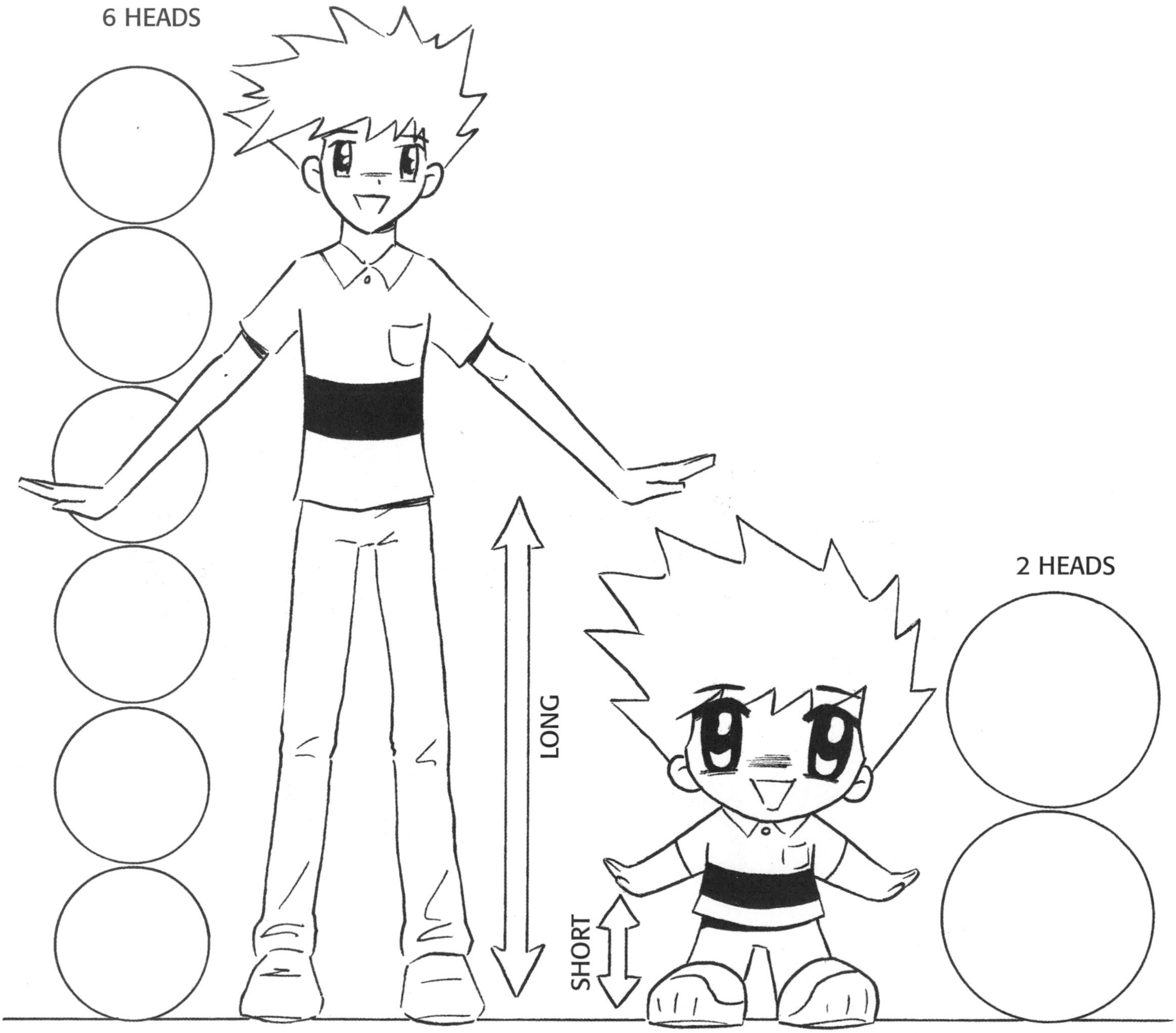

6 HEADS
LONG
SHORT
2 HEADS

Because chibis are so short and round, their bodies are easy to draw. There is a rule of thumb when drawing chibis: Keep it simple. Look at the drawings below. You can see how their bodies are made up of basic shapes put together.

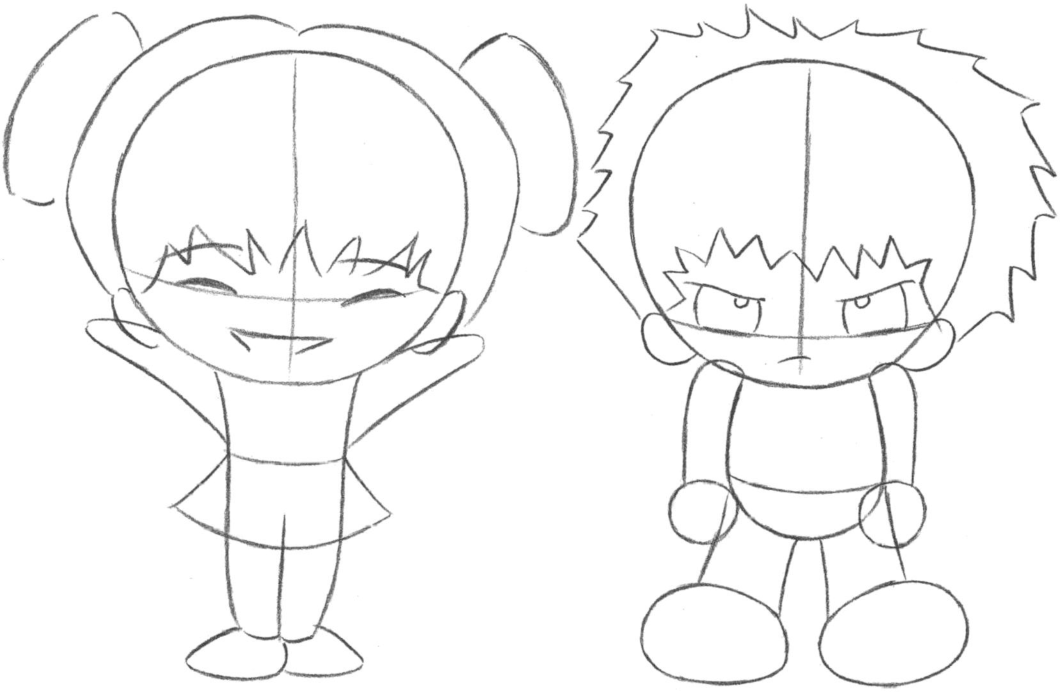

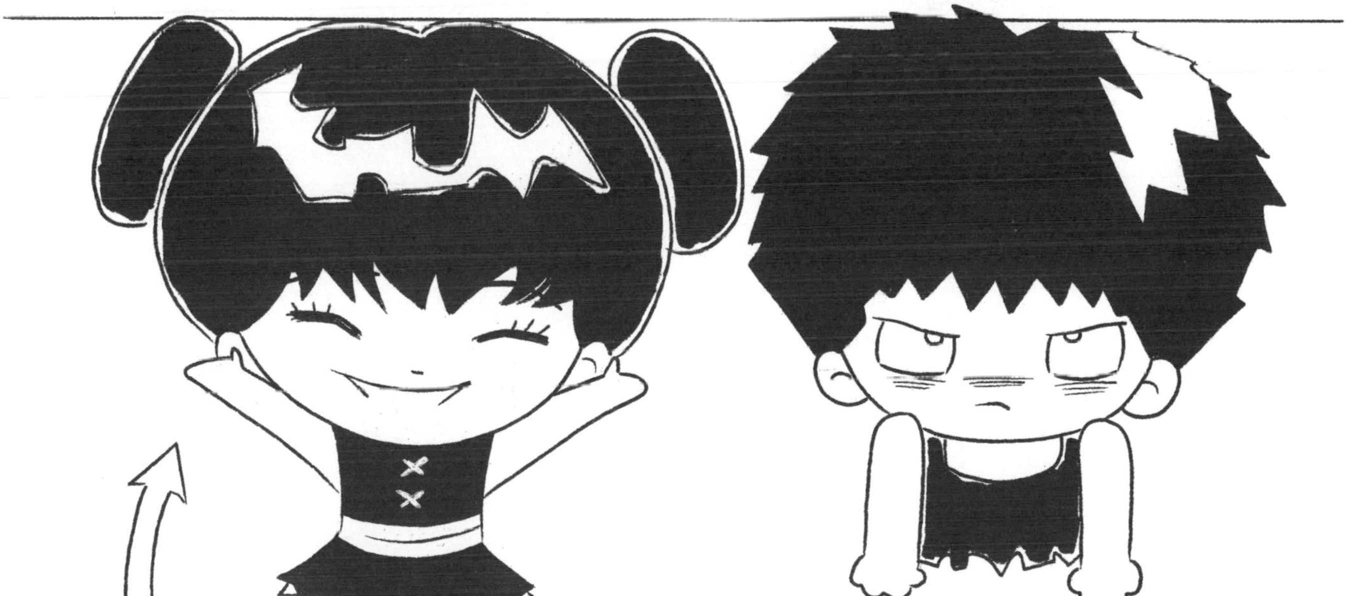

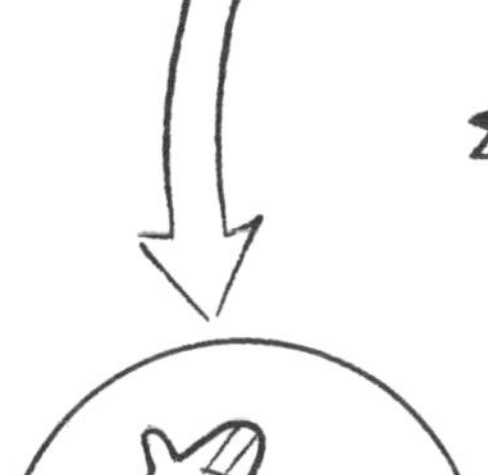

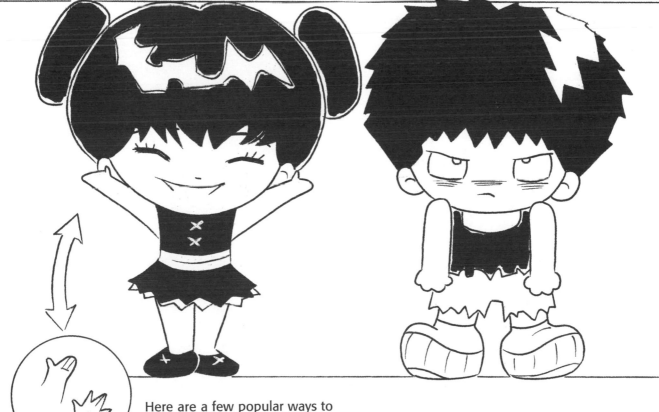

Here are a few popular ways to draw chibi hands and fingers.

Here are some more tips to help you.

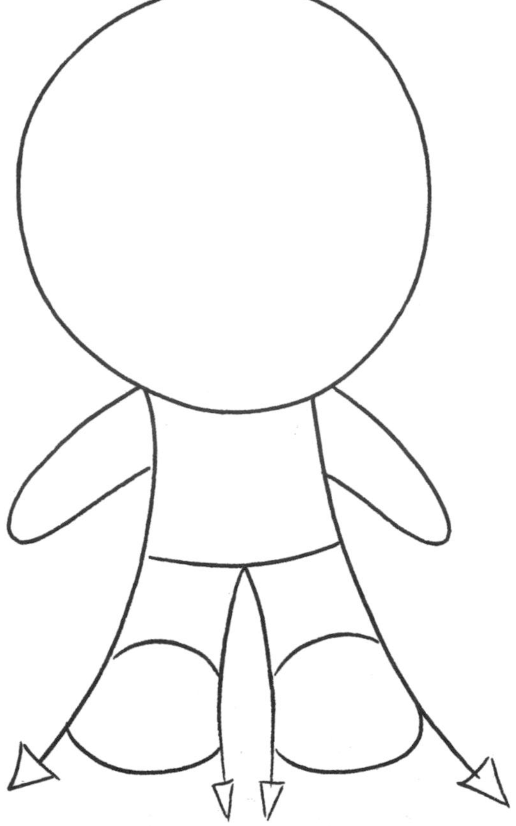

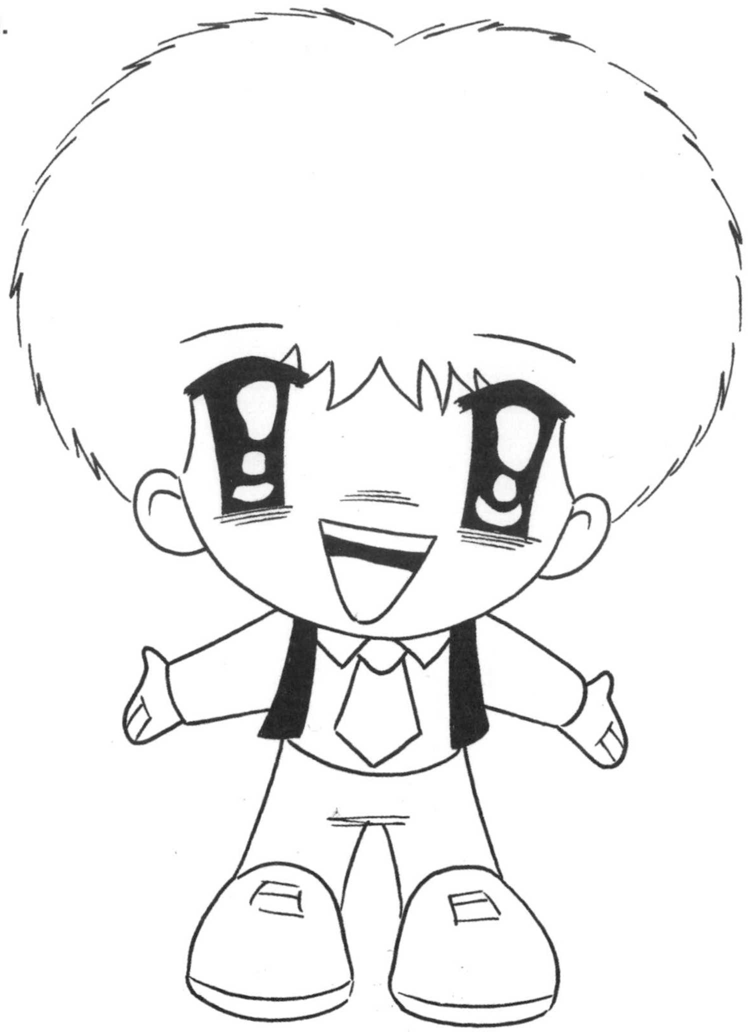

Chibi bodies start off narrow but get wider toward the feet, which can be pretty big.

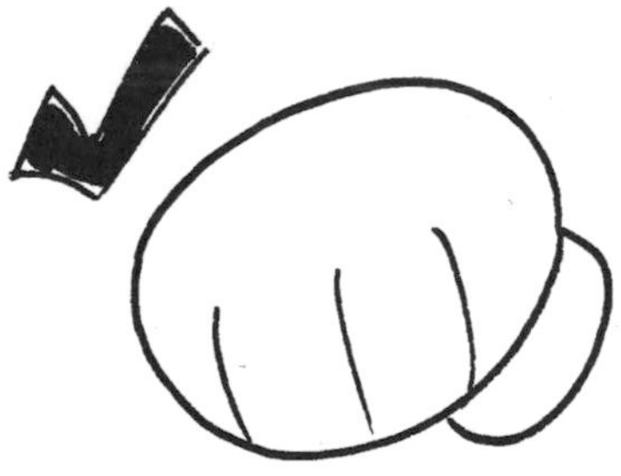

Keep it simple! Draw hands like this...

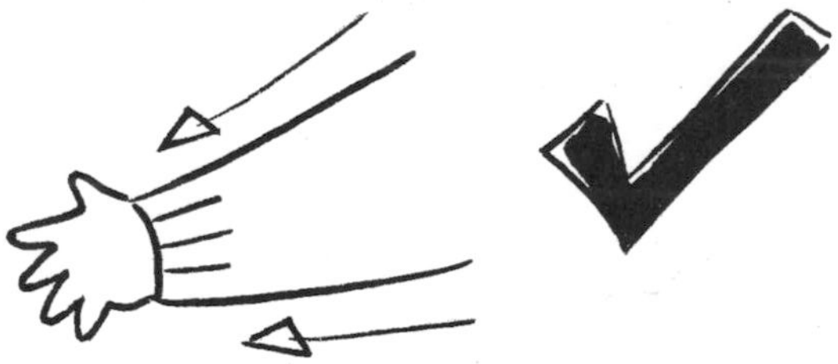

The arms get thinner as they travel toward the hands...

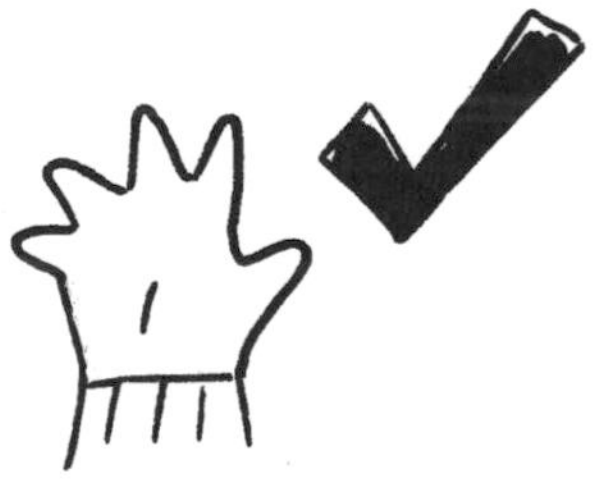

The fingers are tiny and delicate...

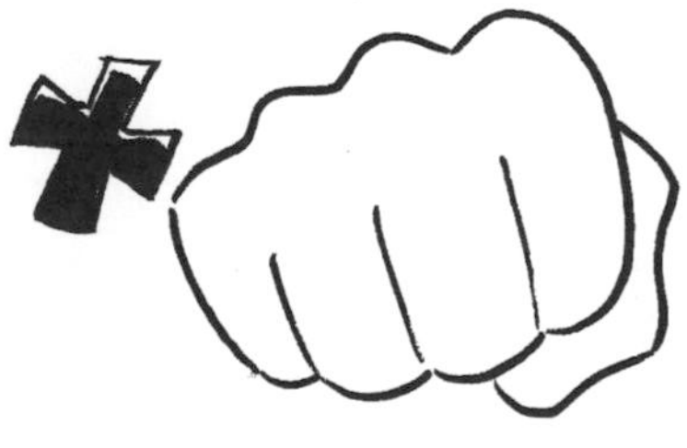

...not like this!

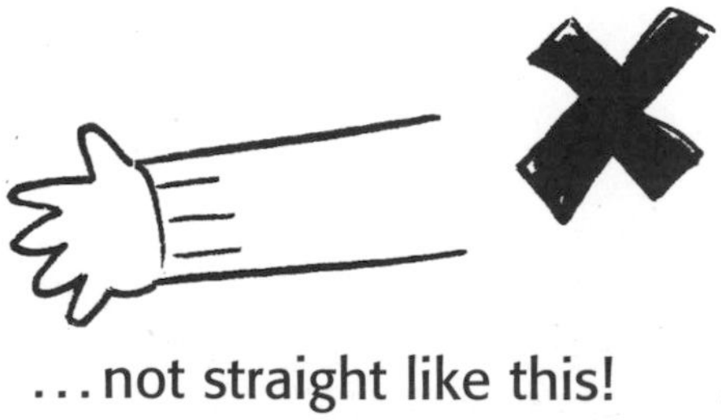

...not straight like this!

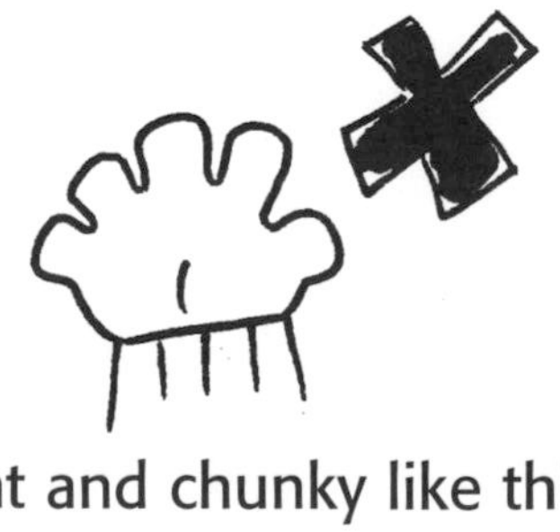

...not fat and chunky like this!

Chibi characters are small, but they usually have big feet. So how do you make small feet look big? You do it by making them short, chunky, and round. Look at the difference between regular cartoon feet and the chibi-style feet below.

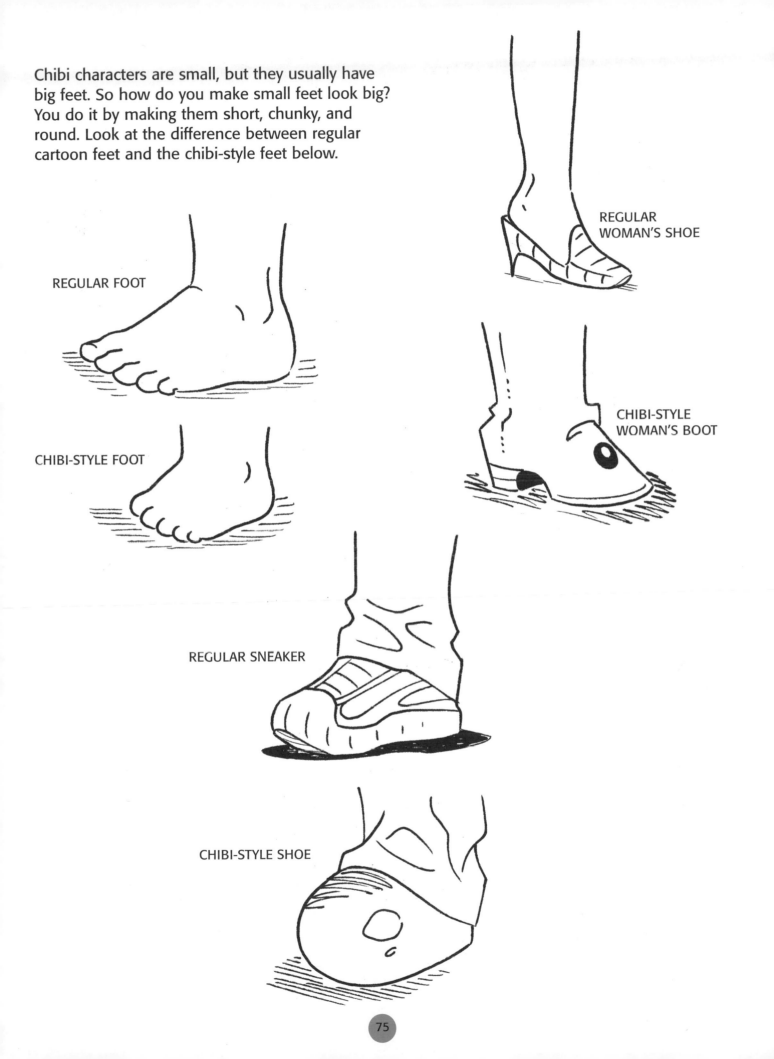

REGULAR WOMAN'S SHOE

REGULAR FOOT

CHIBI-STYLE FOOT

CHIBI-STYLE WOMAN'S BOOT

REGULAR SNEAKER

CHIBI-STYLE SHOE

BABY BUNNY

1

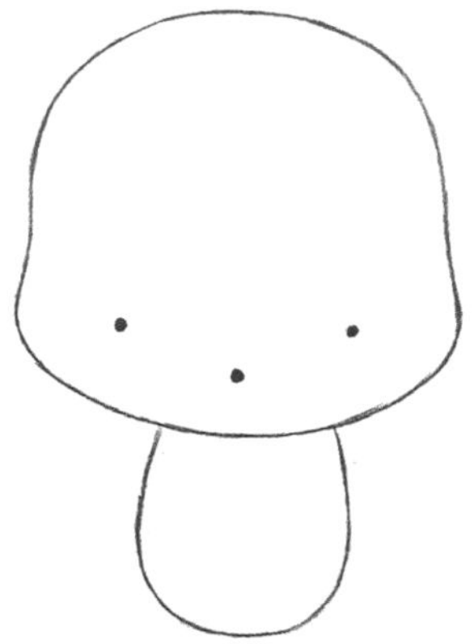

2

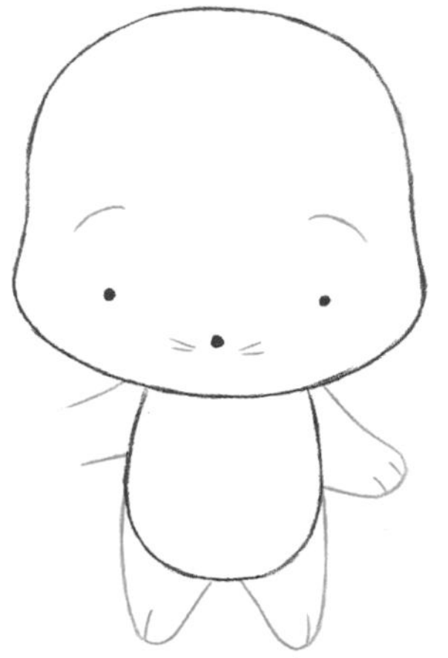

3

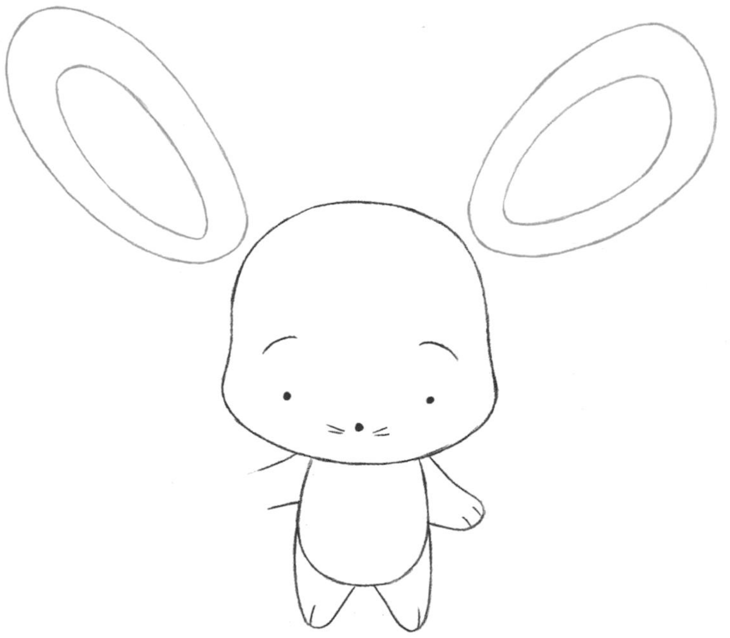

4

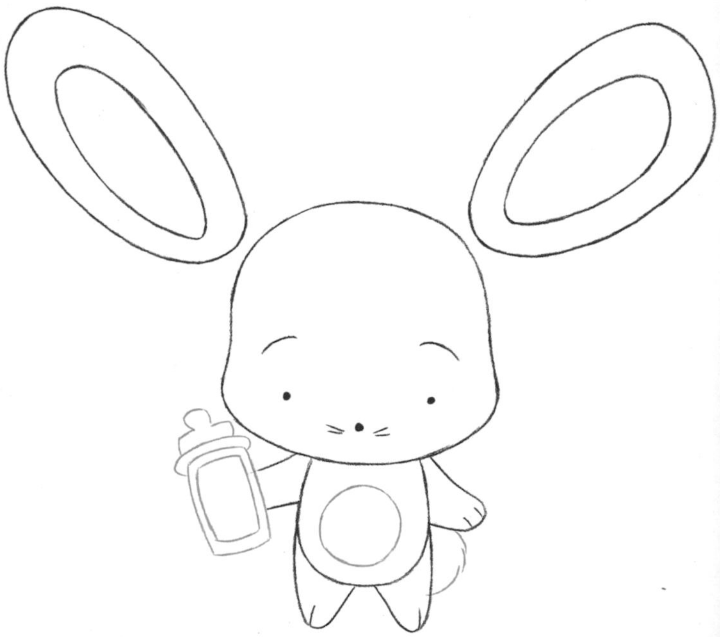

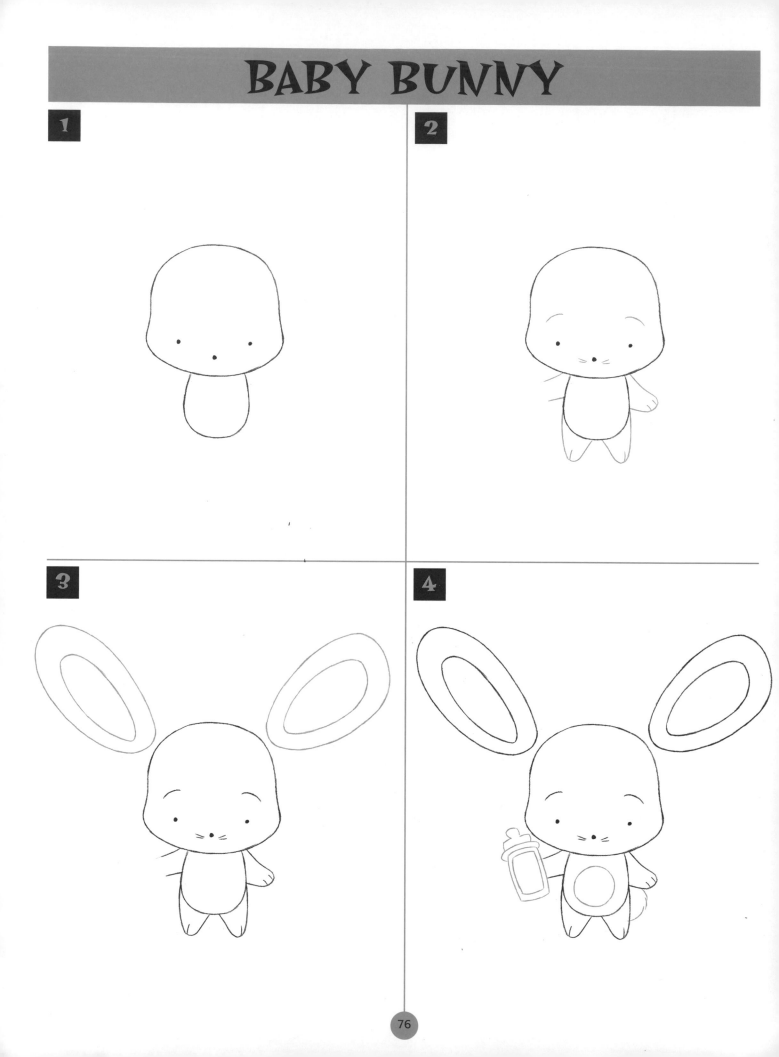

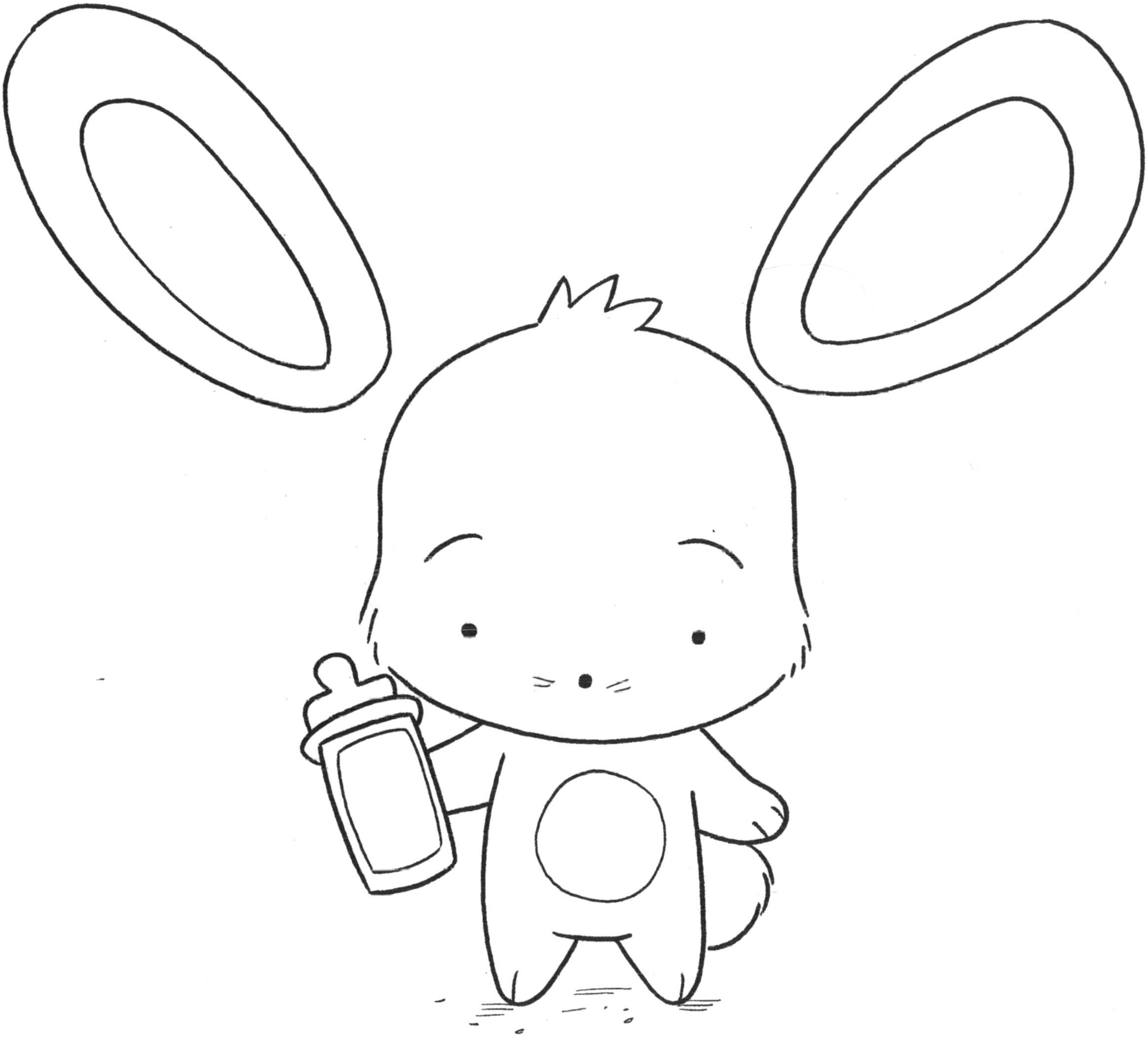

GOOFY GRIN

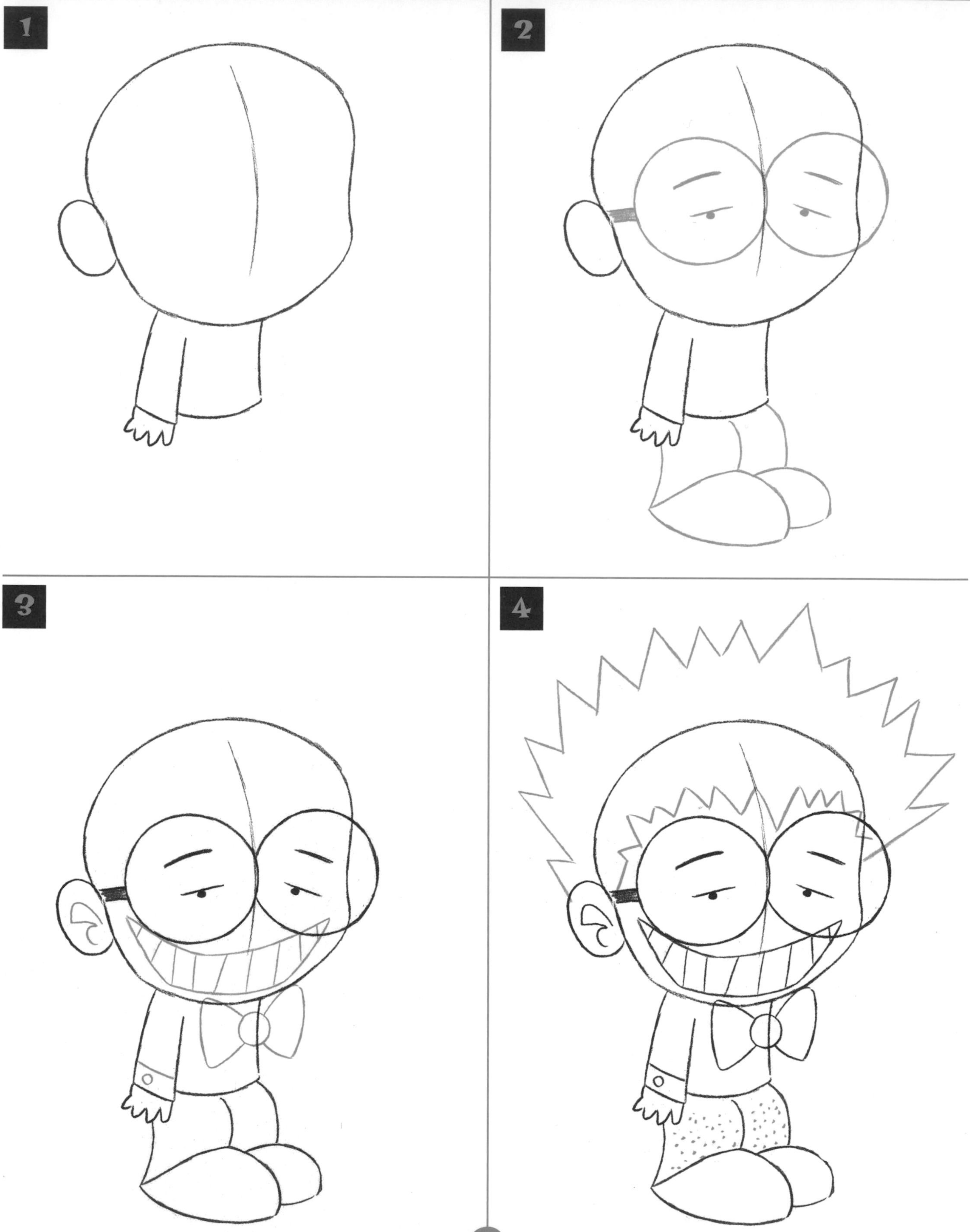
1
2
3
4

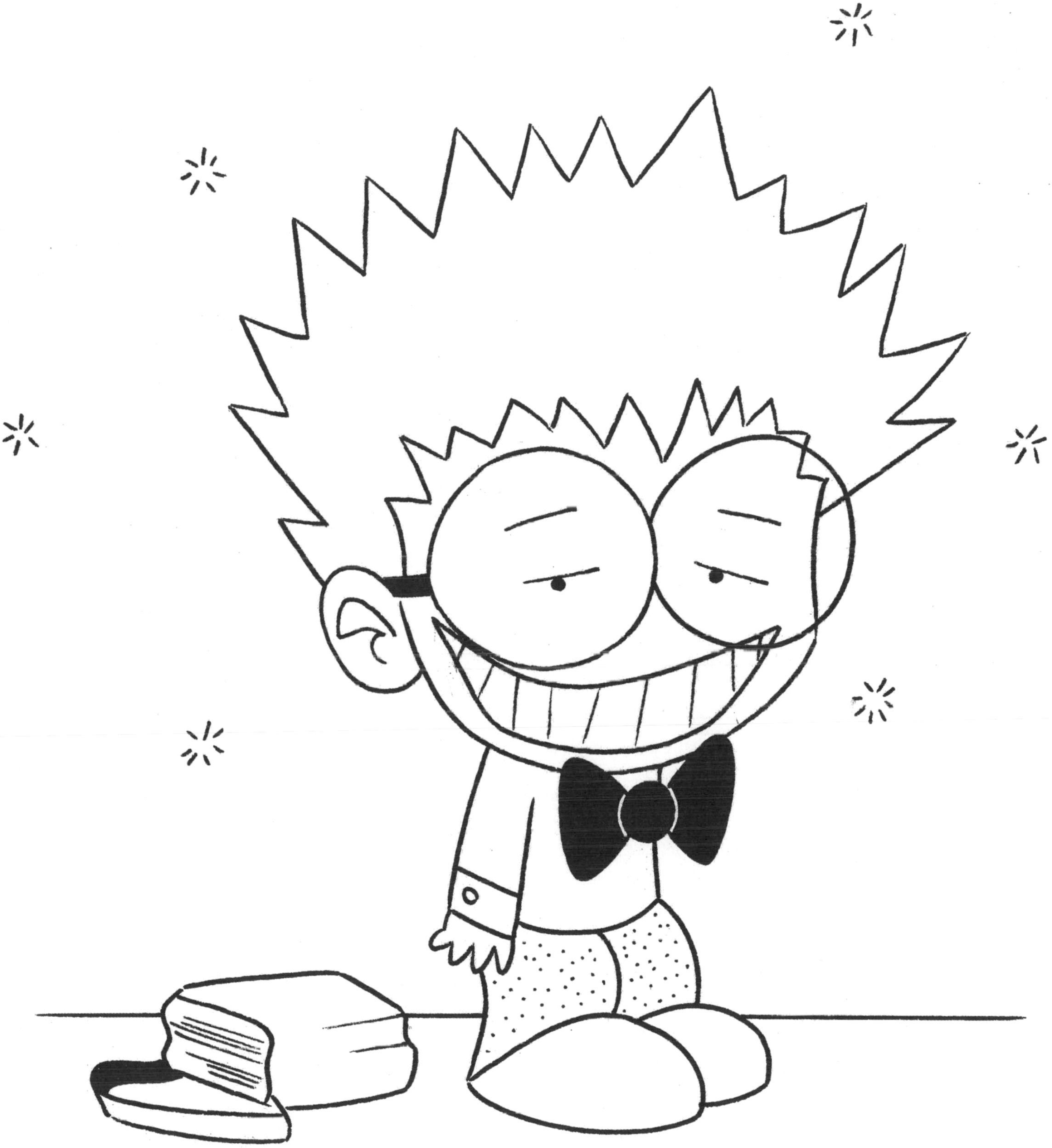

BULLY BOY

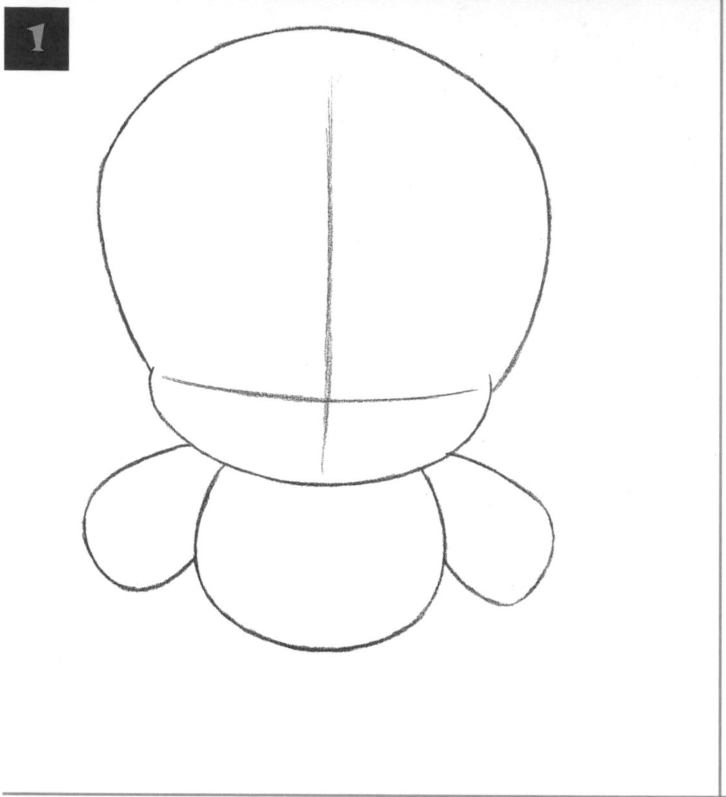

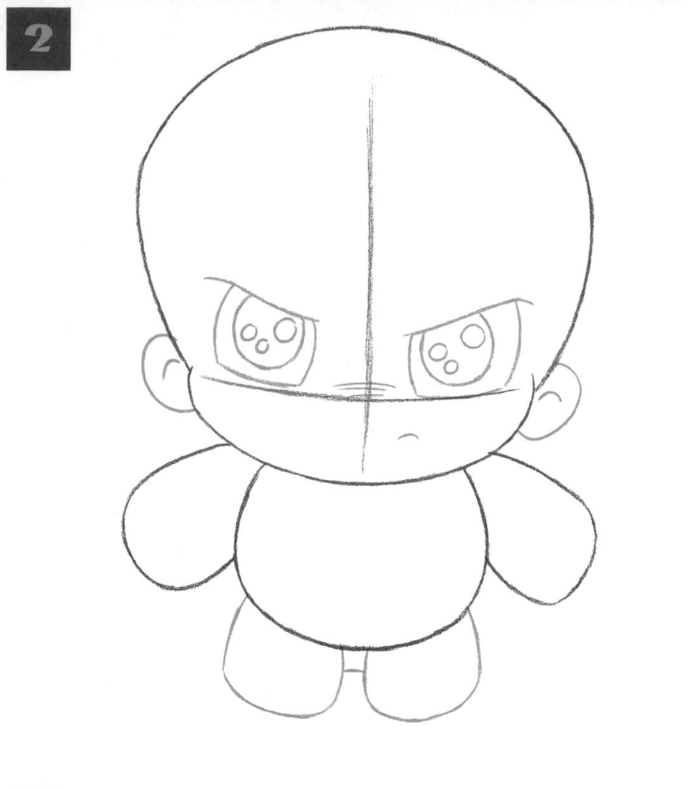

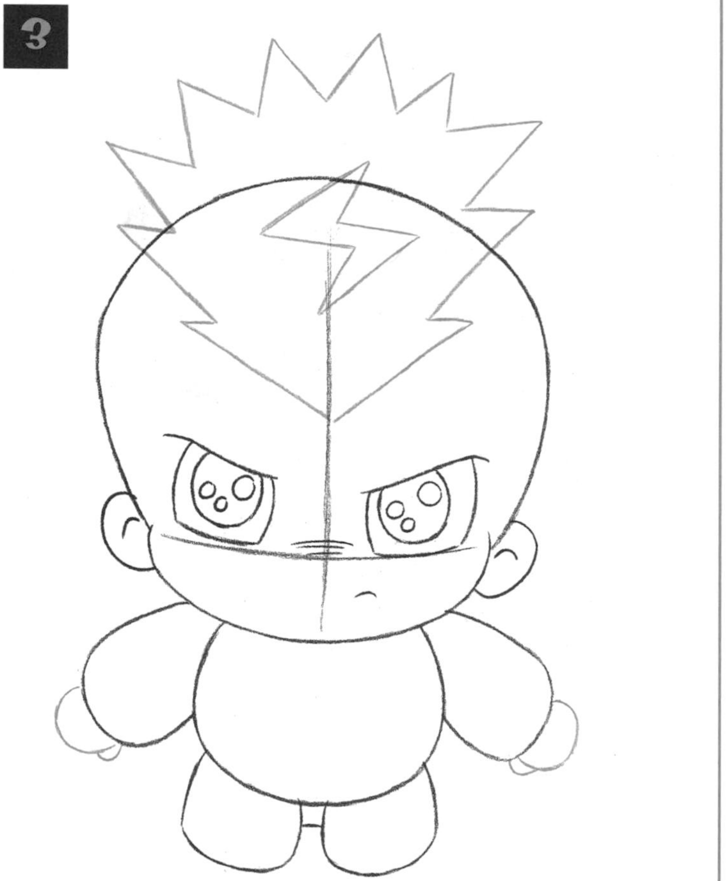

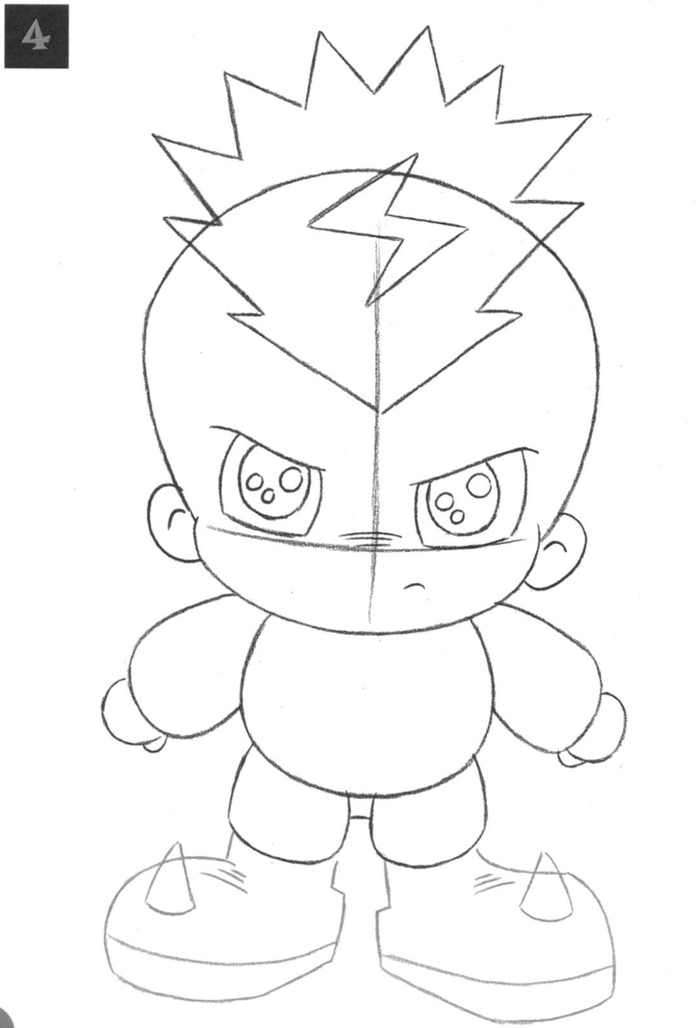

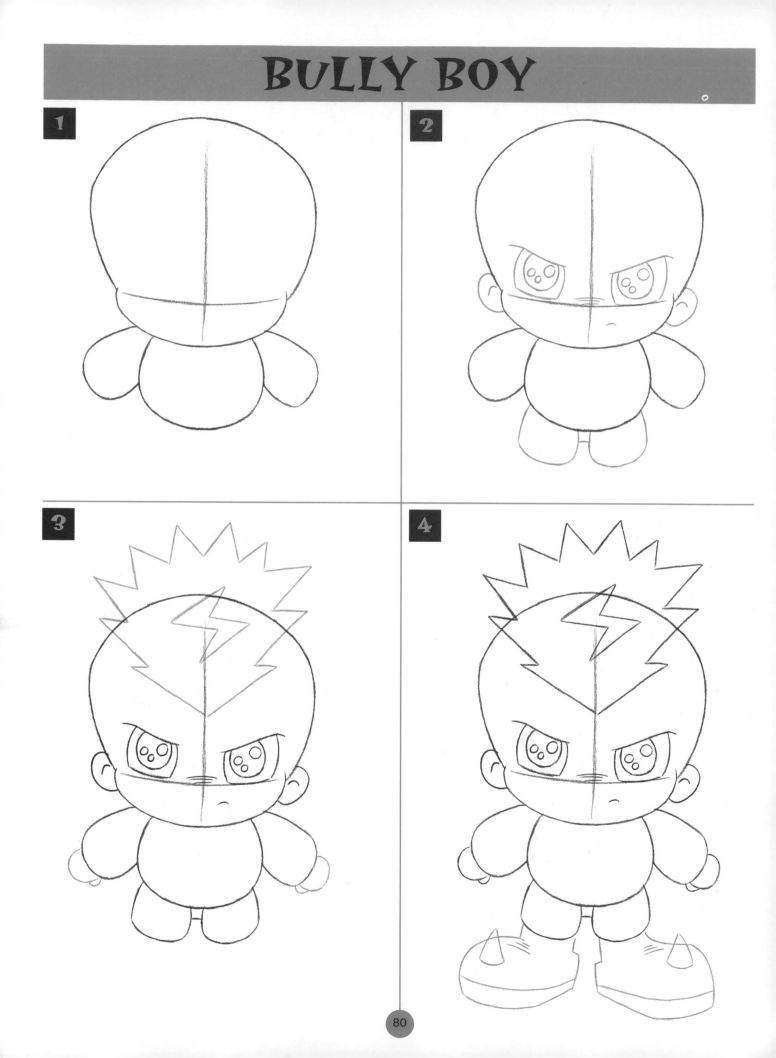

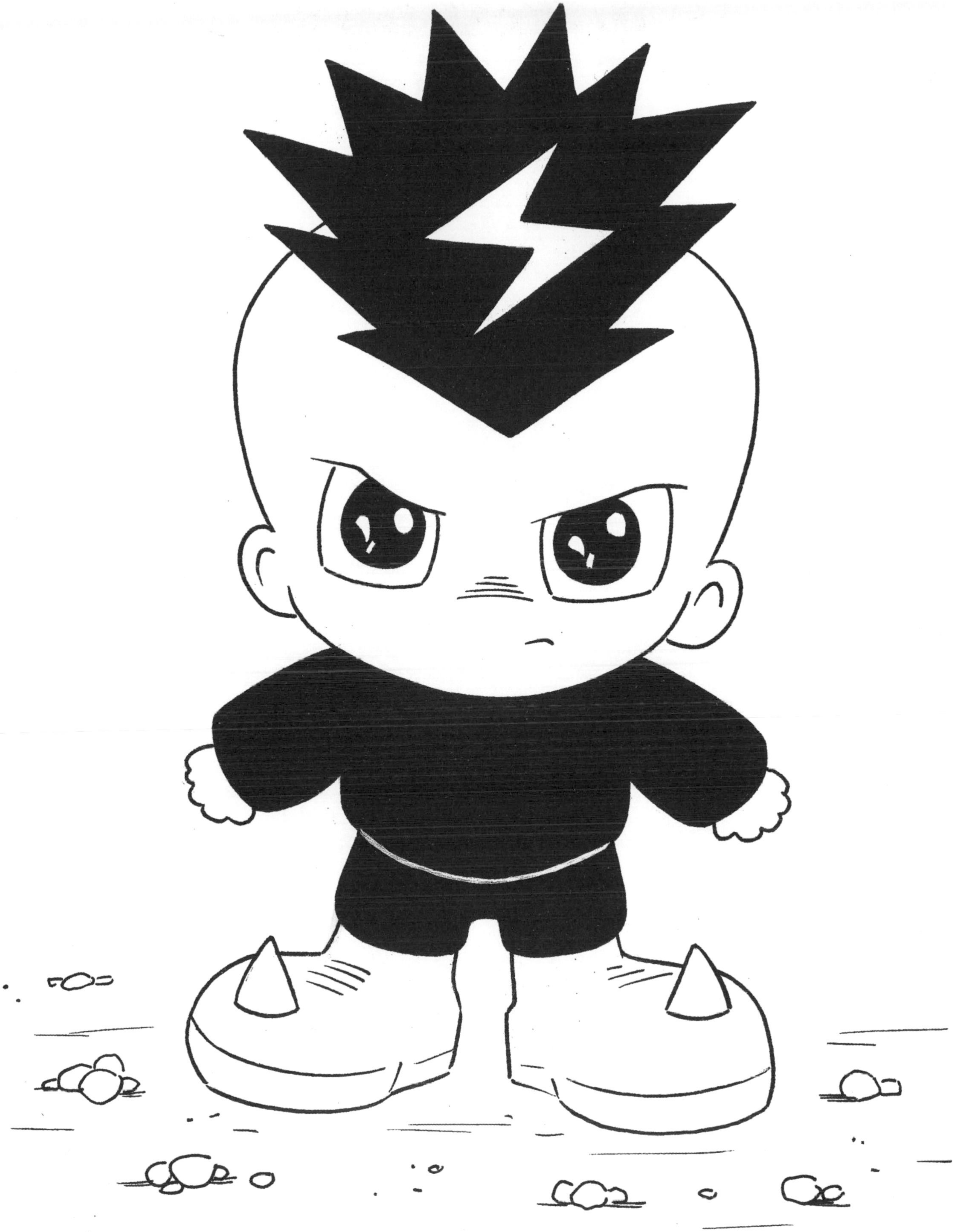

PUFFY PET

1

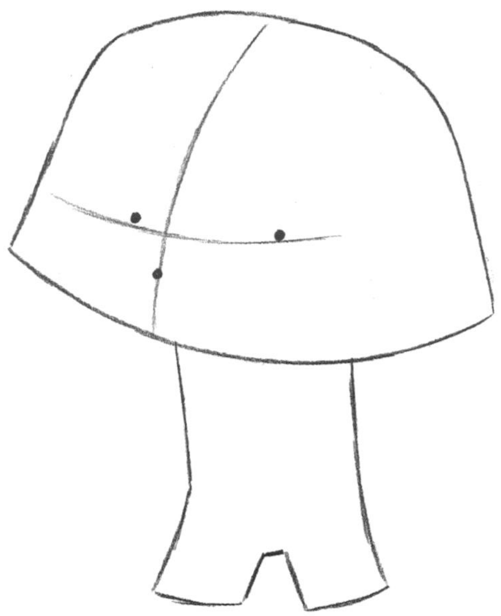

2

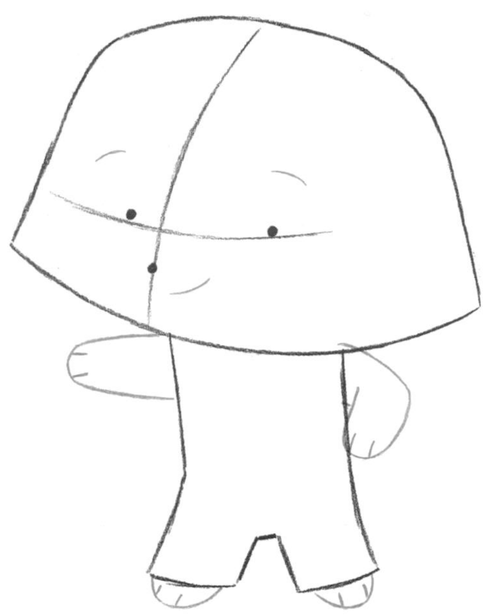

3

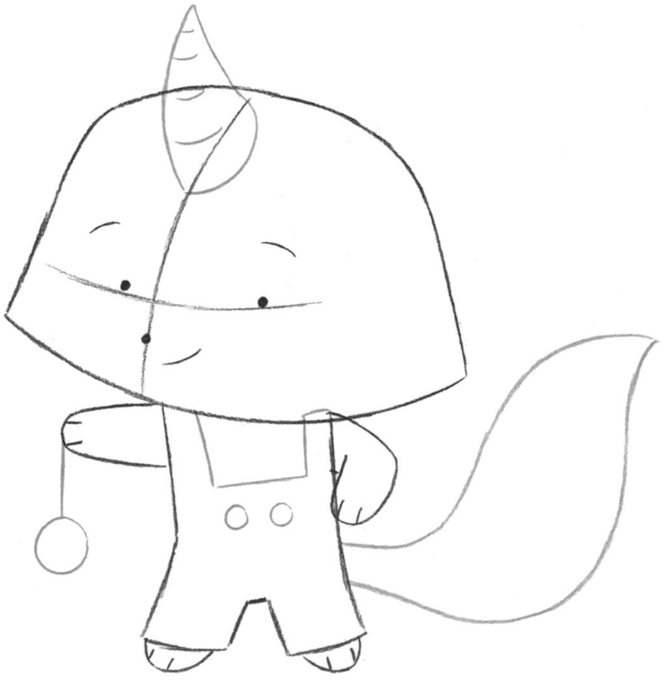

4

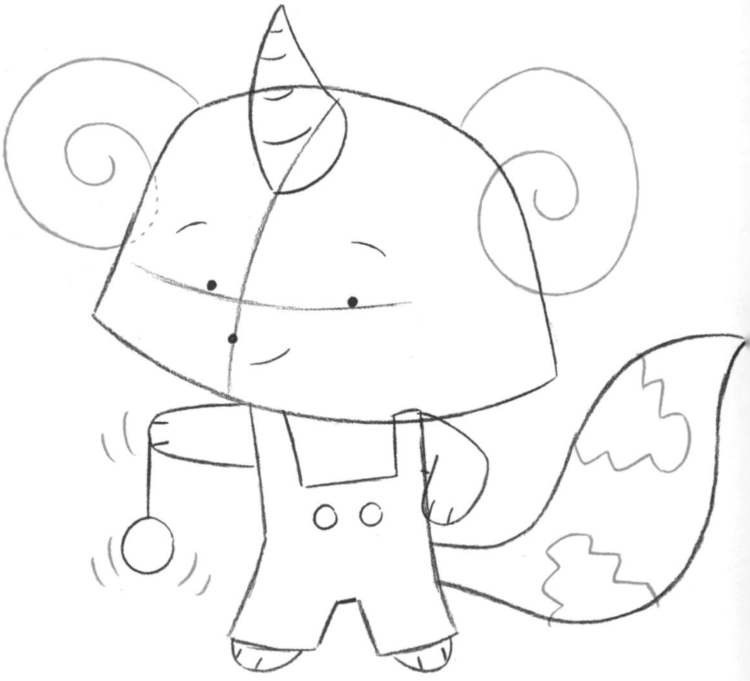

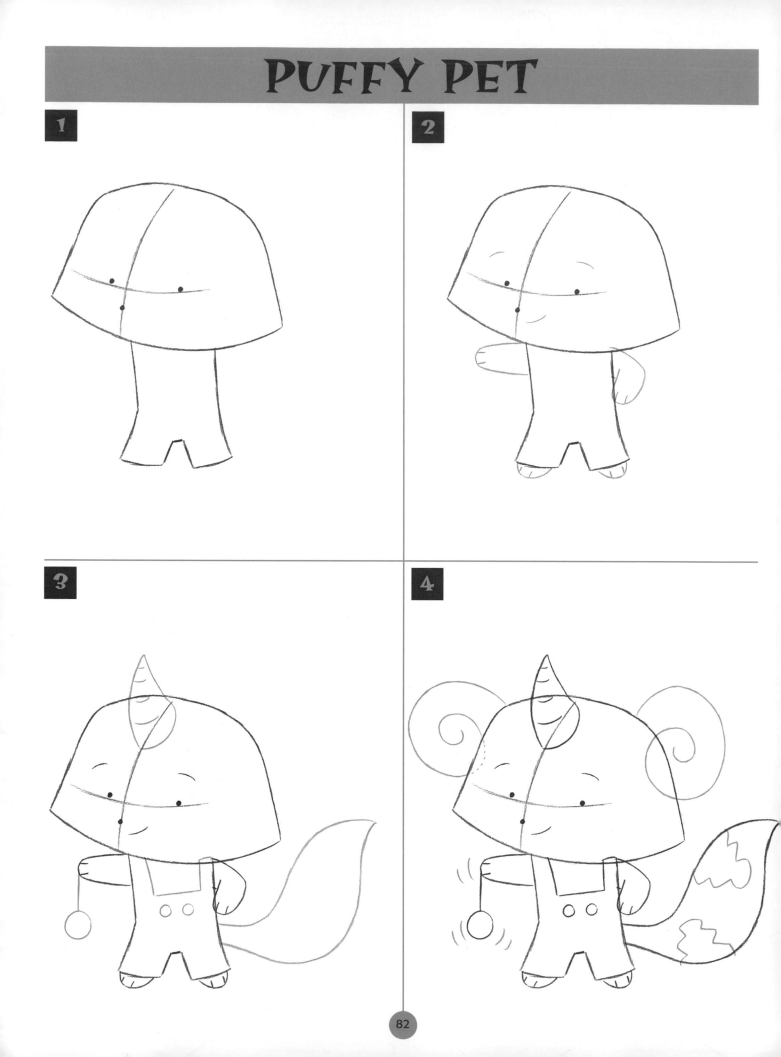

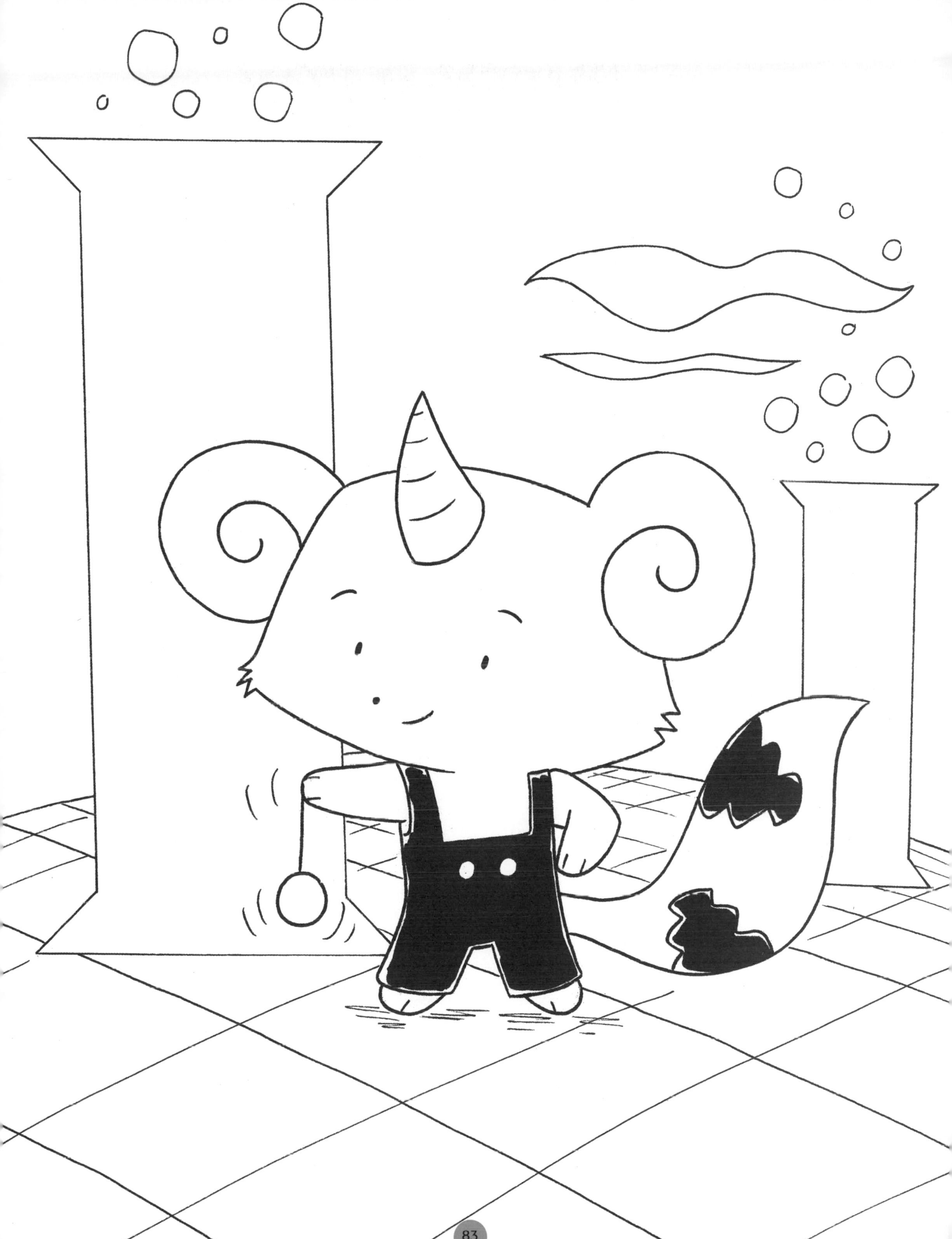

EXPLORER BOY

1

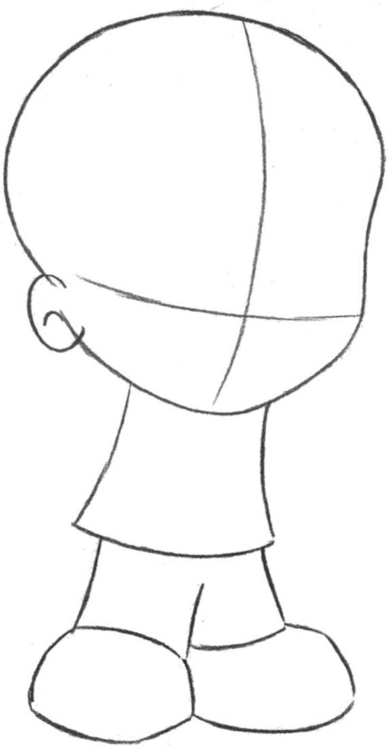

2

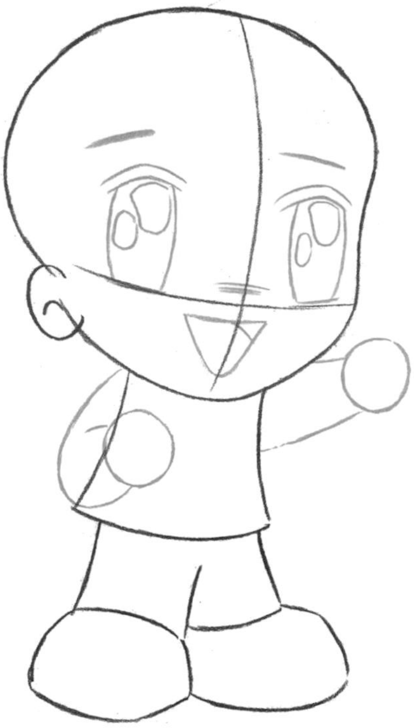

3

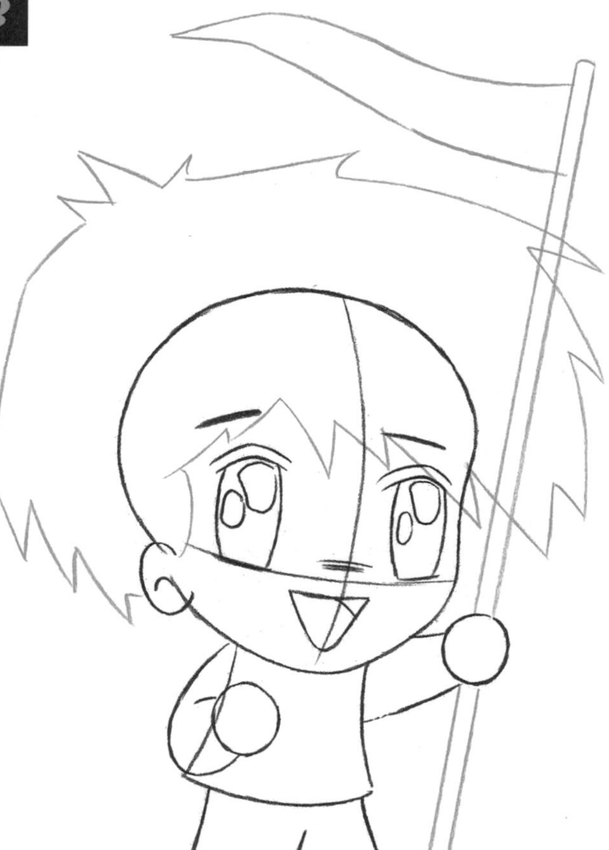

4

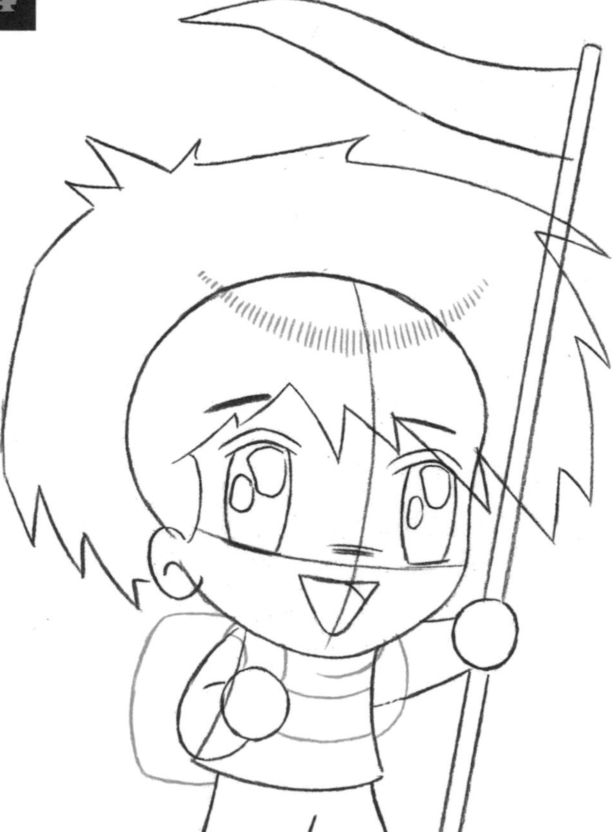

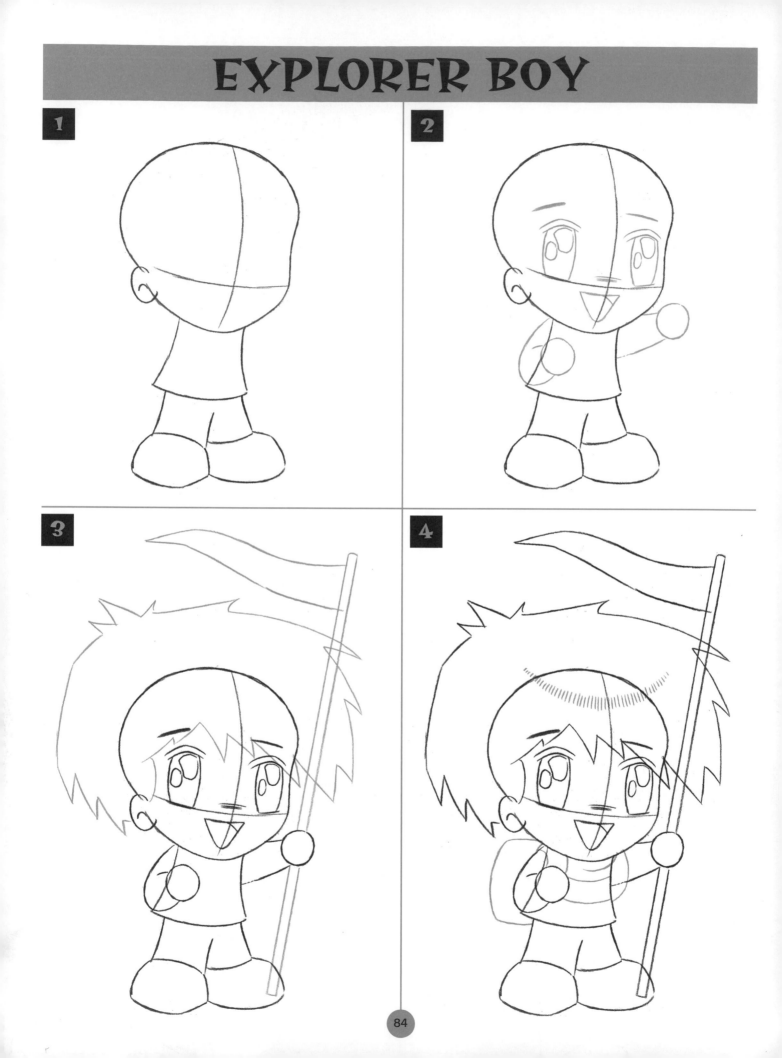

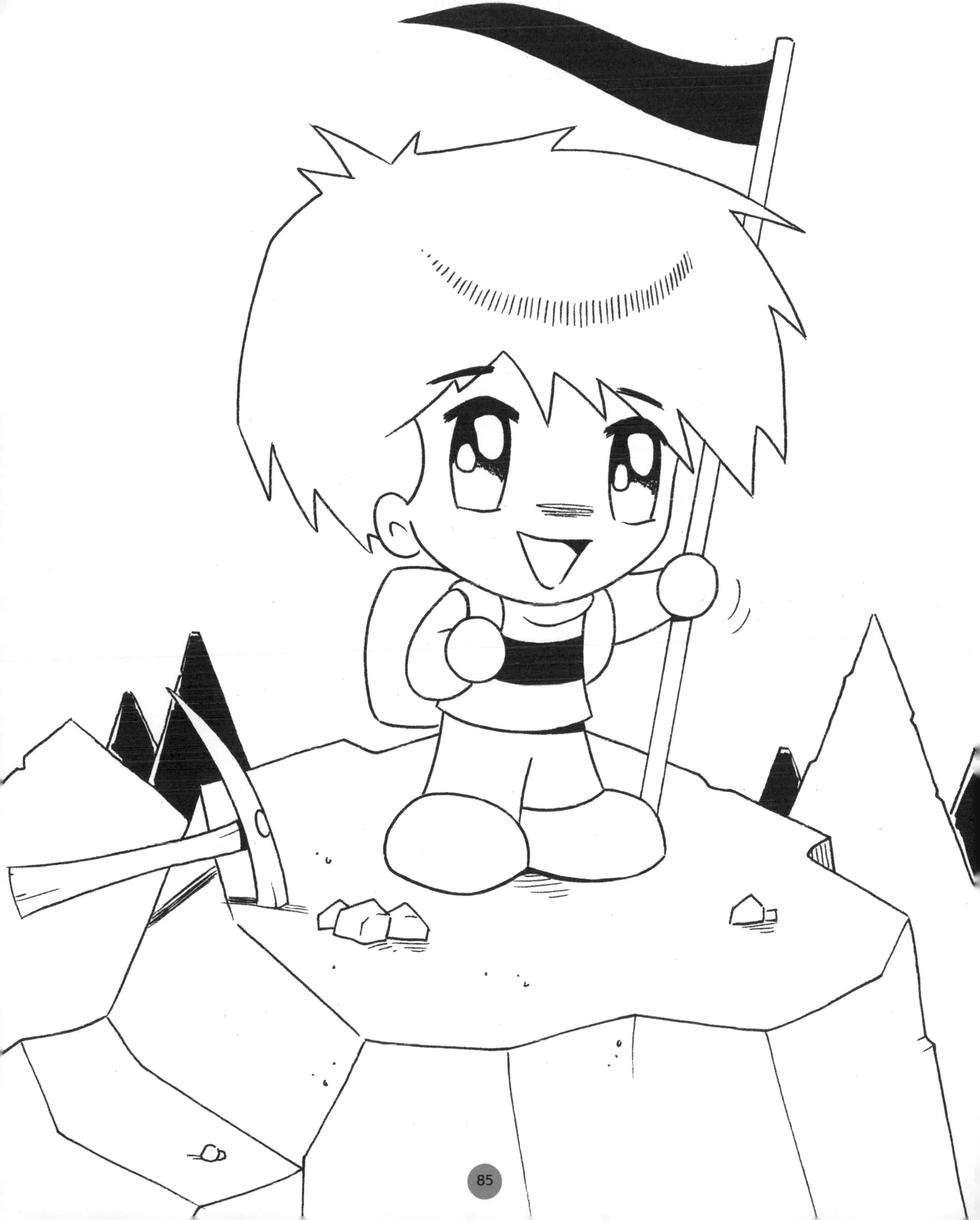

COCOA CAFÉ

1

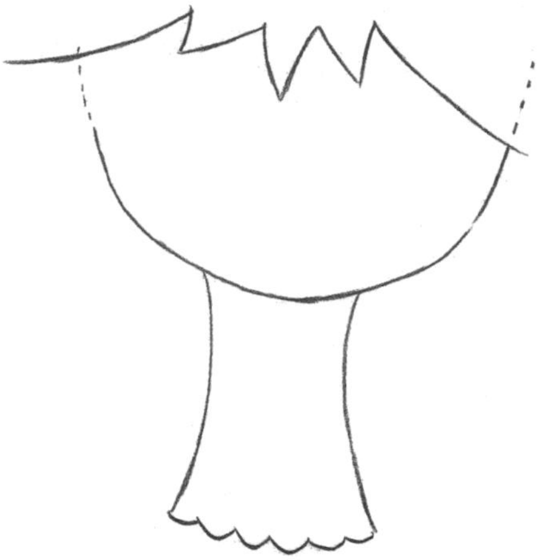

2

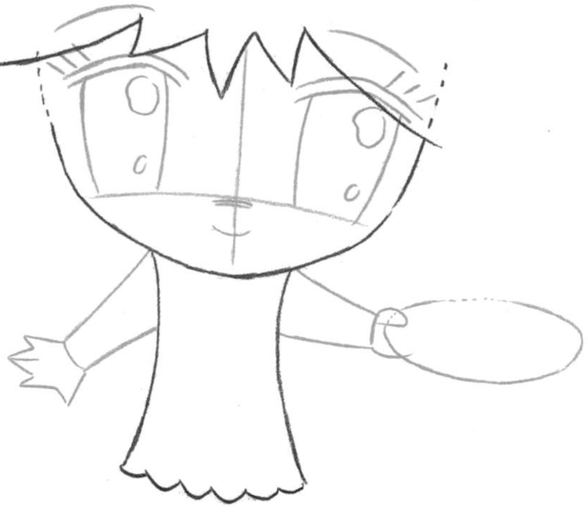

3

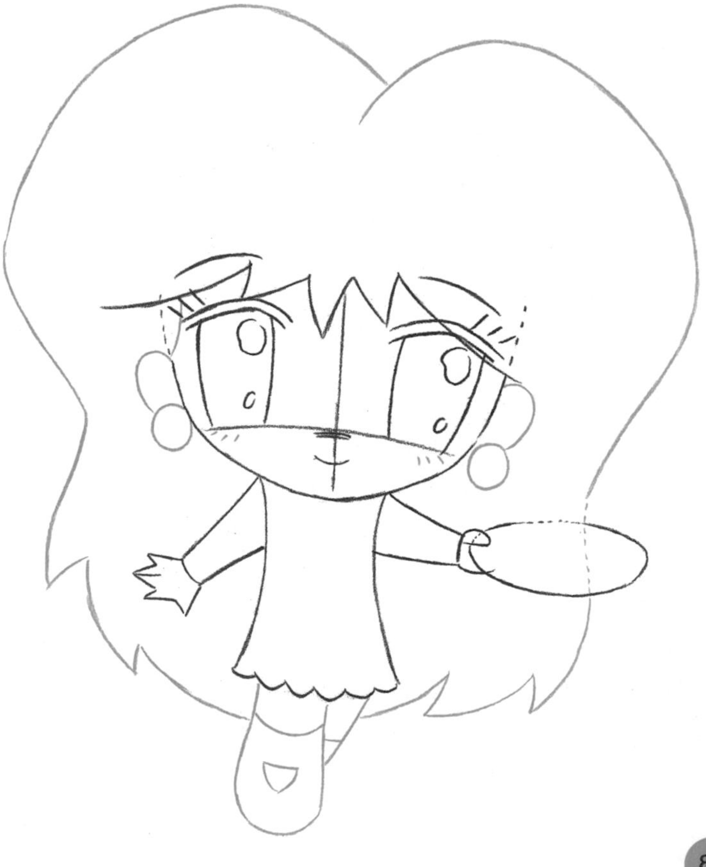

4

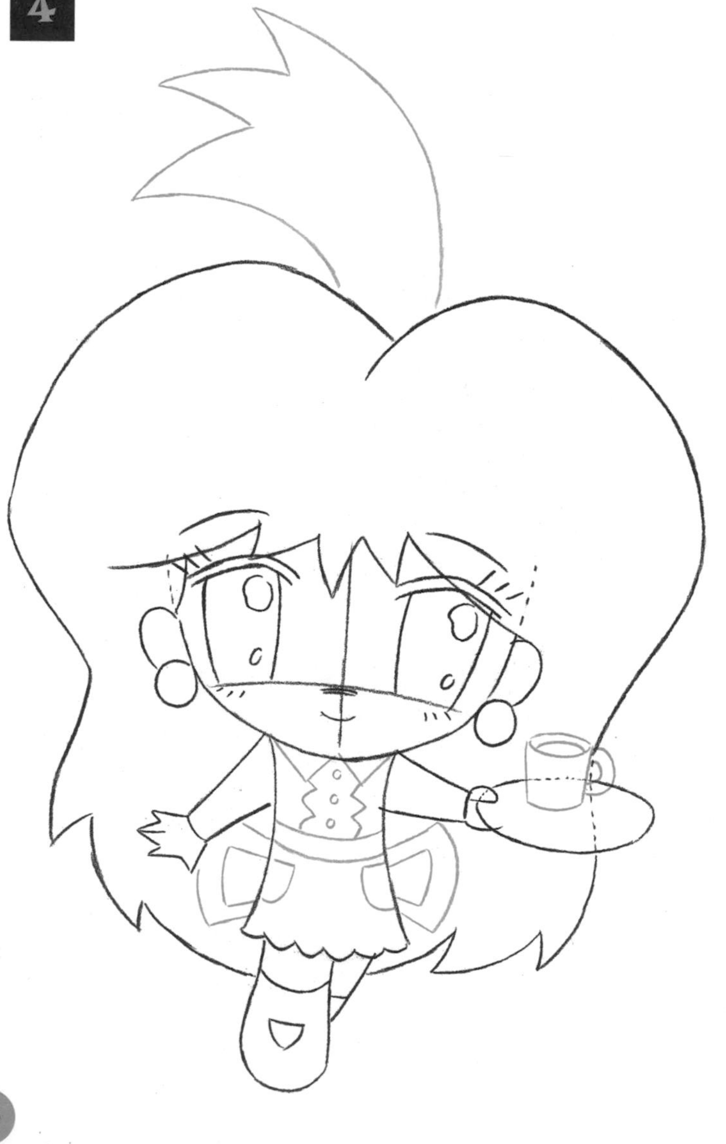

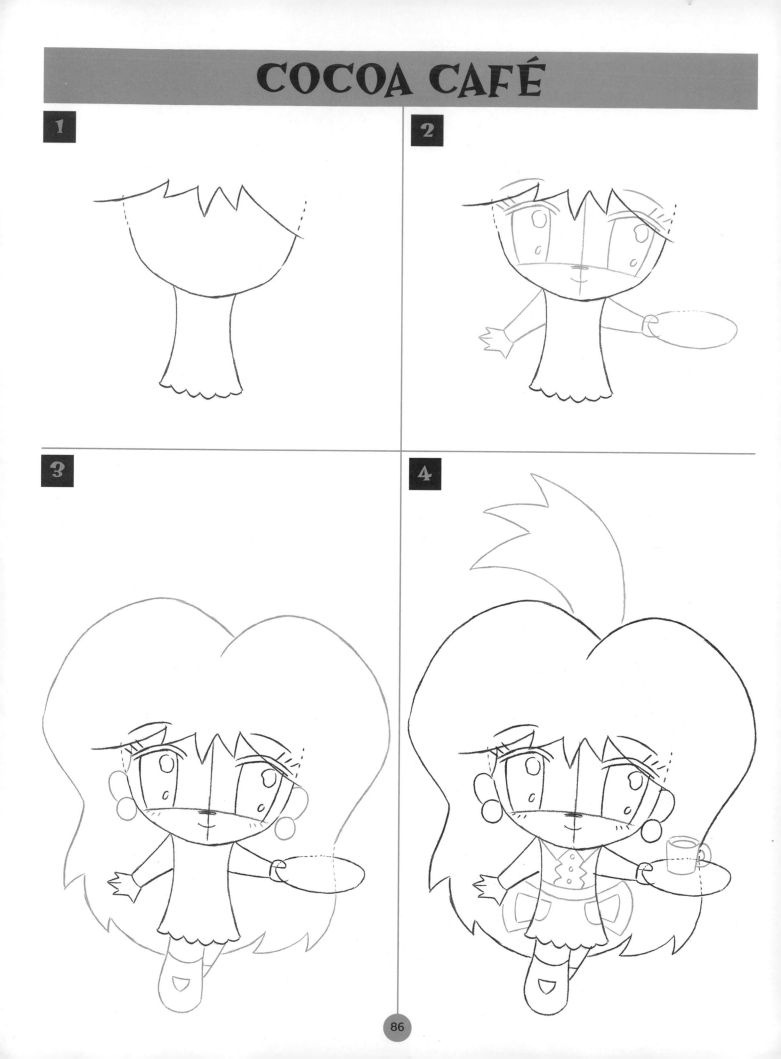

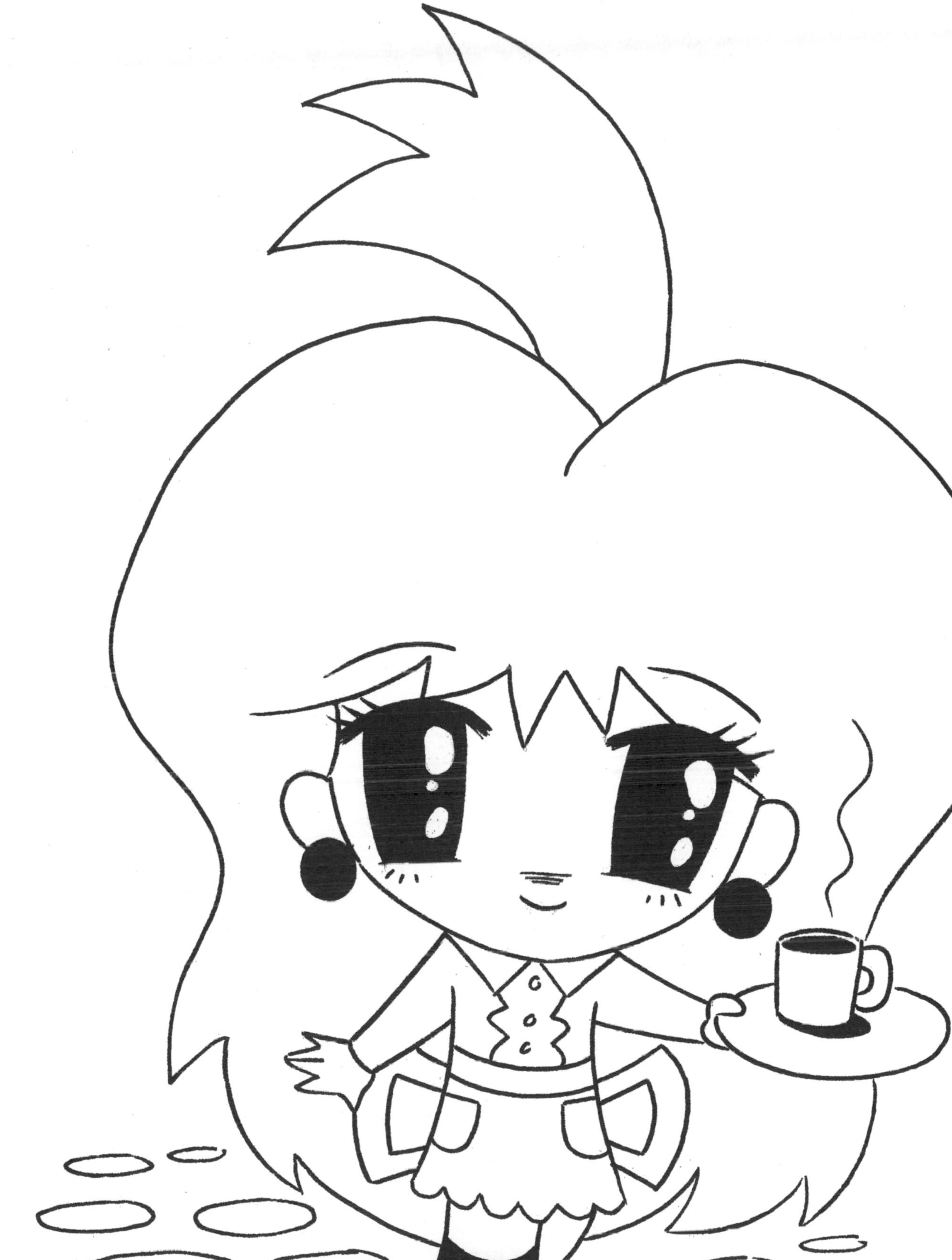

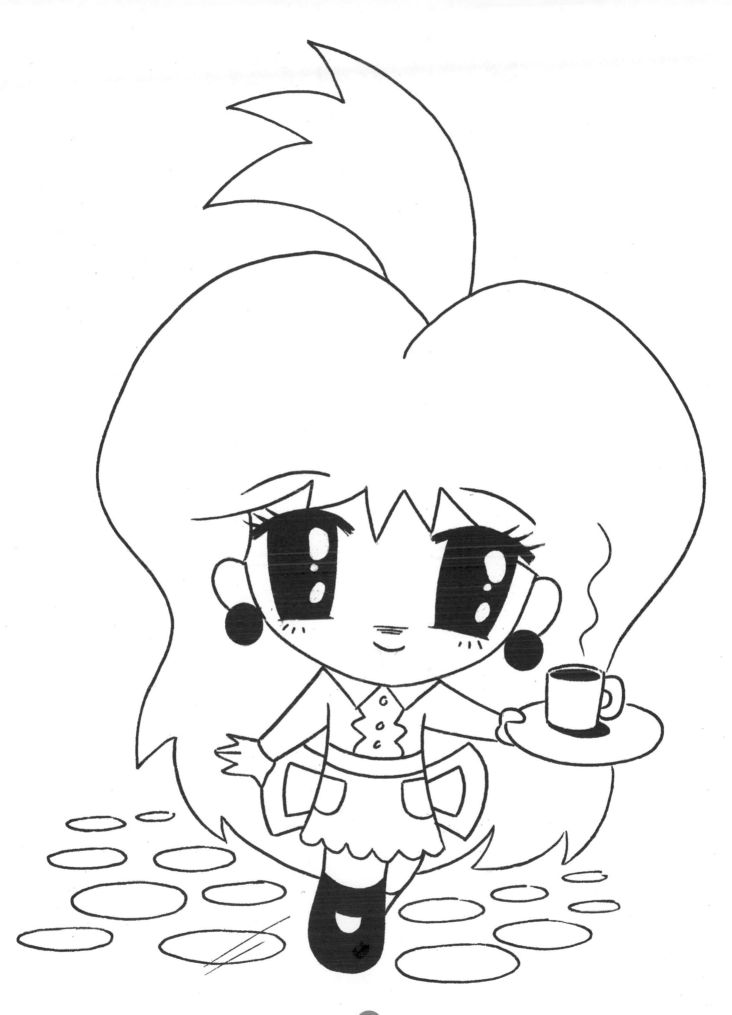

MINI KNIGHT

1

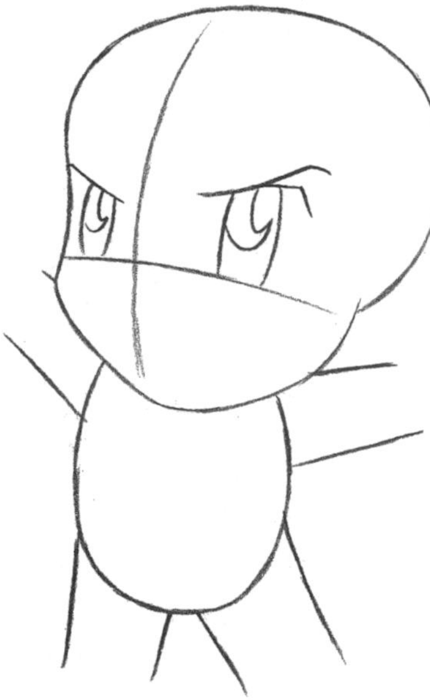

2

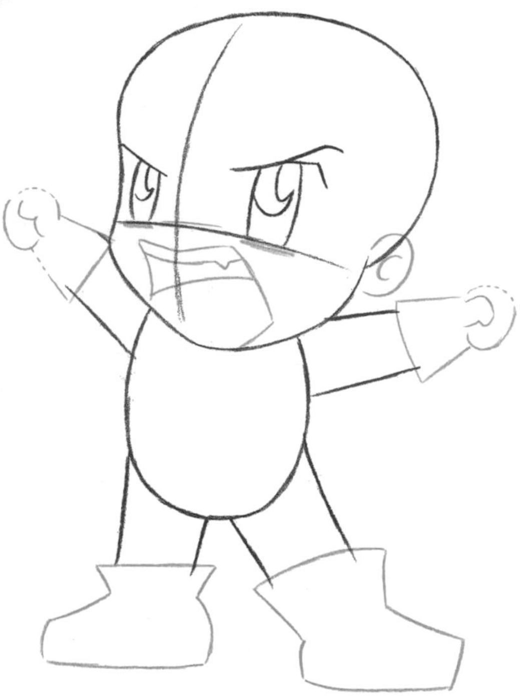

3

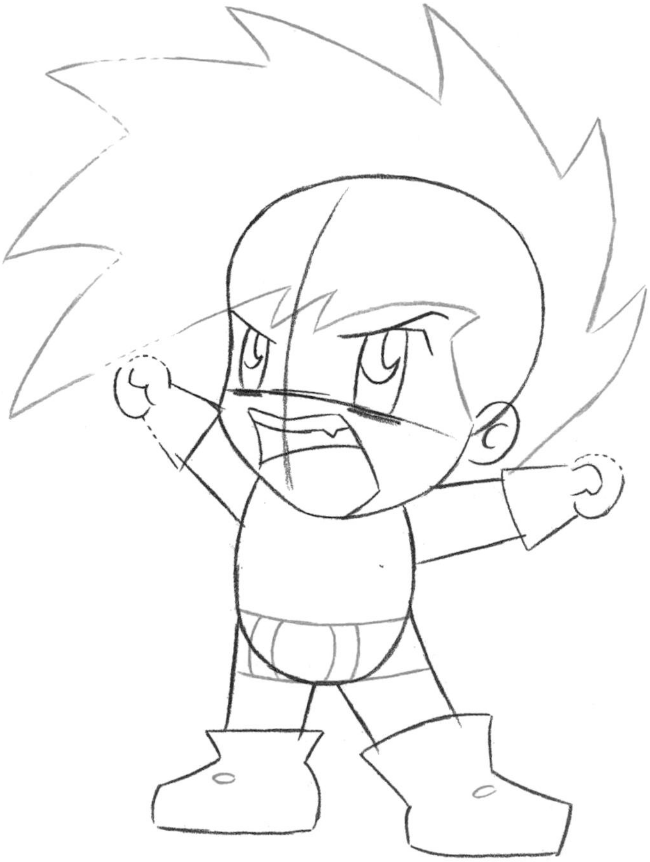

4

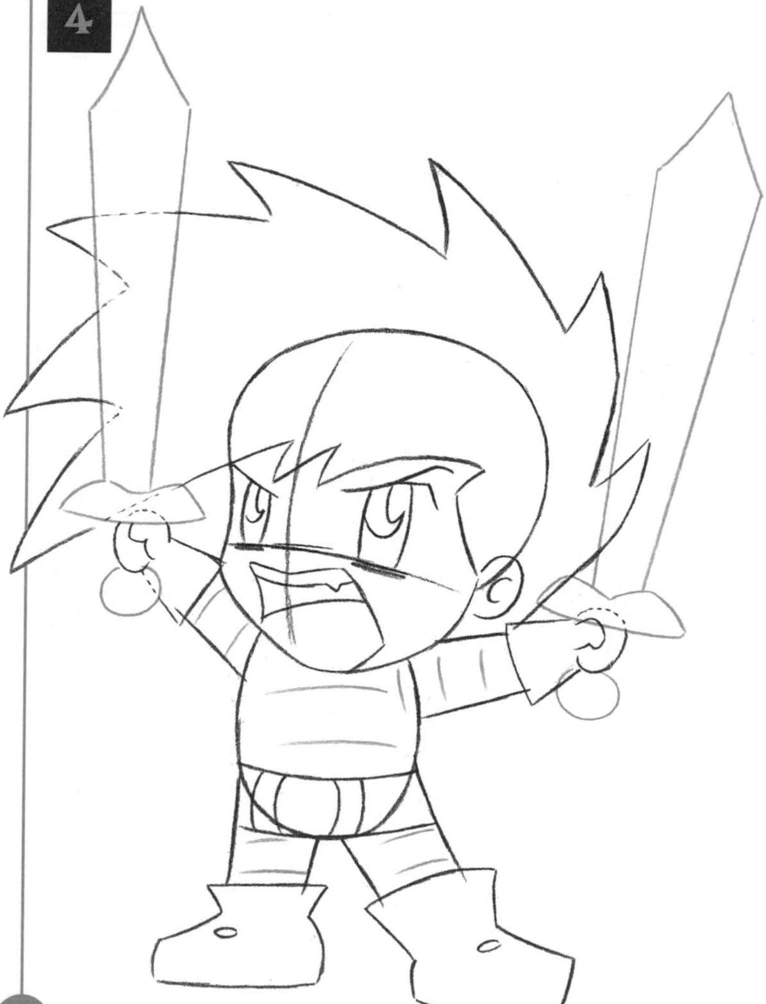

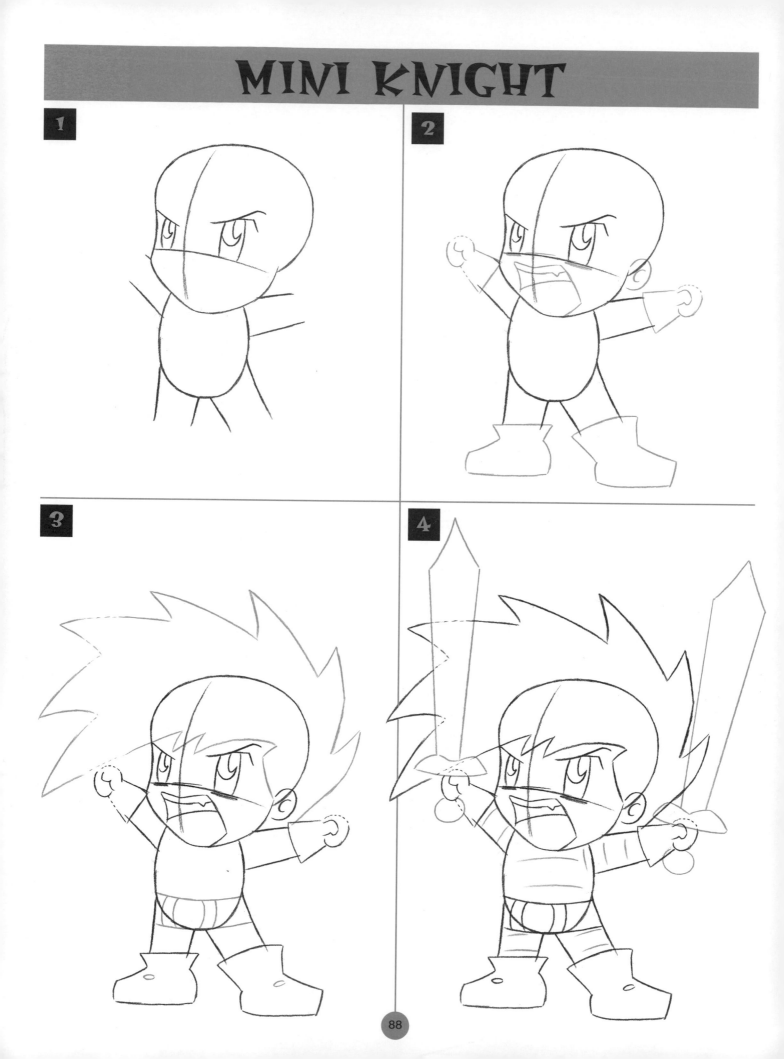

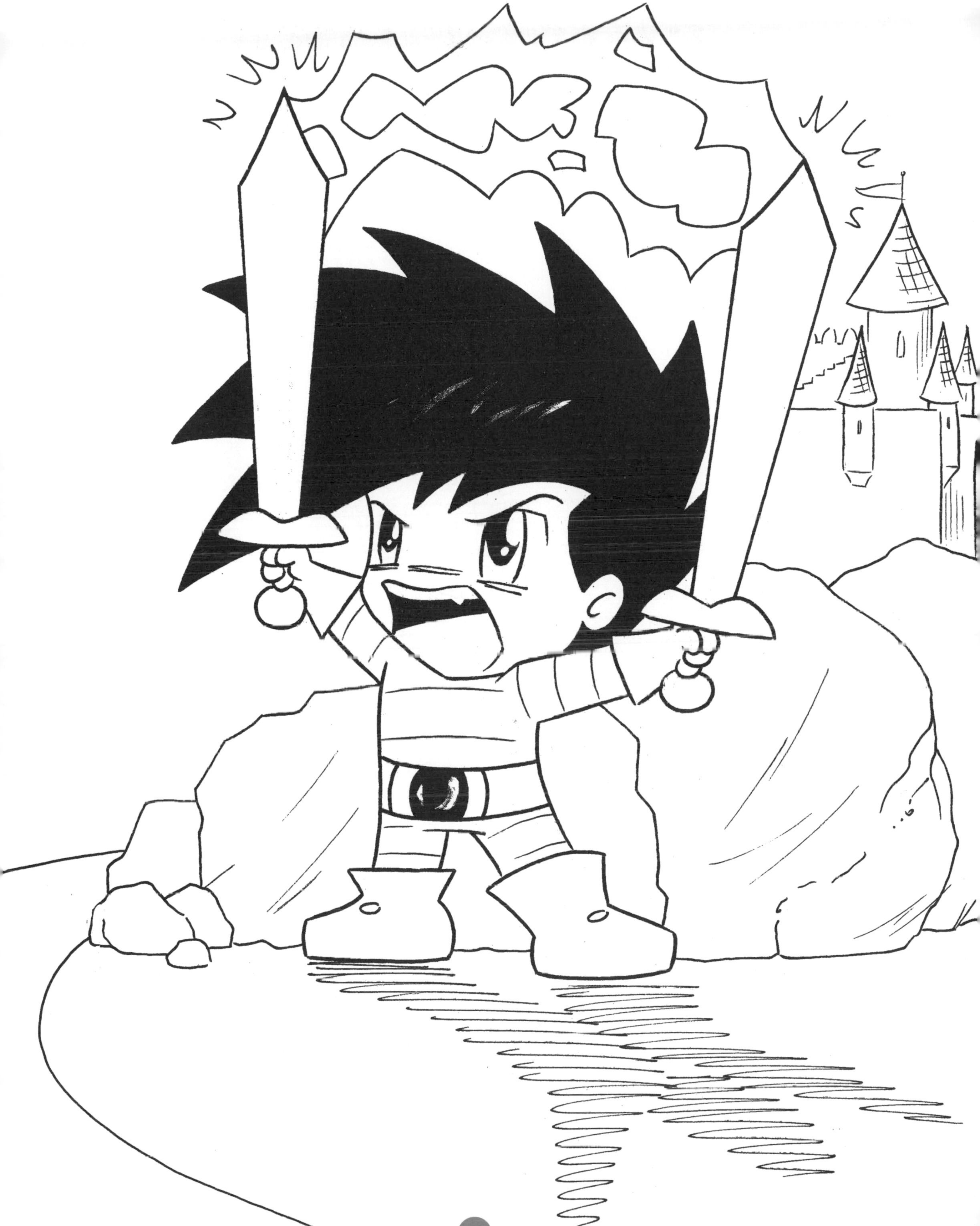

BALLET DANCER

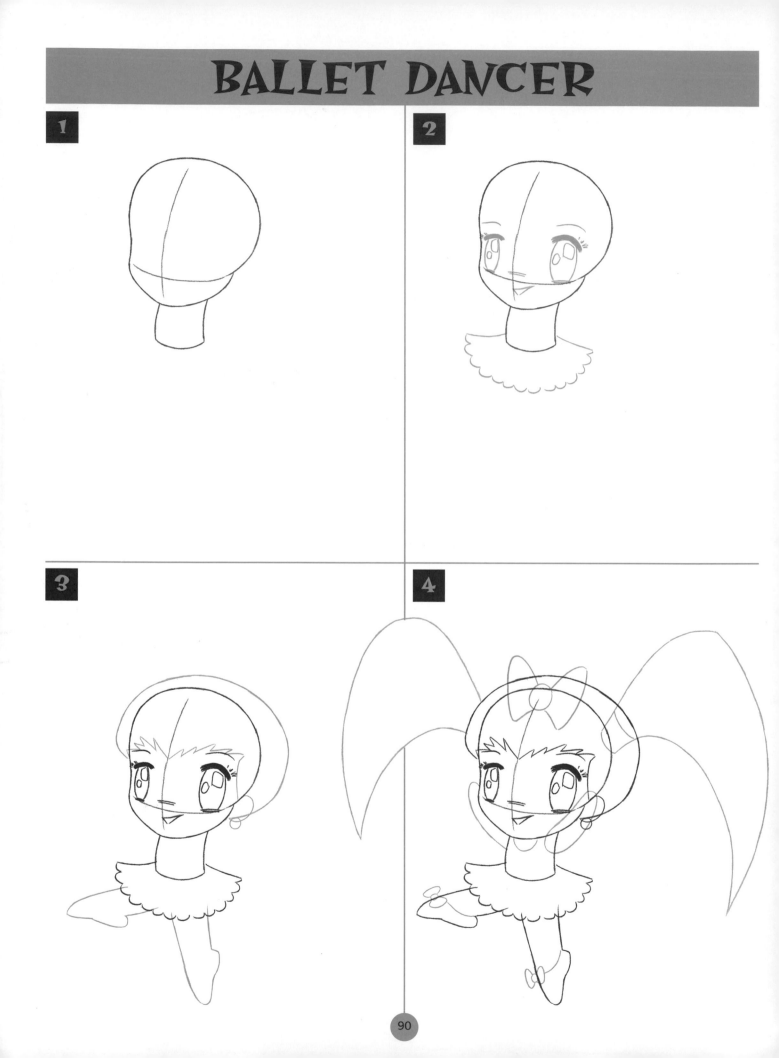

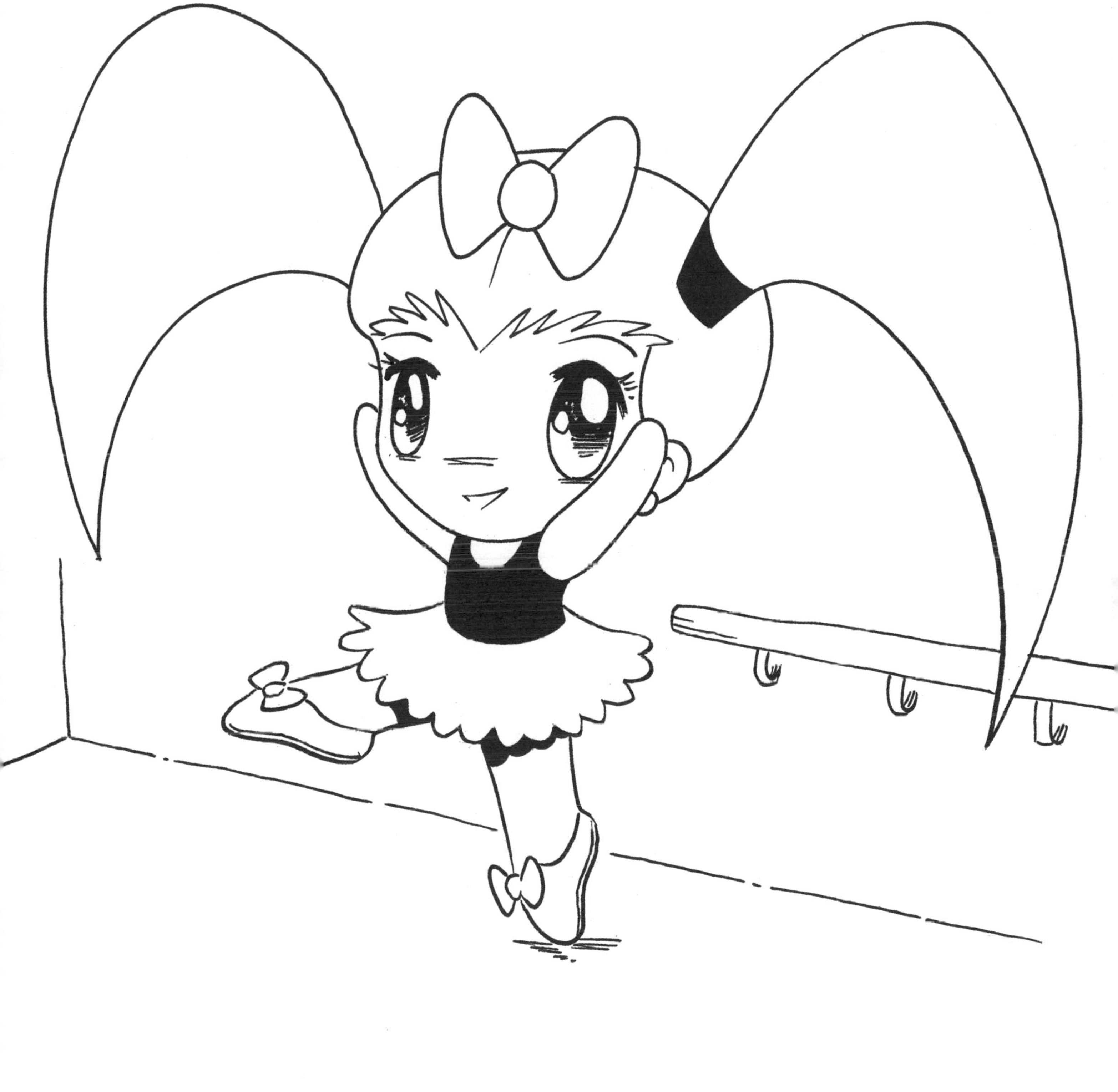

FIGHTING FURBALL

1

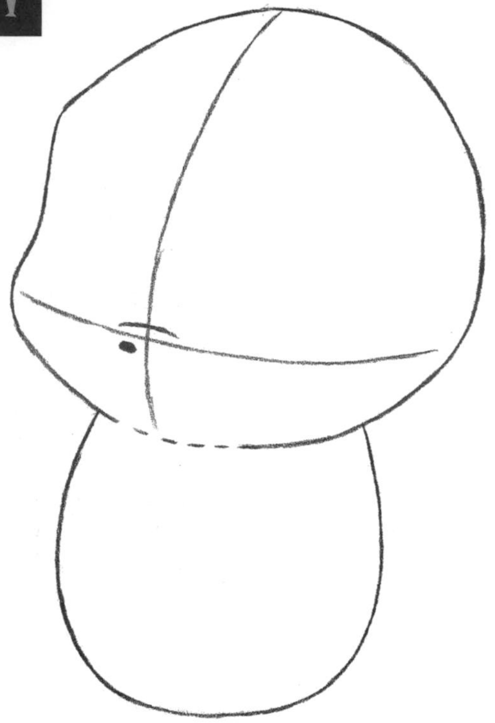

2

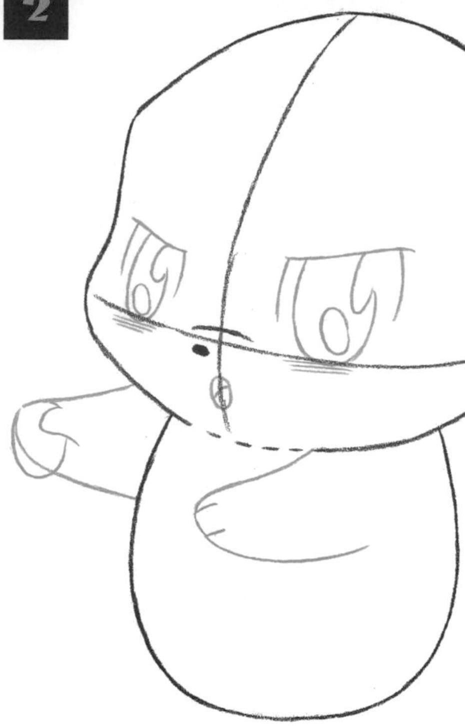

3

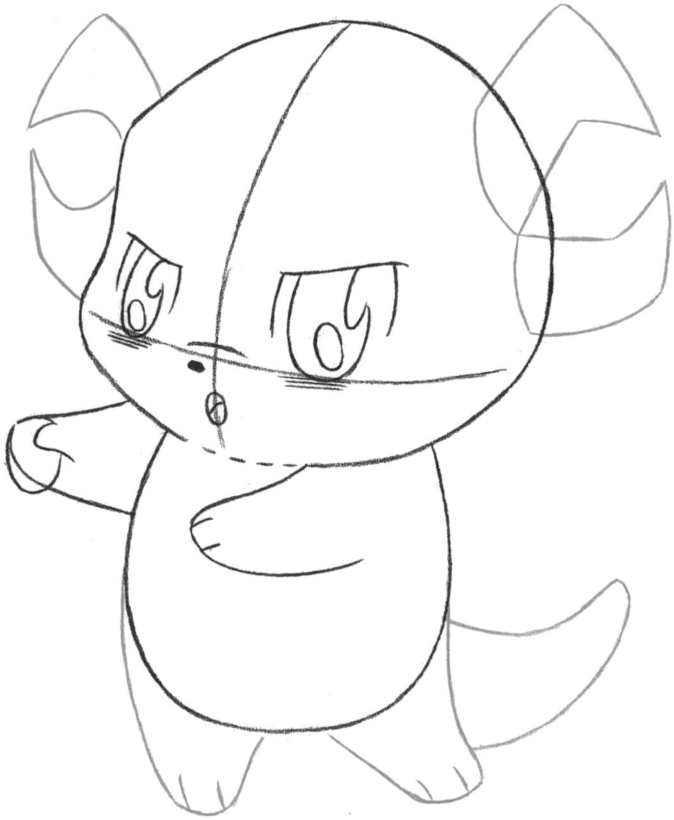

4

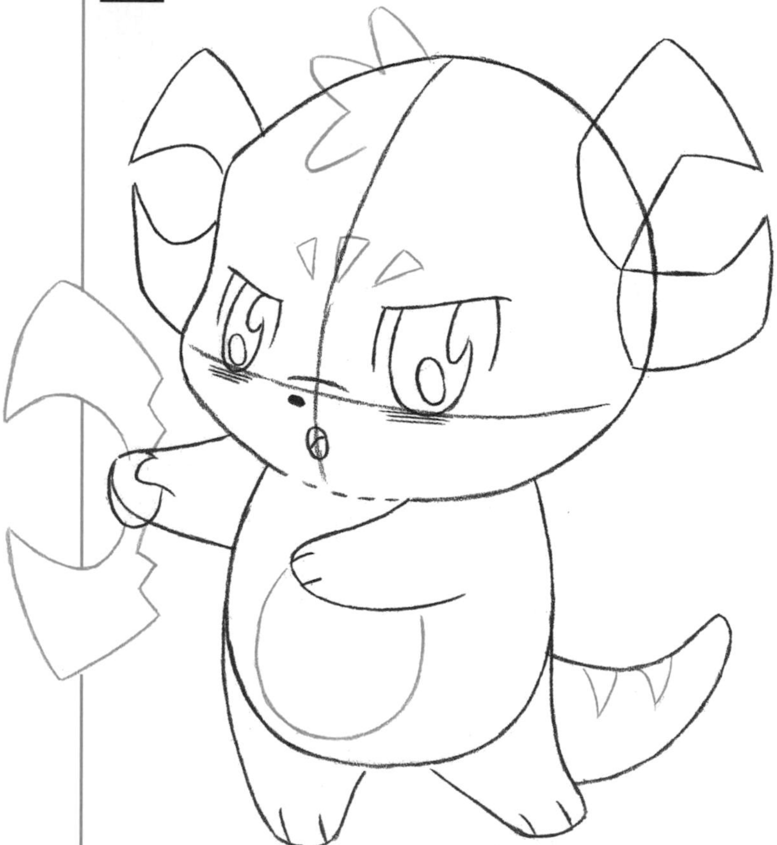

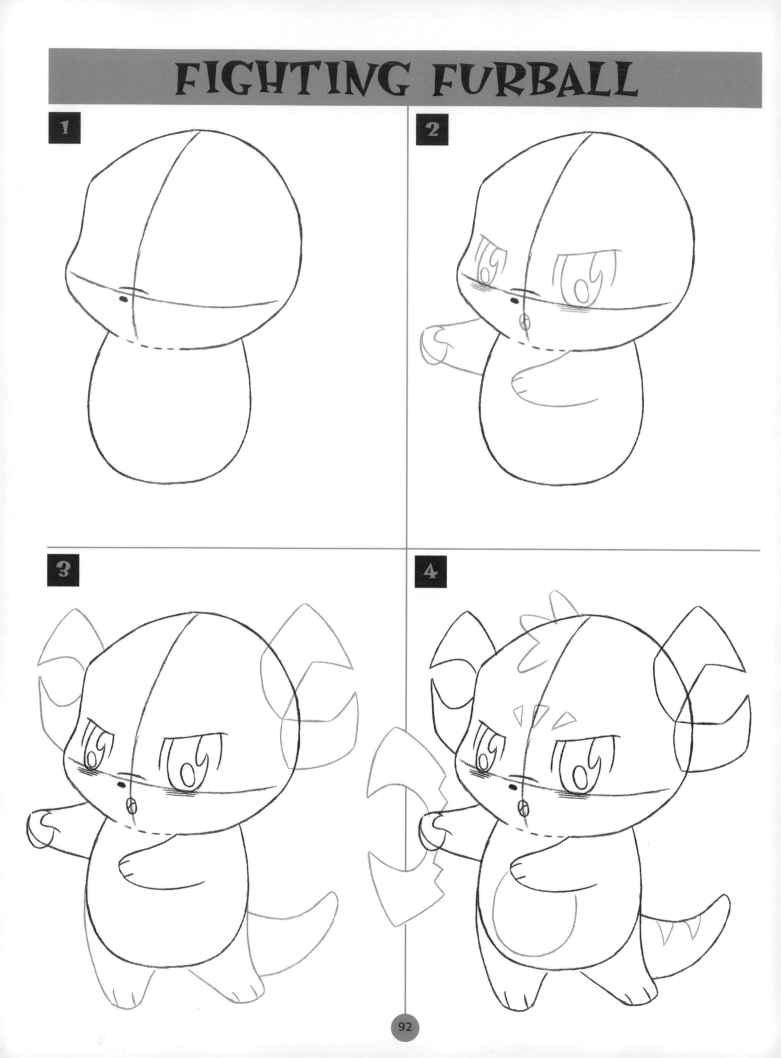

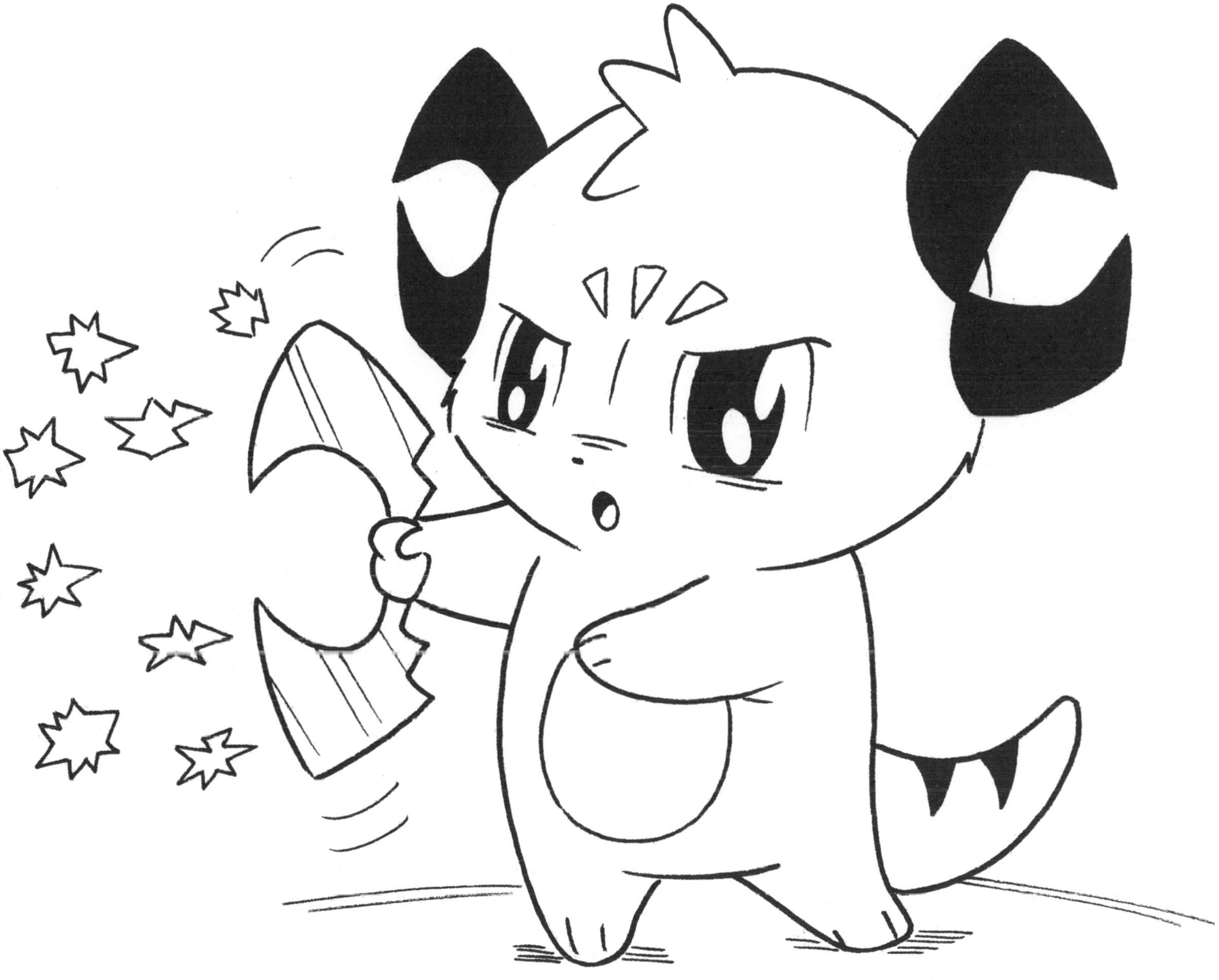

KITTY CRAZY

1

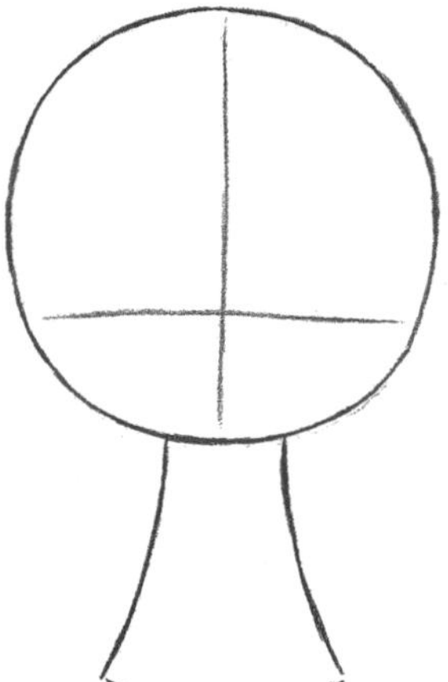

2

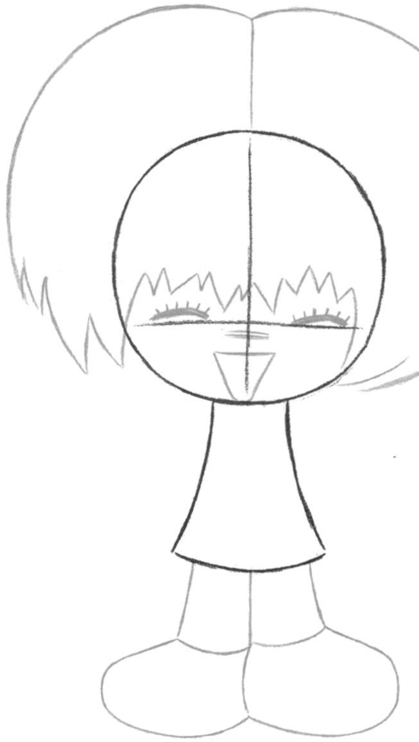

3

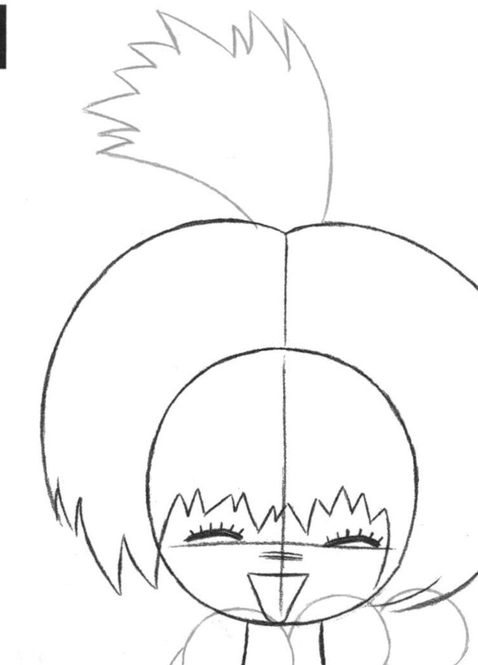

4

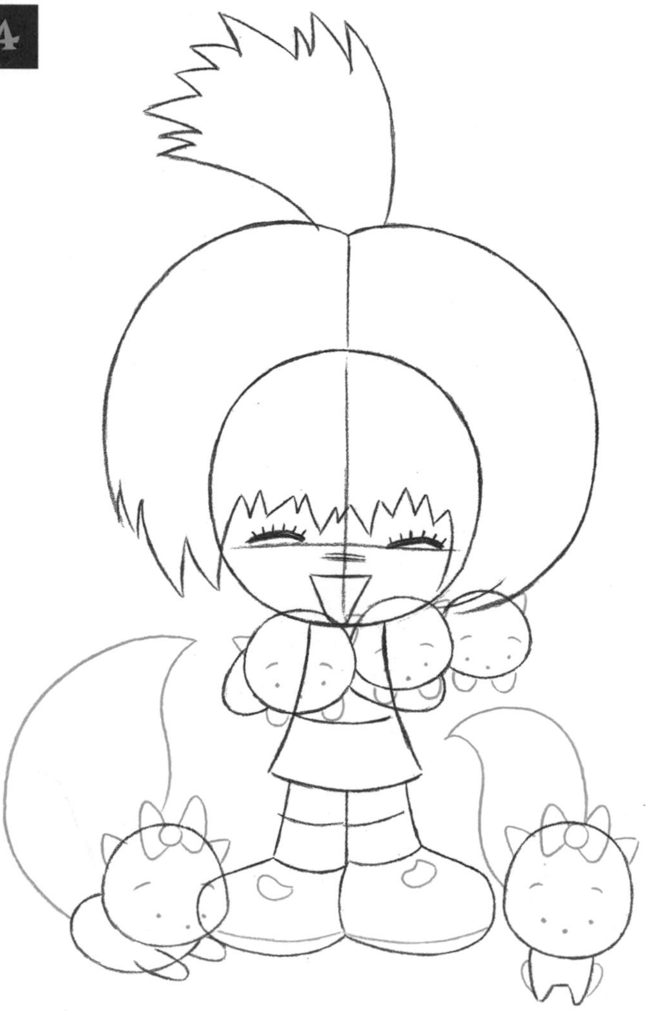

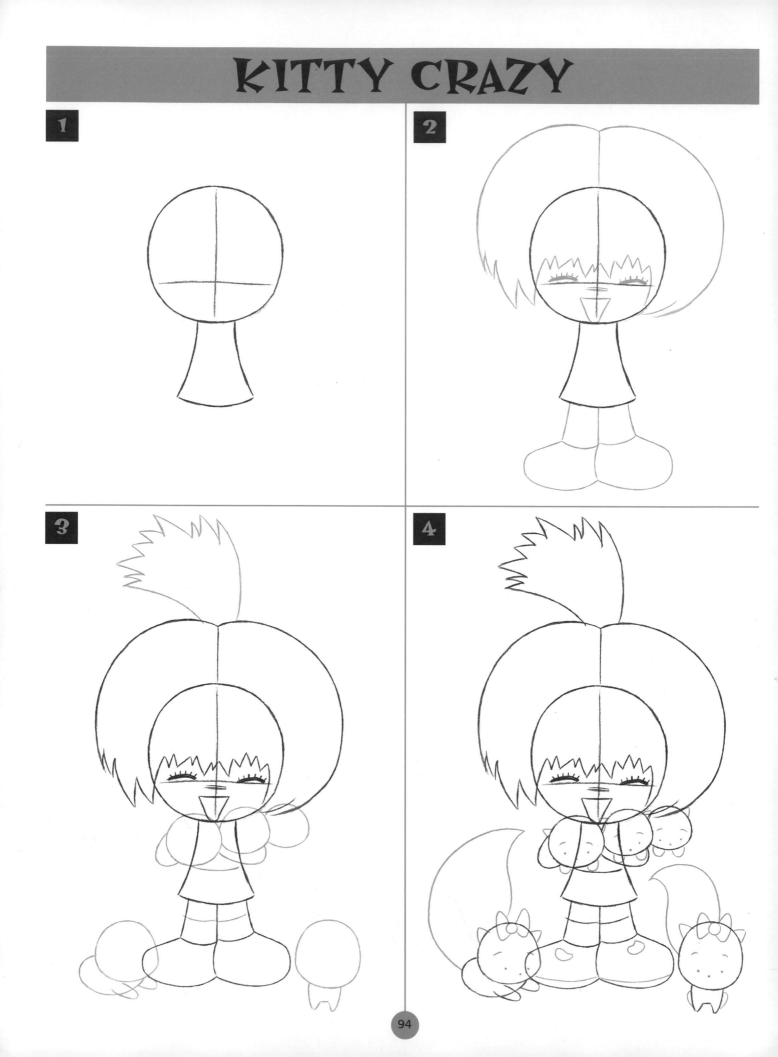

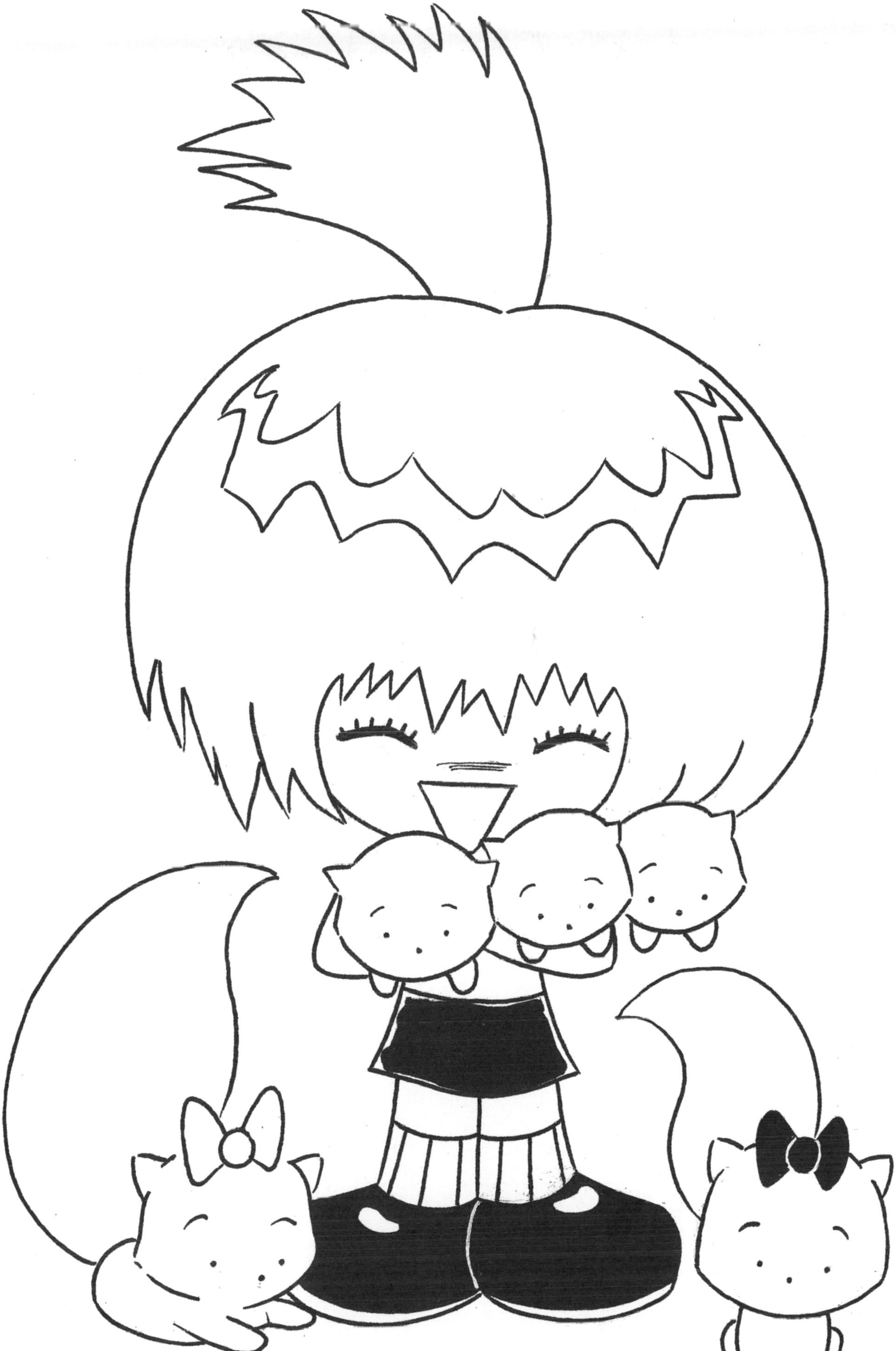

LASER LARRY

1

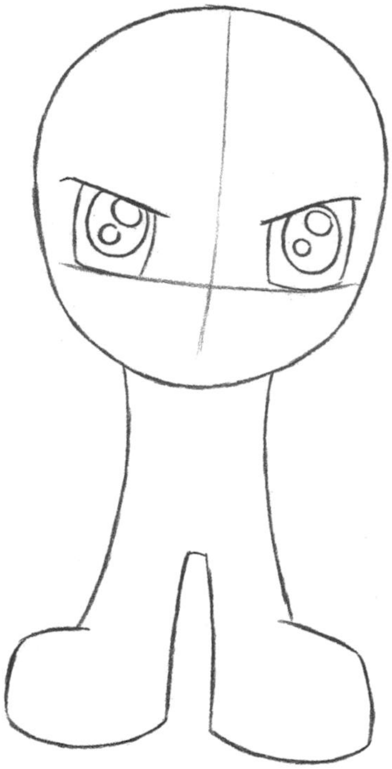

2

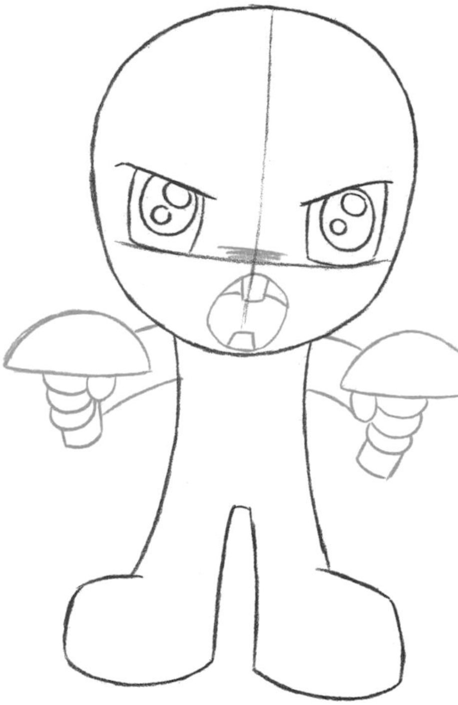

3

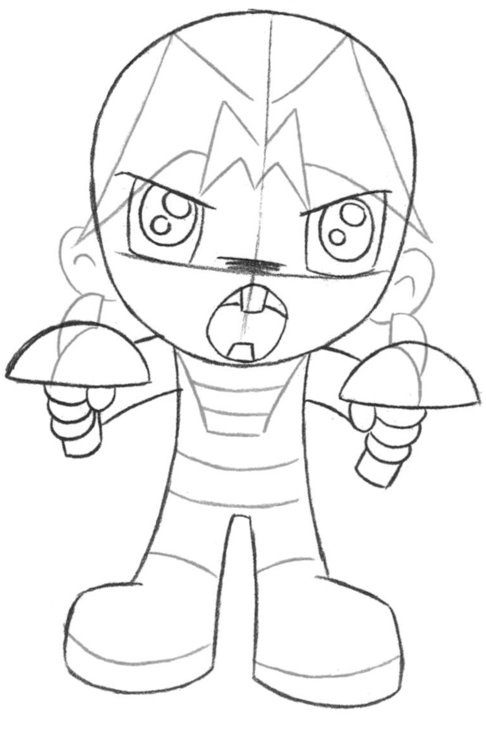

4

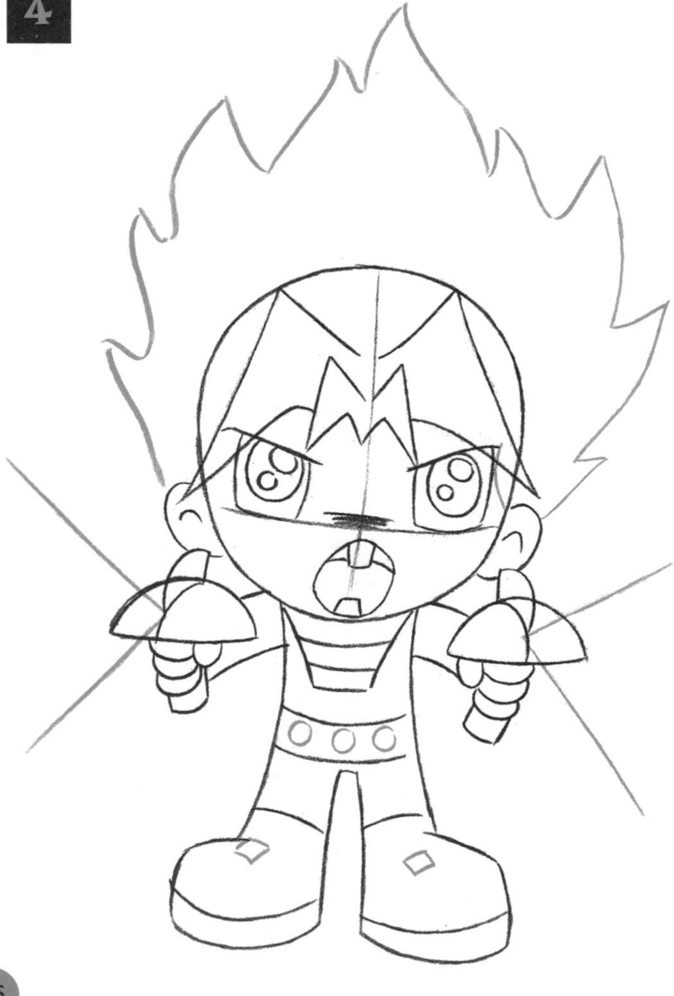

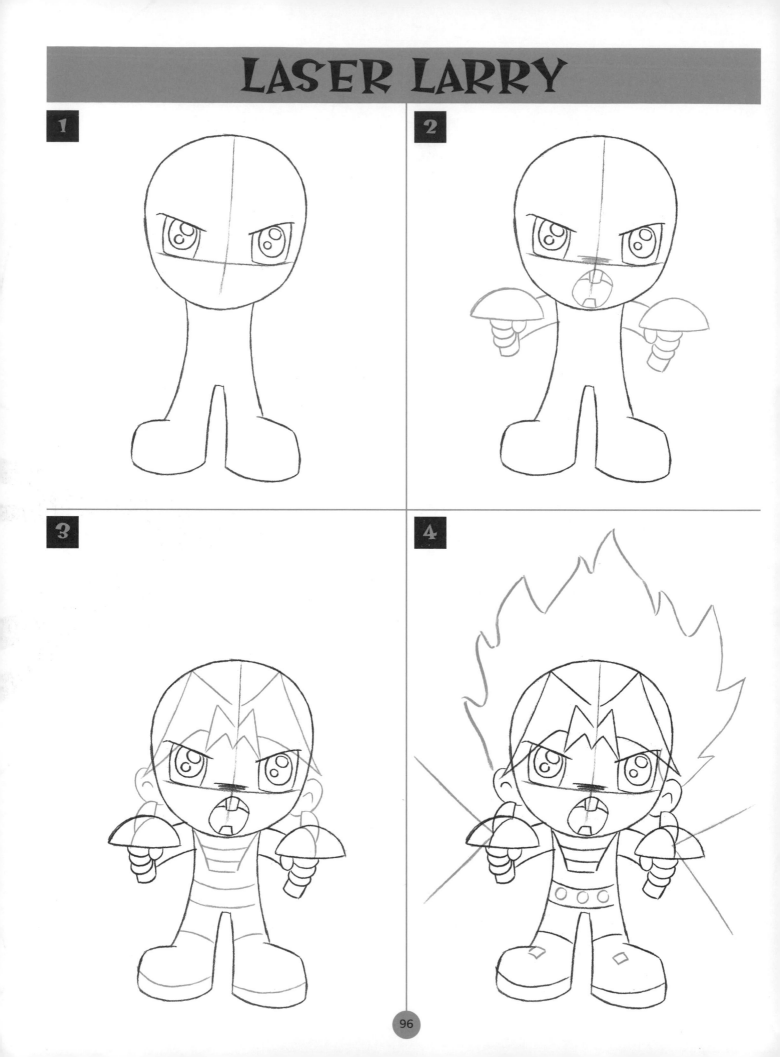

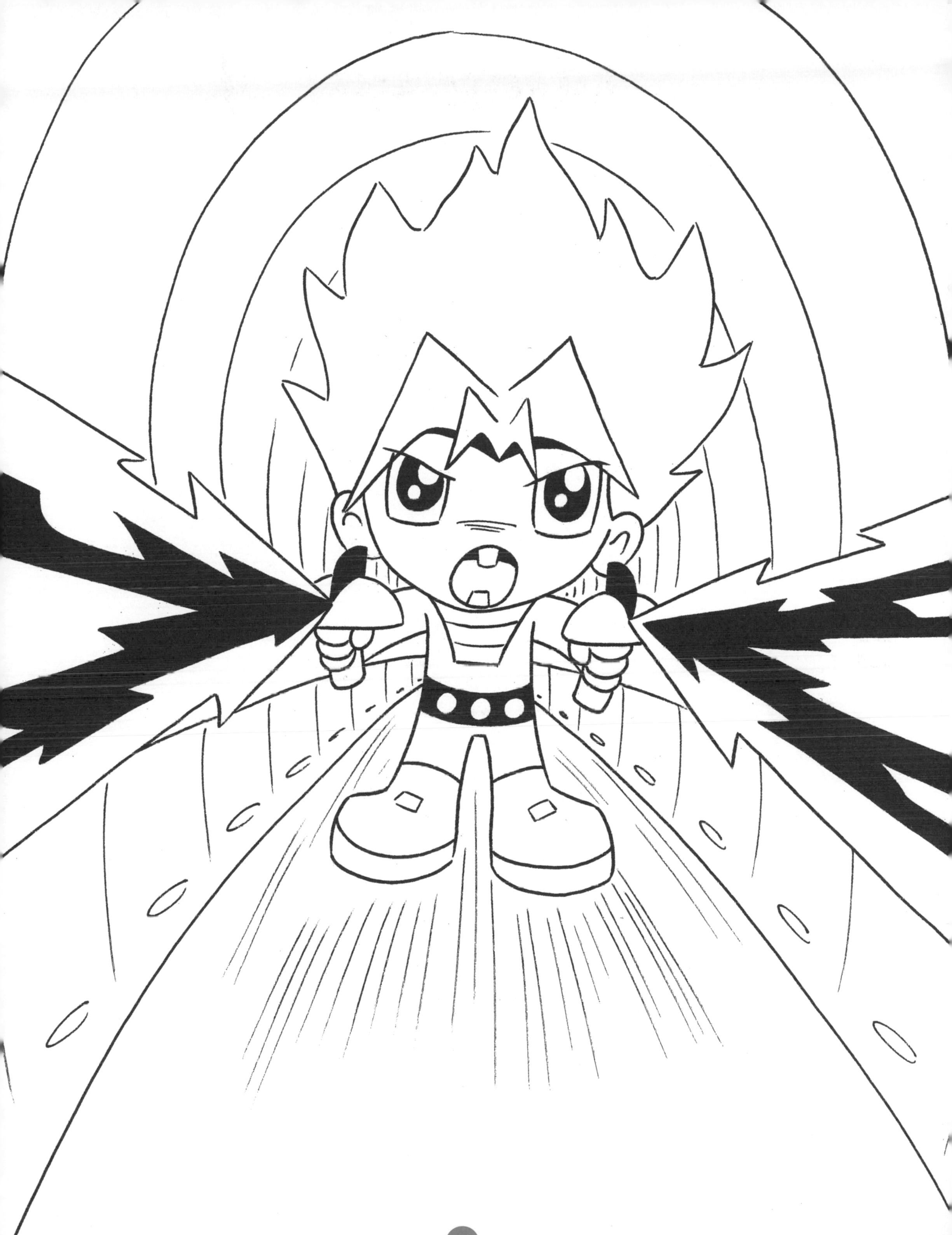

SLICK SAM

1

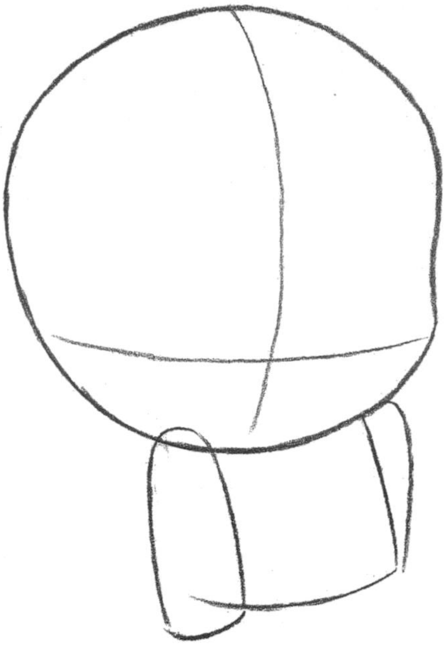

2

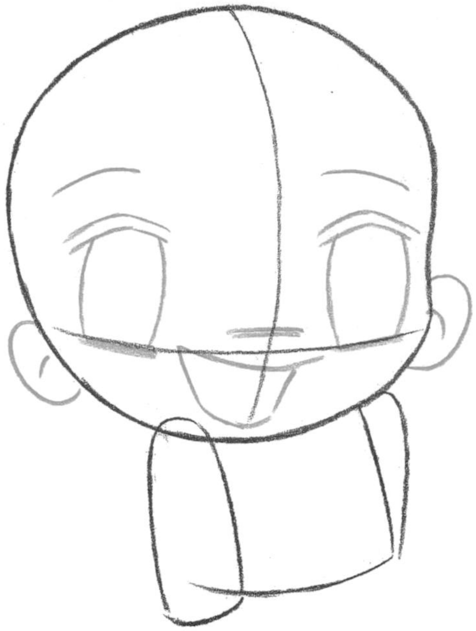

3

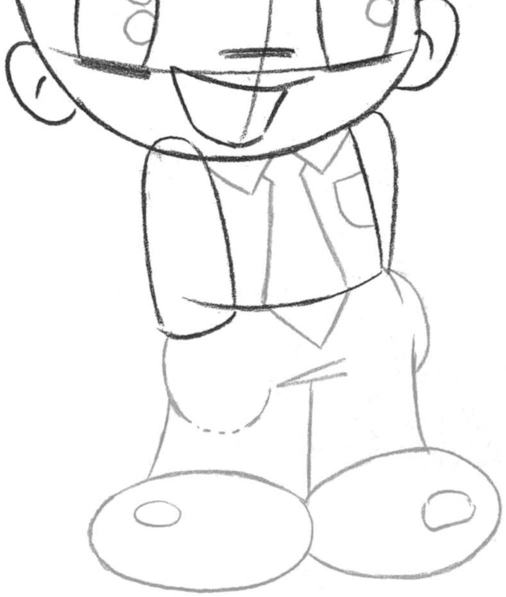

4

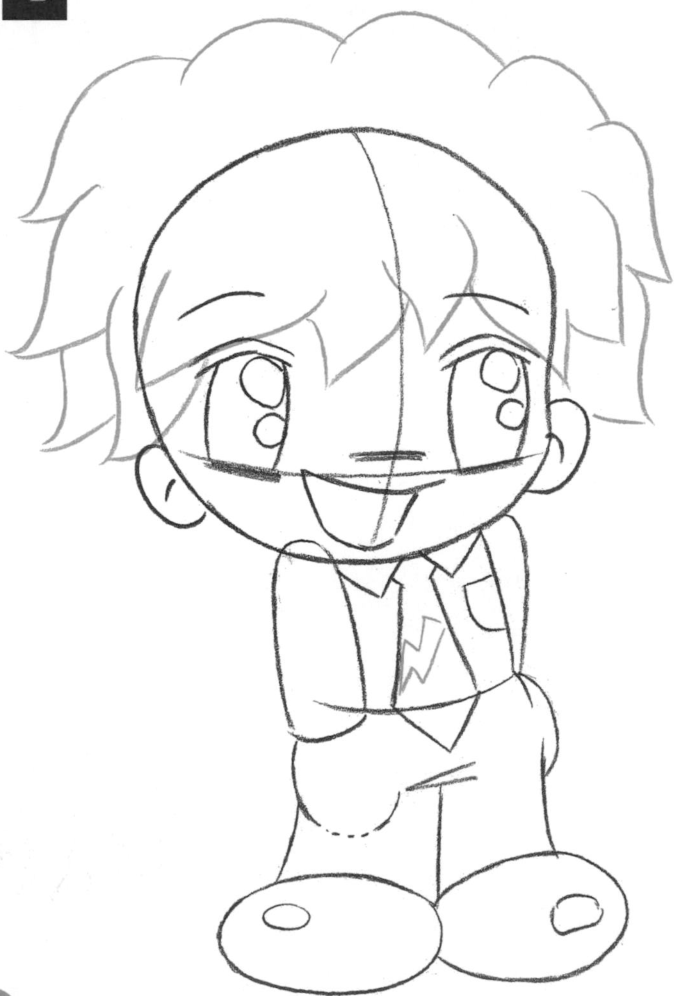

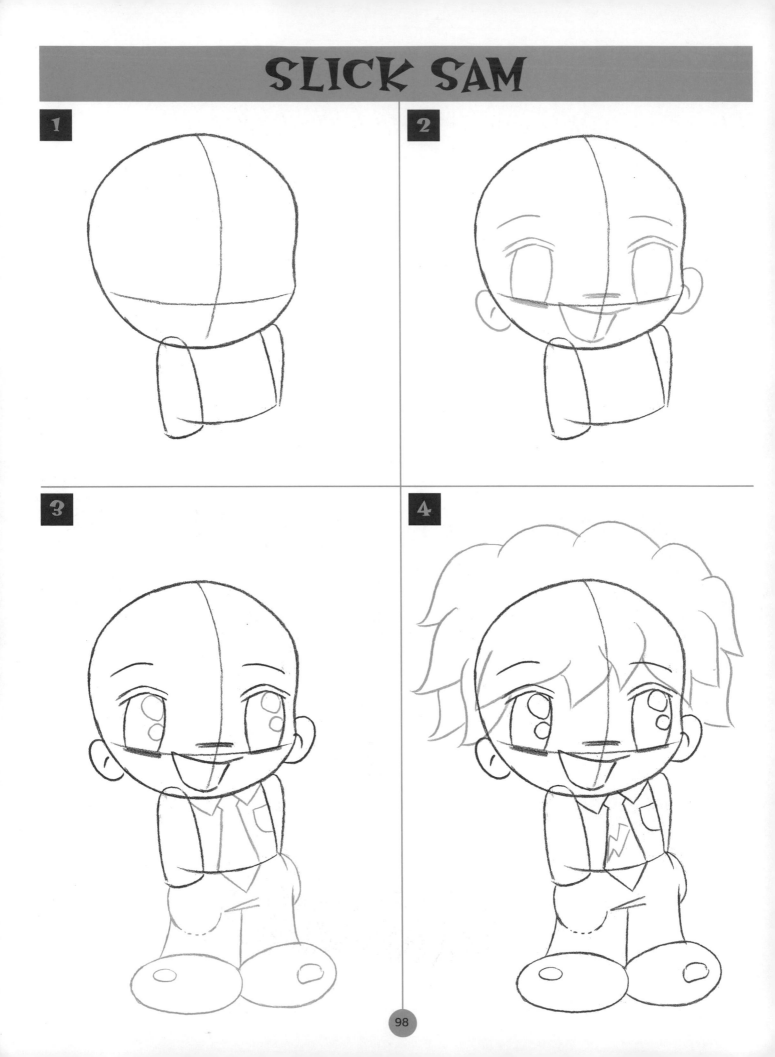

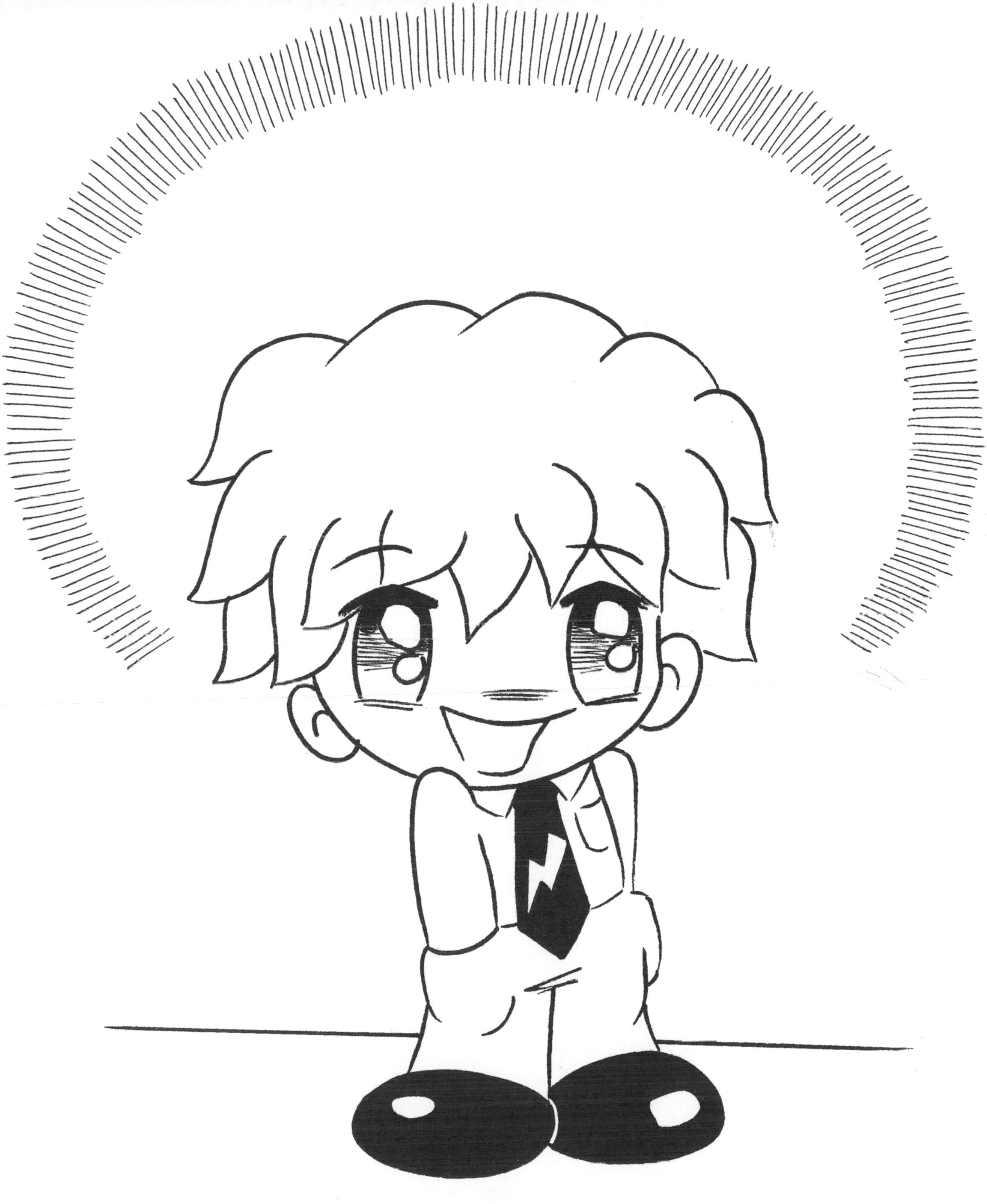

WIZARD KING

1

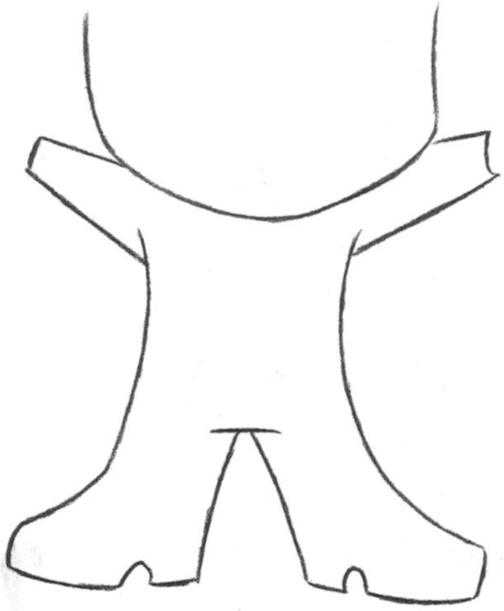

2

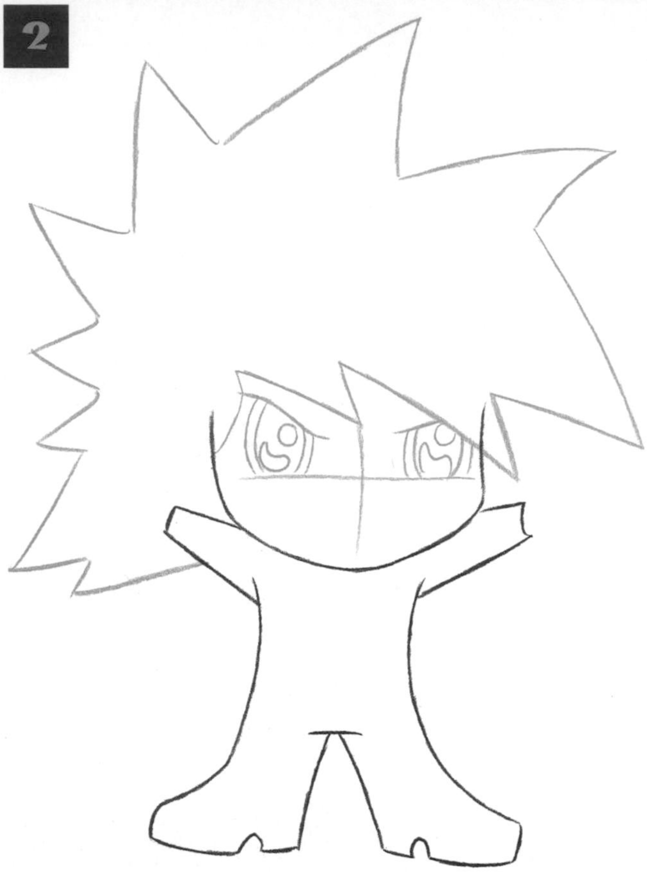

3

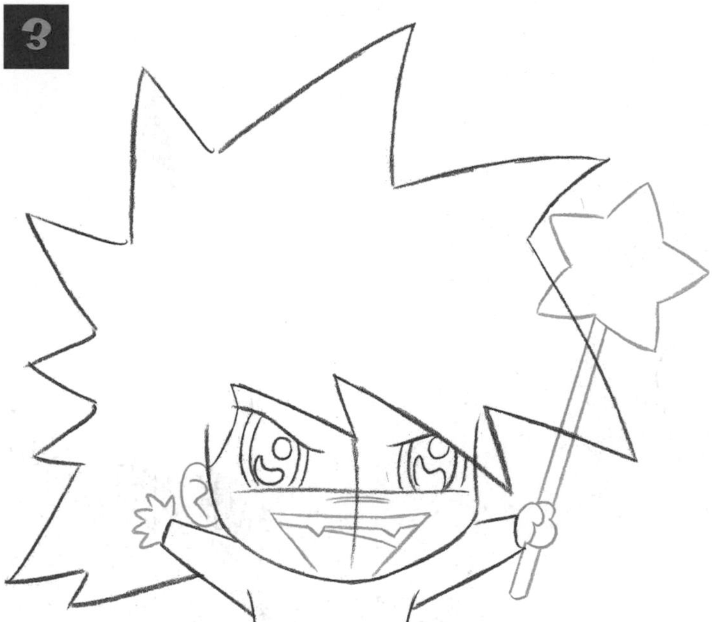

4

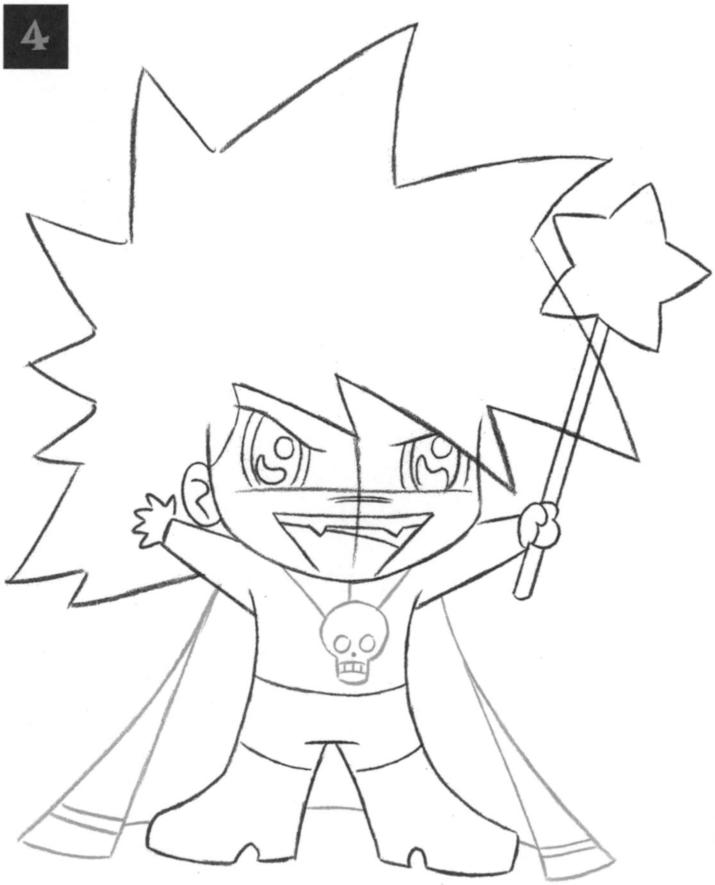

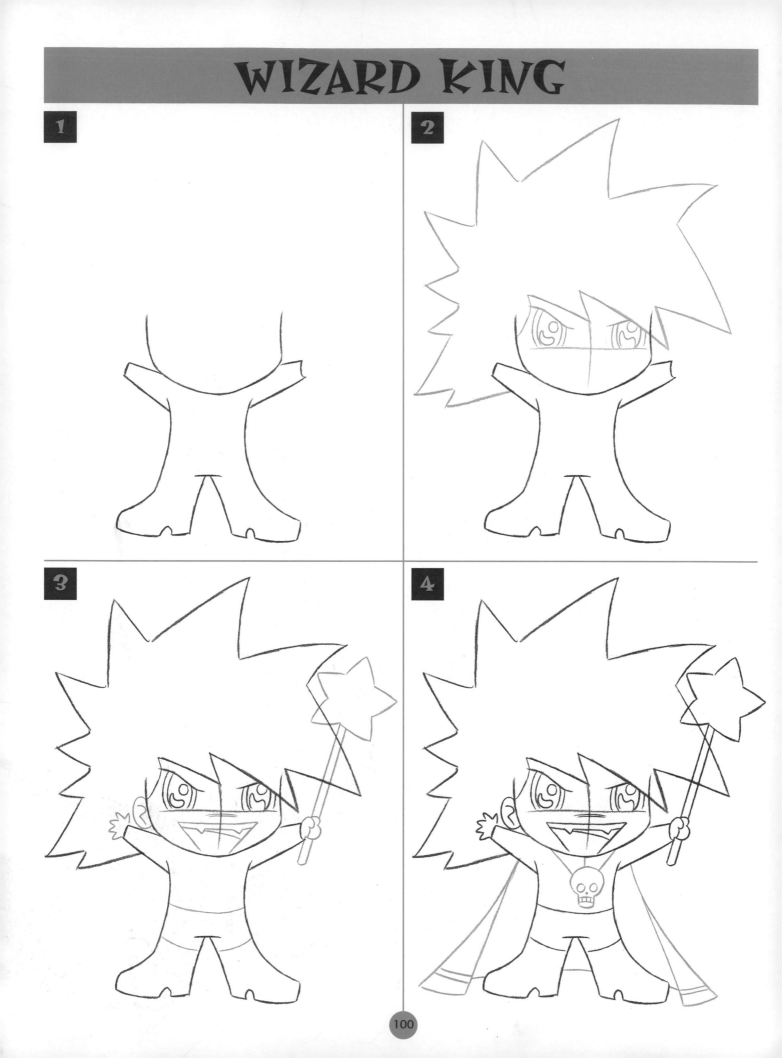

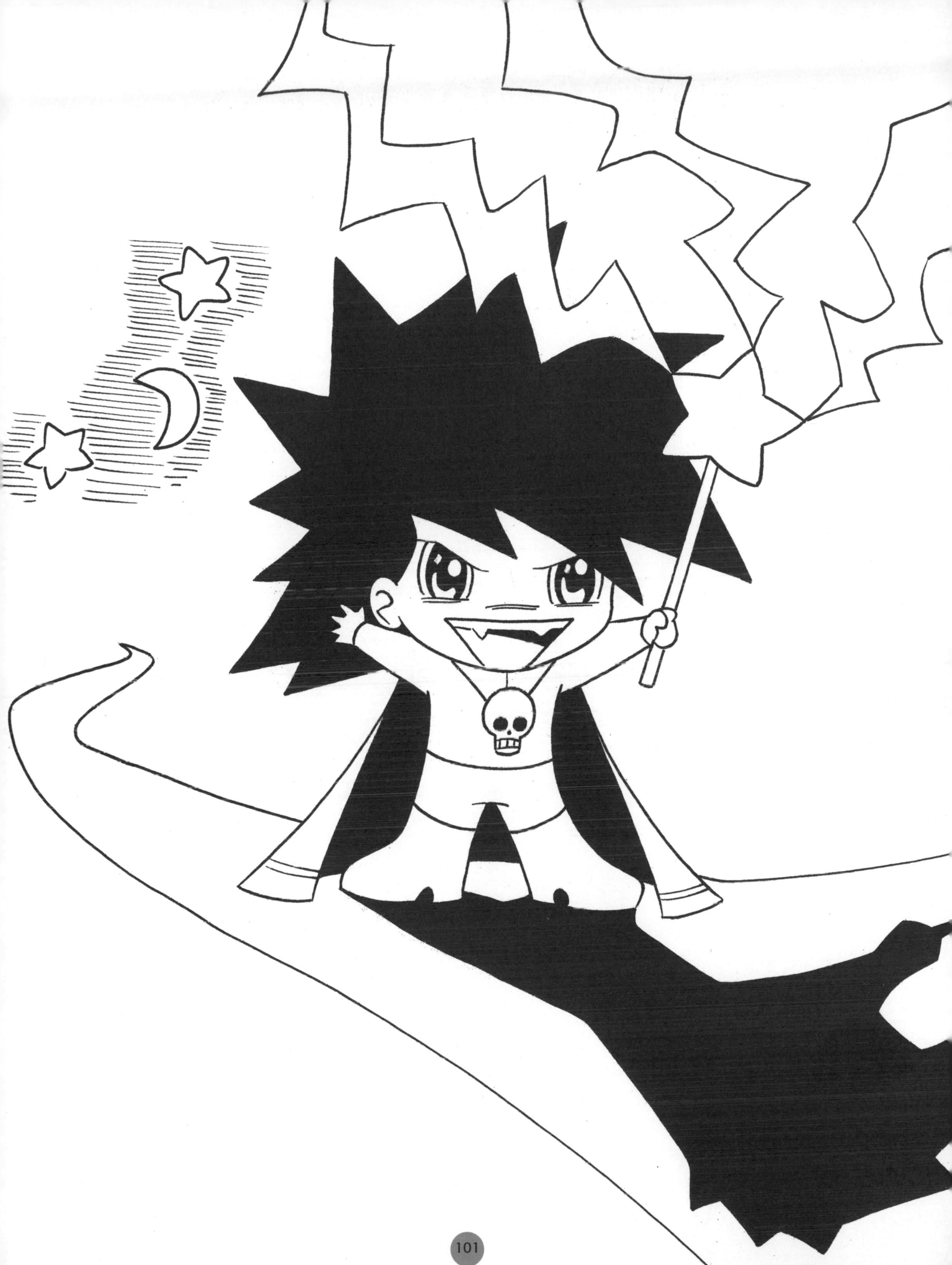

BATTLE PRINCESS

1

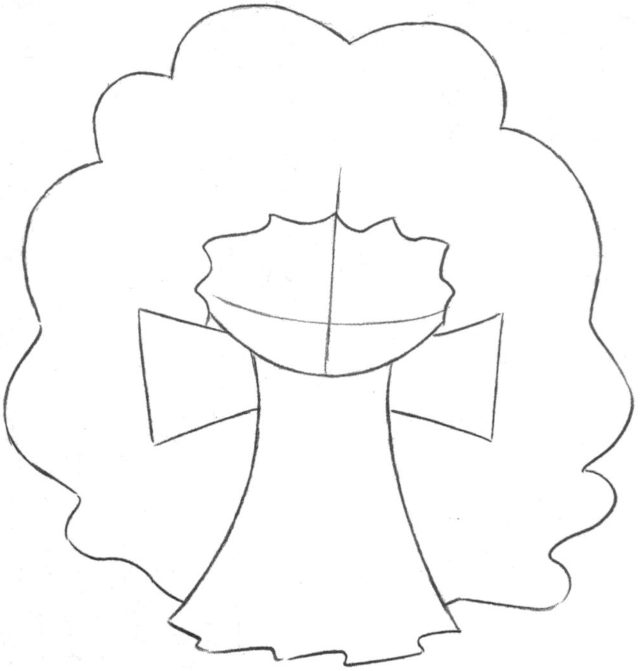

2

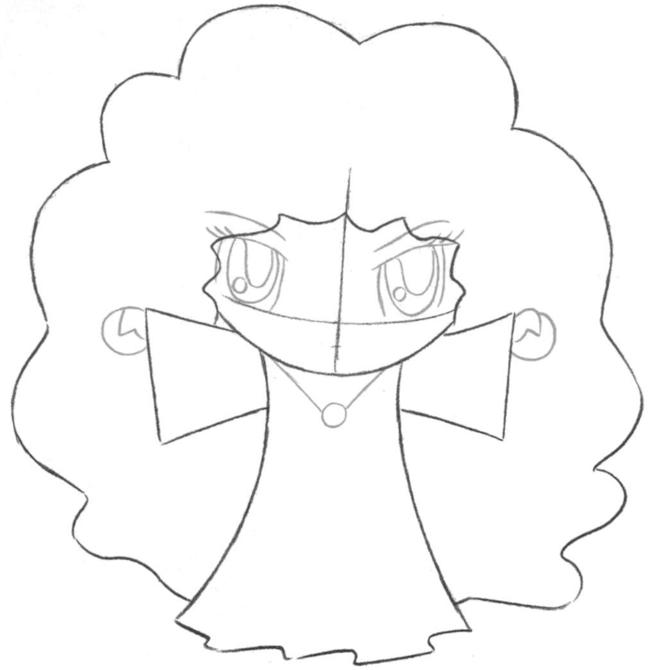

3

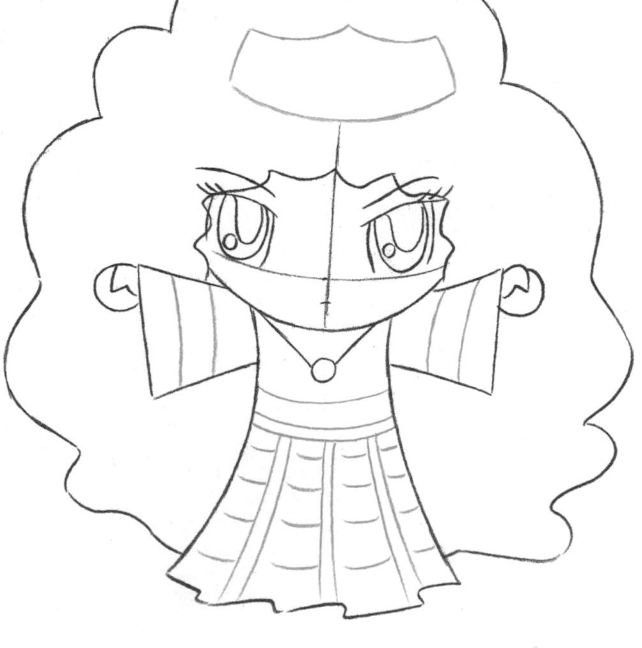

4

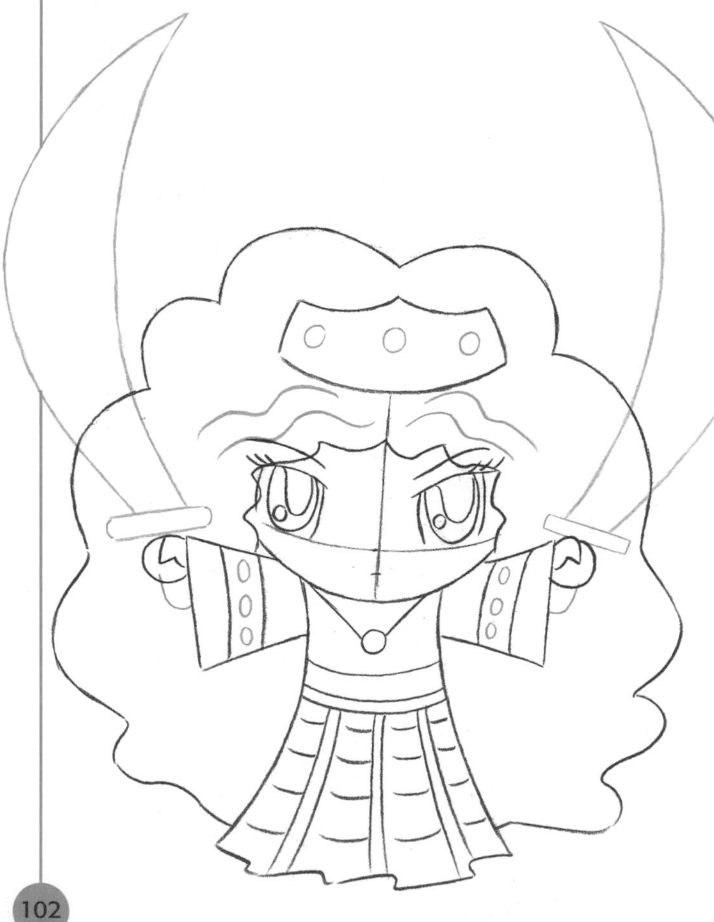

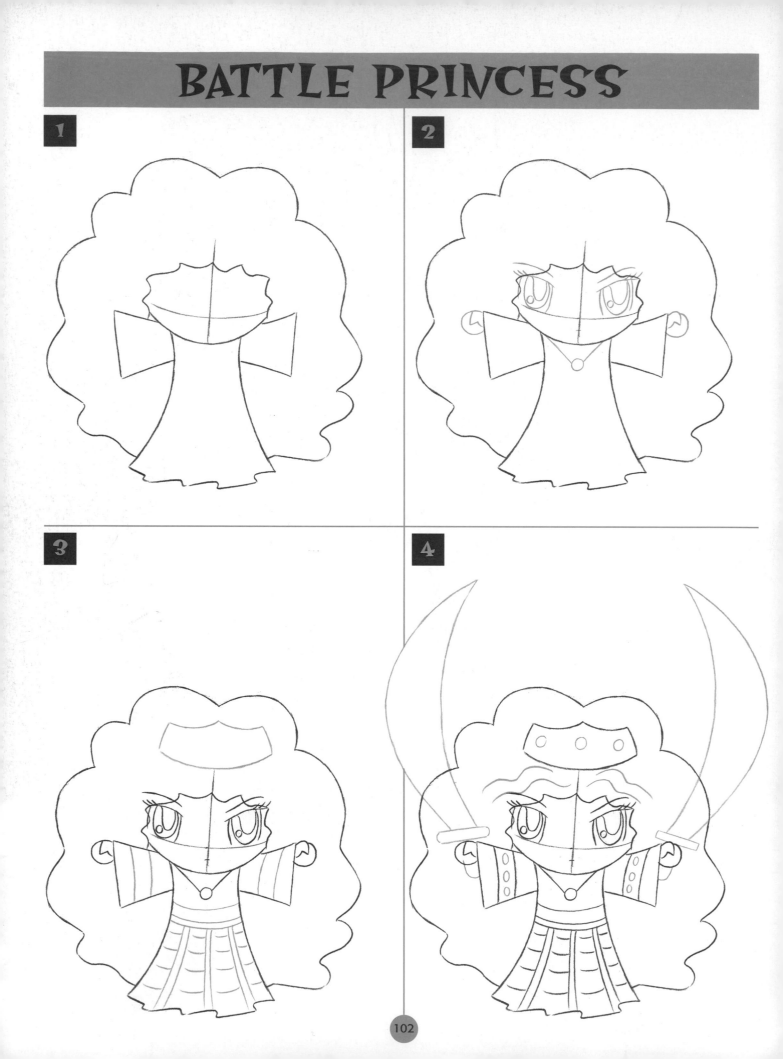

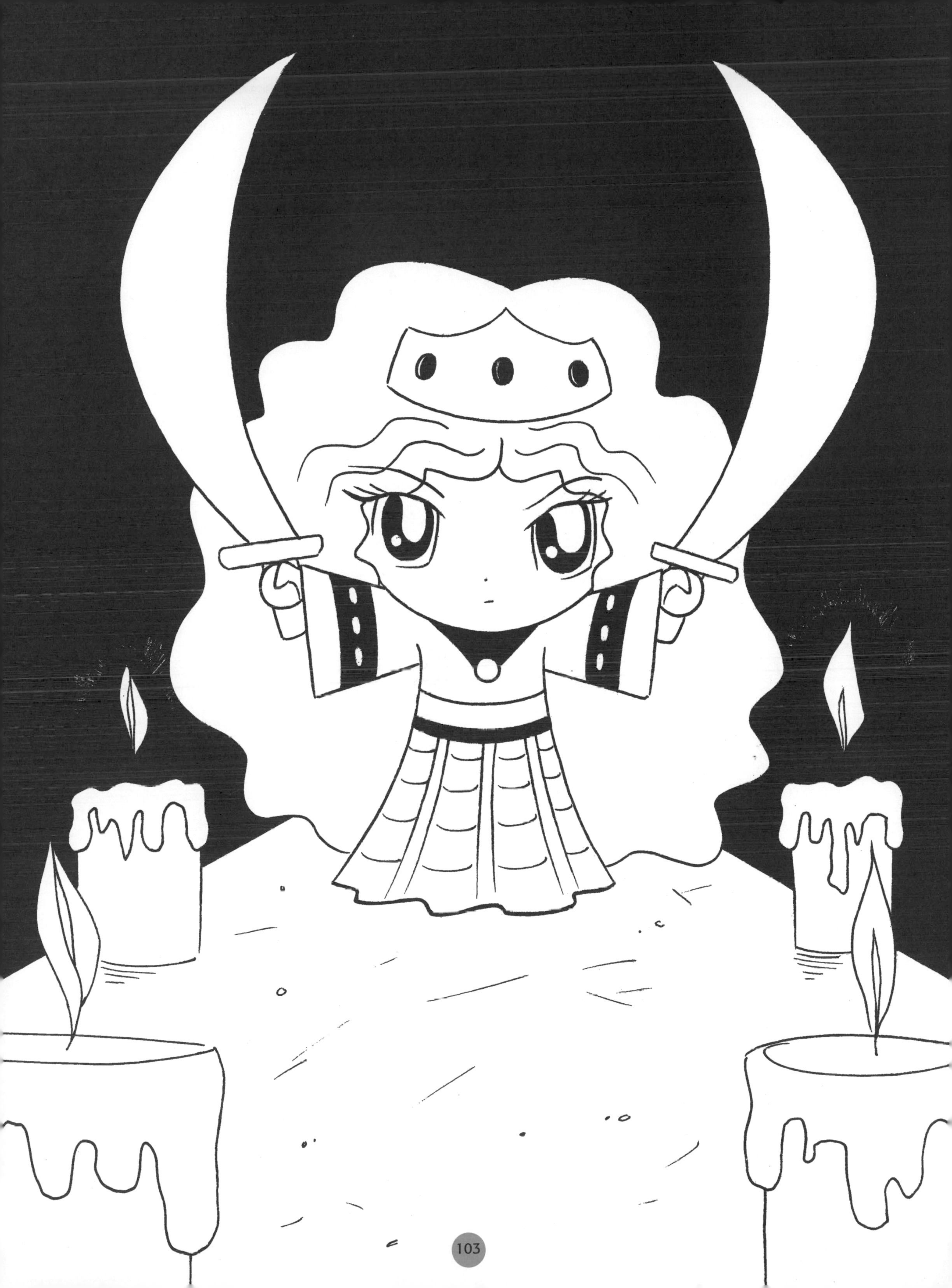

SUMO-SAMURAI

1

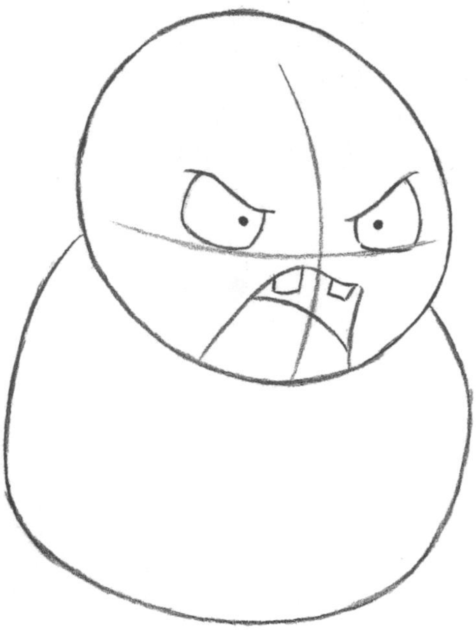

2

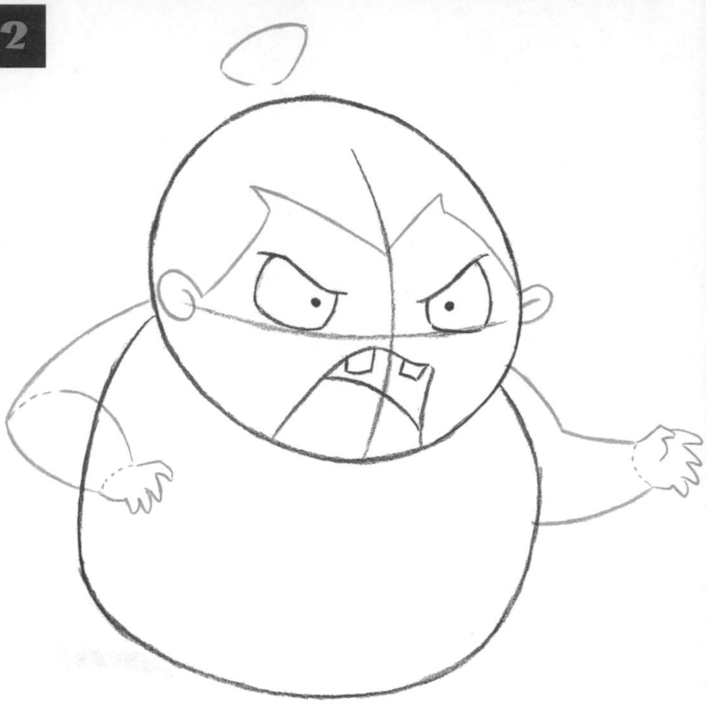

3

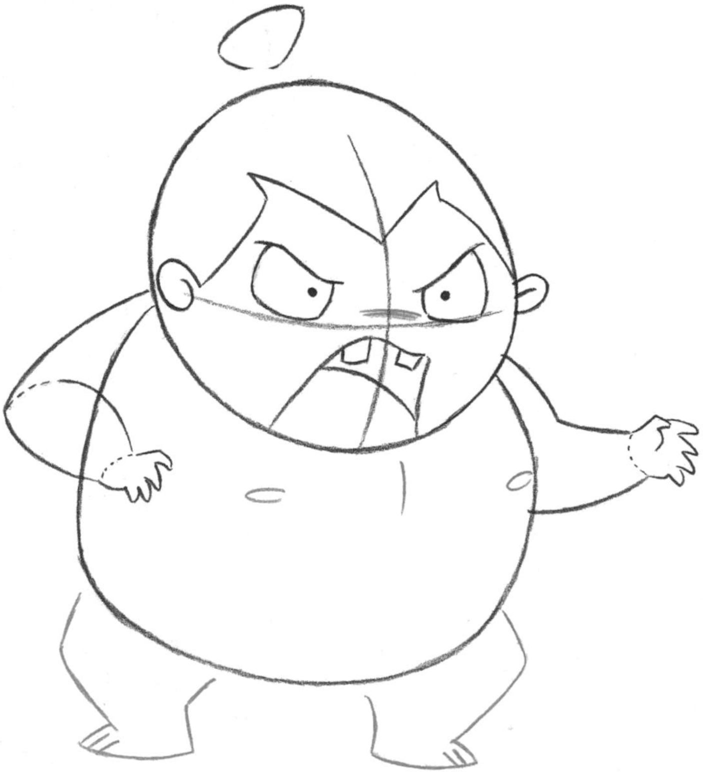

4

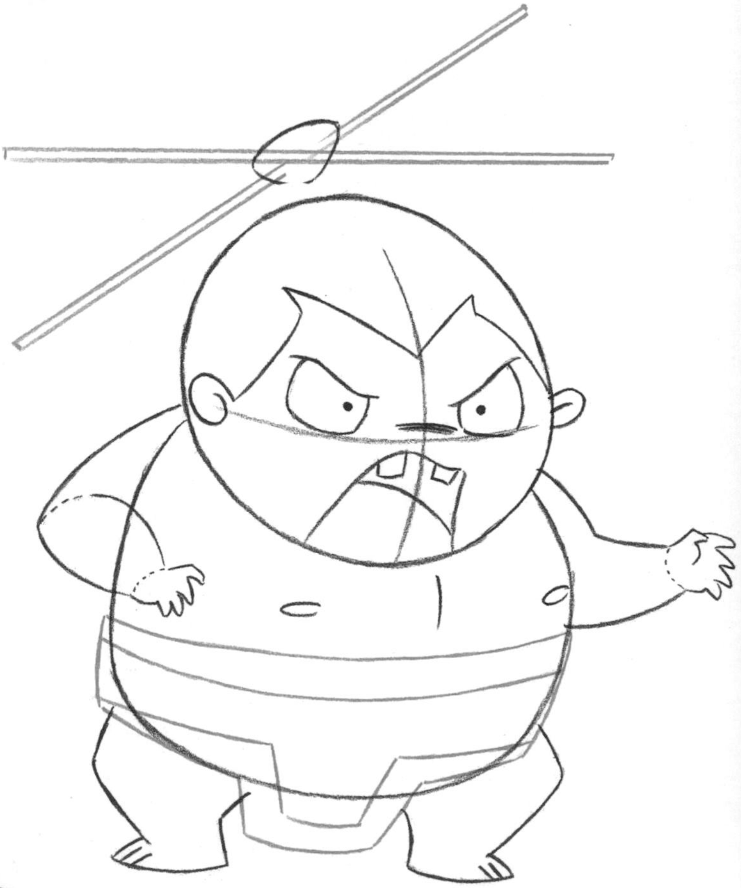

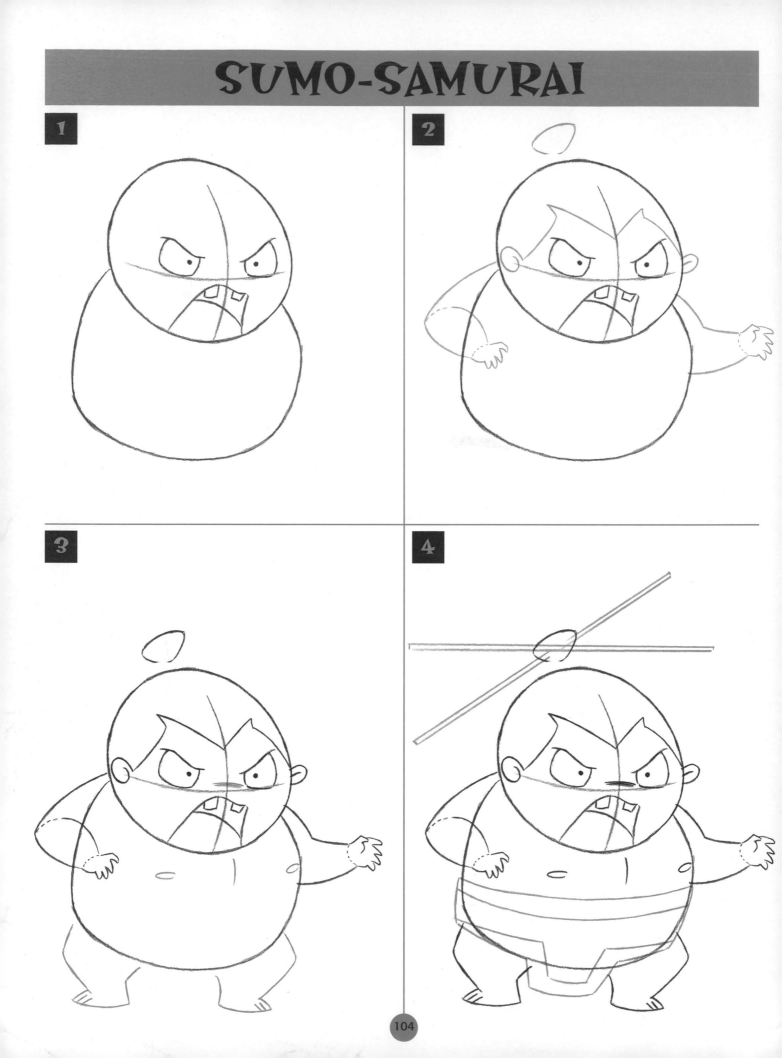

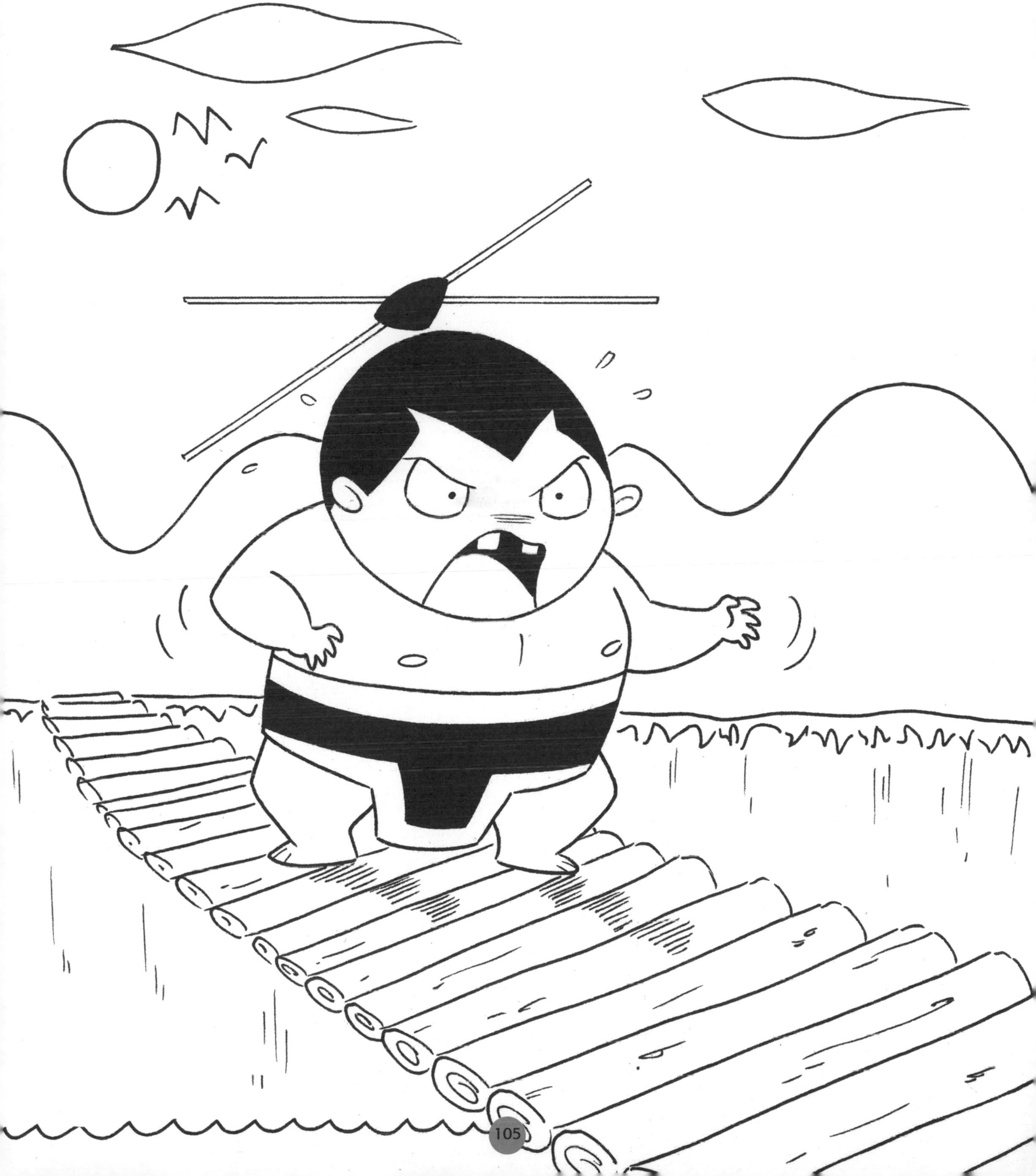

HIPPO-HORN

1

2

3

4

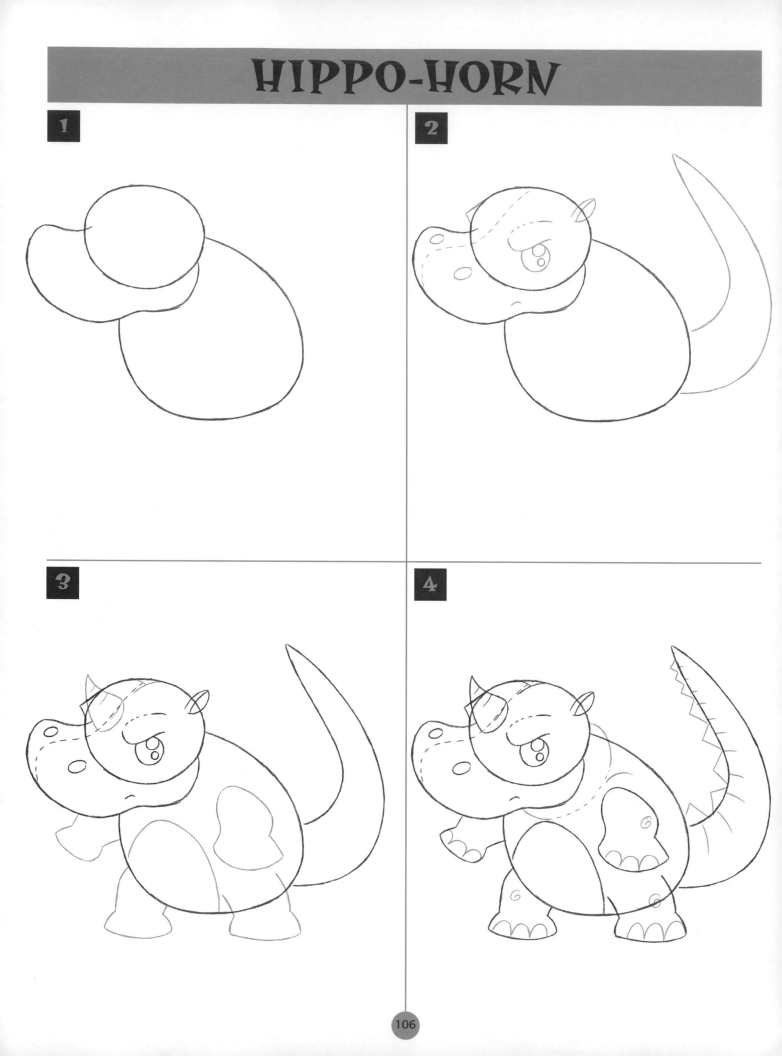

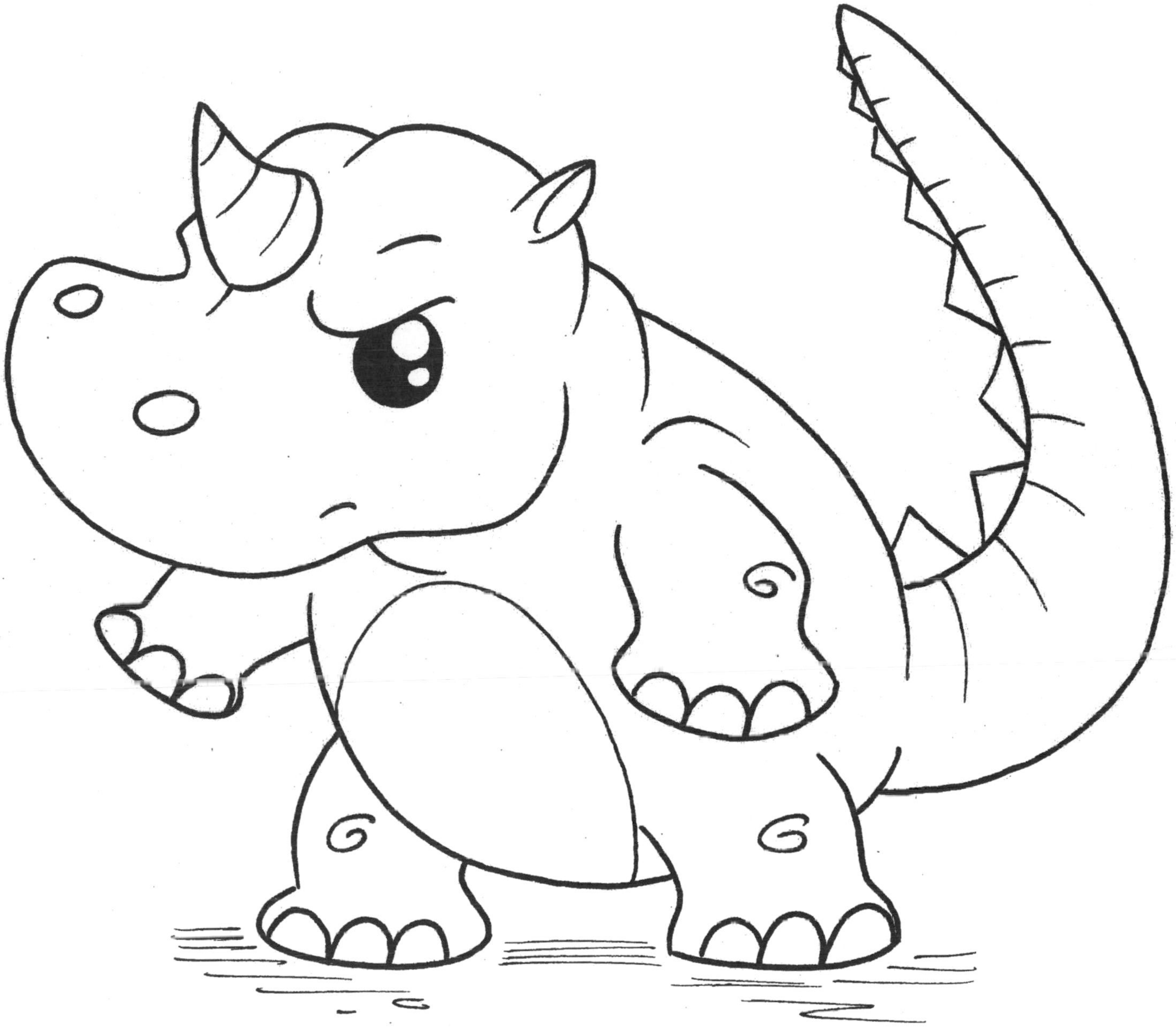

MAGIC EMPRESS

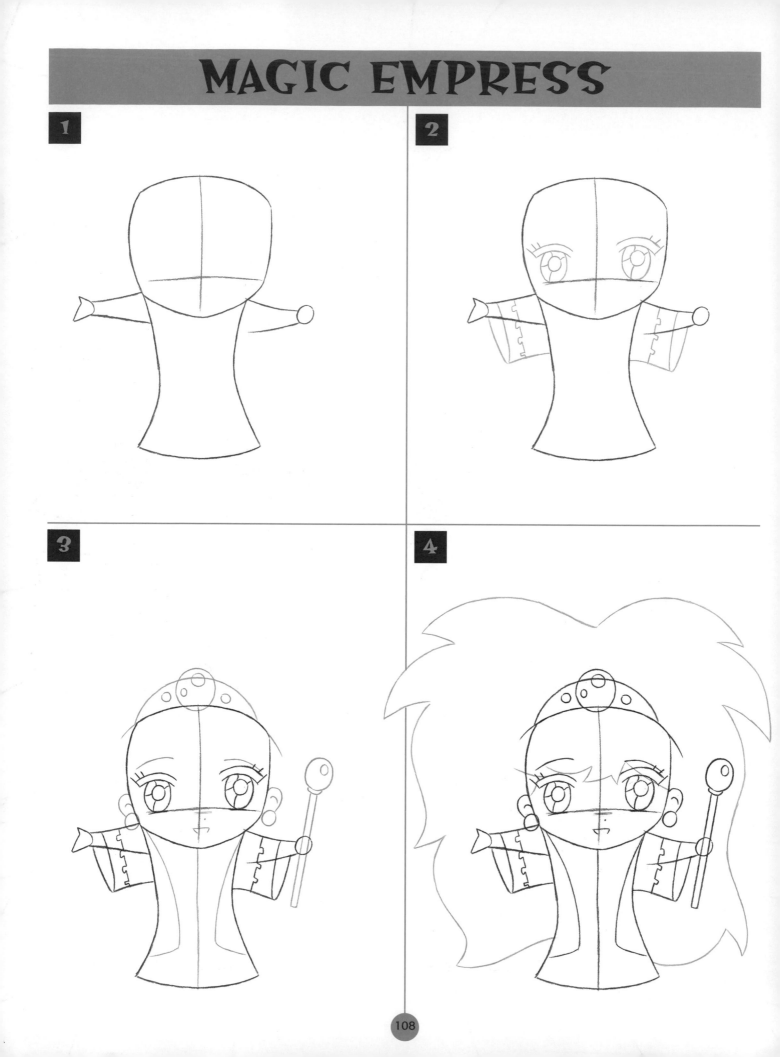

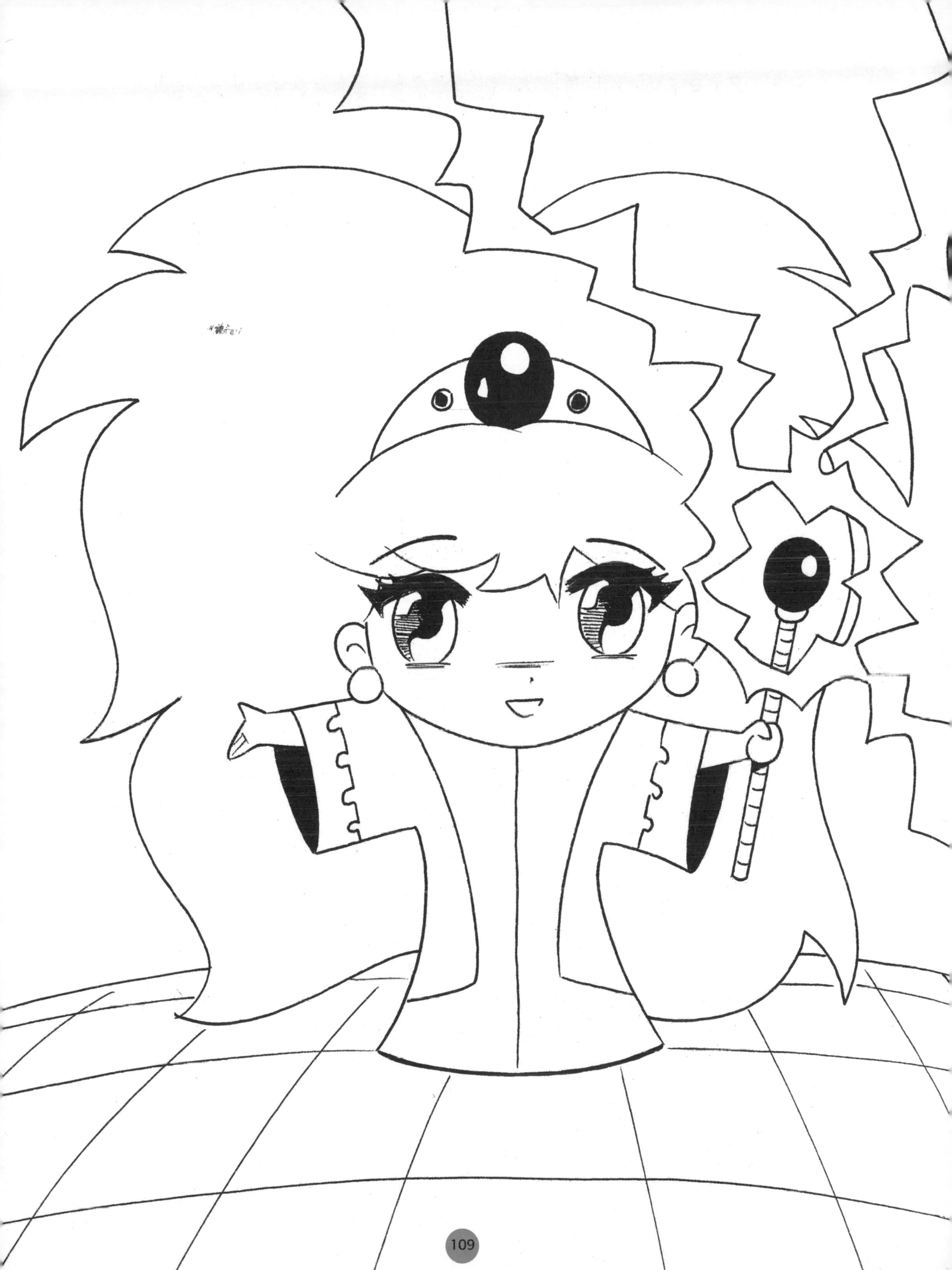

FRUSTRATED FREDDY

1

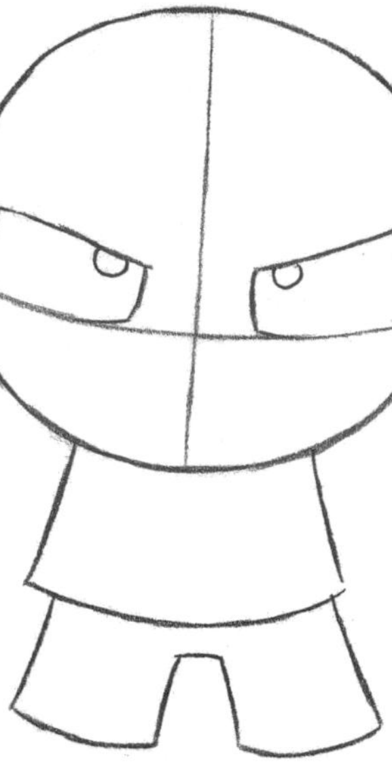

2

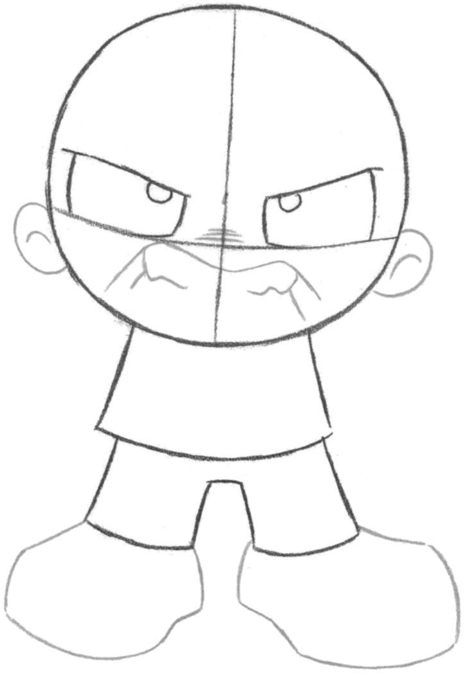

3

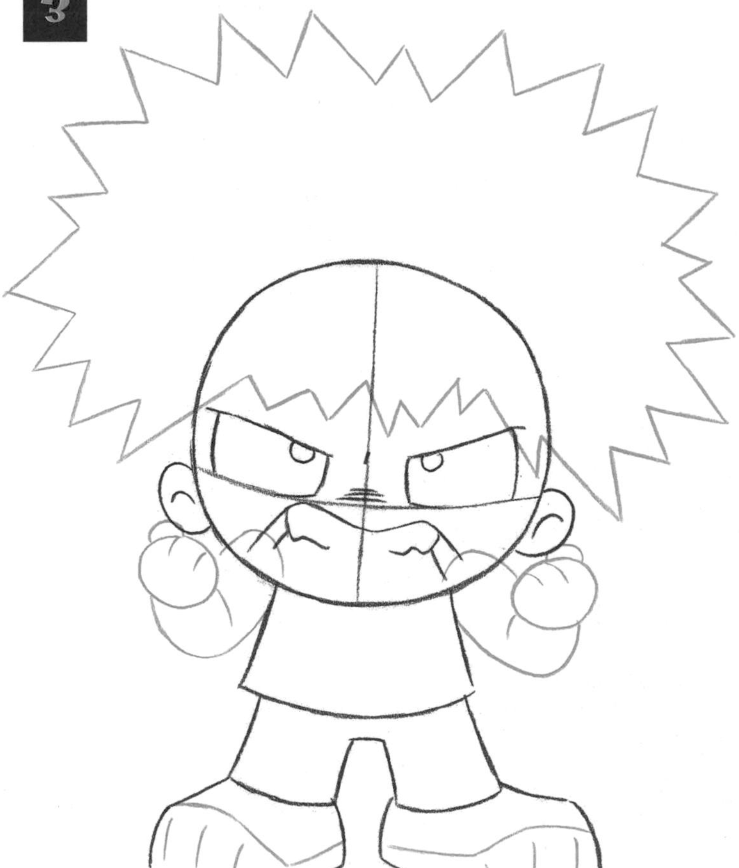

4

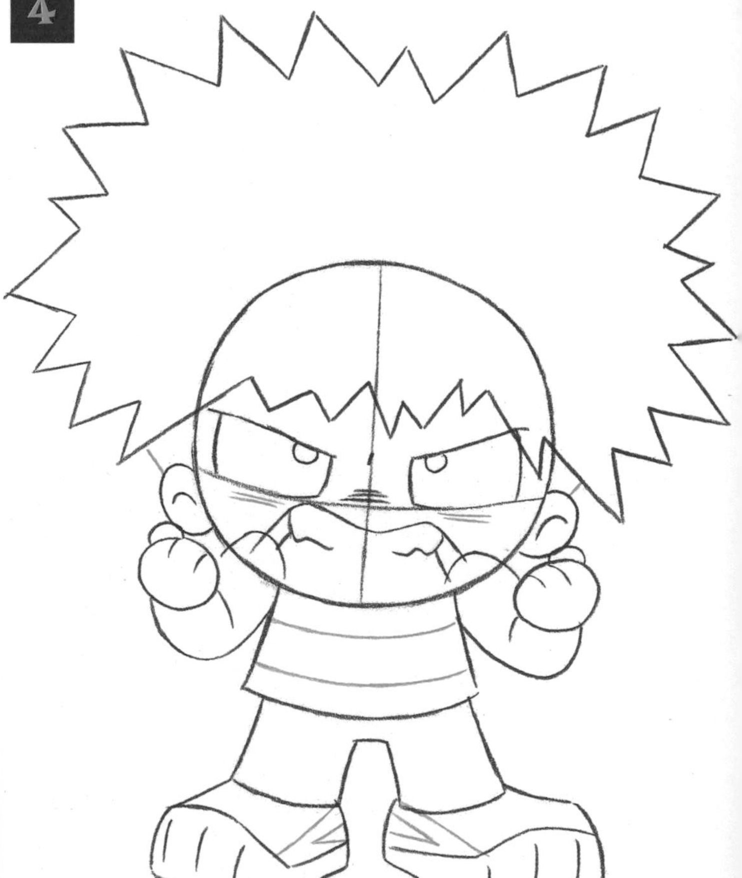

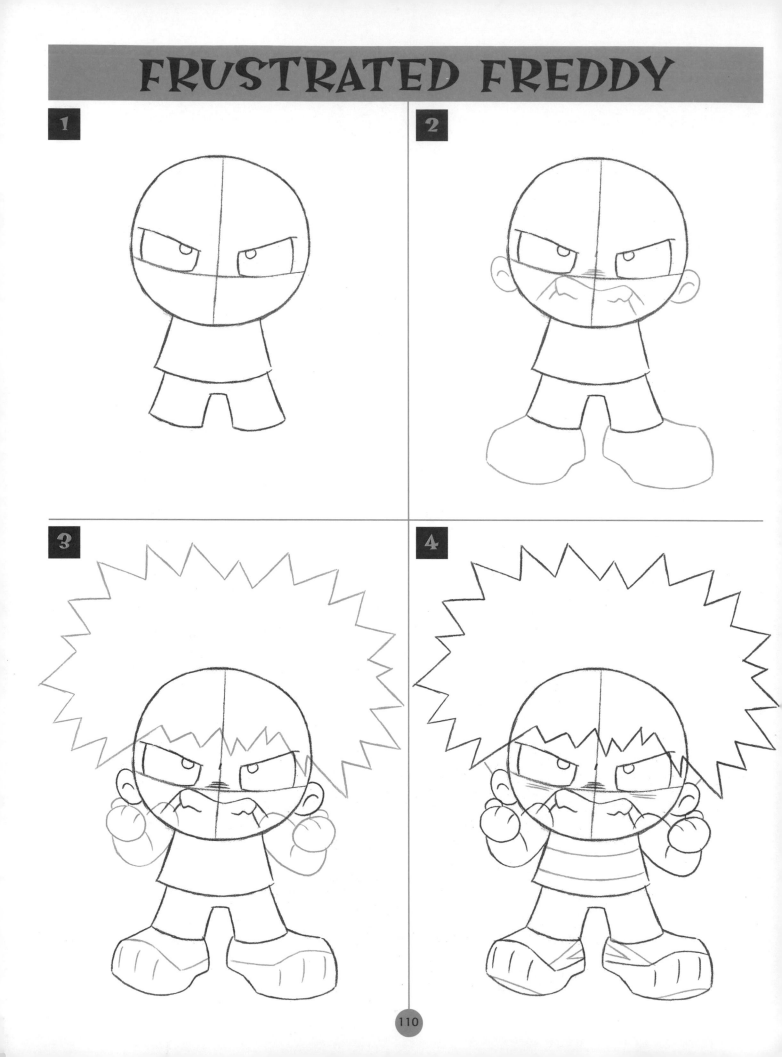

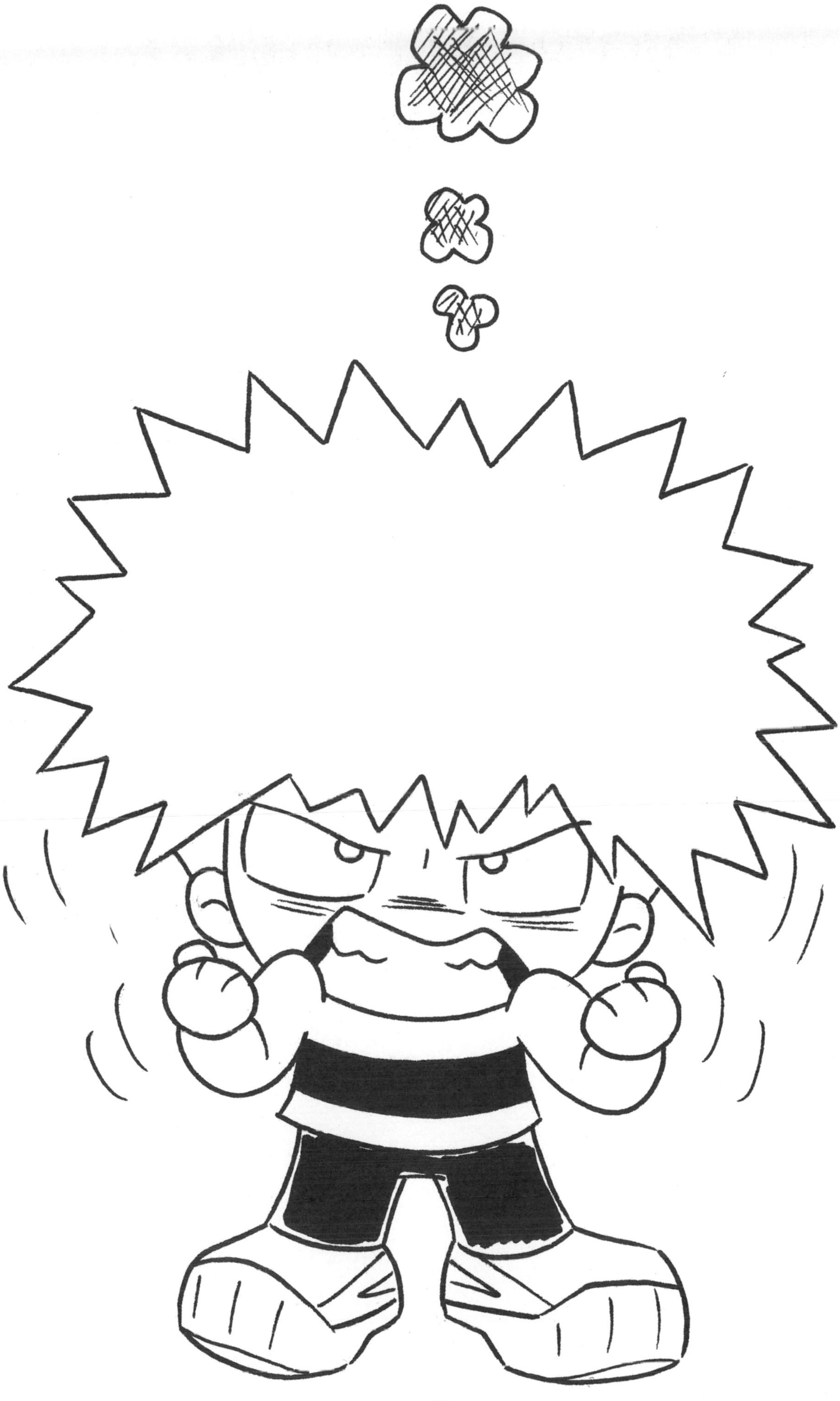

SNOWBALL FIGHT

1

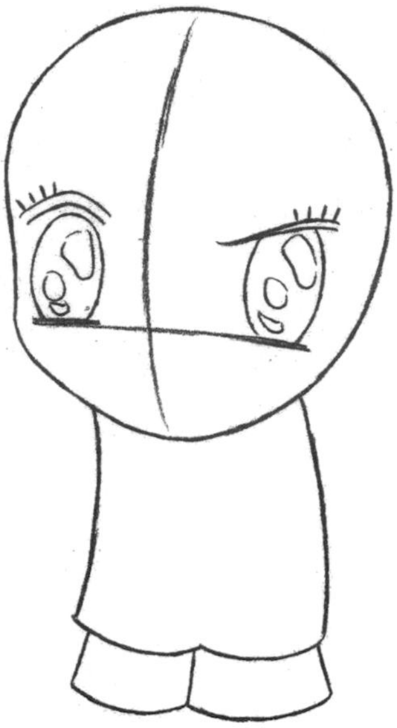

2

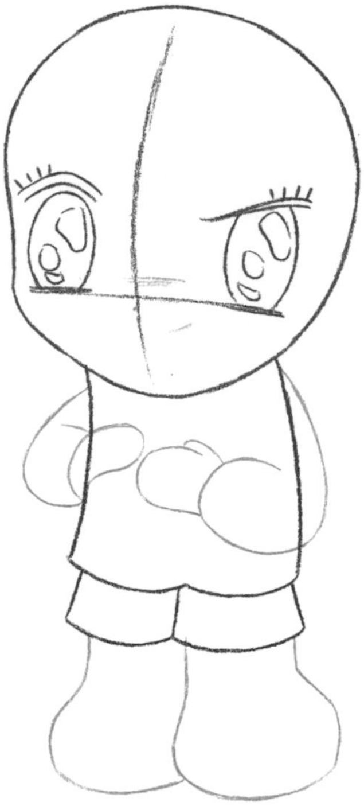

3

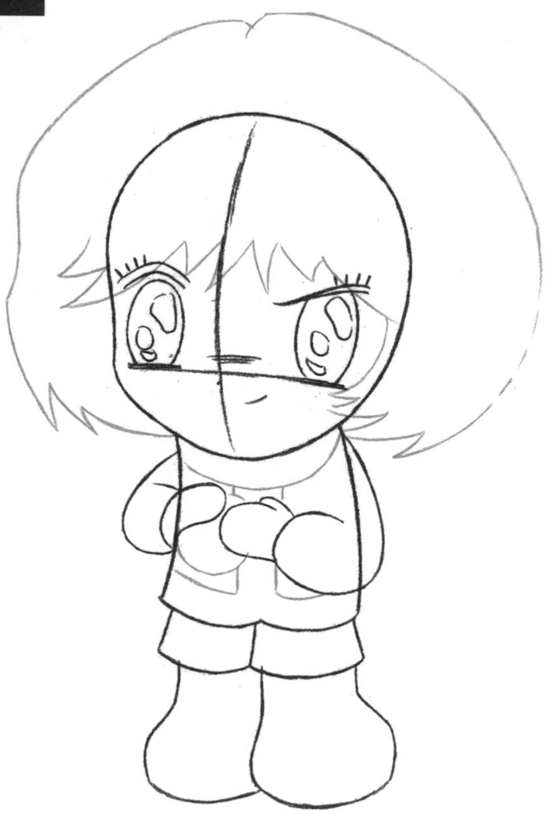

4

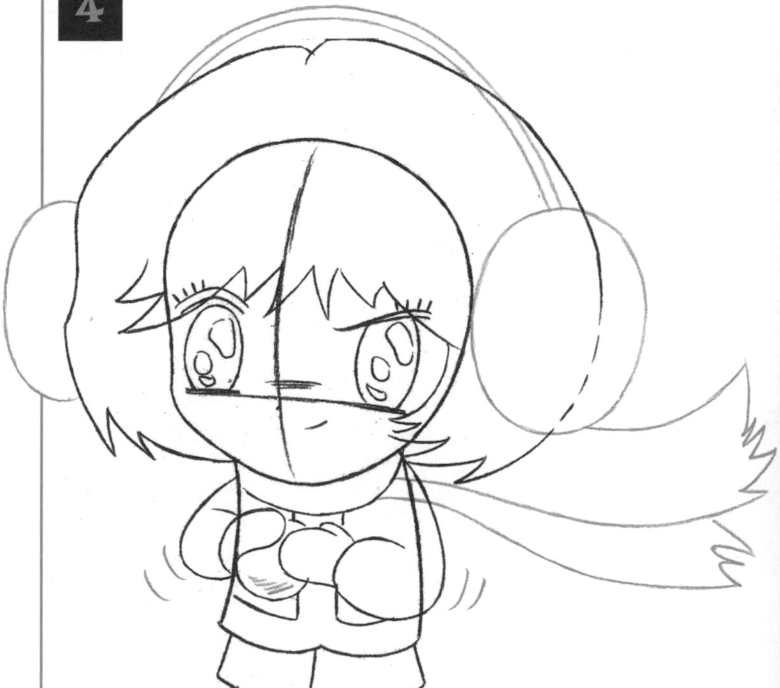

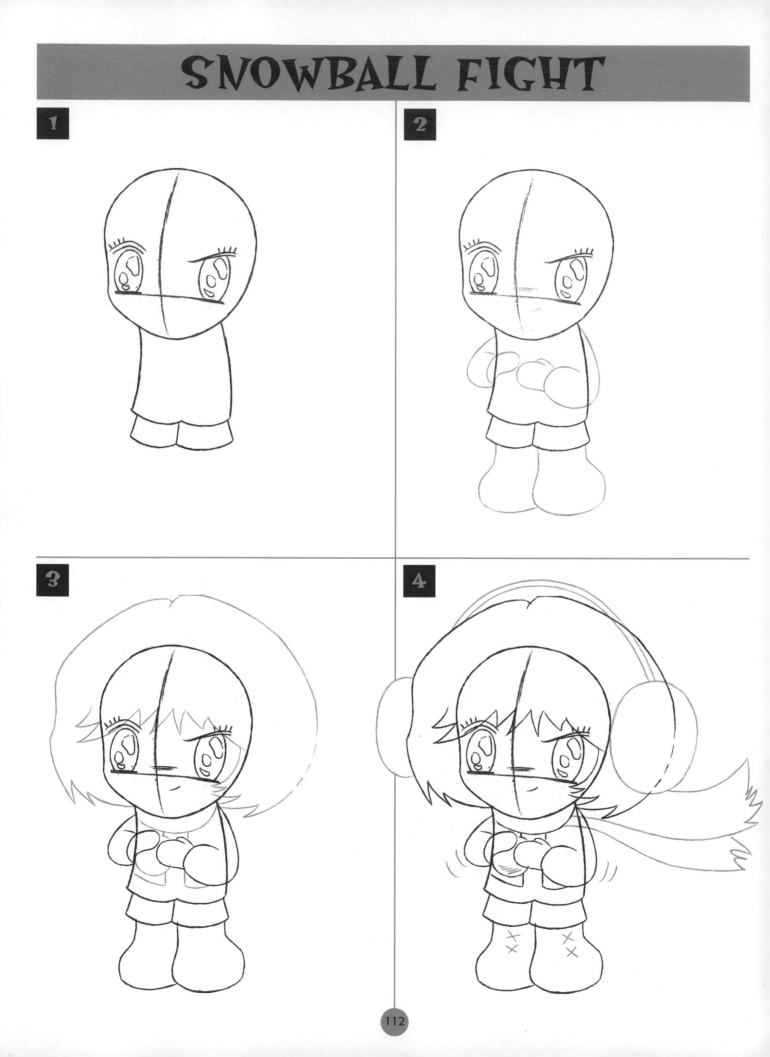

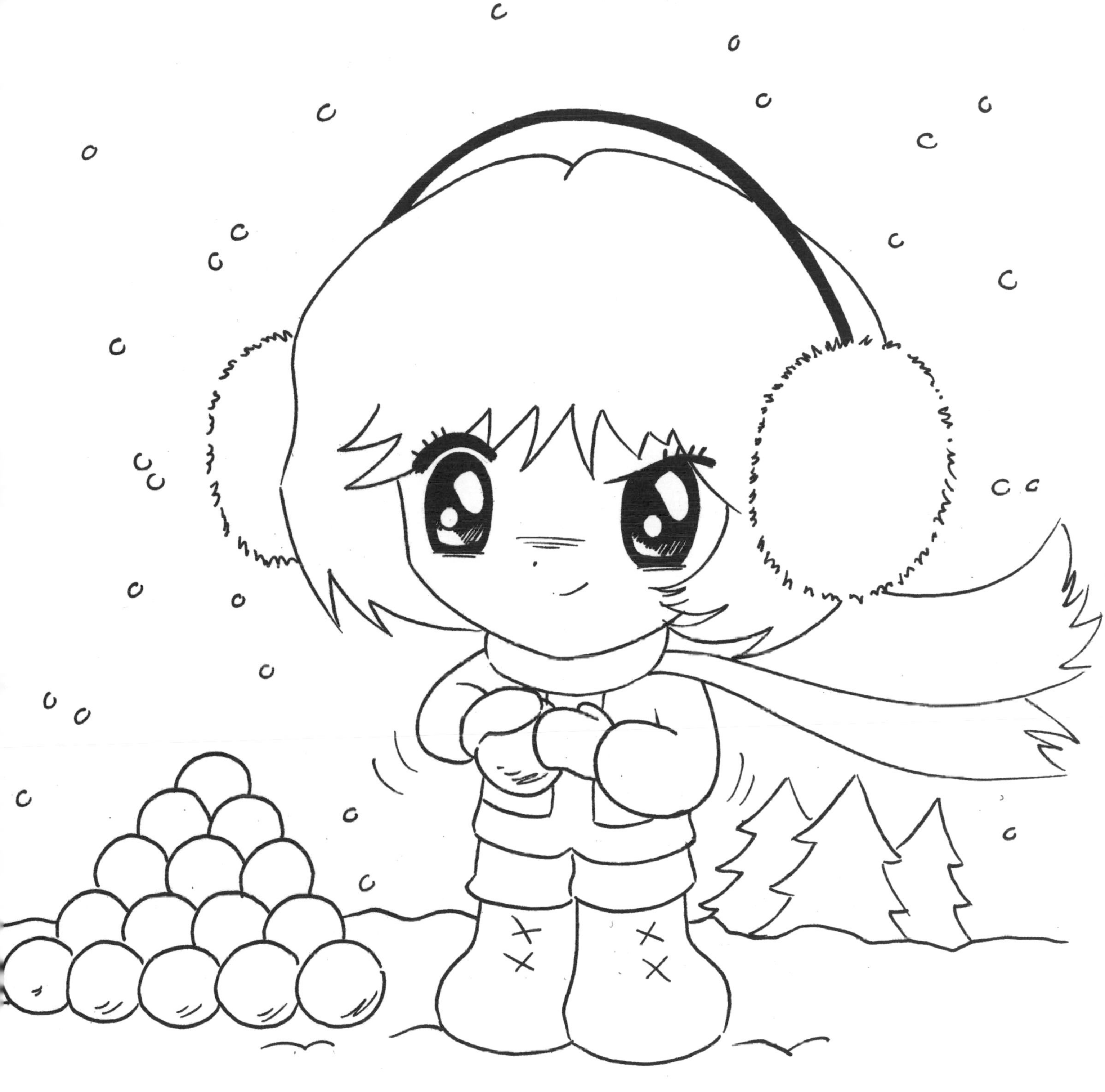

BIG IDEA

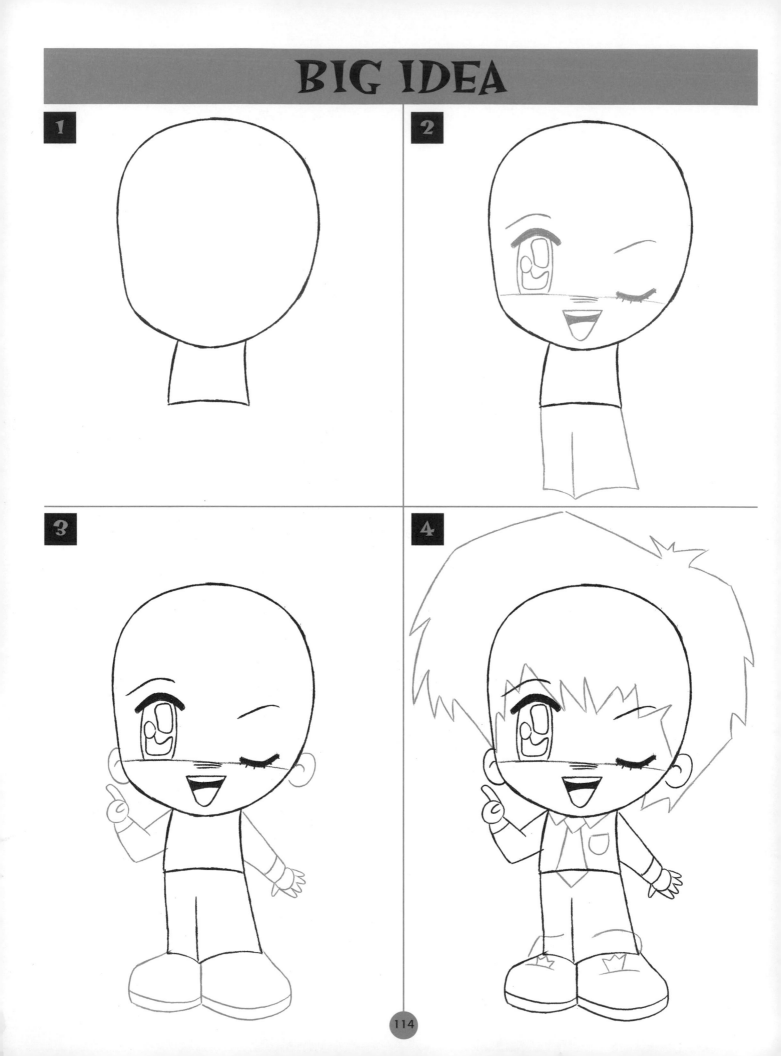

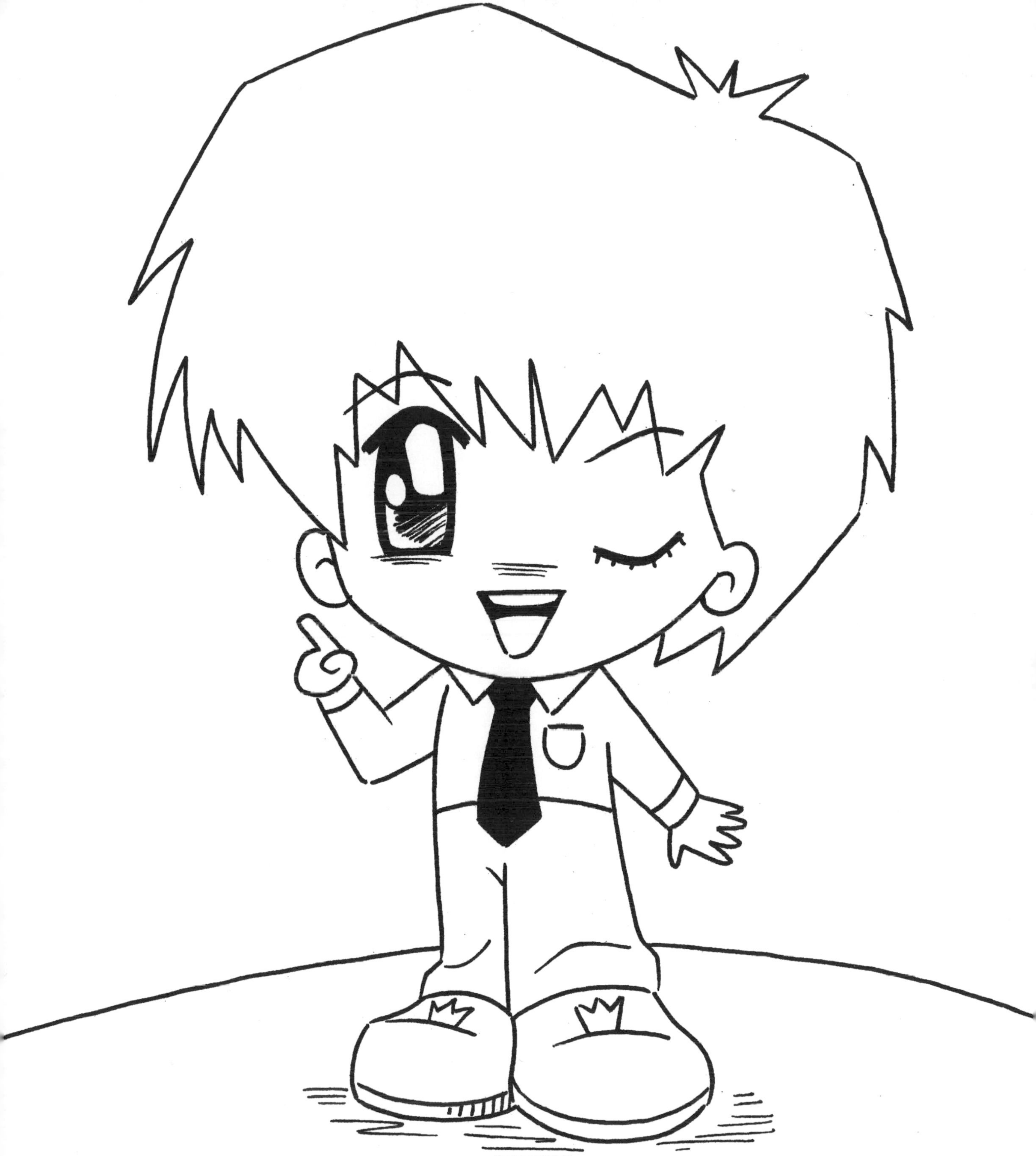

ROCKIN' GIRL

1

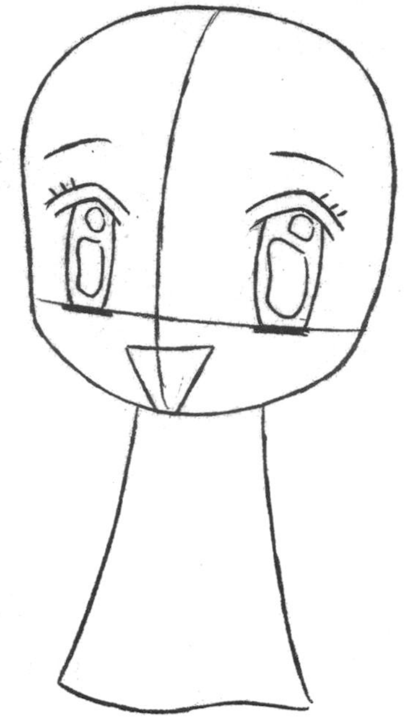

2

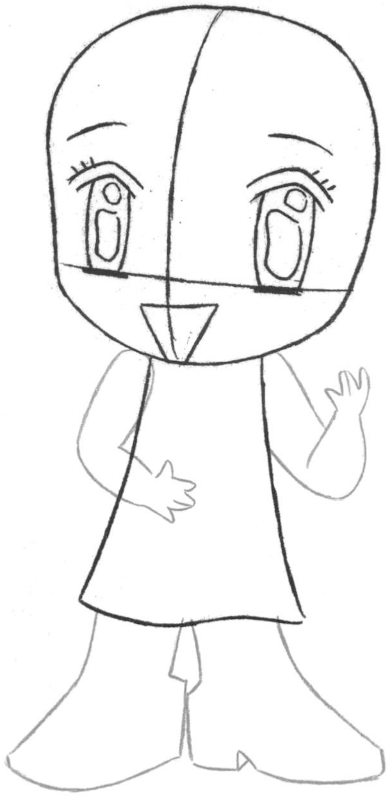

3

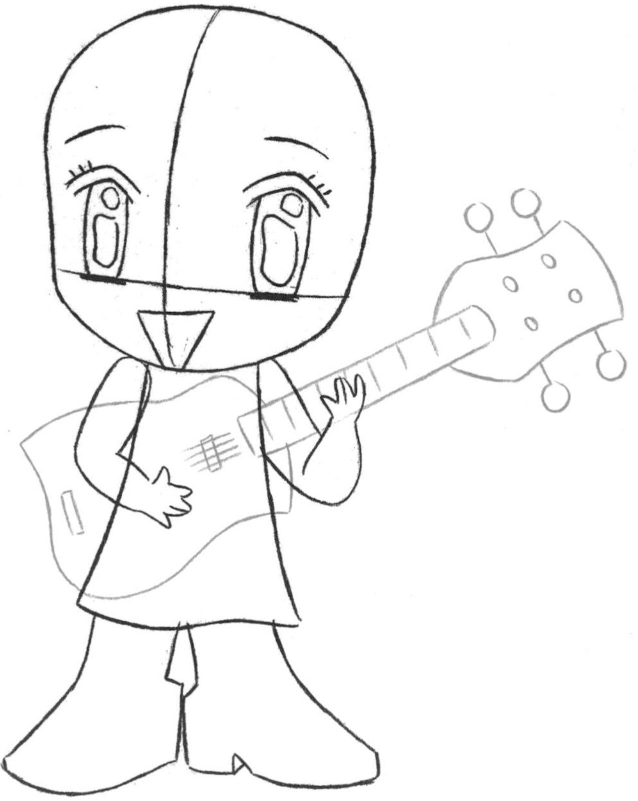

4

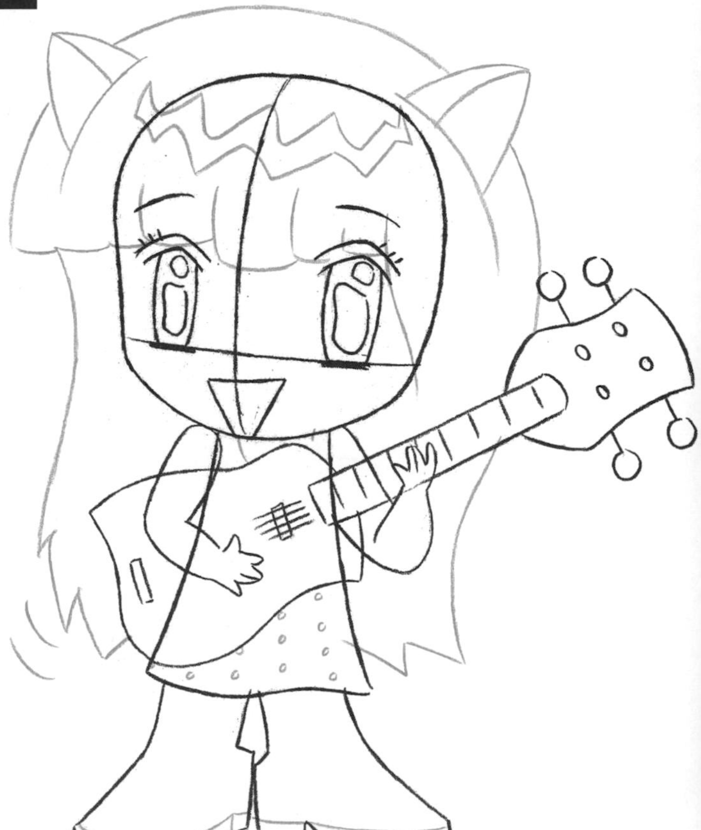

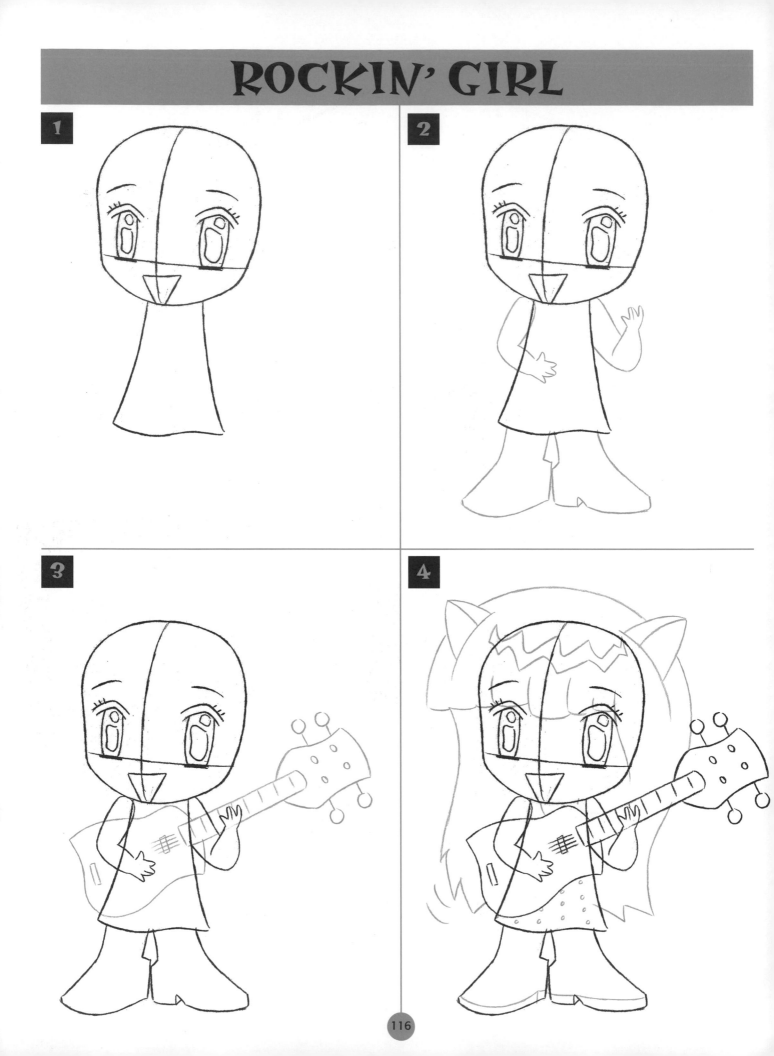

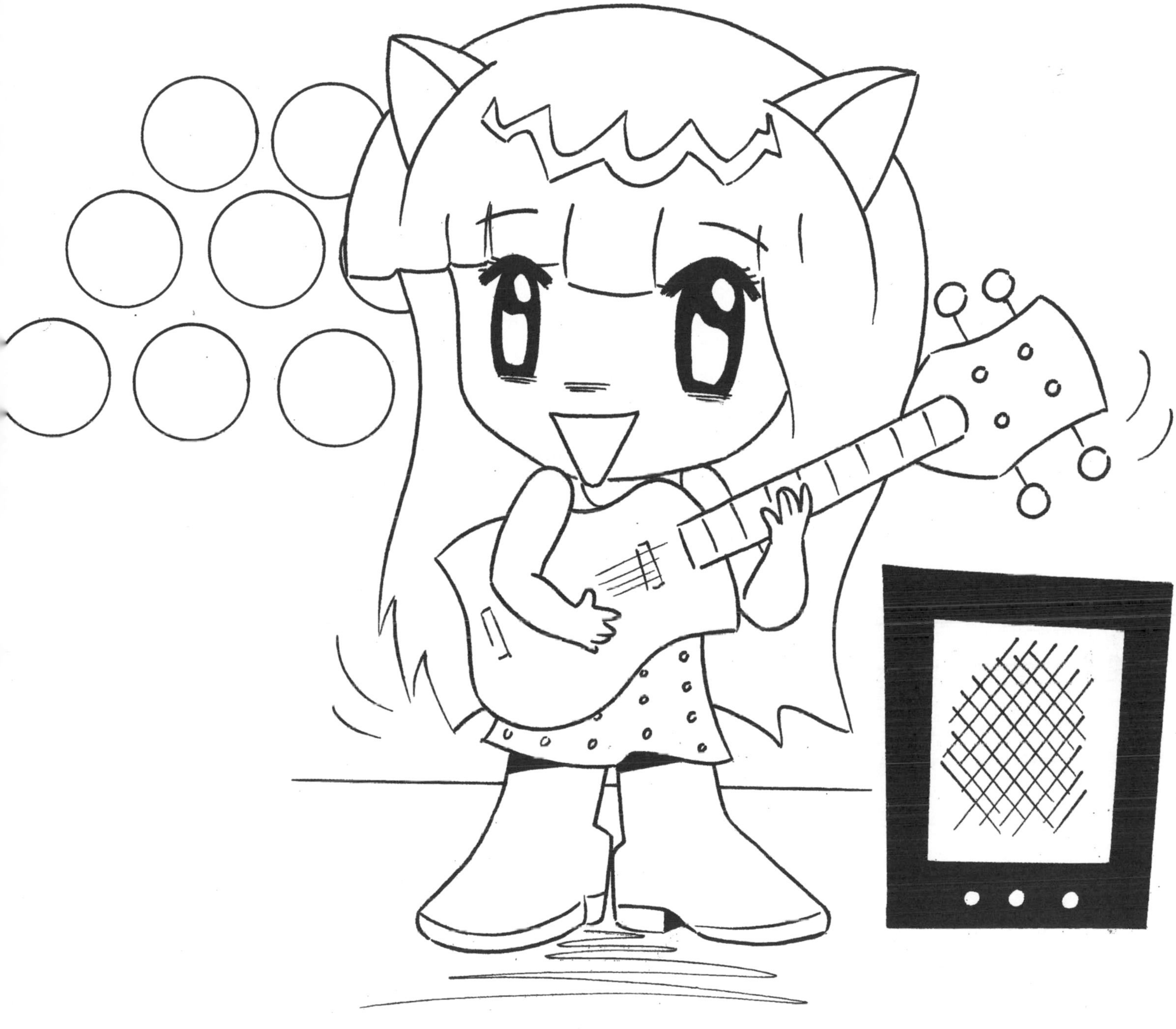

TRAINING KID

1

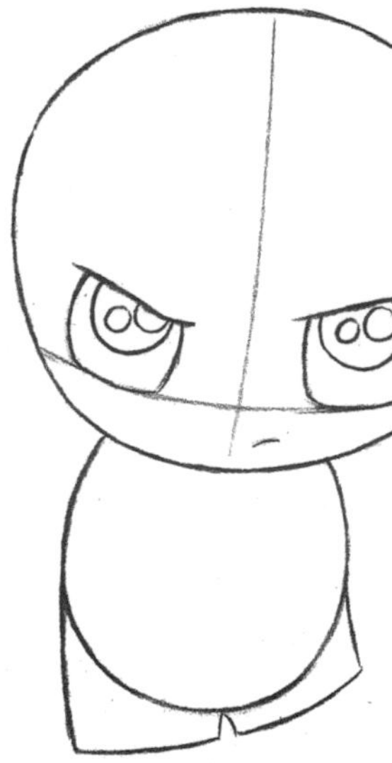

2

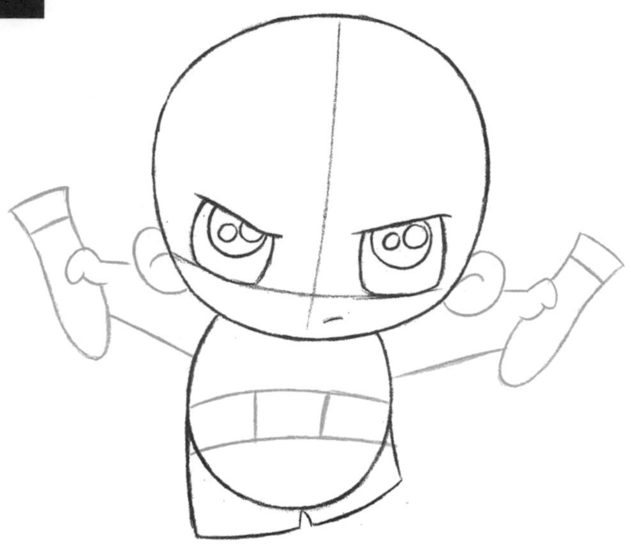

3

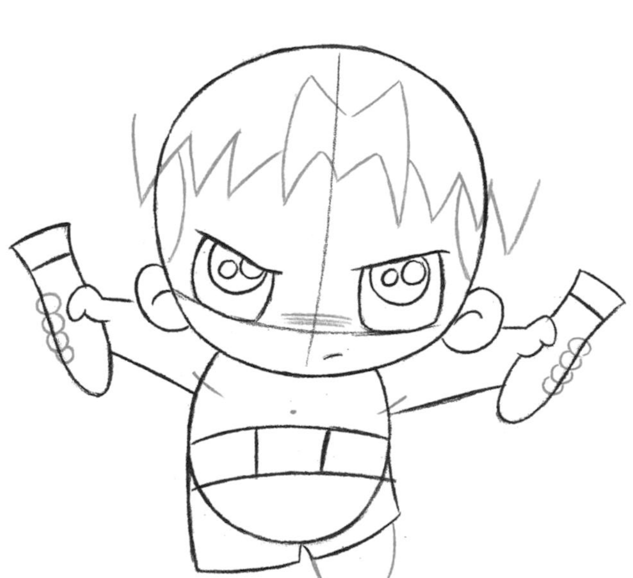

4

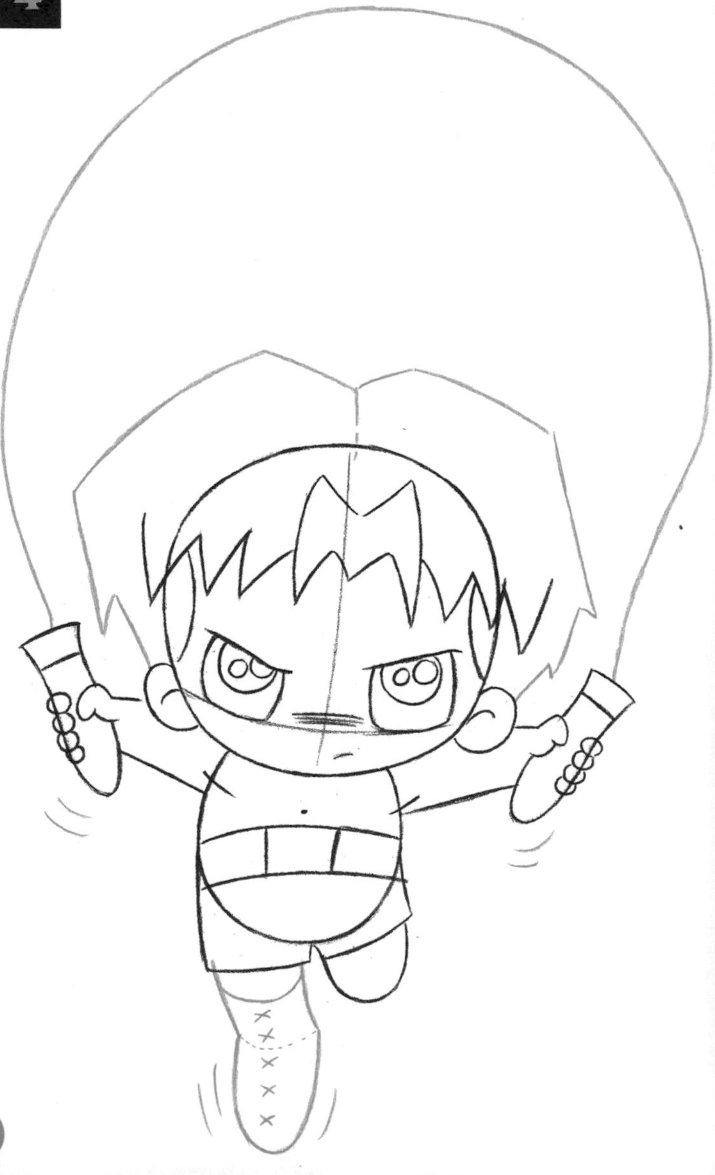

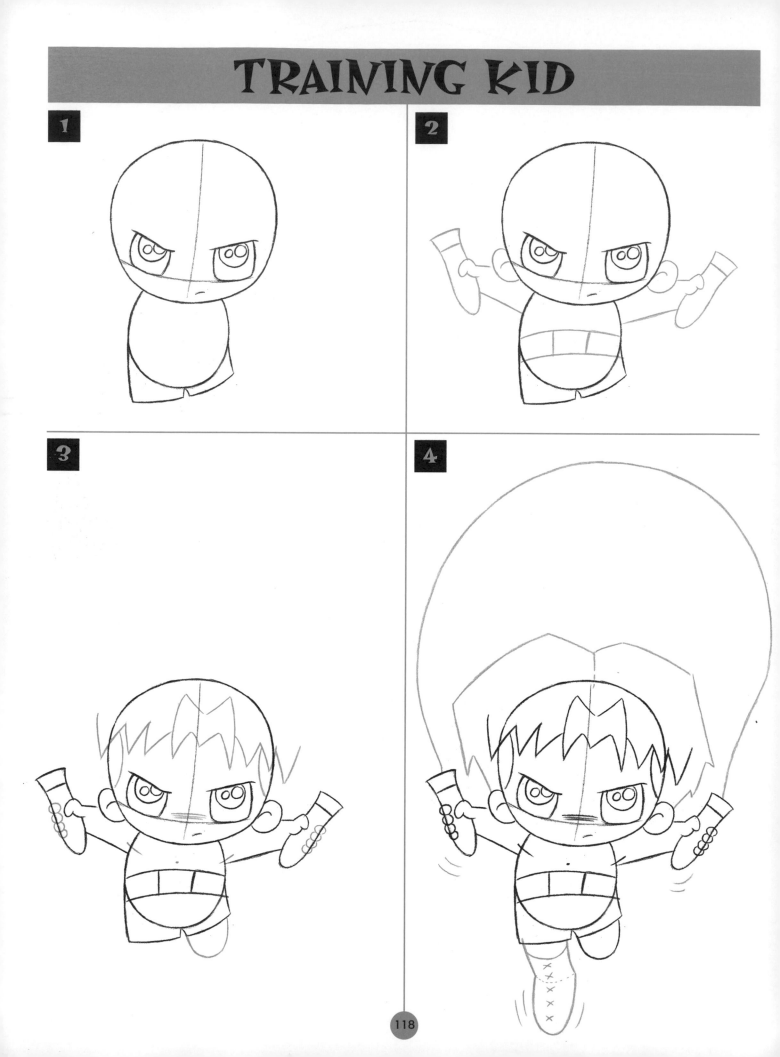

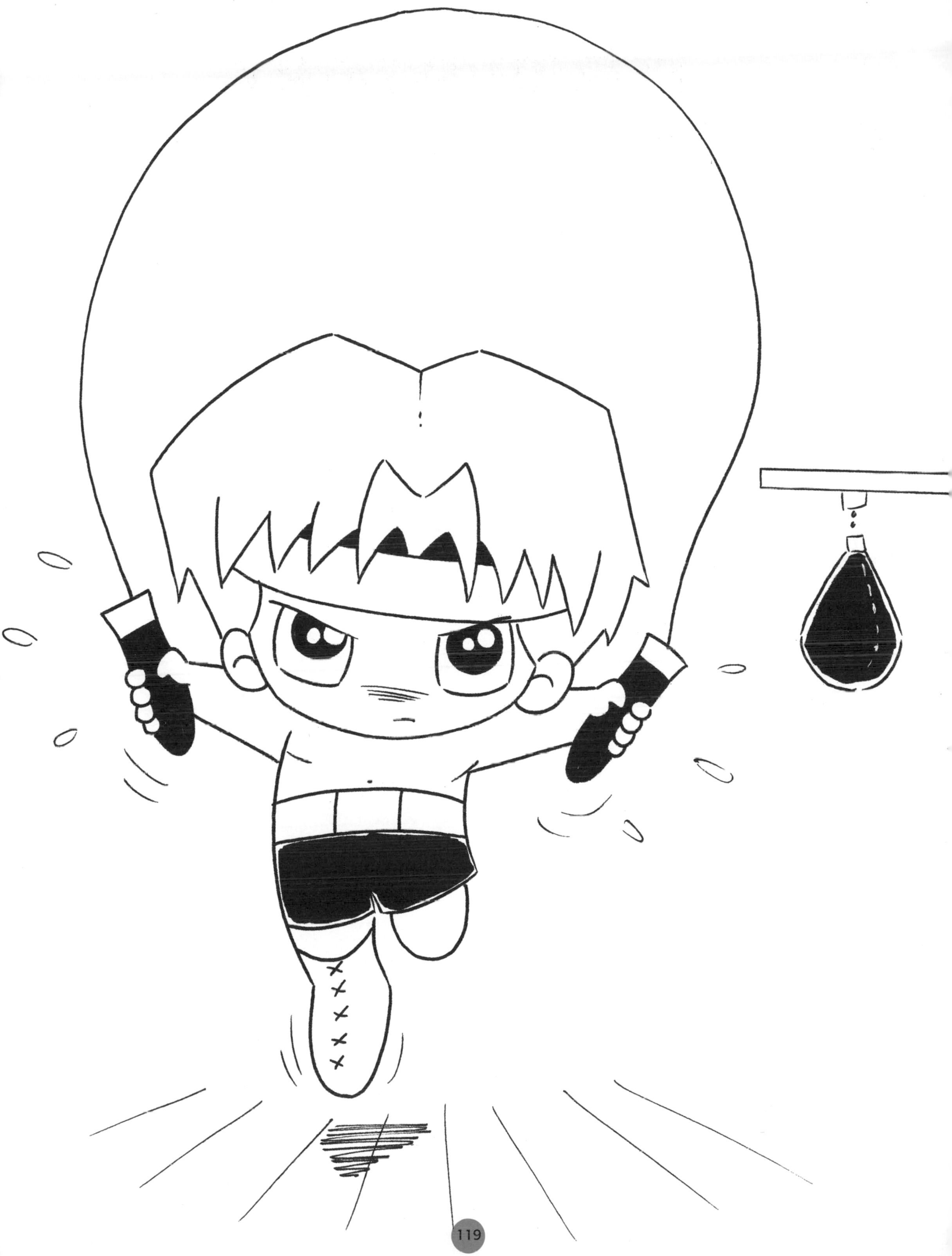

FURIOUS FAIRY

1

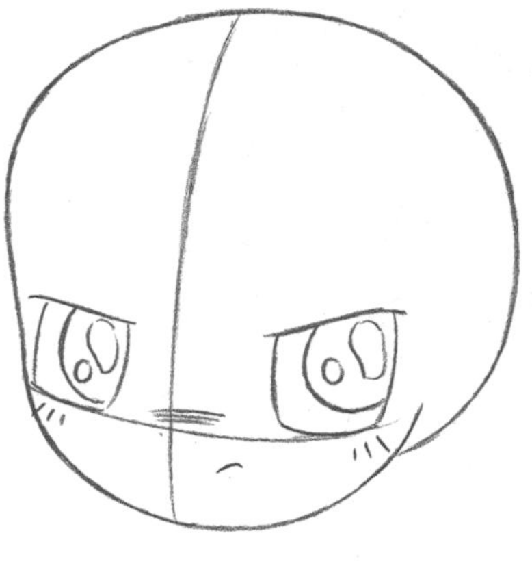

2

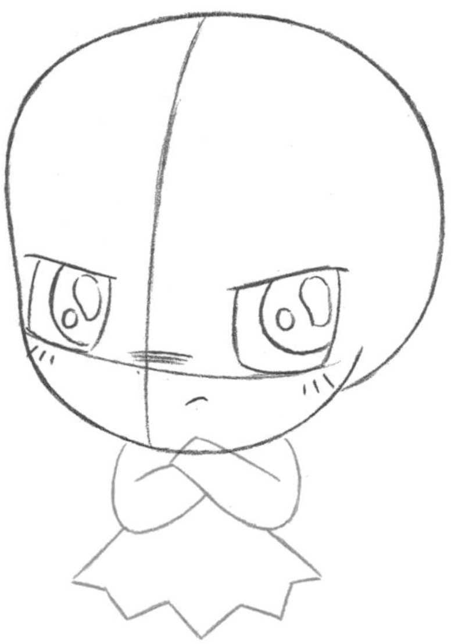

3

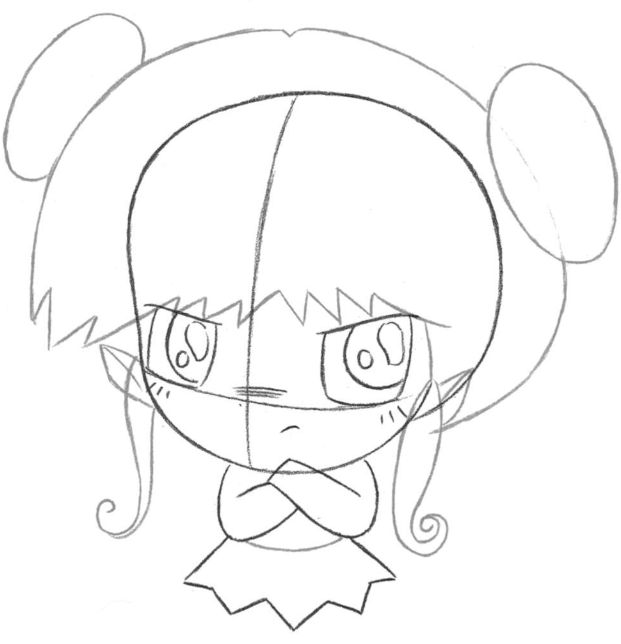

4

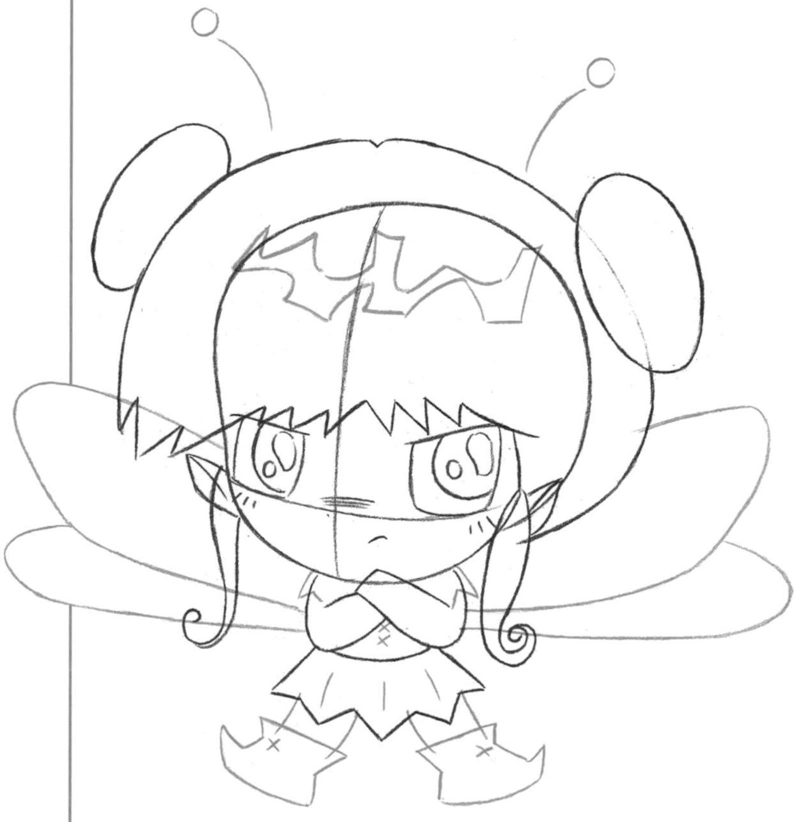

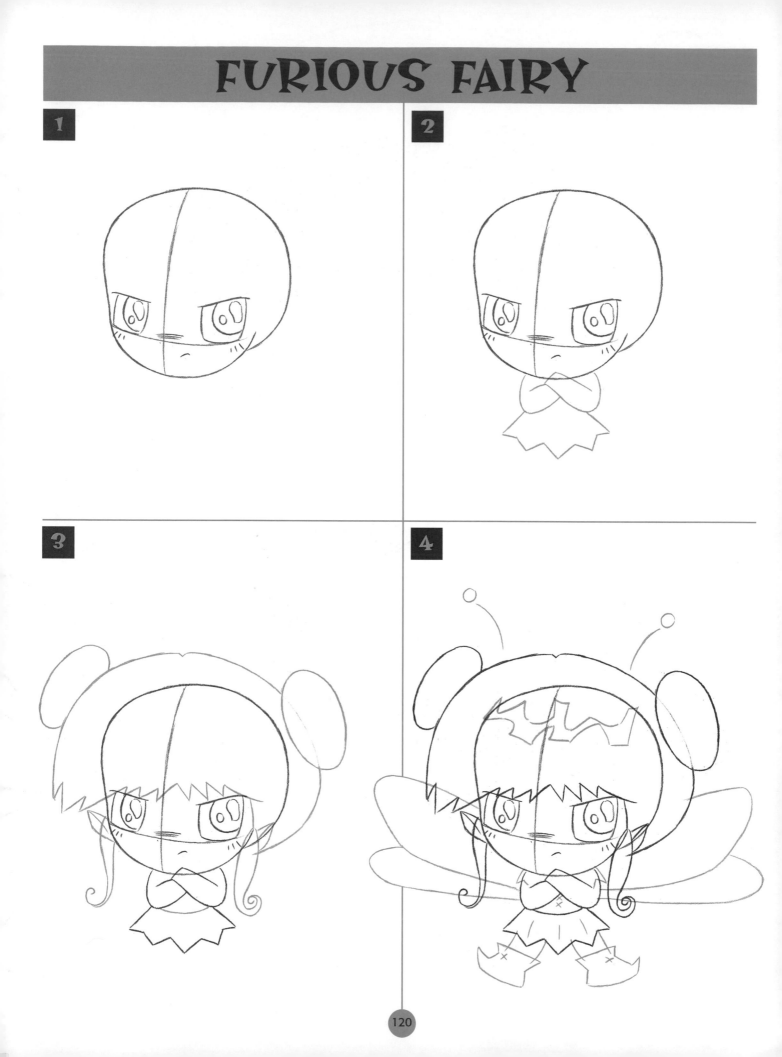

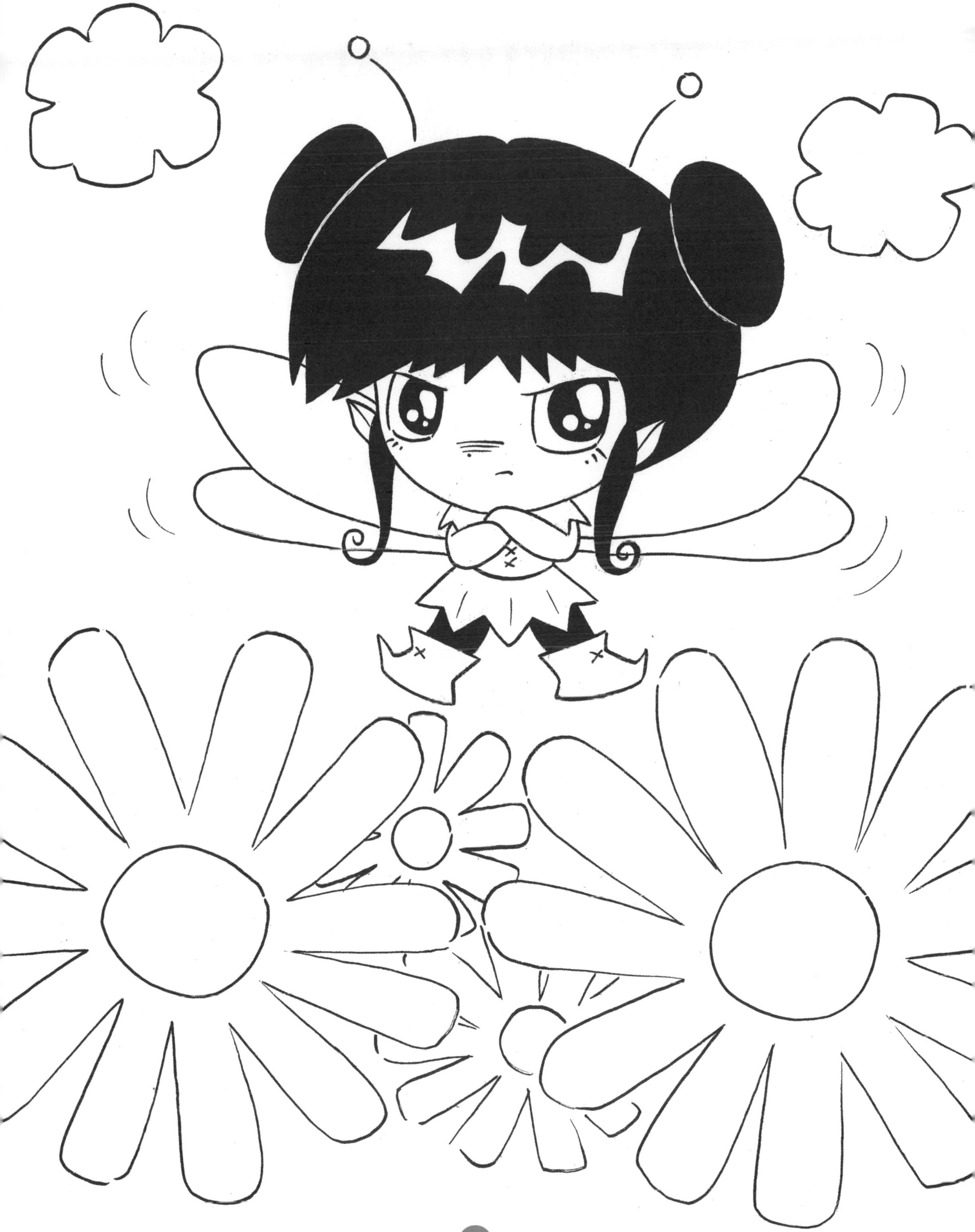

SURFIN' SALLY

1

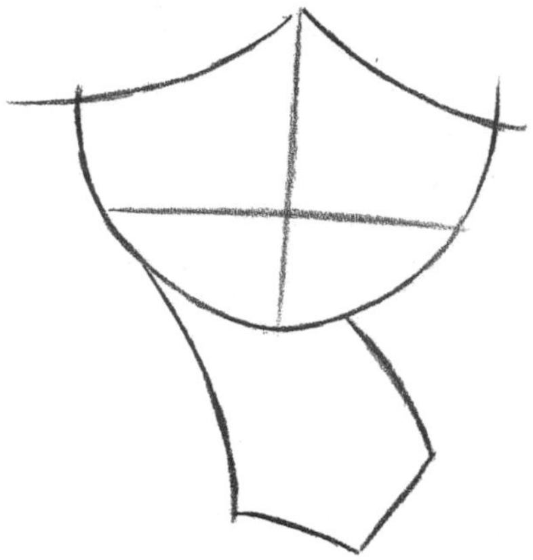

2

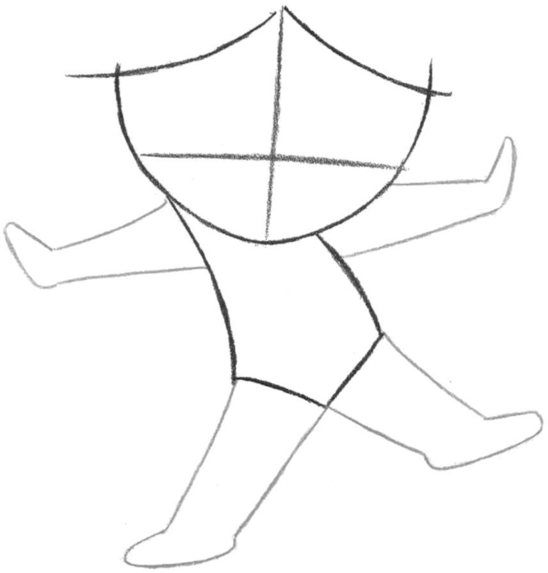

3

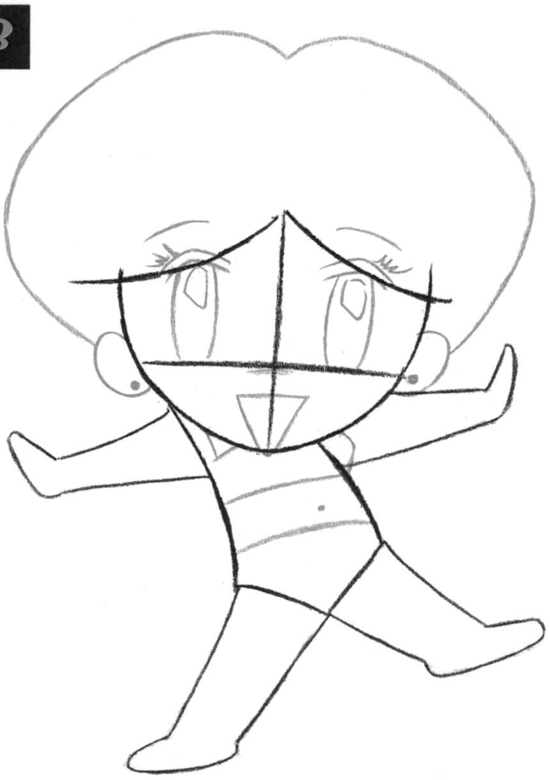

4

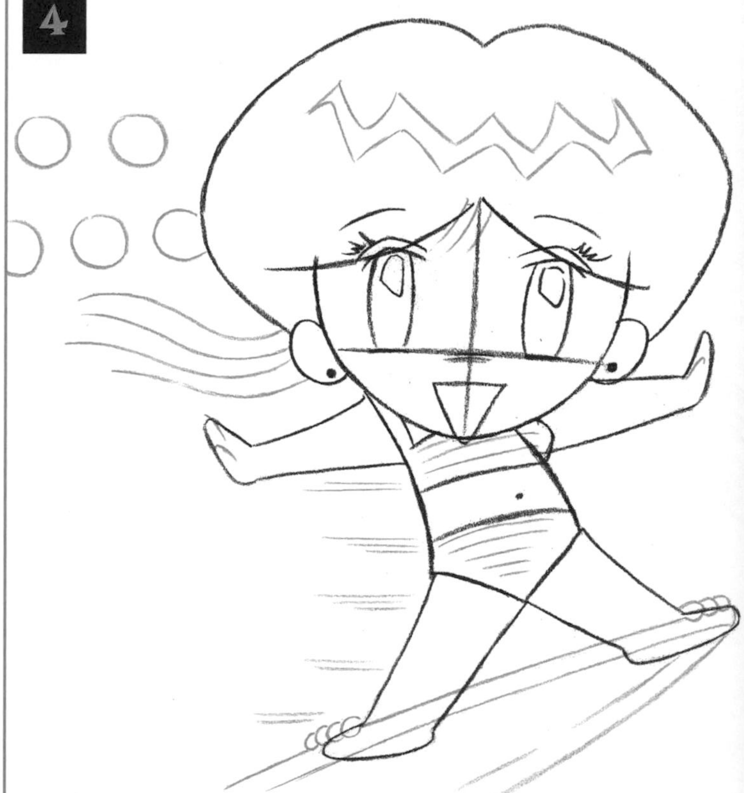

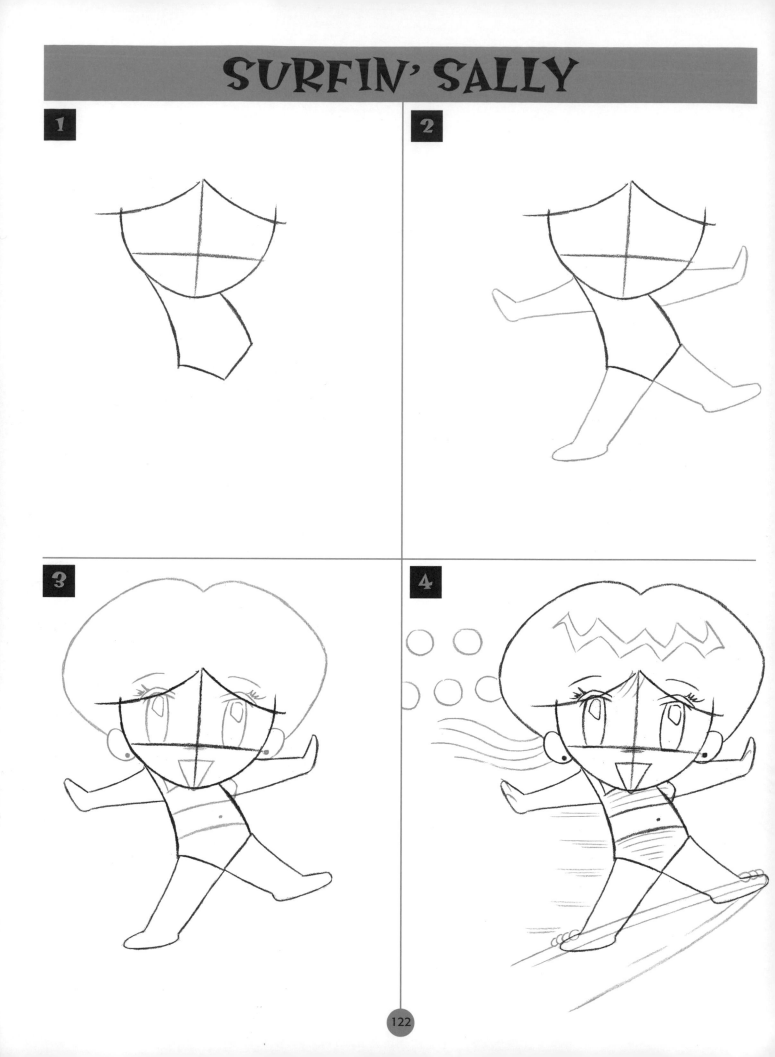

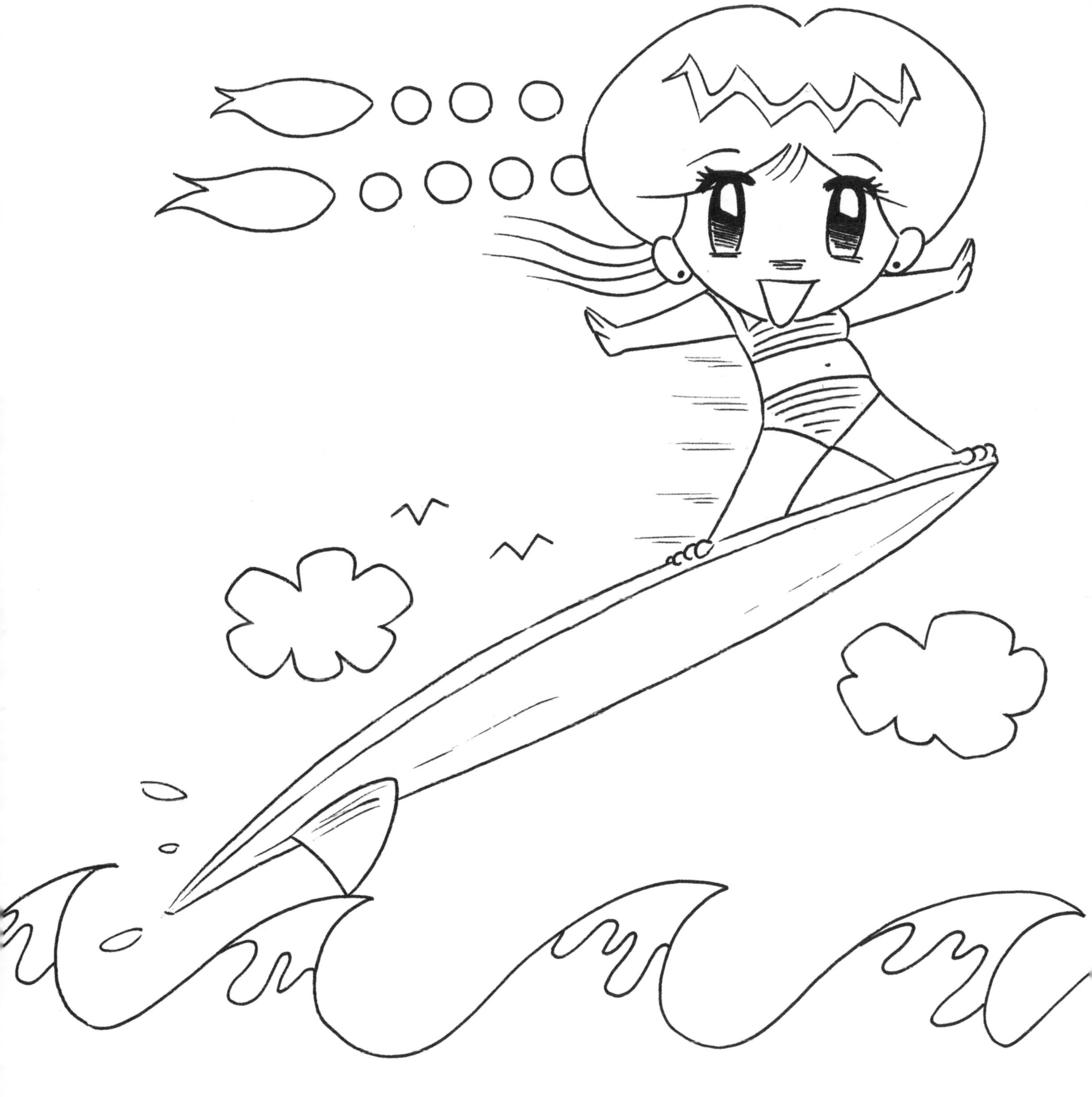

SURPRISED SERENA

1

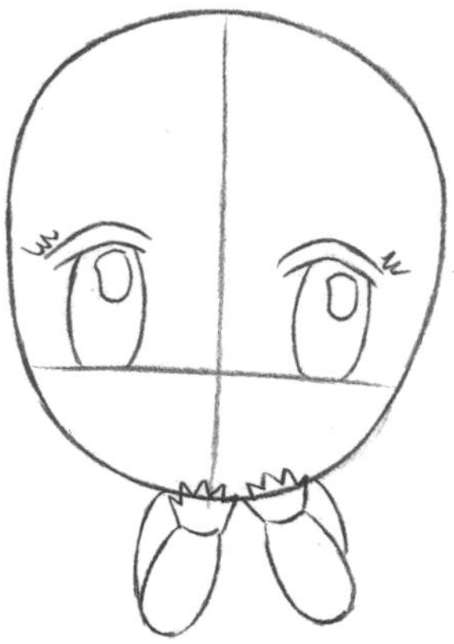

2

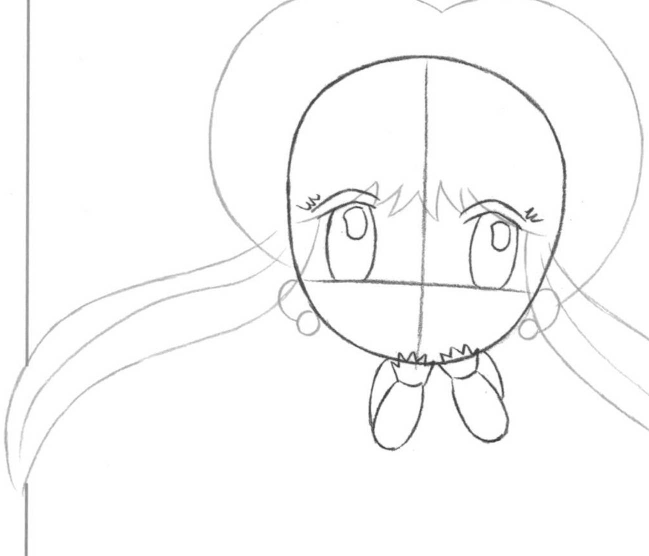

3

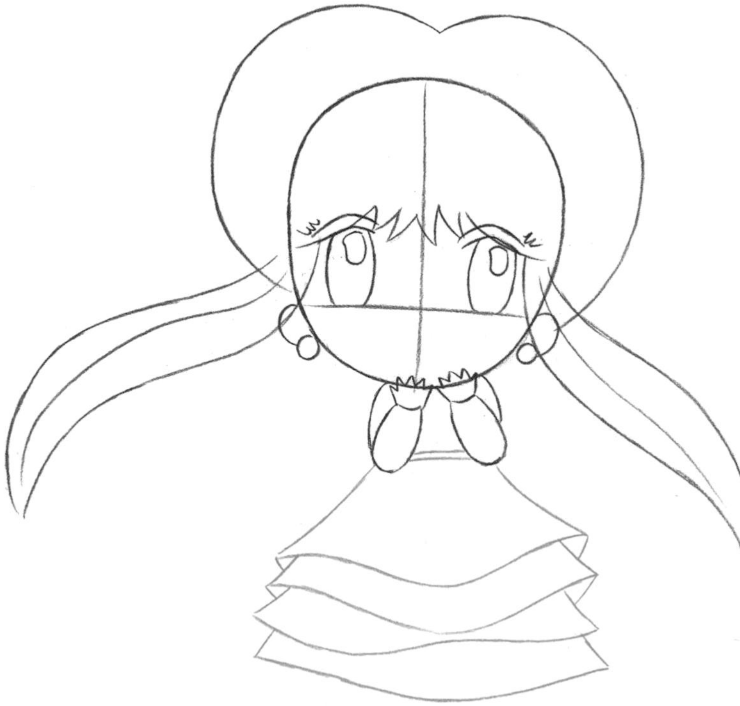

4

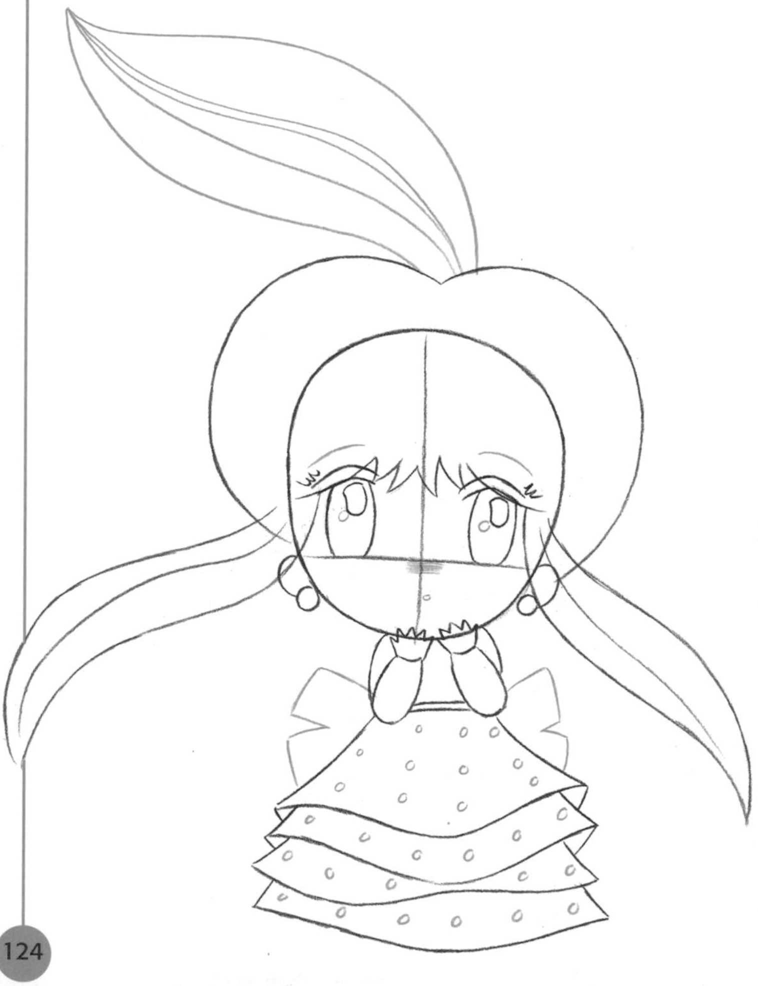

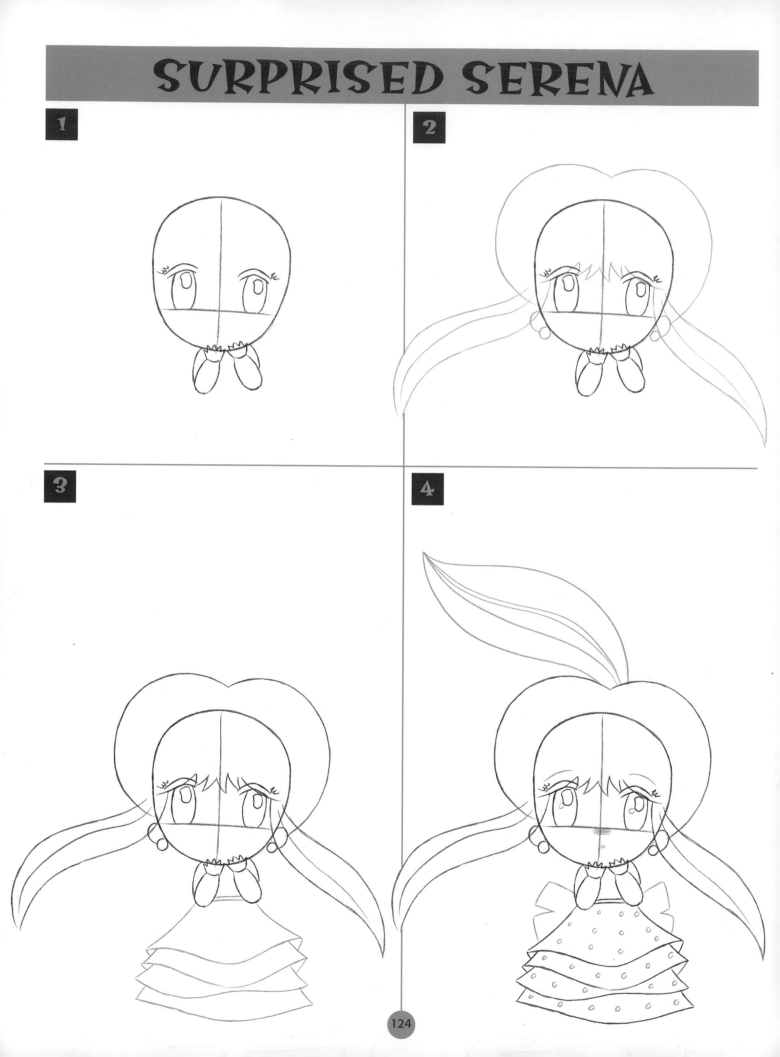

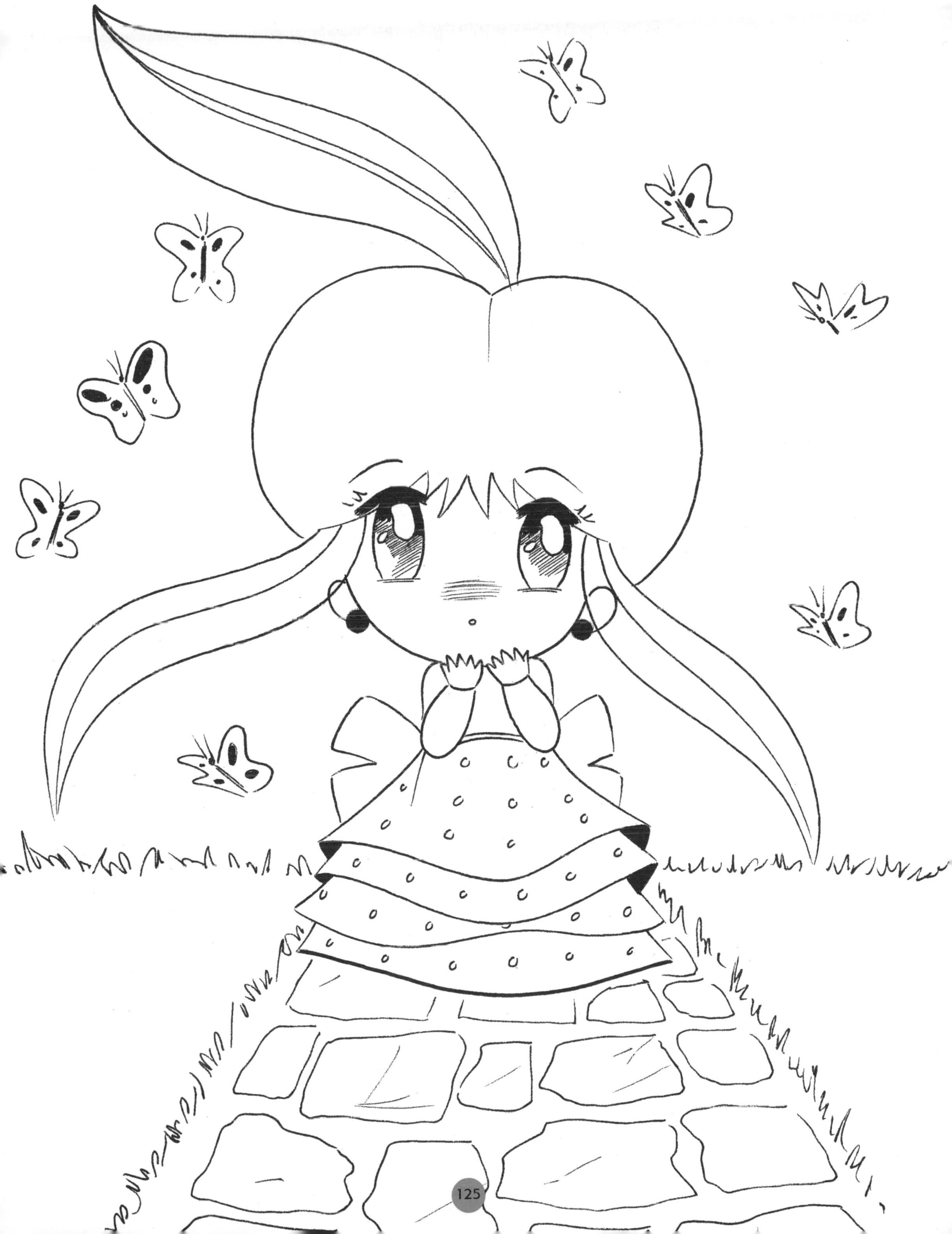

ROCKET GIRL

1

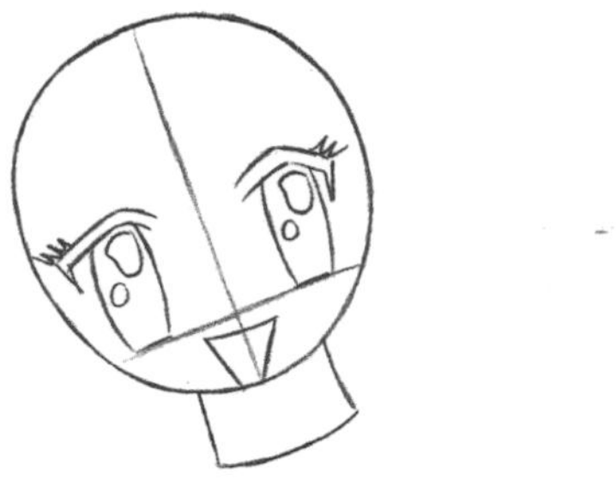

2

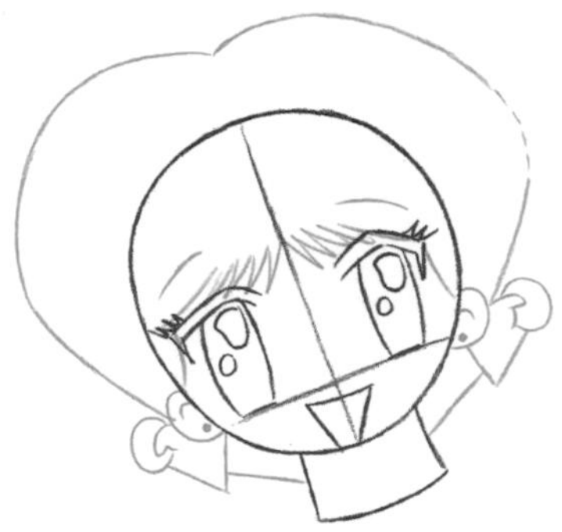

3

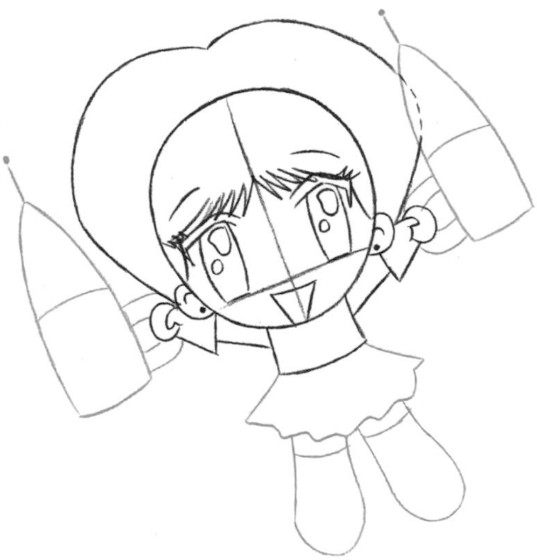

4

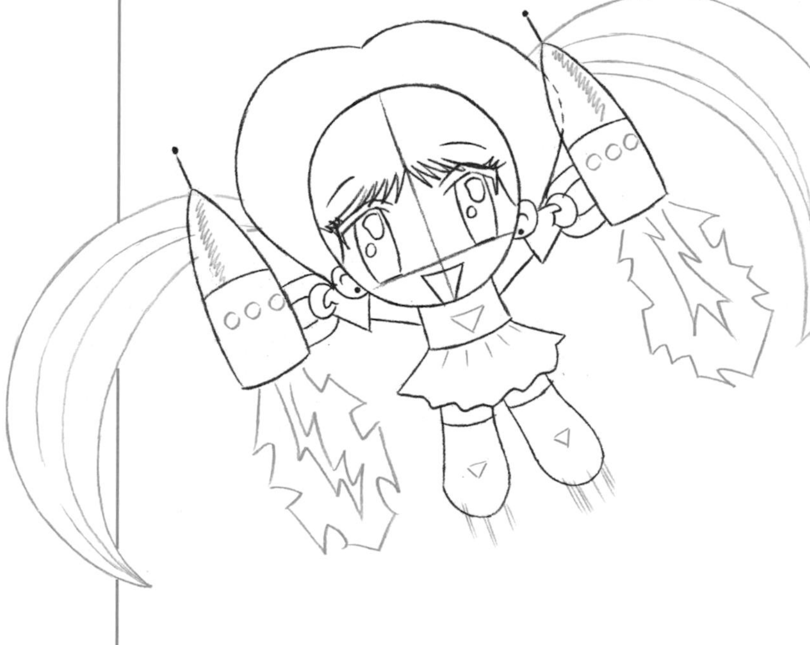

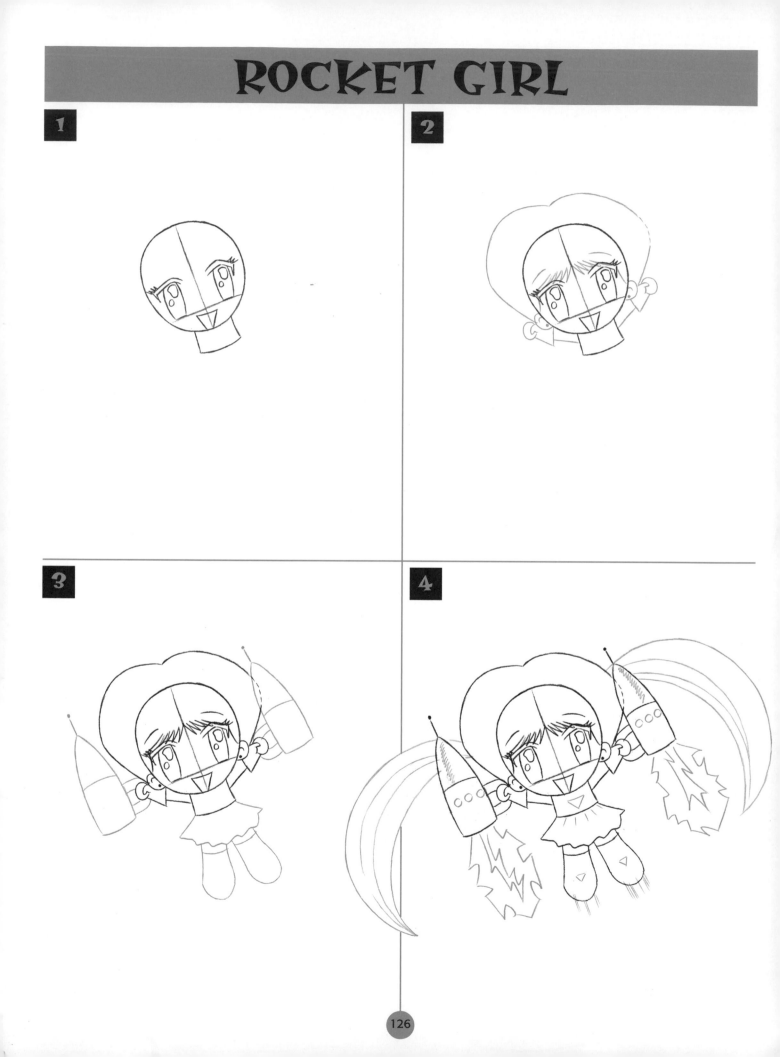

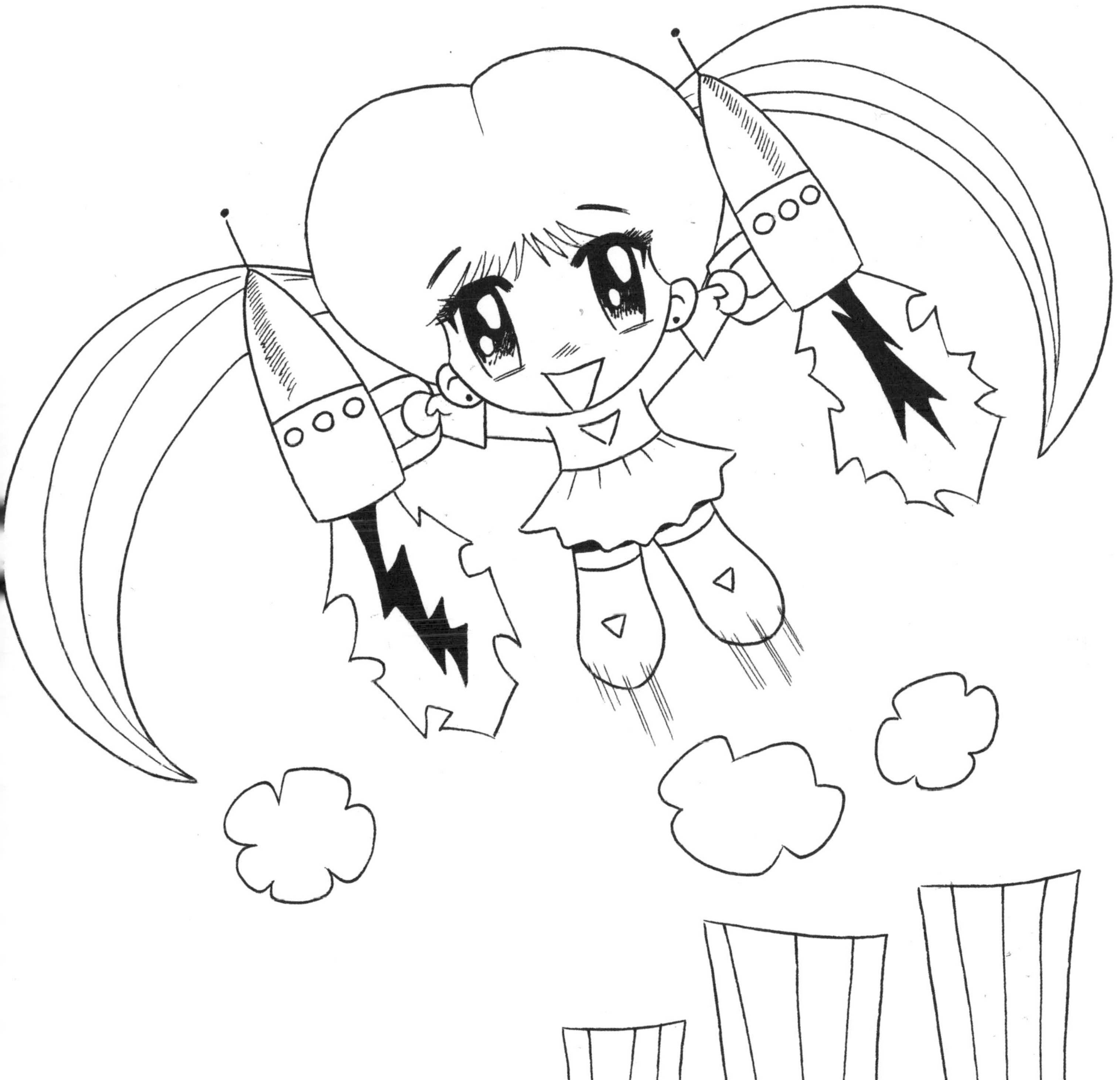

PUPS & KISSES

1

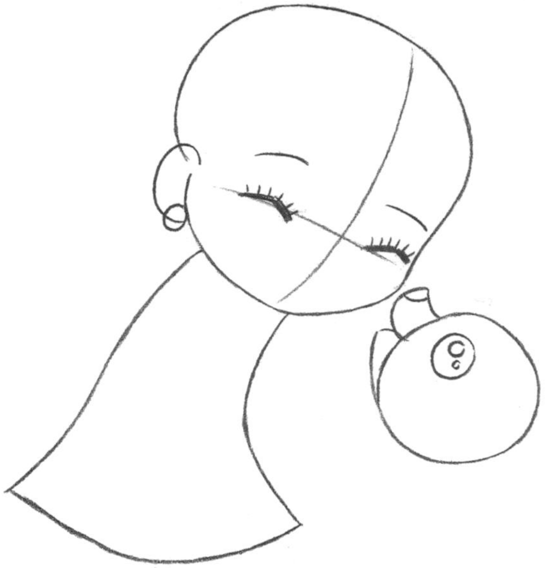

2

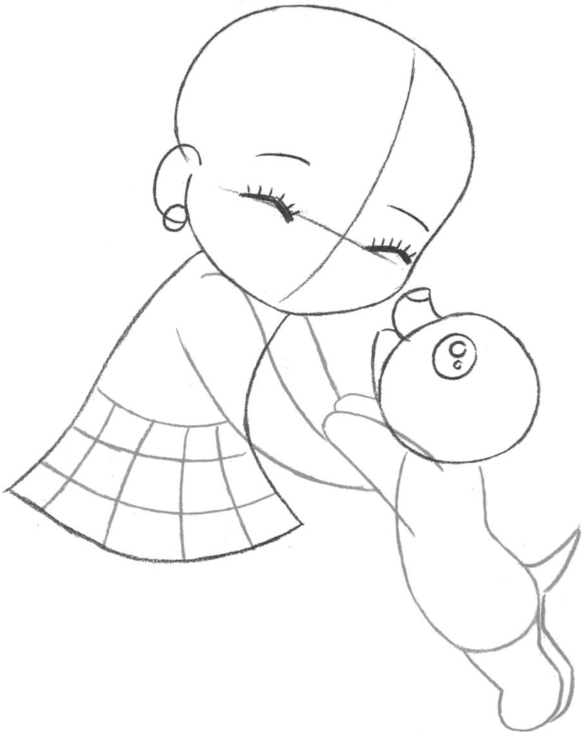

3

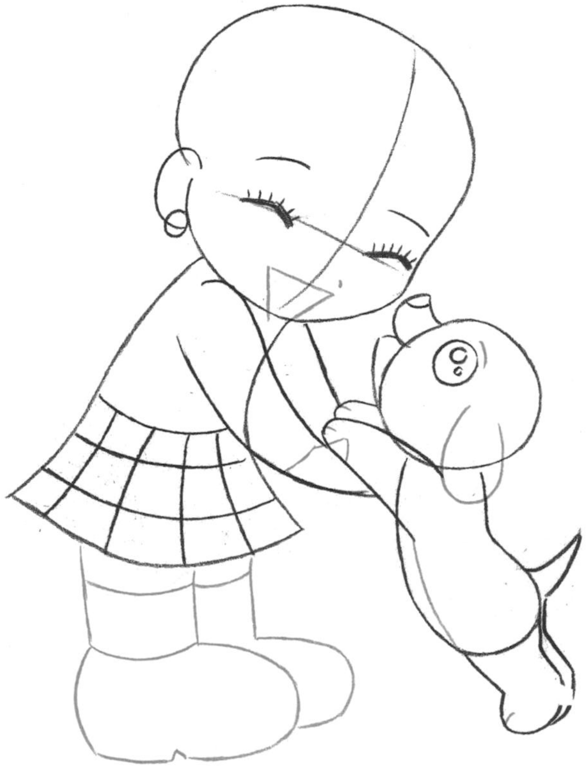

4

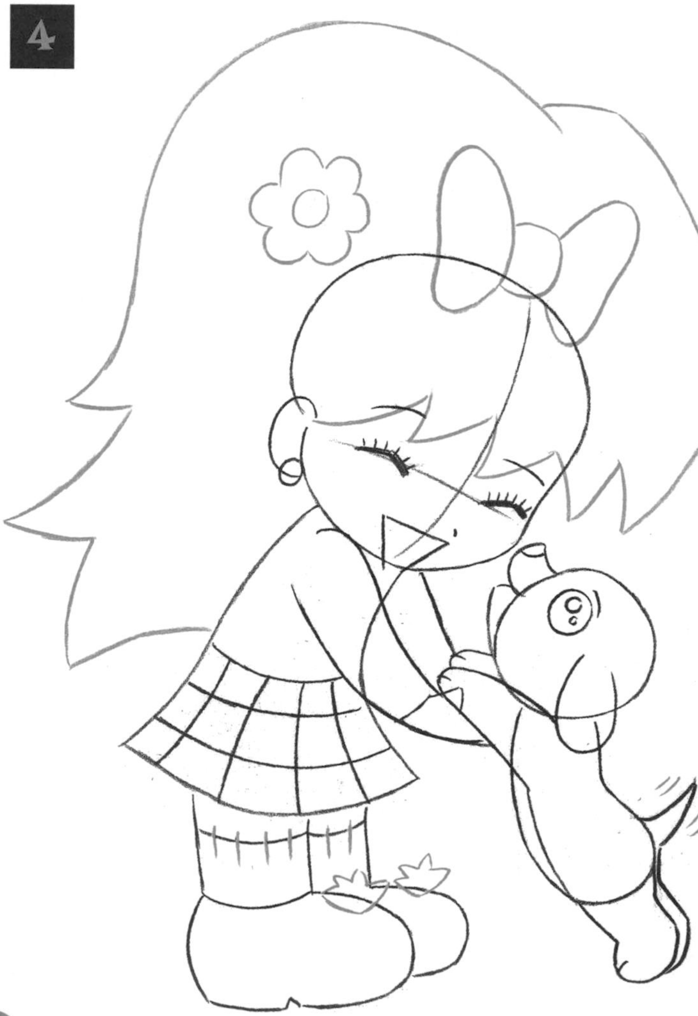

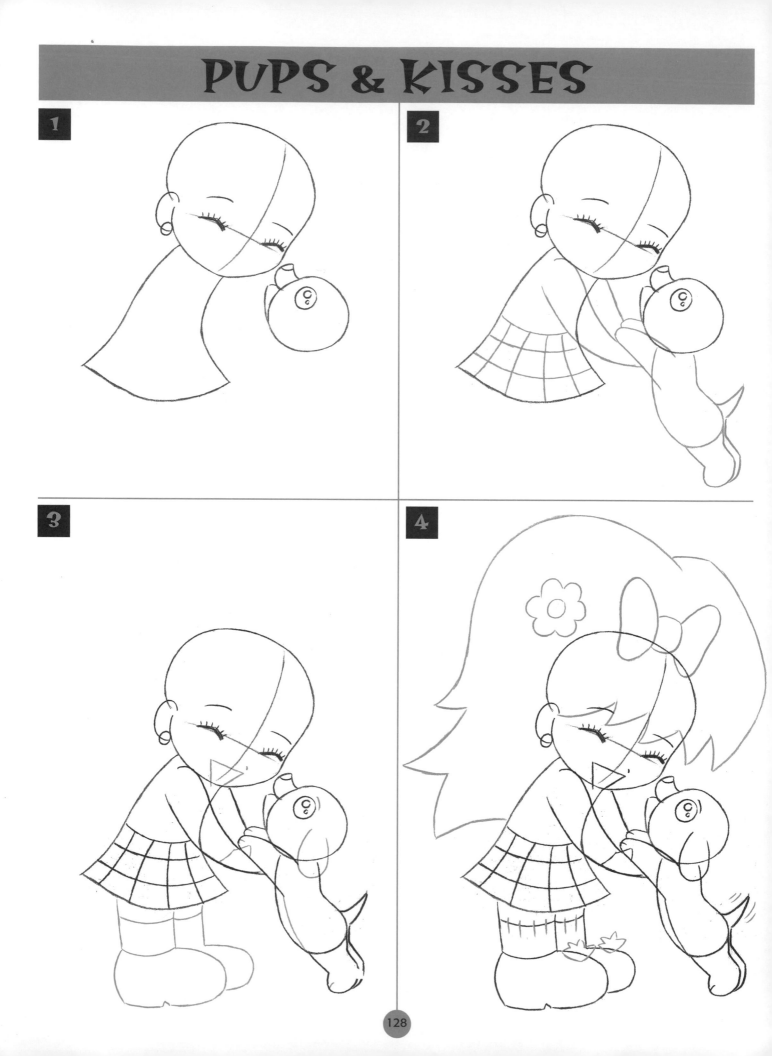

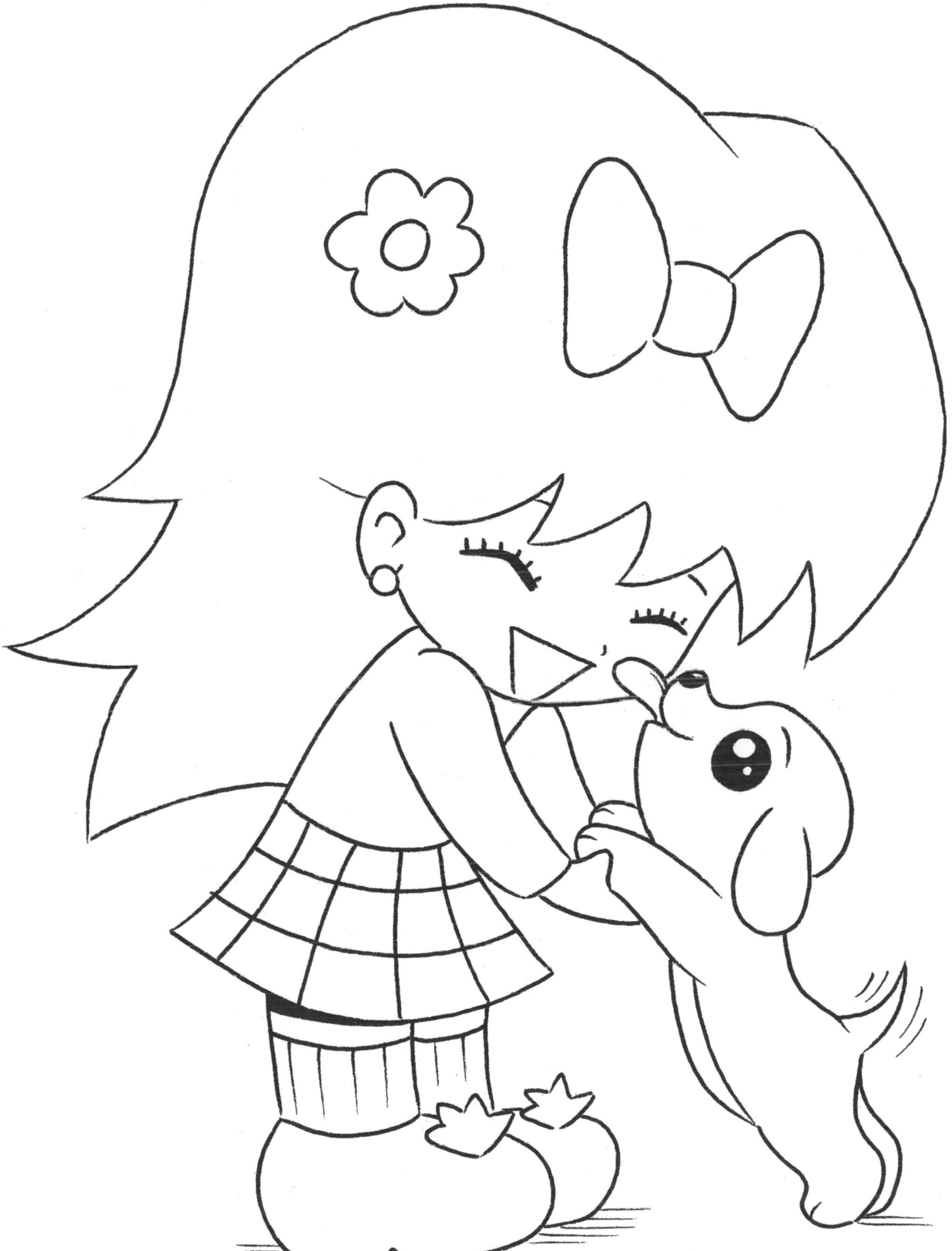

PART 3
DRAW MANGA MONSTERS!

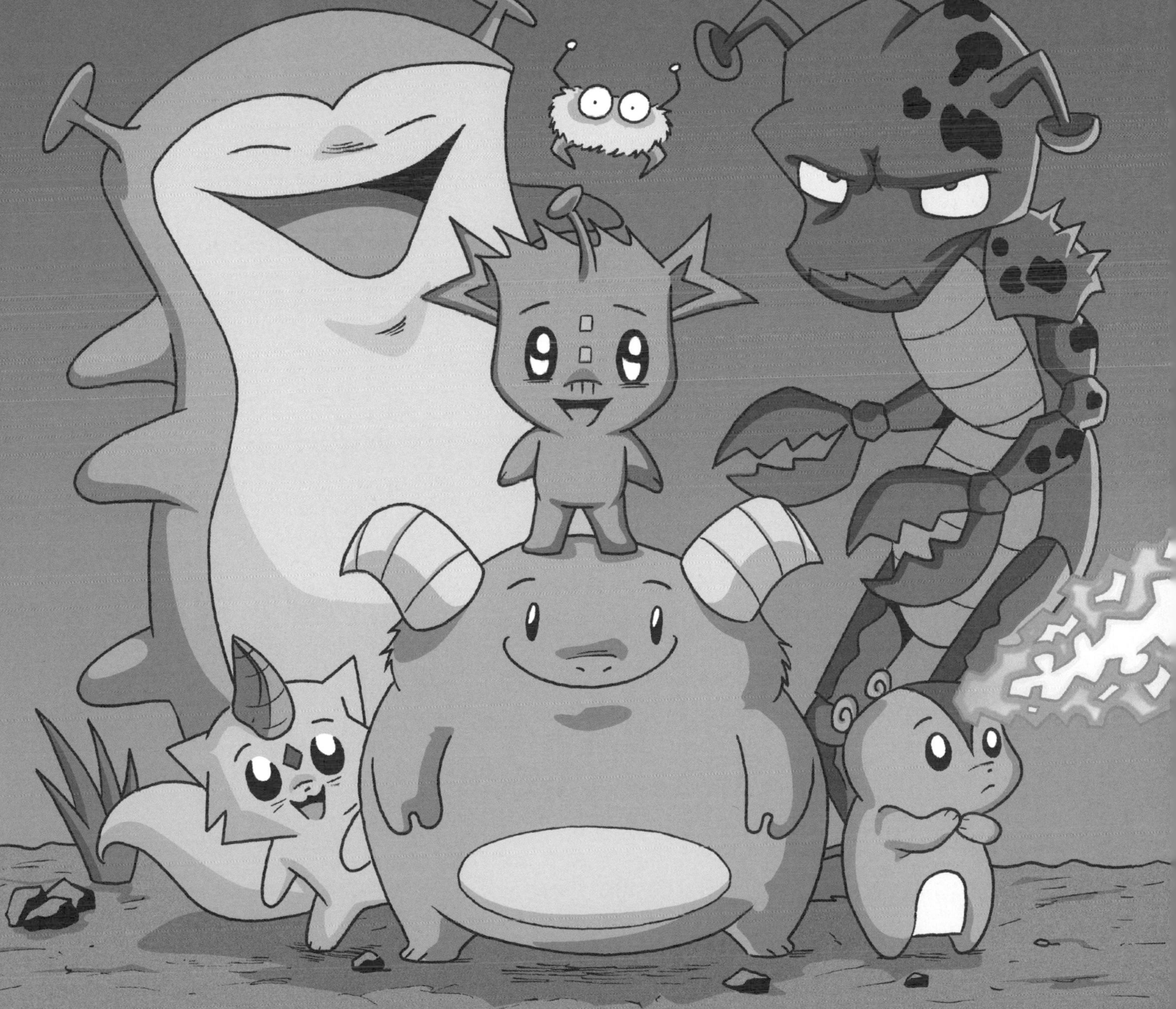

THE BASICS

How do you make a monster? Surprisingly, it often begins with a chubby, simple, little character. By adding bits and pieces as you go, you gradually build a unique creature. Only you can decide whether it will fight on the side of good...or evil!

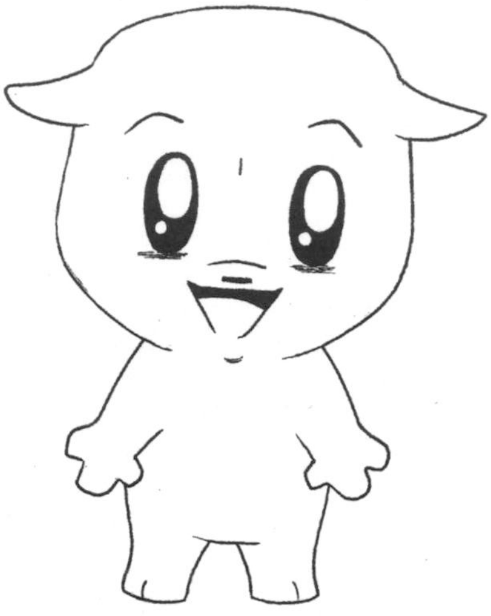

1. START WITH A CHUBBY SHAPE.

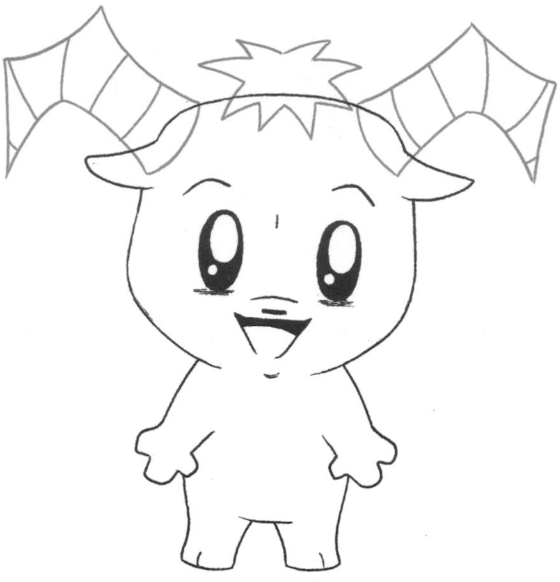

2. ADD HORNS AND HAIR.

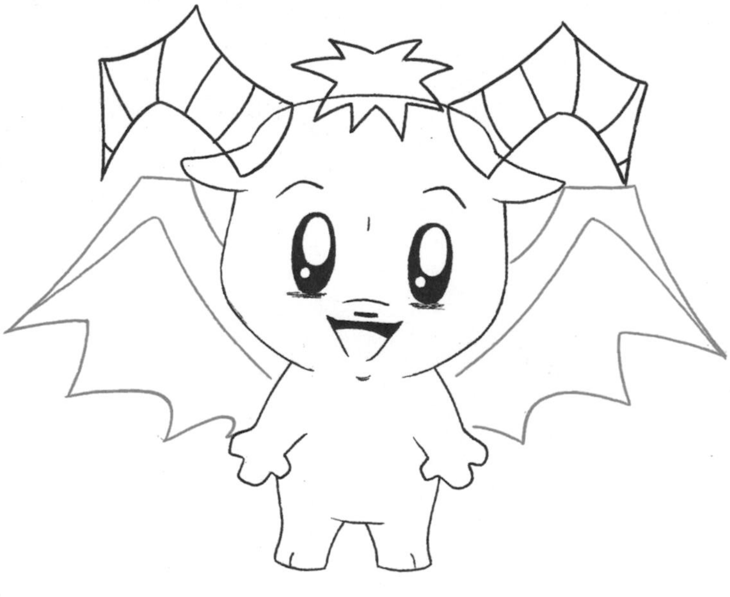

3. BIG WINGS MAKE IT MORE IMPRESSIVE.

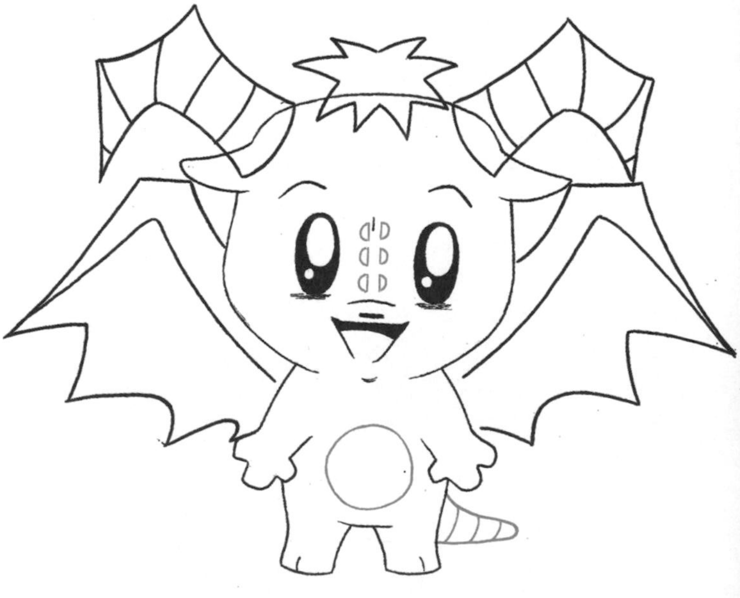

4. NOW ADD FUN DETAILS, LIKE MARKINGS, A TUMMY CIRCLE, AND A TAIL!

Manga artists often use body shapes from real animals that they combine or change to create an original manga monster. Let's take a look at some popular sources of inspiration.

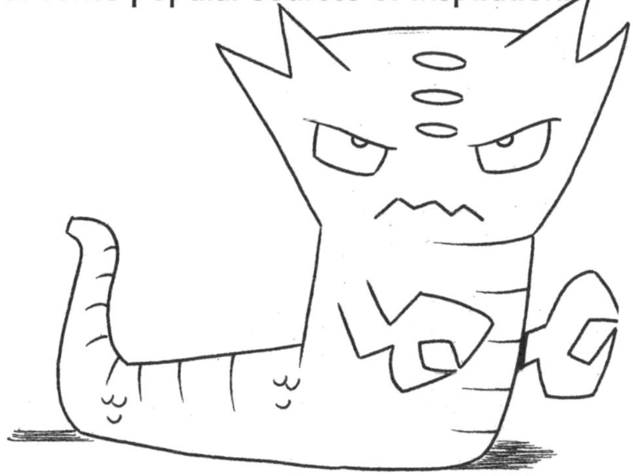

Worms, Crustaceans, and Insects

Worms, crustaceans, and insects are good beginnings for manga monsters. A worm body with crab-like hands does the trick for this character.

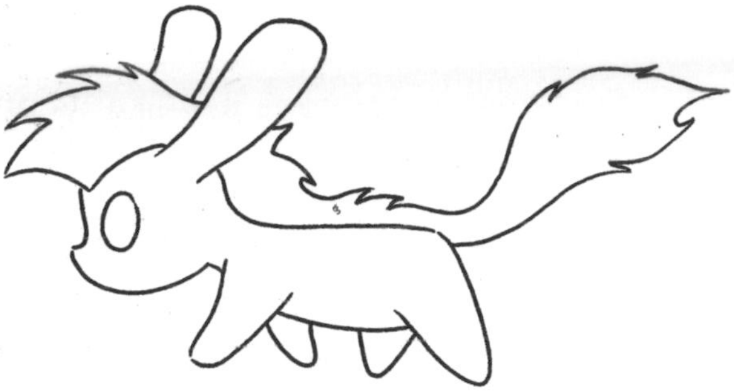

Little Animals

This one has the body of a cat and the ears of a rabbit. The mane and long tail are additions that turn it into a manga monster.

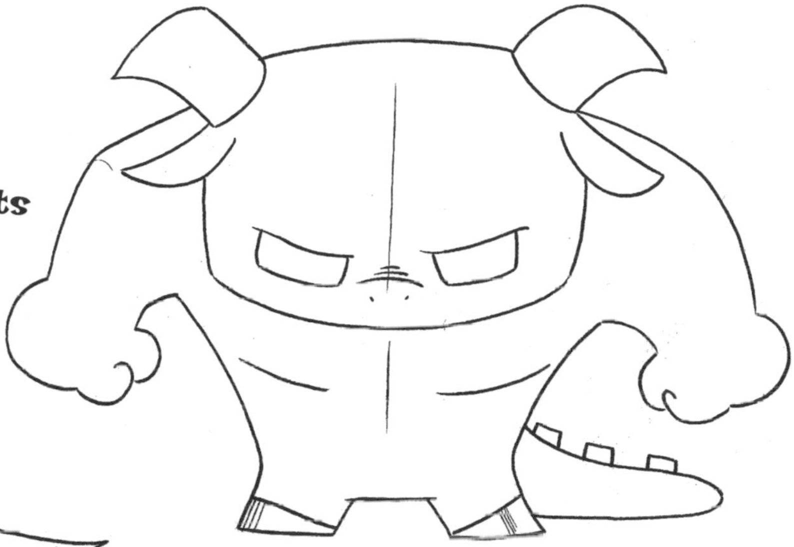

Animals That Stand Like People

Giving an animal the posture of a human is a common way to make a manga monster. This one looks like a bull, but the tail has been changed to make it monster-ish.

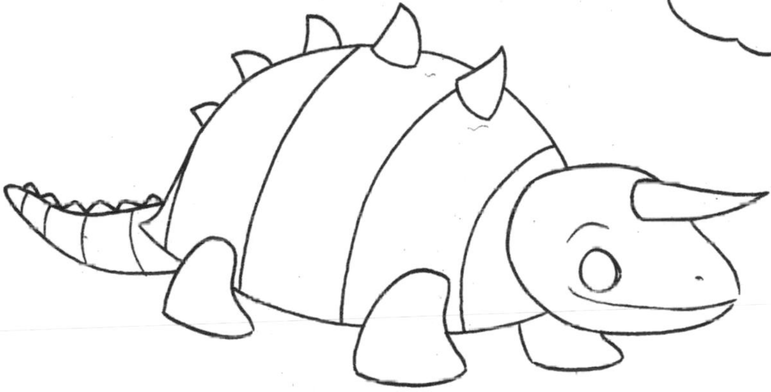

Exotic Animals and Lizards

Lizards and weird creatures like armadillos are great inspirations for manga monsters.

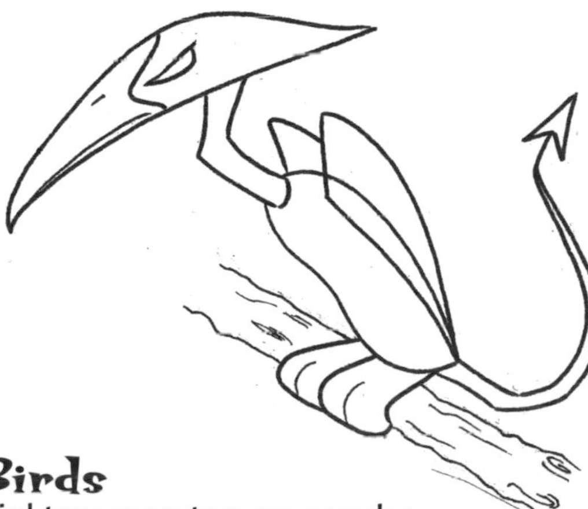

Birds

Bird-type monsters are popular, especially those based on birds from the time of the dinosaurs, like the pterodactyl.

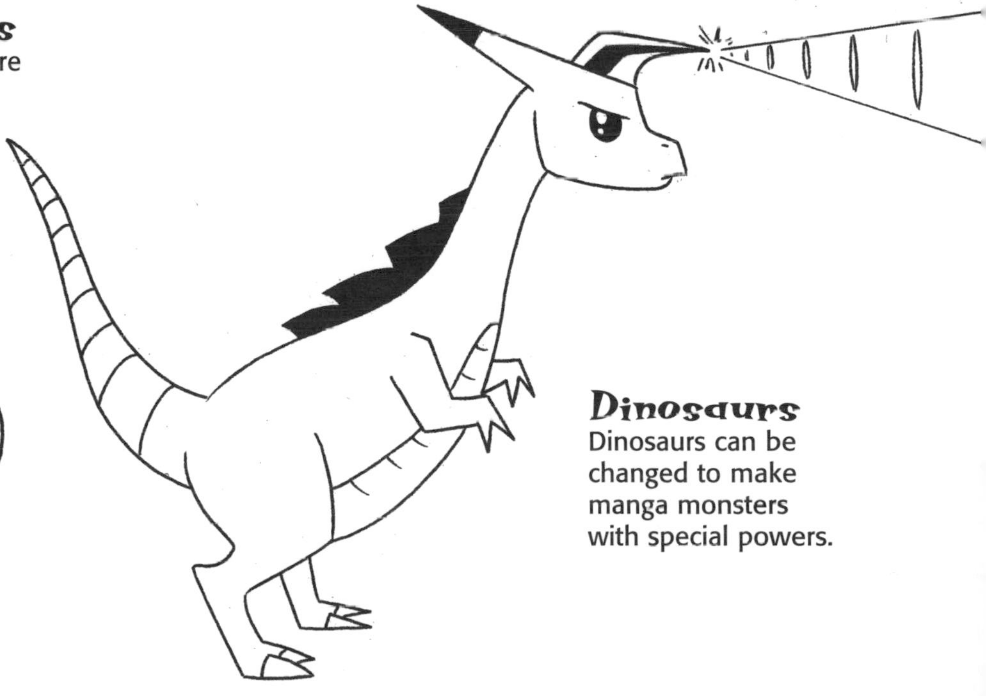

Dinosaurs

Dinosaurs can be changed to make manga monsters with special powers.

A manga monster may look just like its animal inspiration, or nothing like it at all. As an artist, it's up to you to decide how much you want to change it. Take a look at these examples.

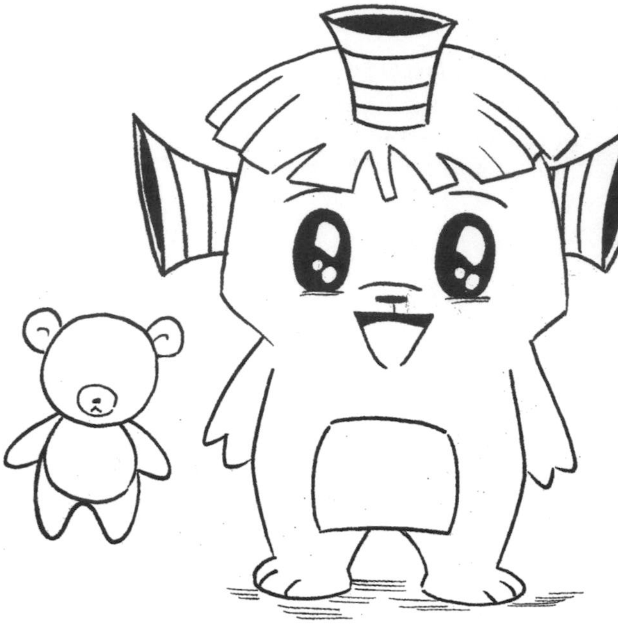

MANGA MONSTER BASED ON A TEDDY BEAR

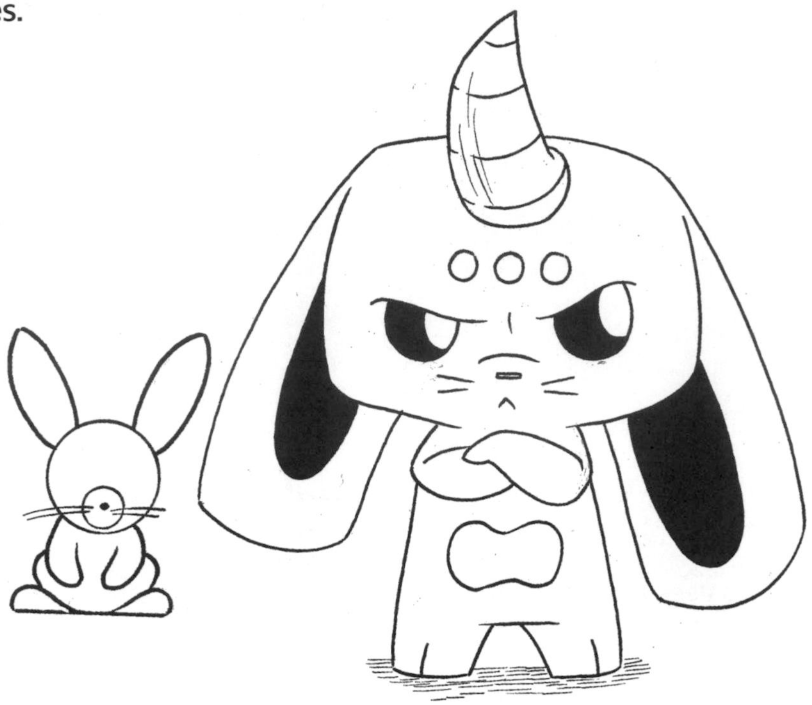

MANGA MONSTER BASED ON A RABBIT

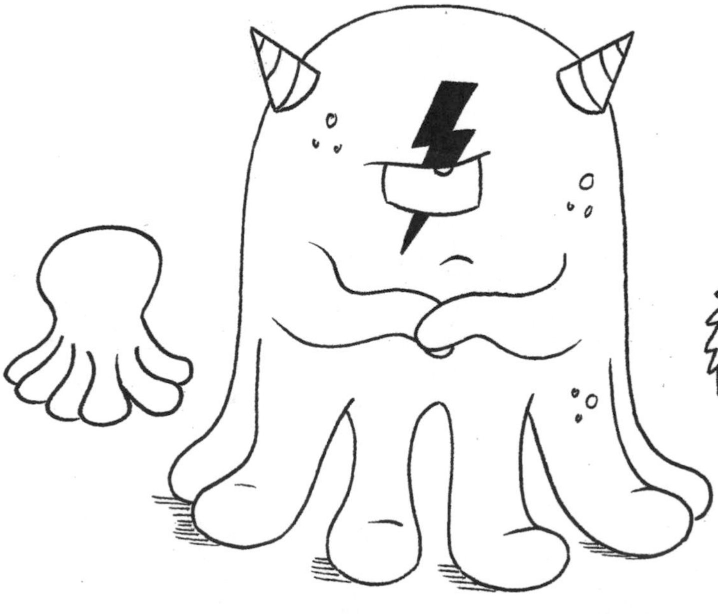

MANGA MONSTER BASED ON AN OCTOPUS

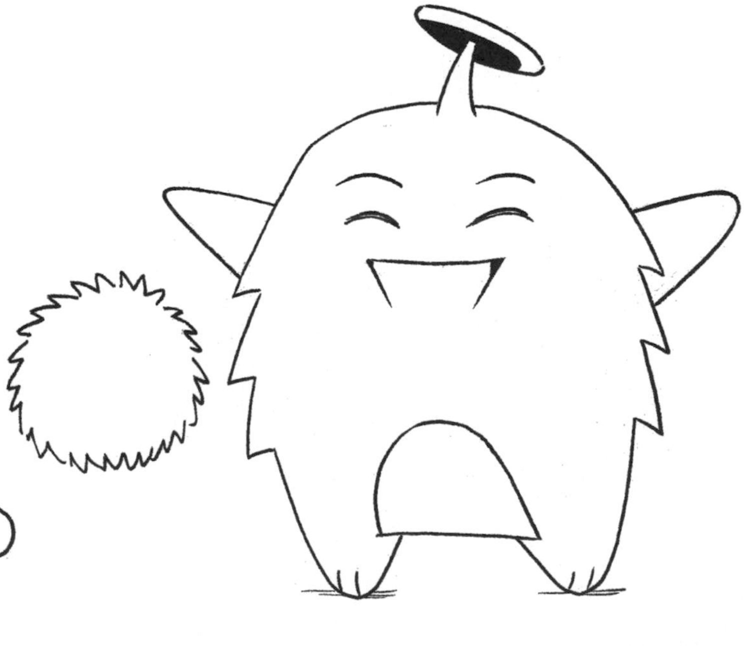

MANGA MONSTER BASED ON A FUR BALL!

It's important that the hands and feet look as though they belong to the same monster. A sea creature would have sea-creature hands and sea-creature feet, not sea-creature hands and hooves for feet. See how the hands and feet on this page go together?

Hands   Feet

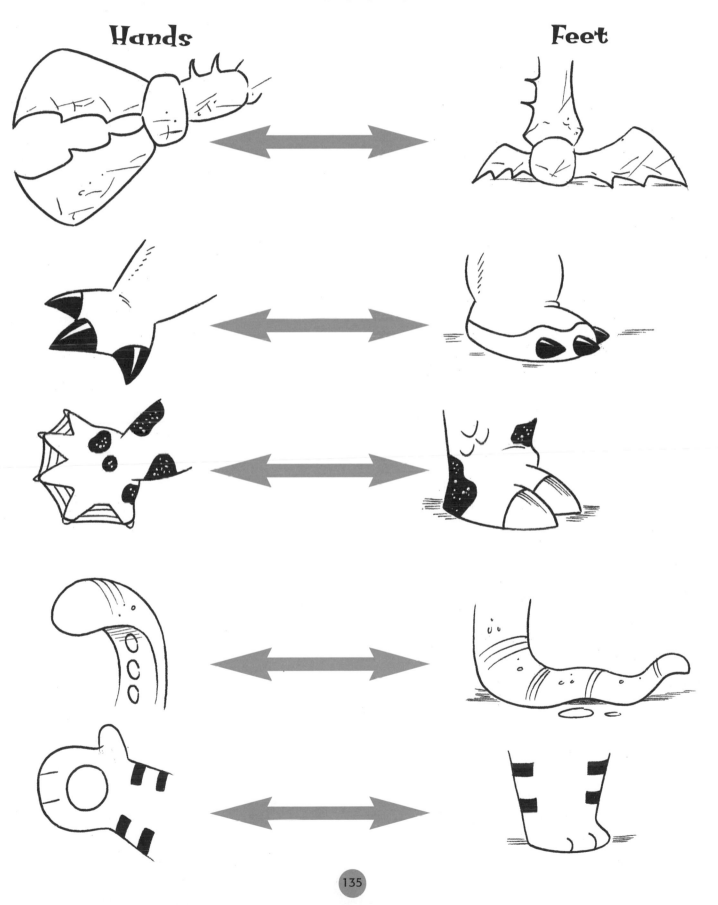

Eyes are a very important feature in manga characters, and they're especially important in manga monsters. Each monster should have its own, distinct type of eyes. Here are some popular types that you can draw.

BIG SHINE

SKINNY SHINE

EVIL EYES

DOUBLE SHINES

ALMOND-SHAPED EYES

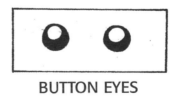

BUTTON EYES

AQUAZAR

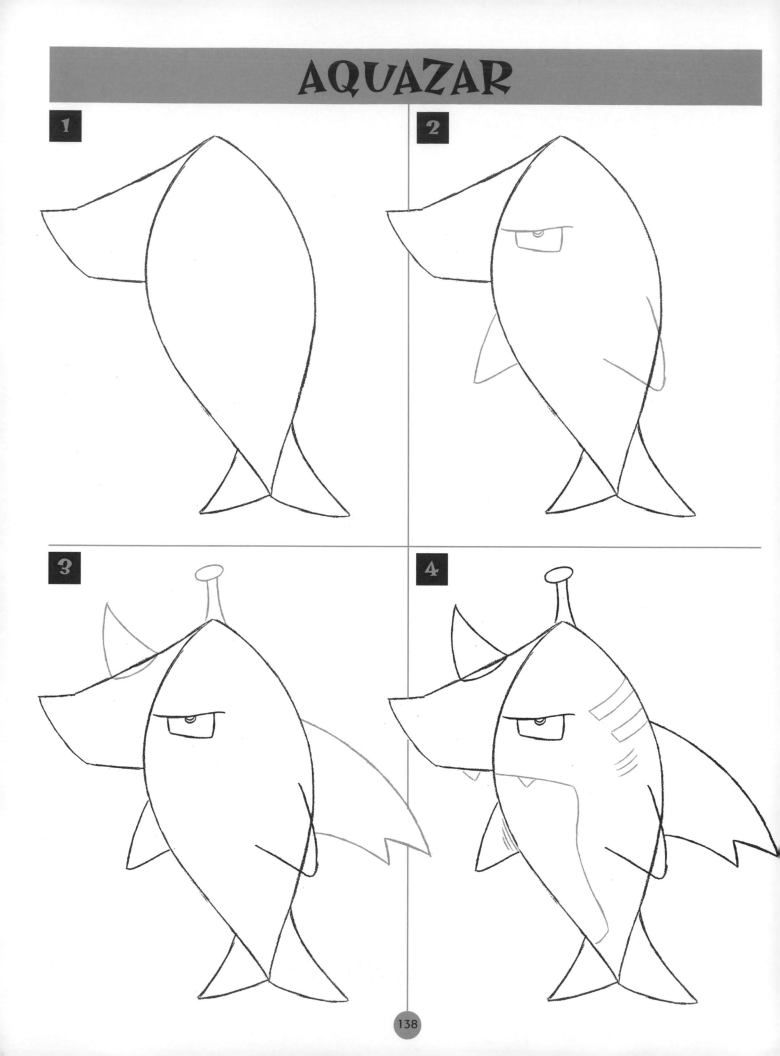

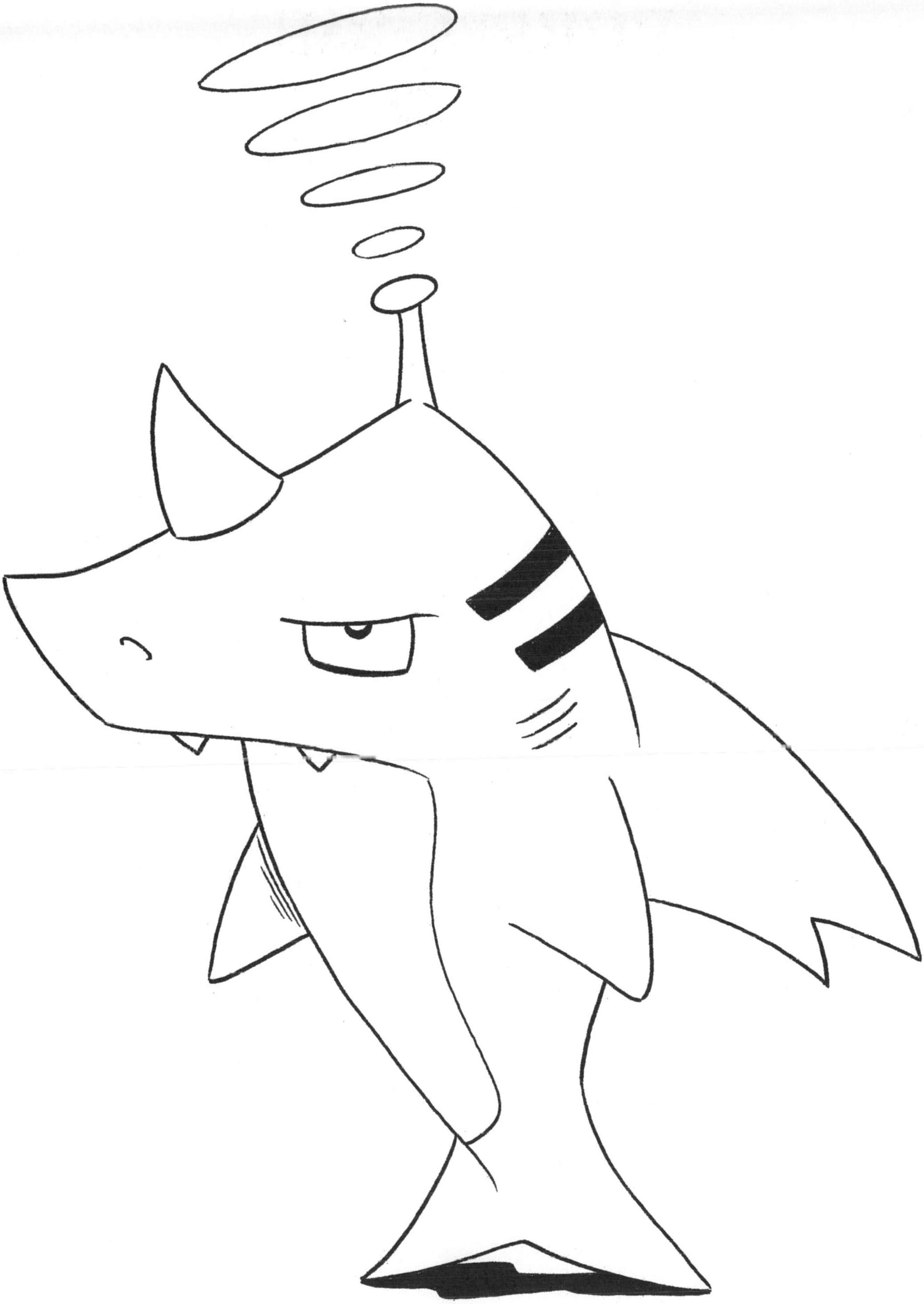

BUBBLE BABY

1

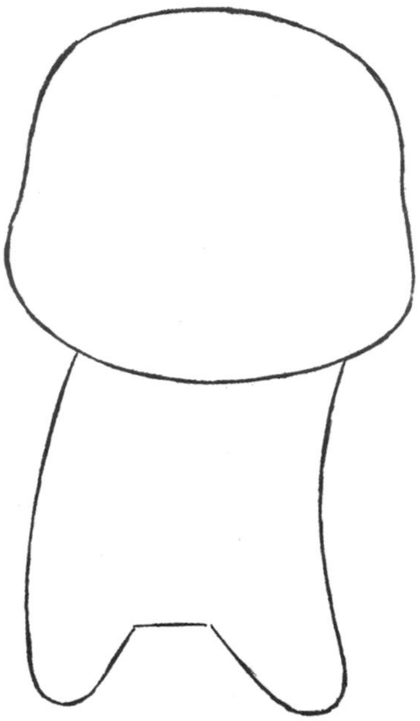

2

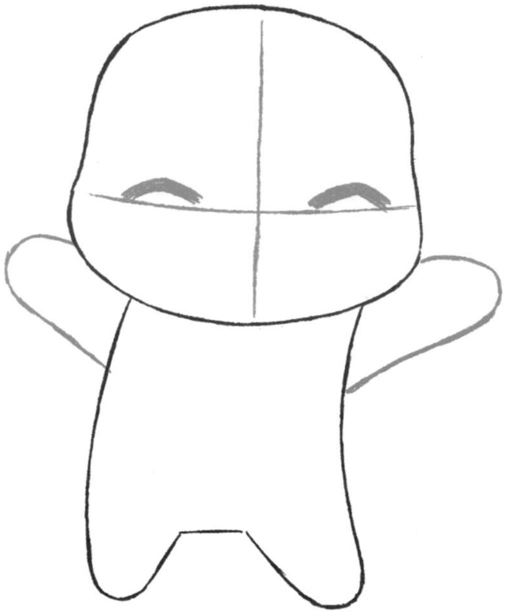

3

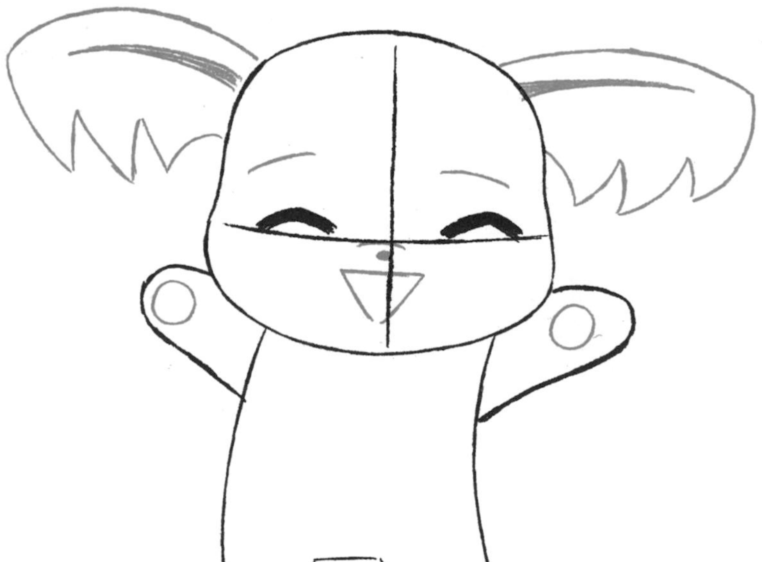

4

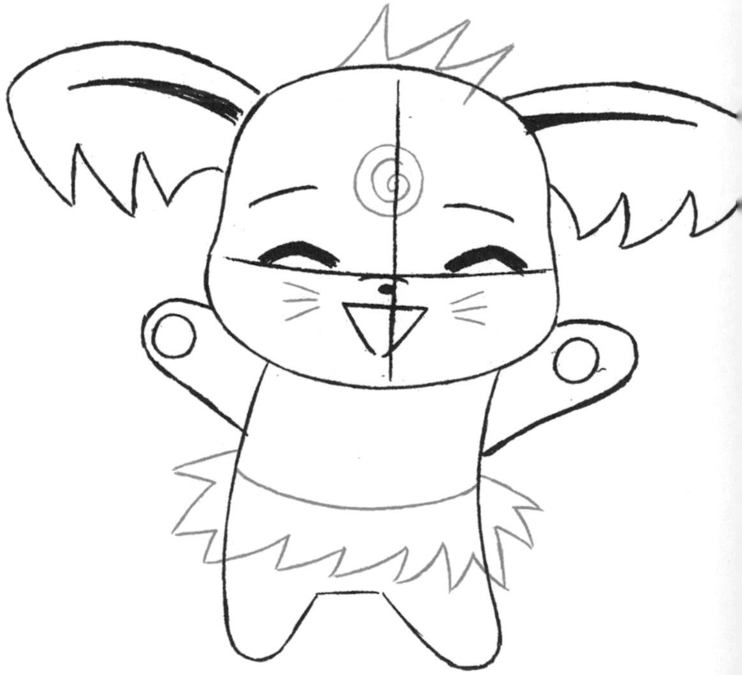

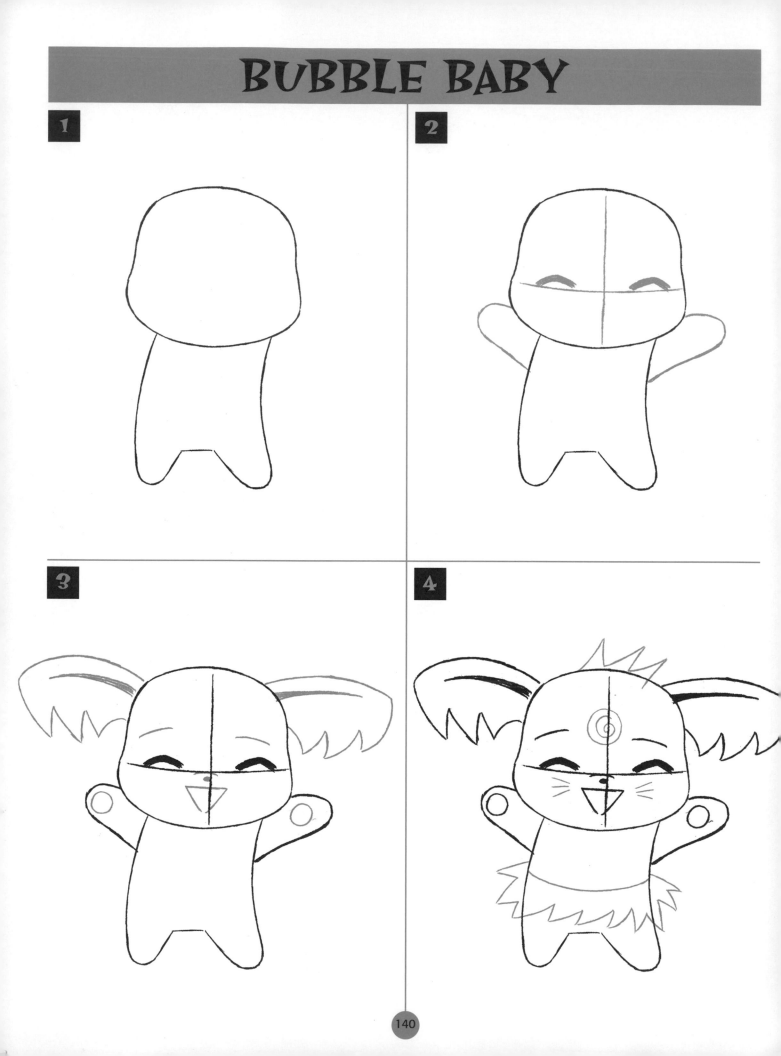

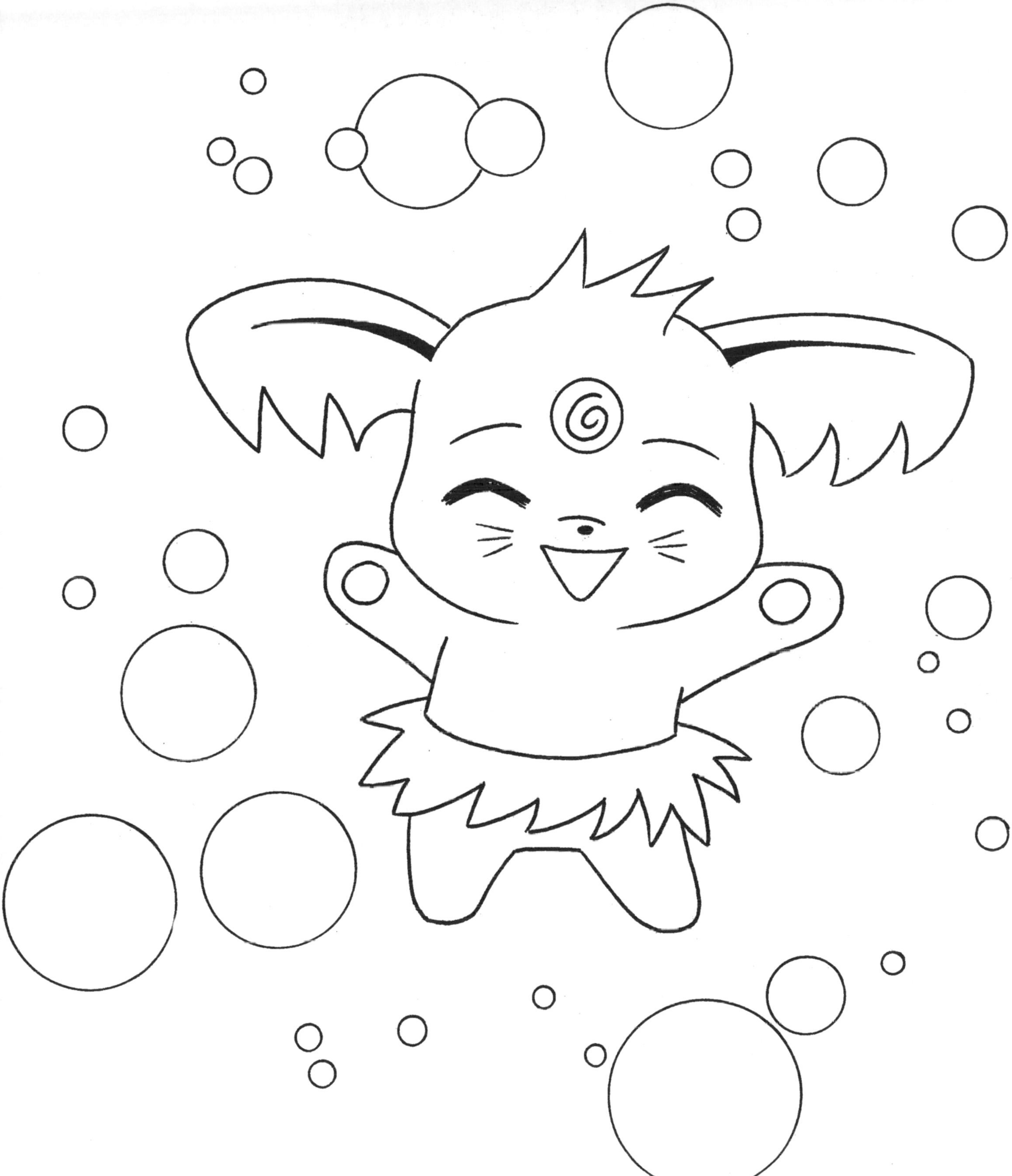

PLUMPOON

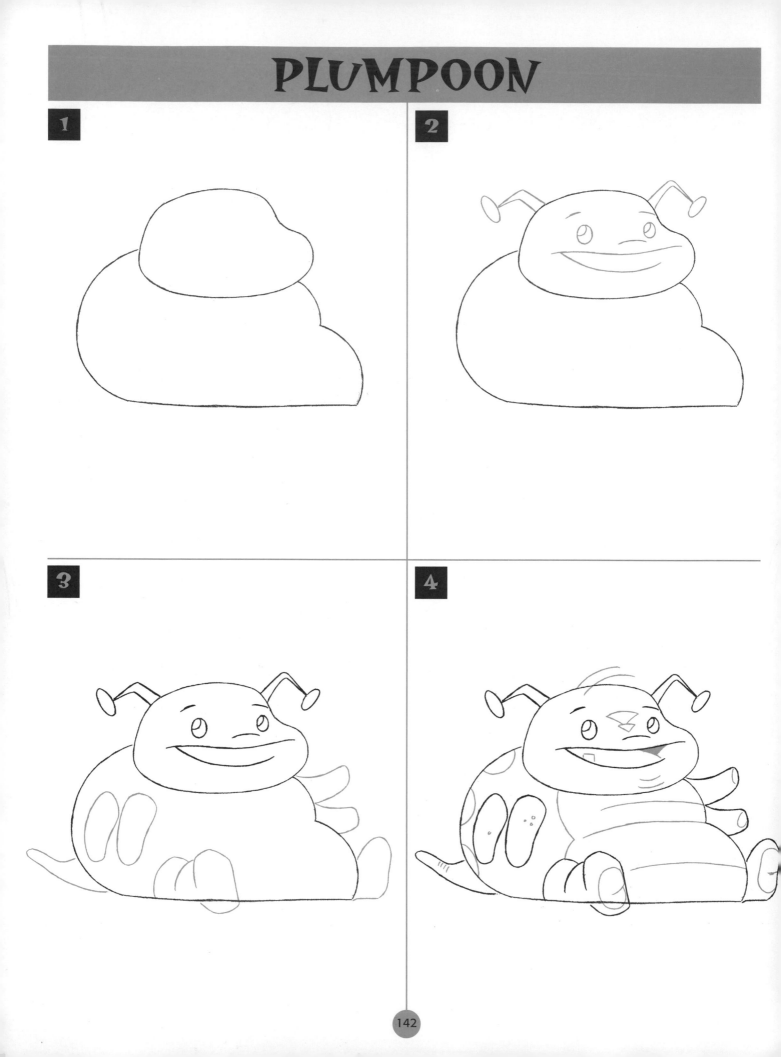

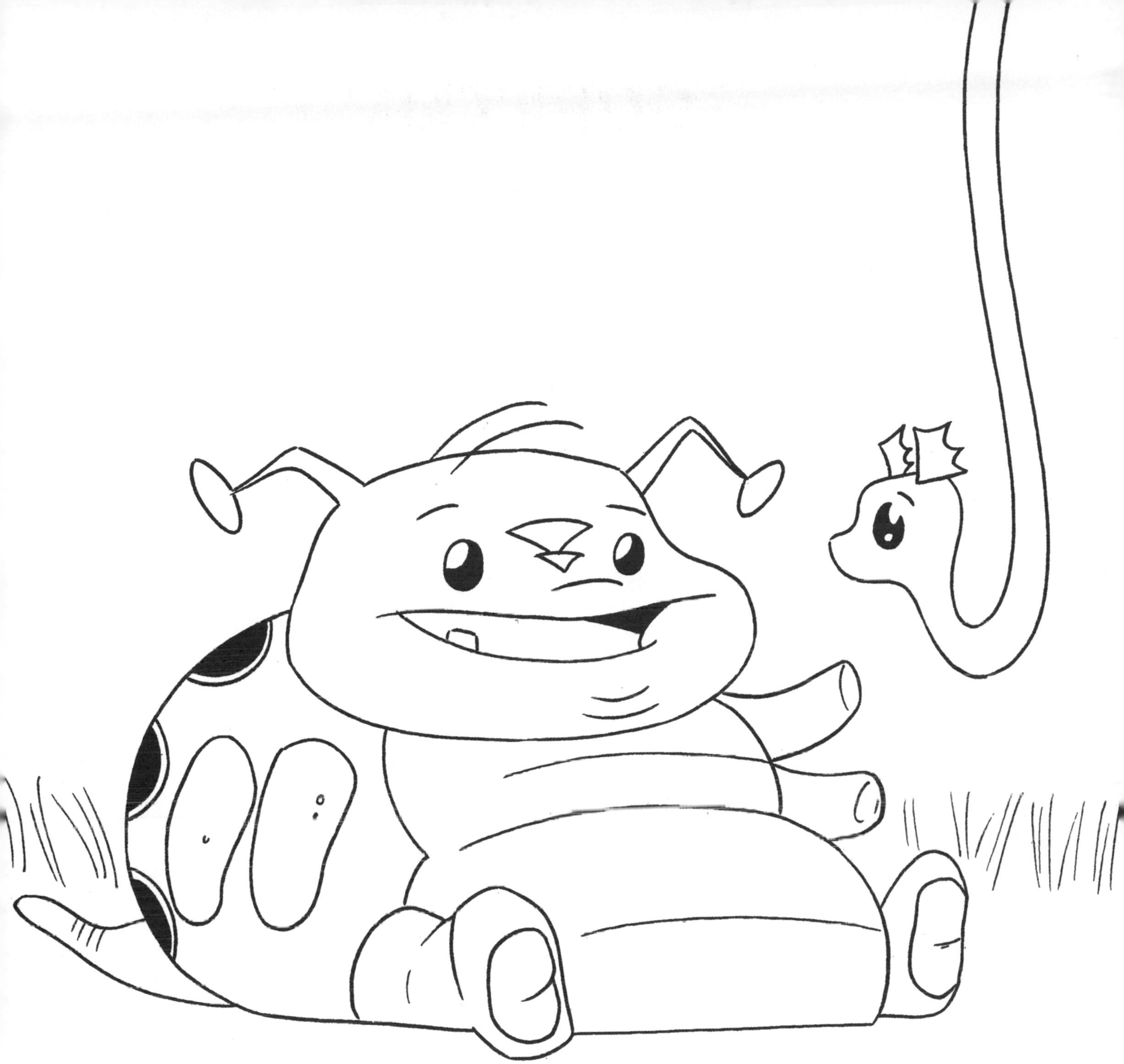

QUEETLE

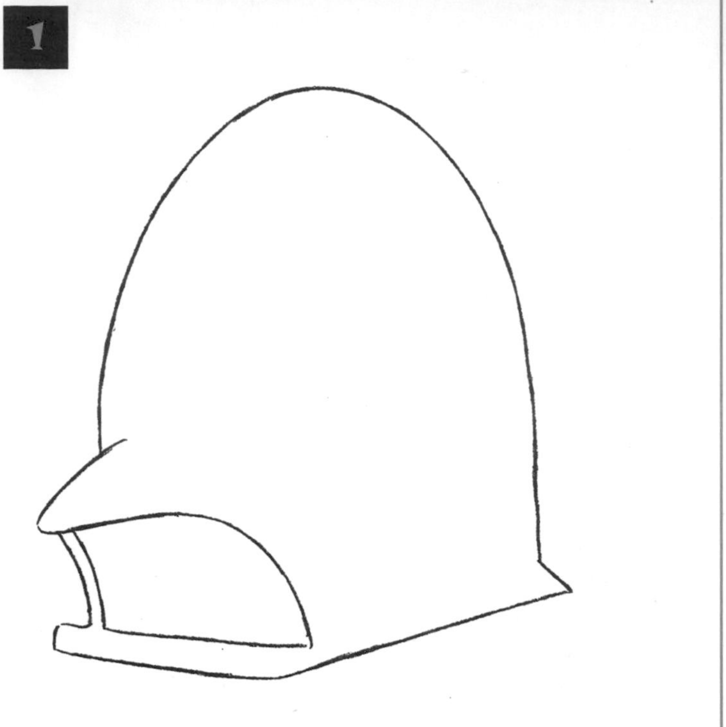
1

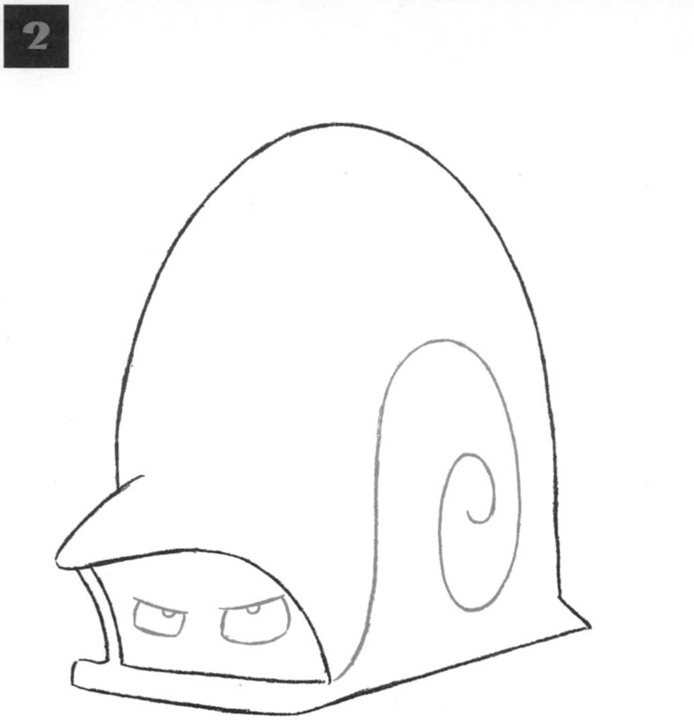
2

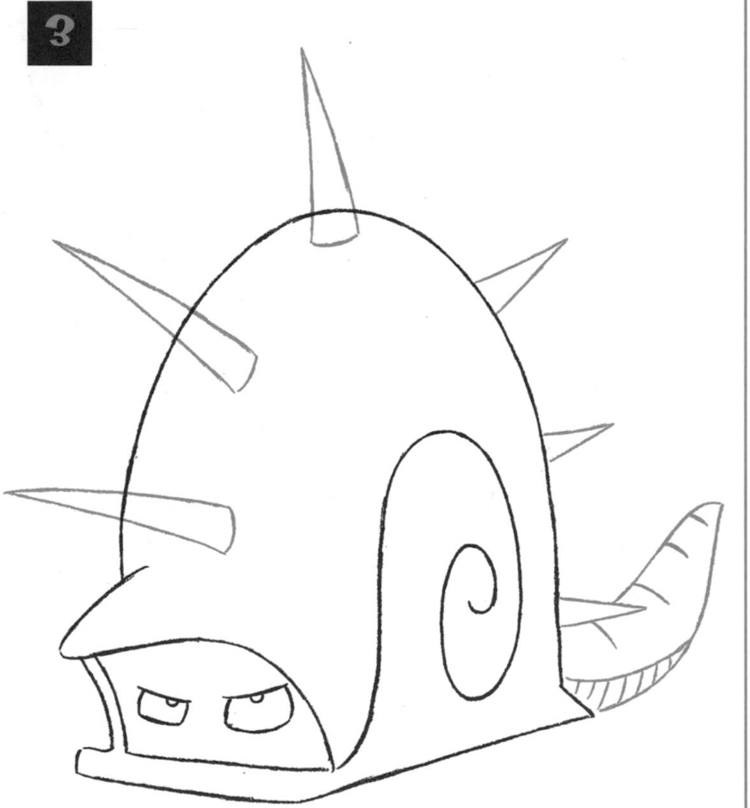
3

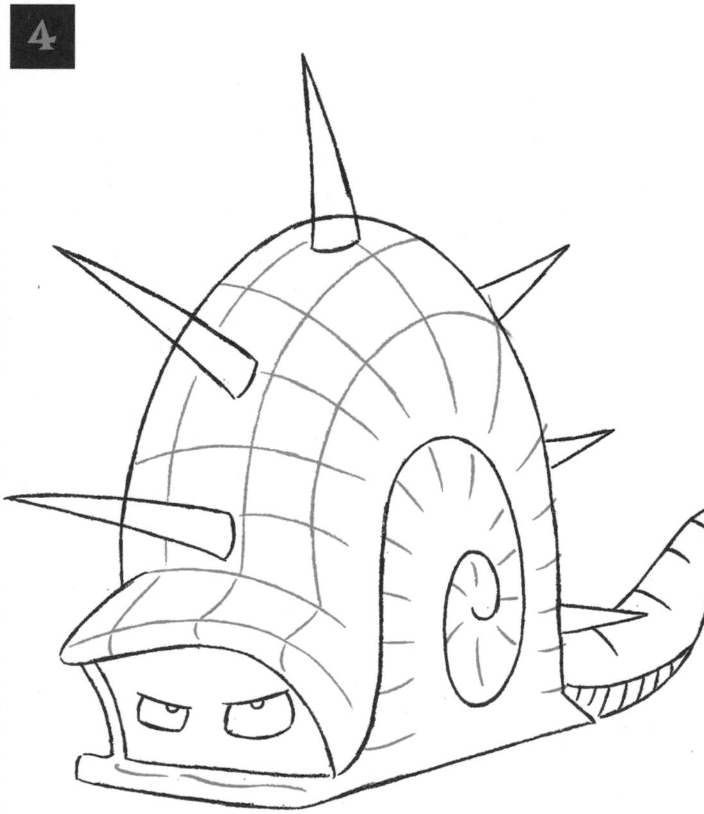
4

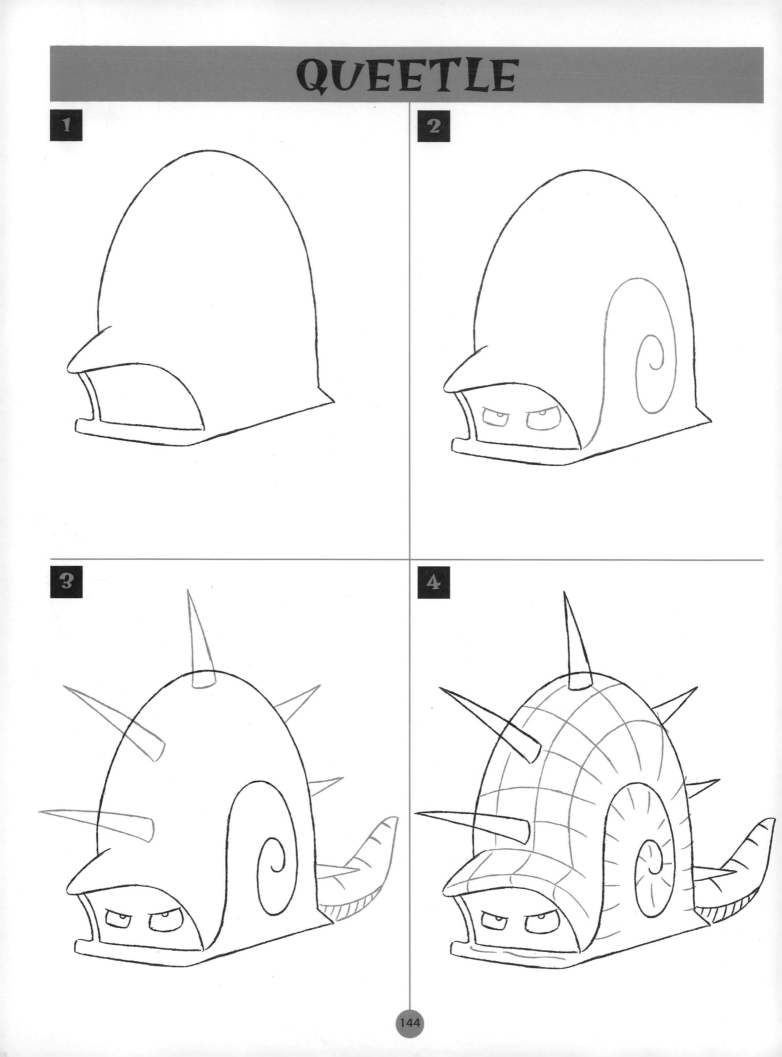

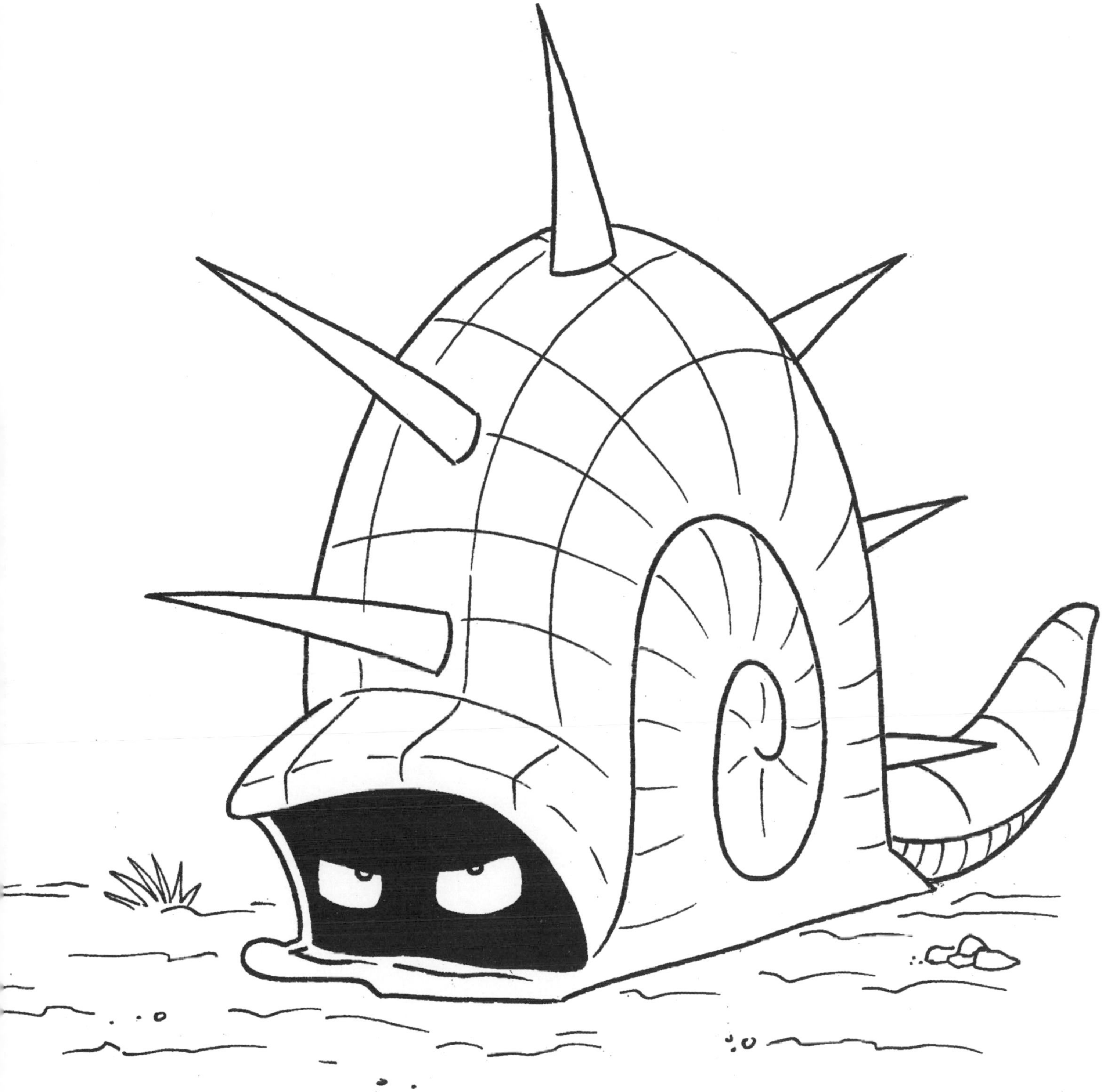

BINKTAR

1

2

3

4

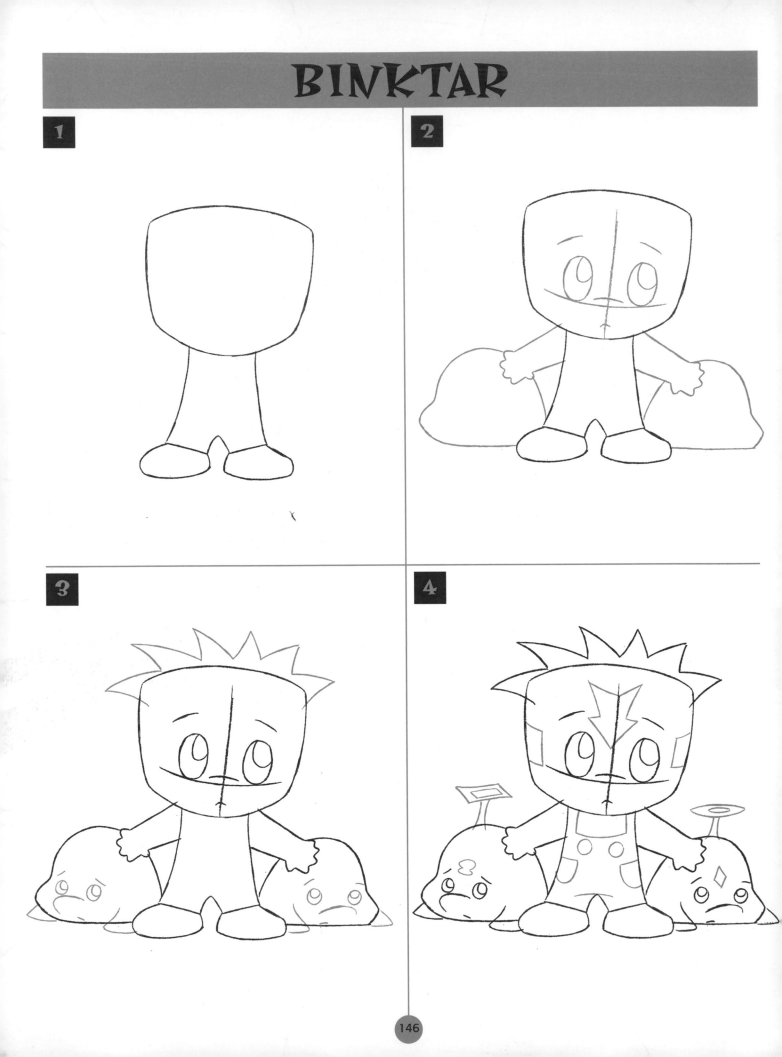

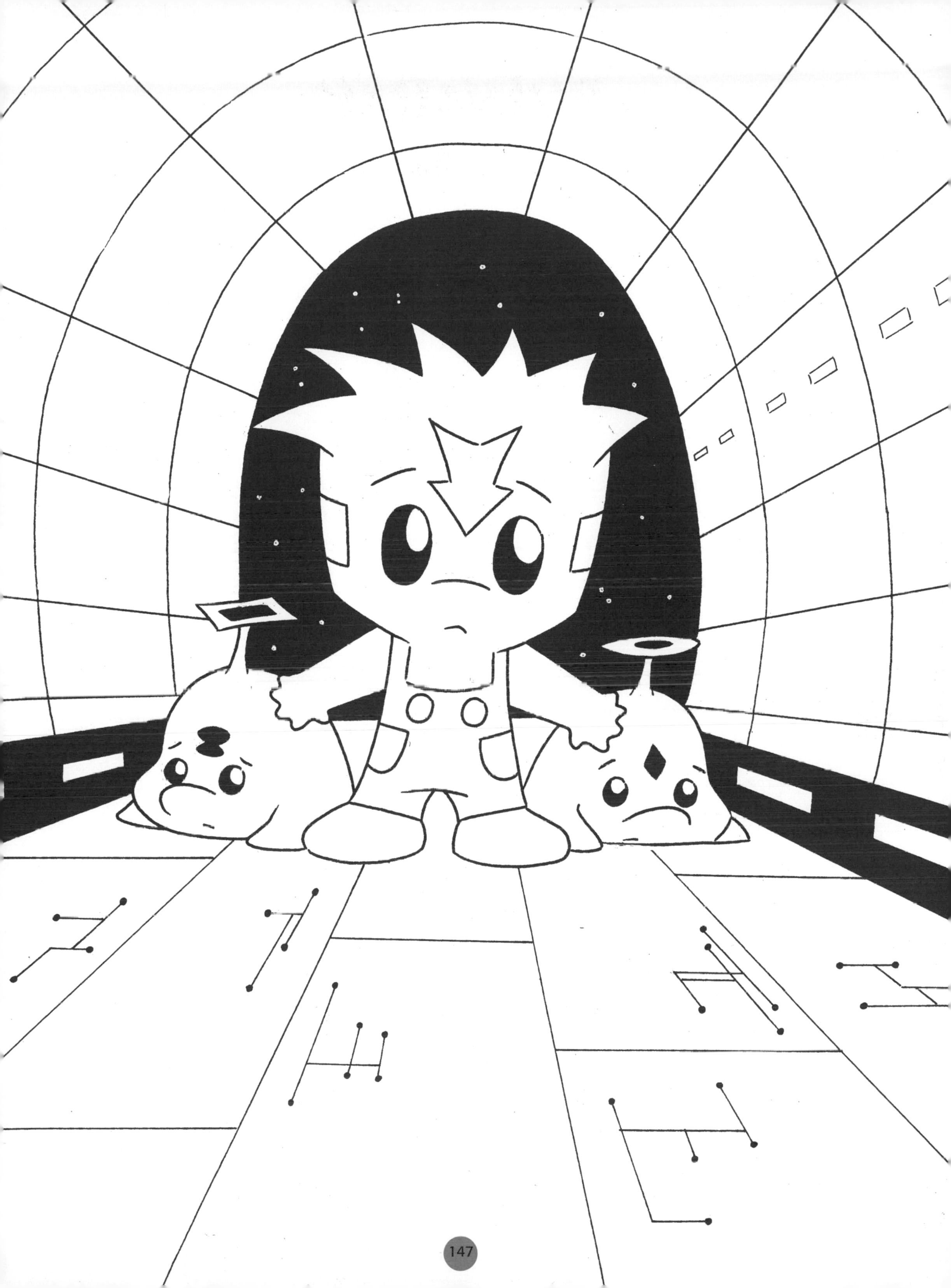

PULVARAK

1

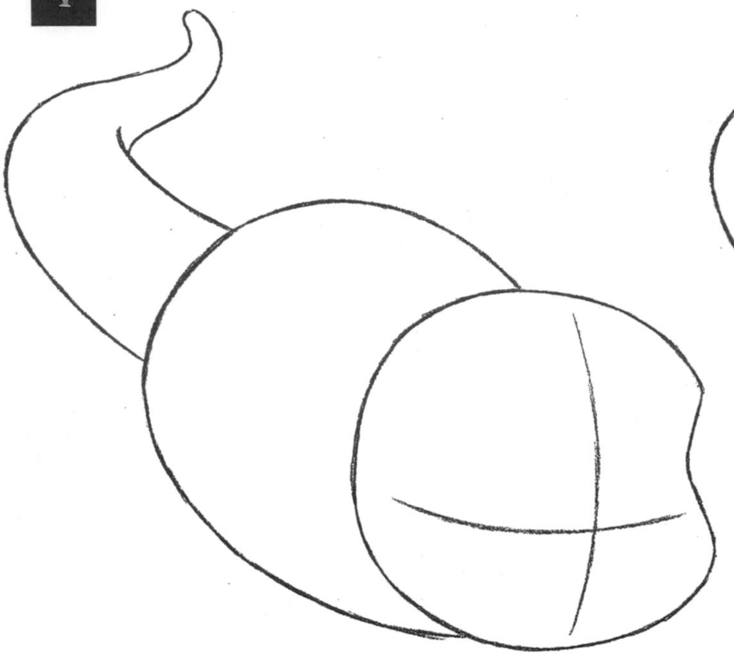

2

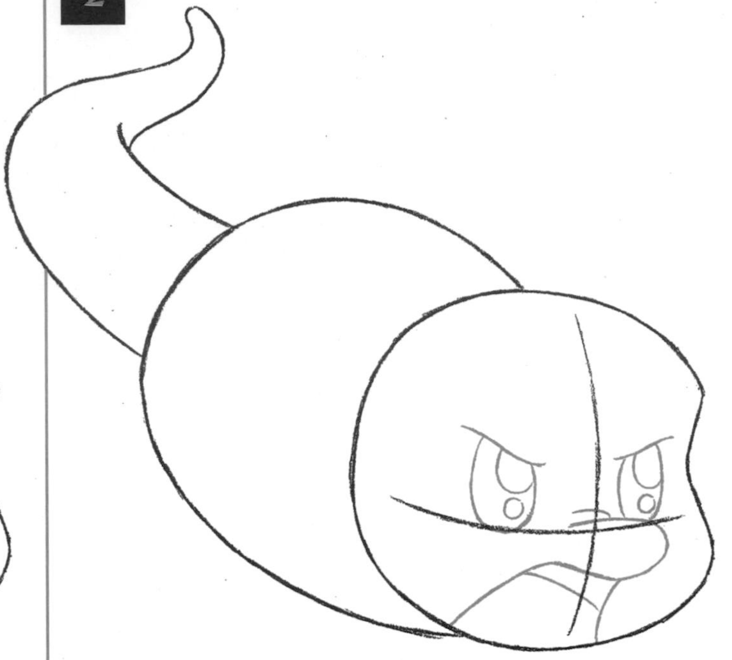

3

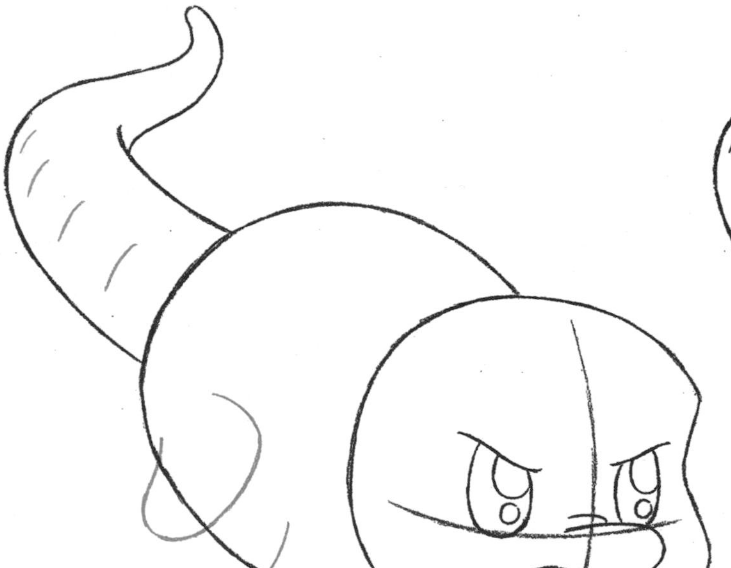

4

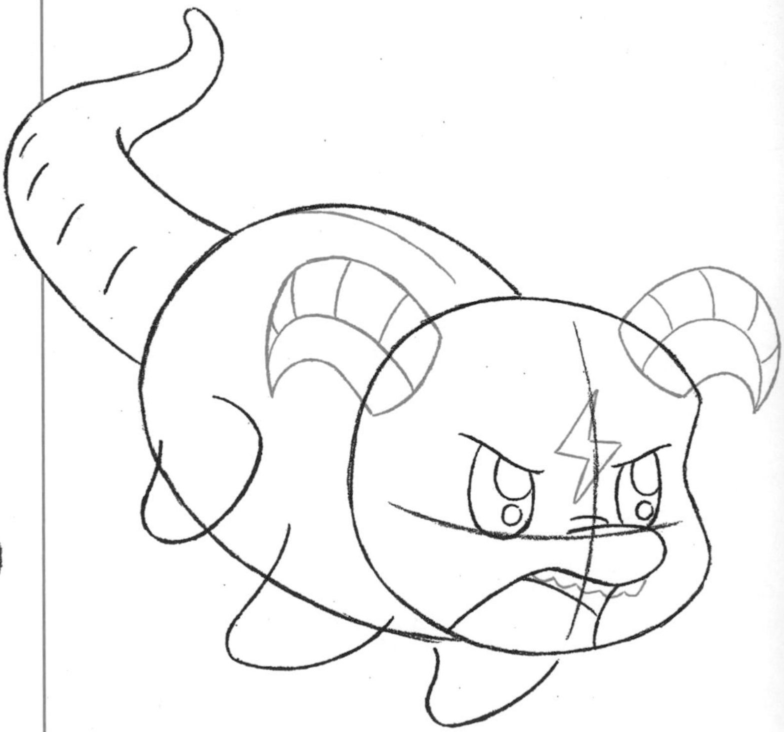

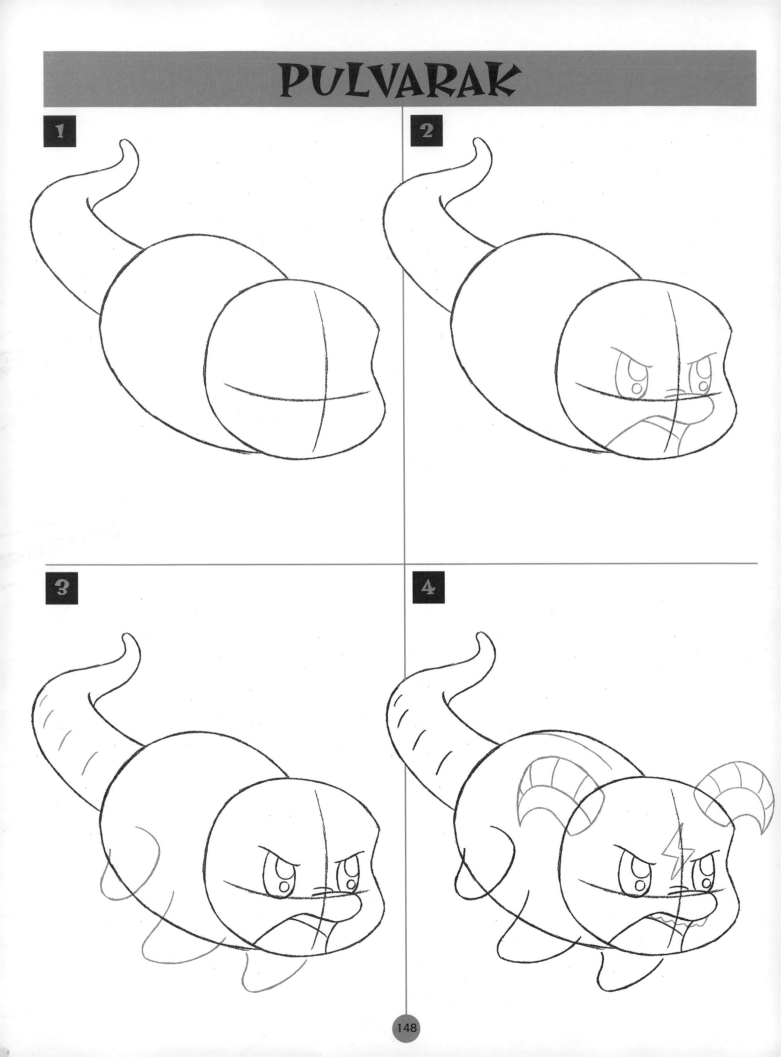

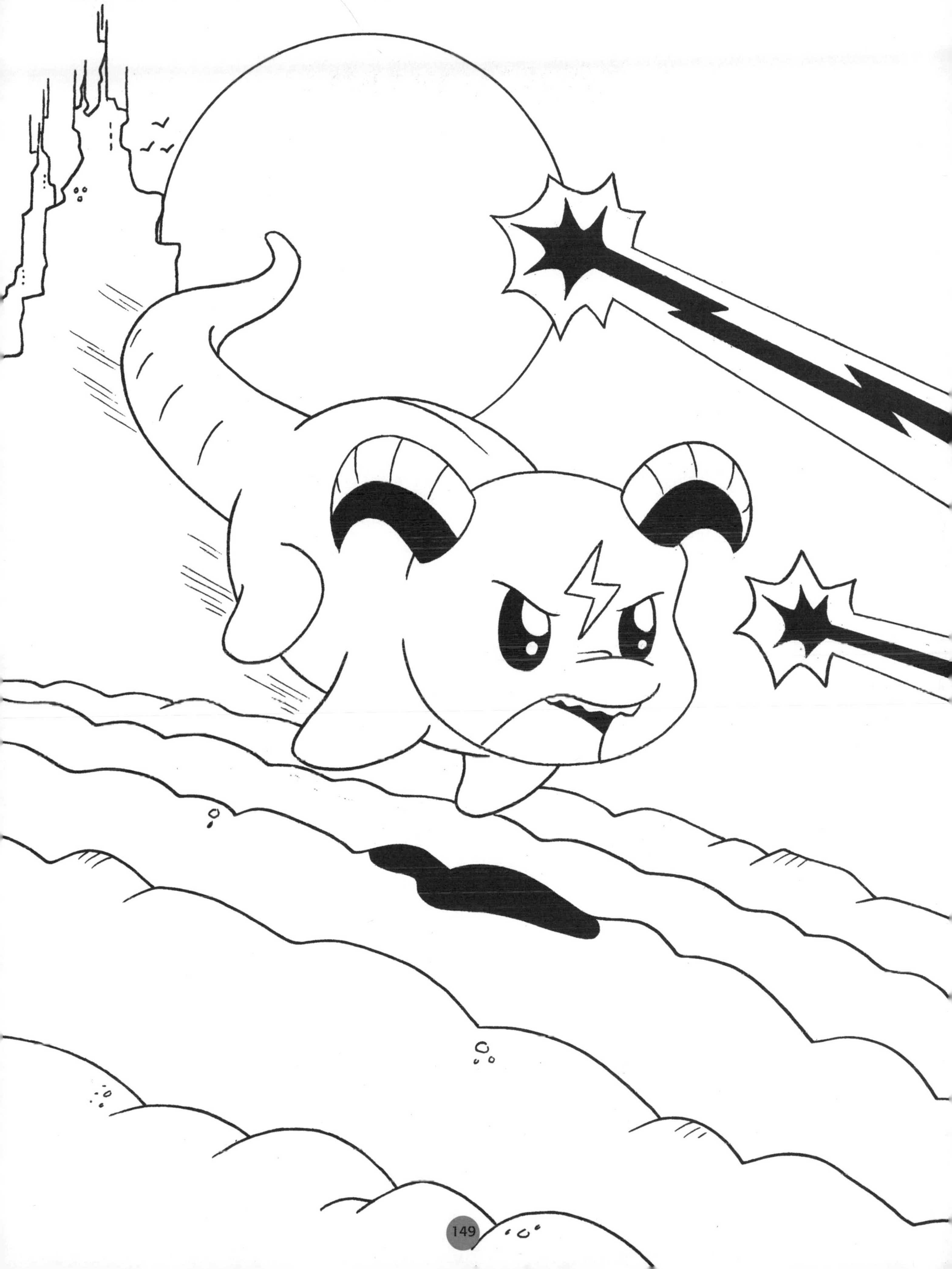

MOONWING

1

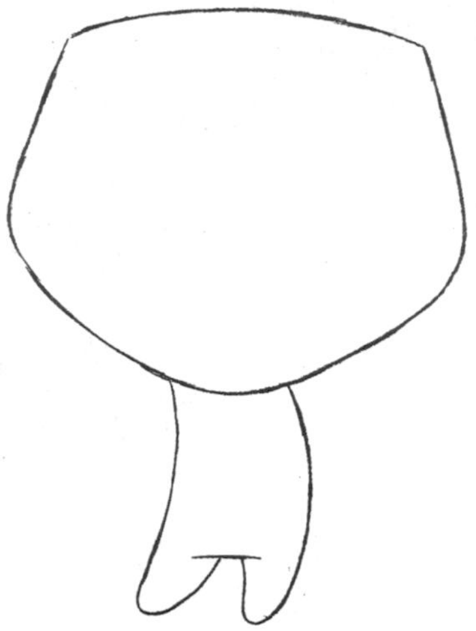

2

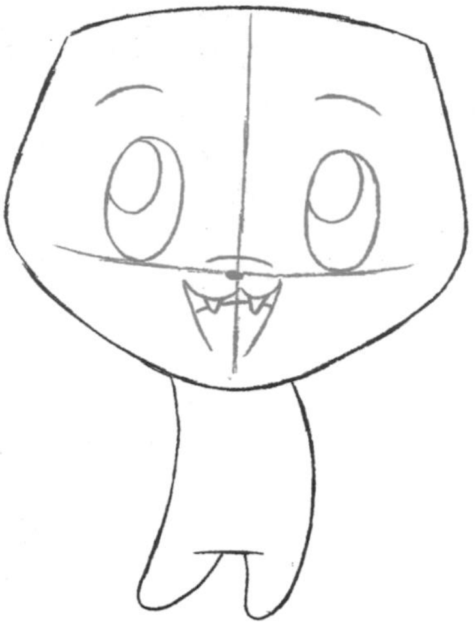

3

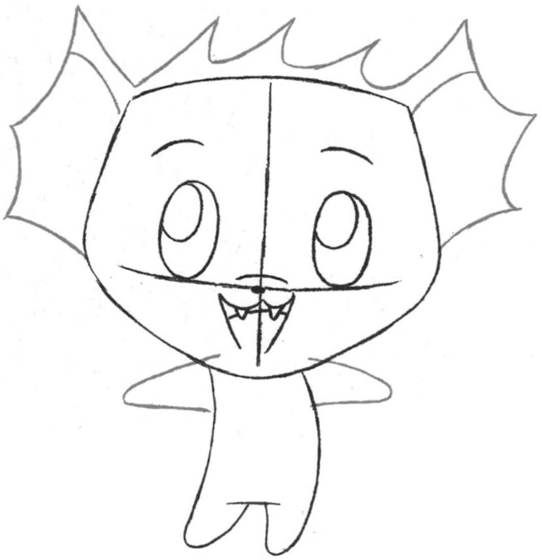

4

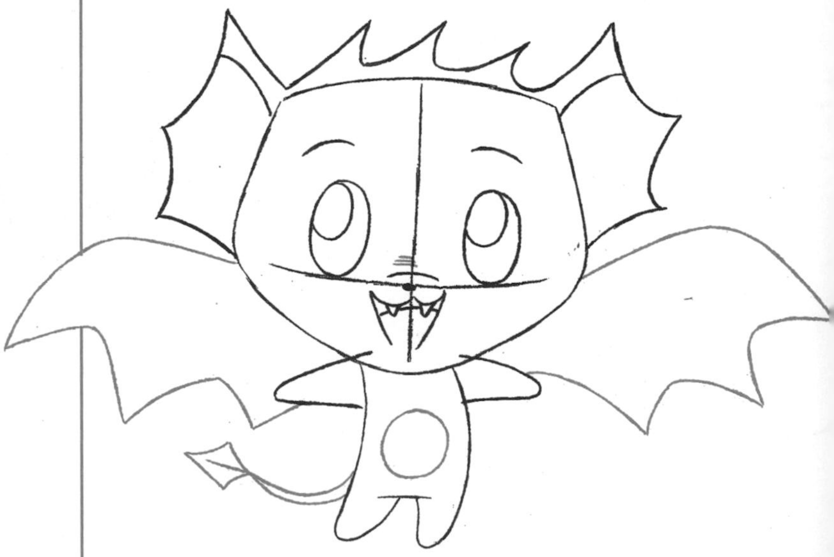

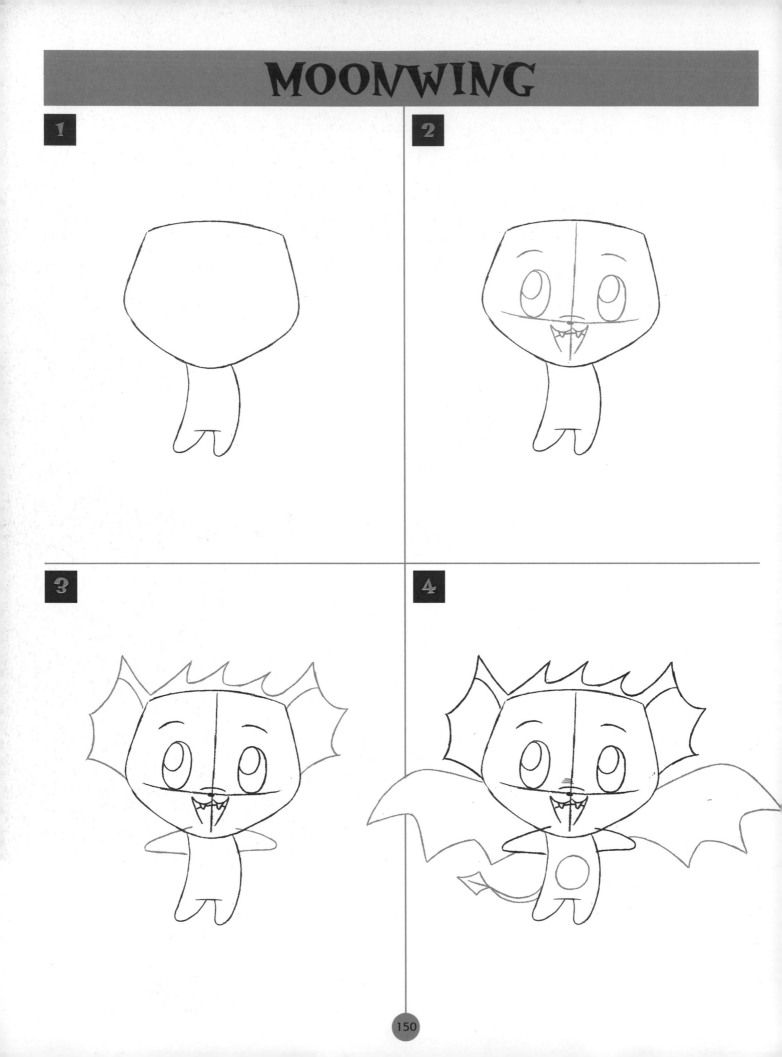

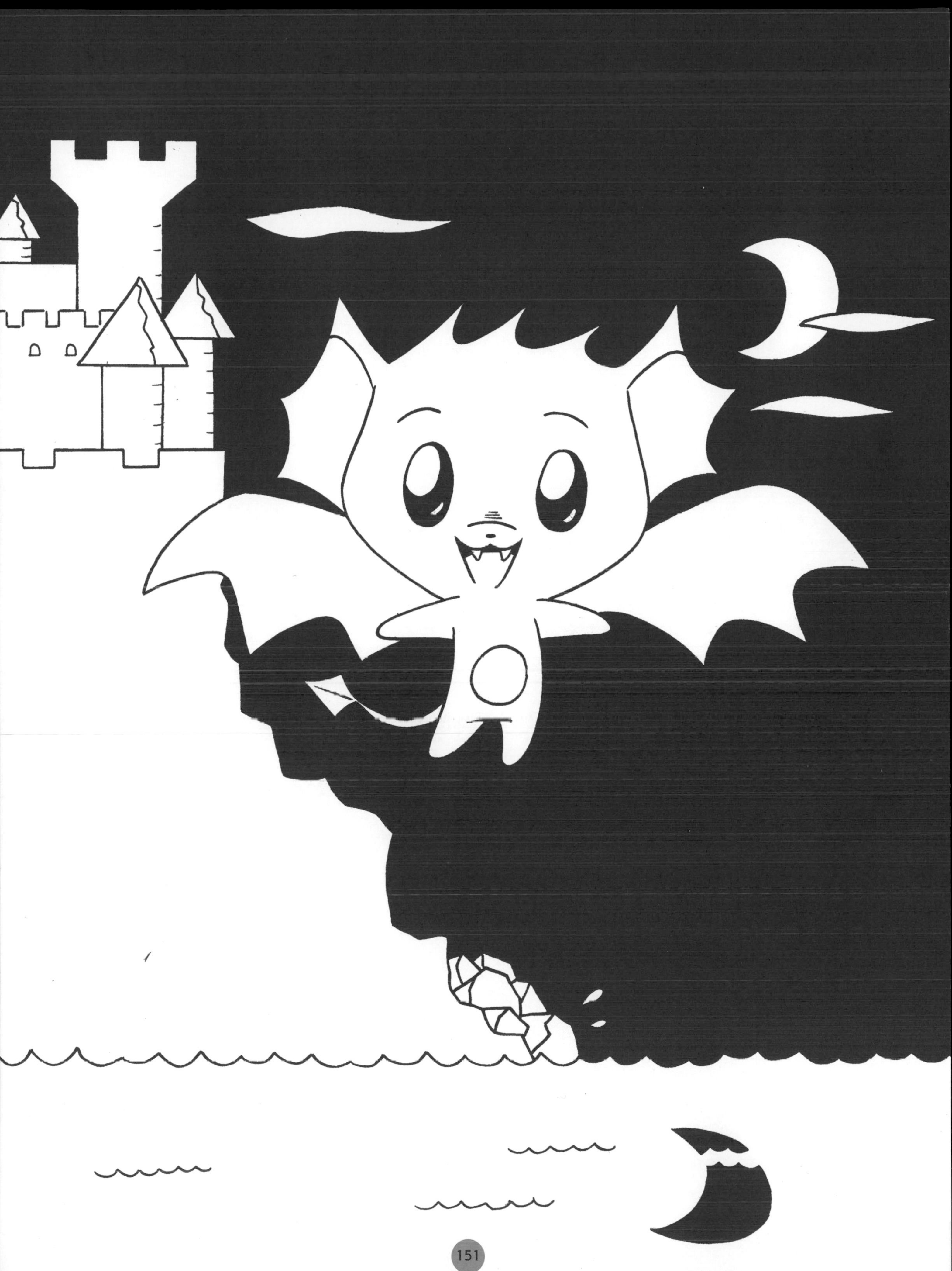

BRAINSTORMER

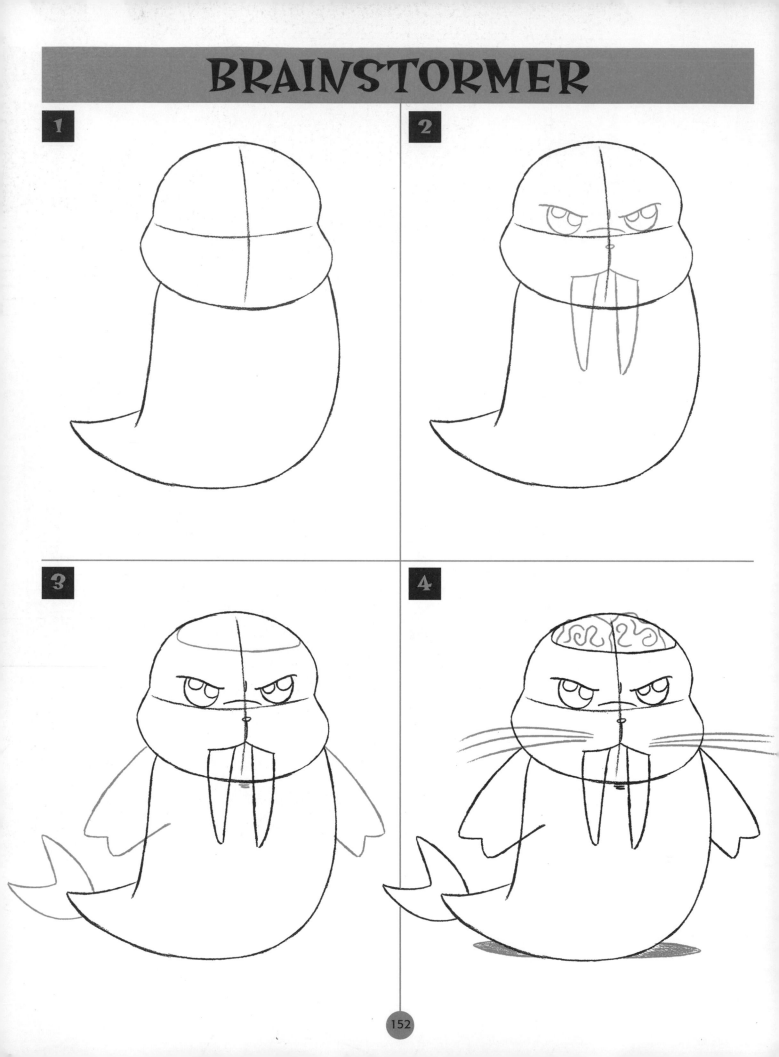

1

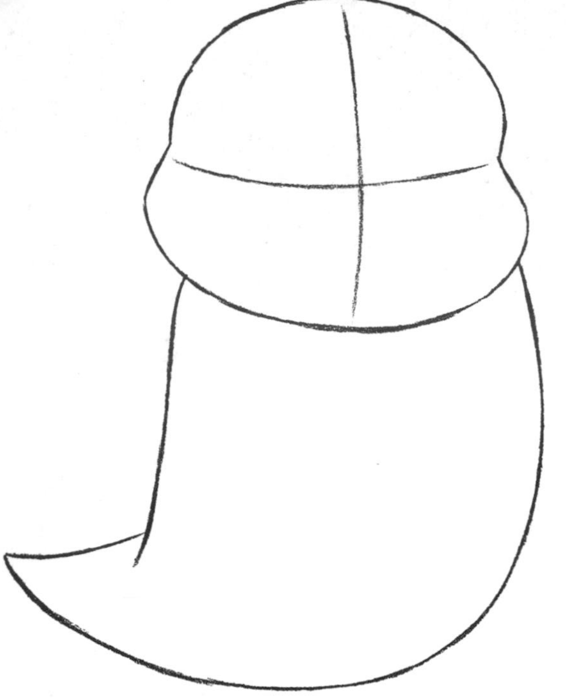

2

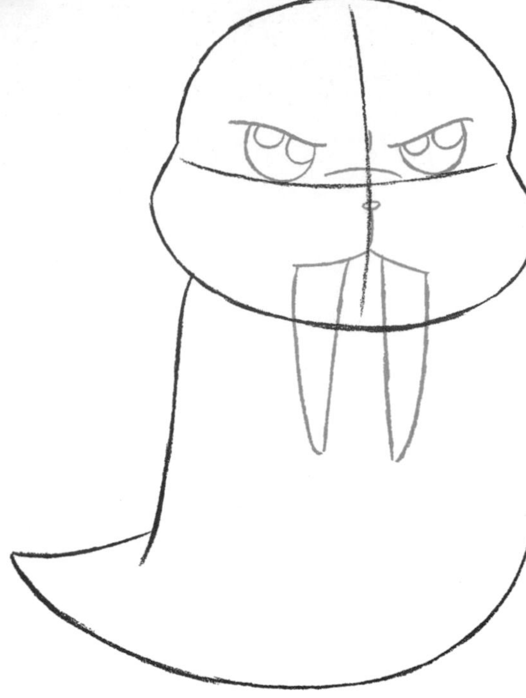

3

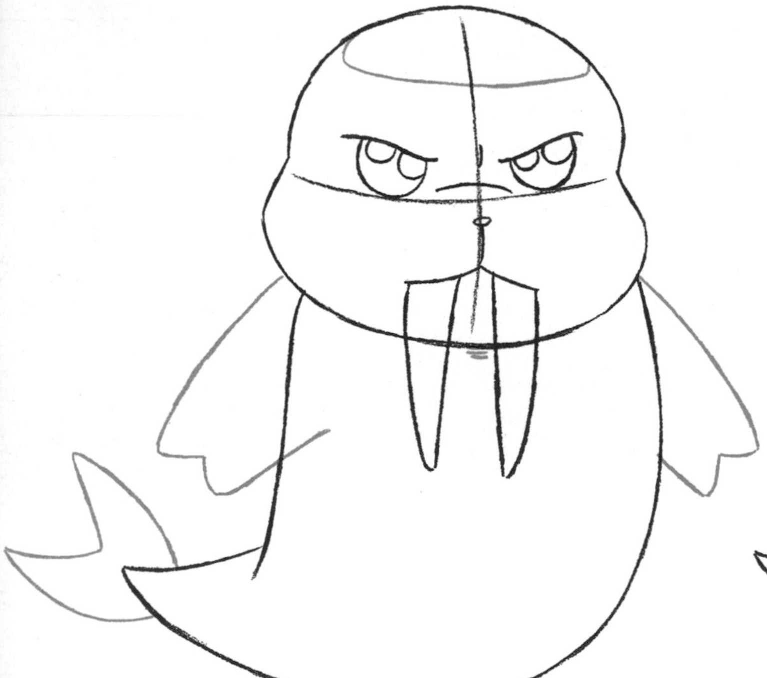

4

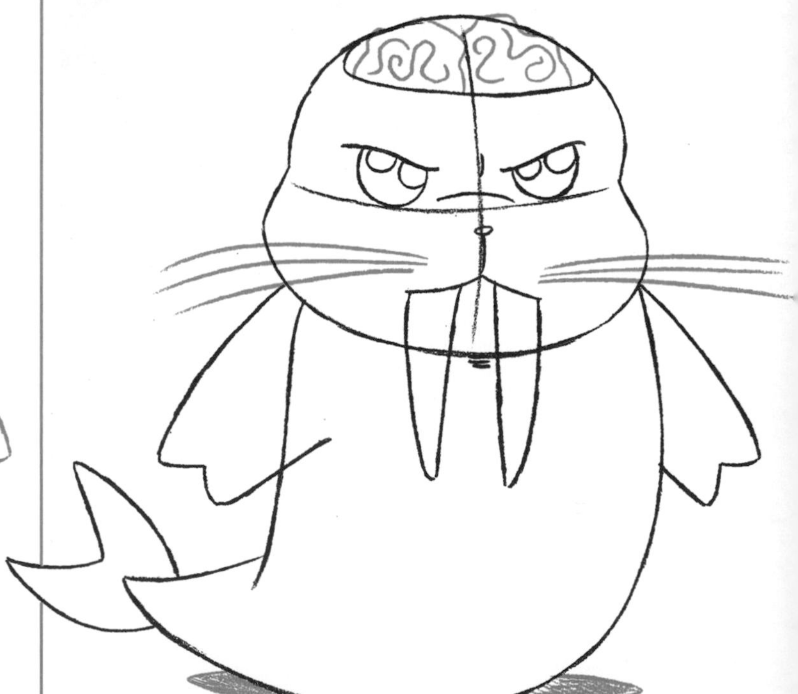

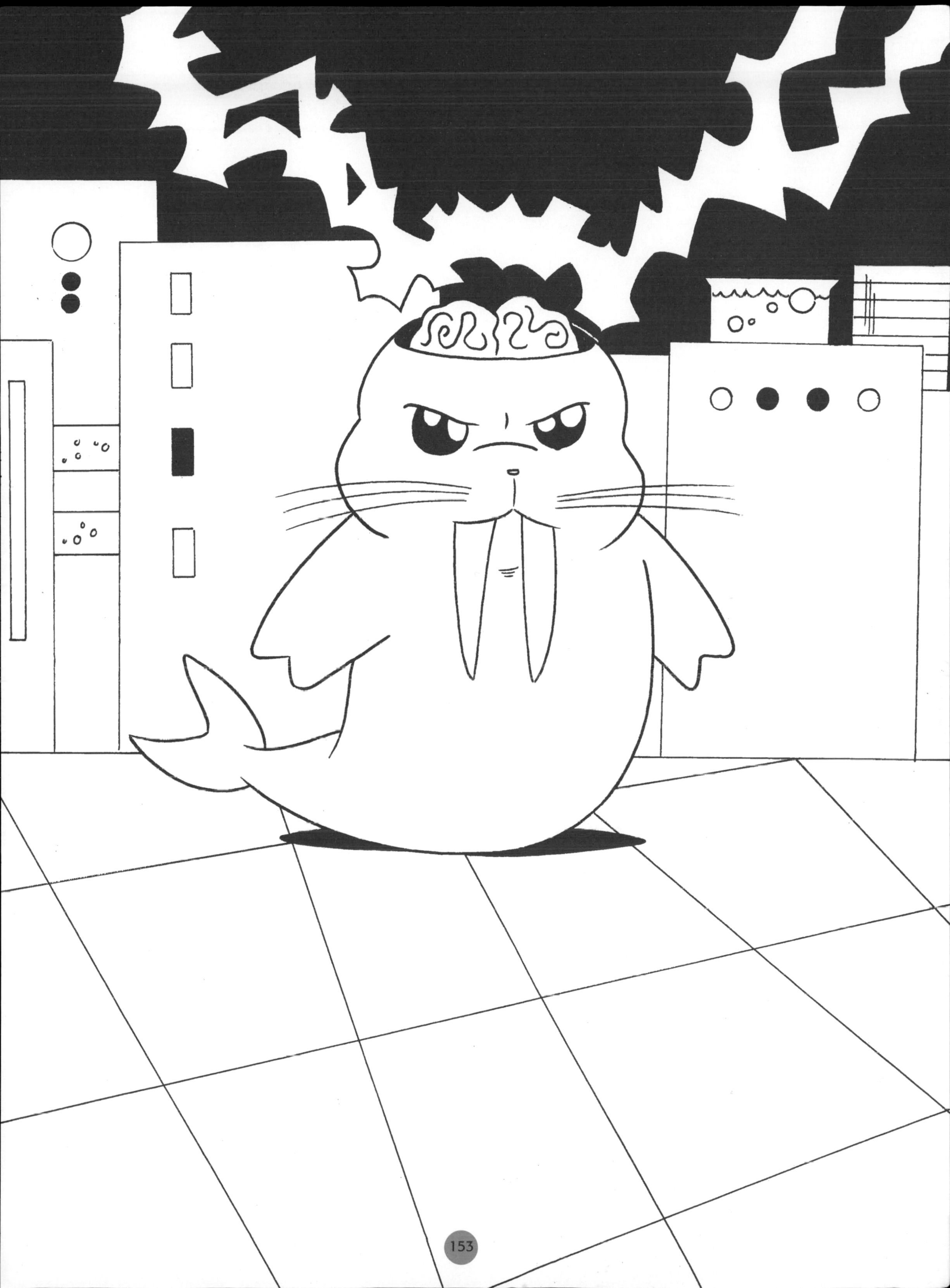

FURTRON

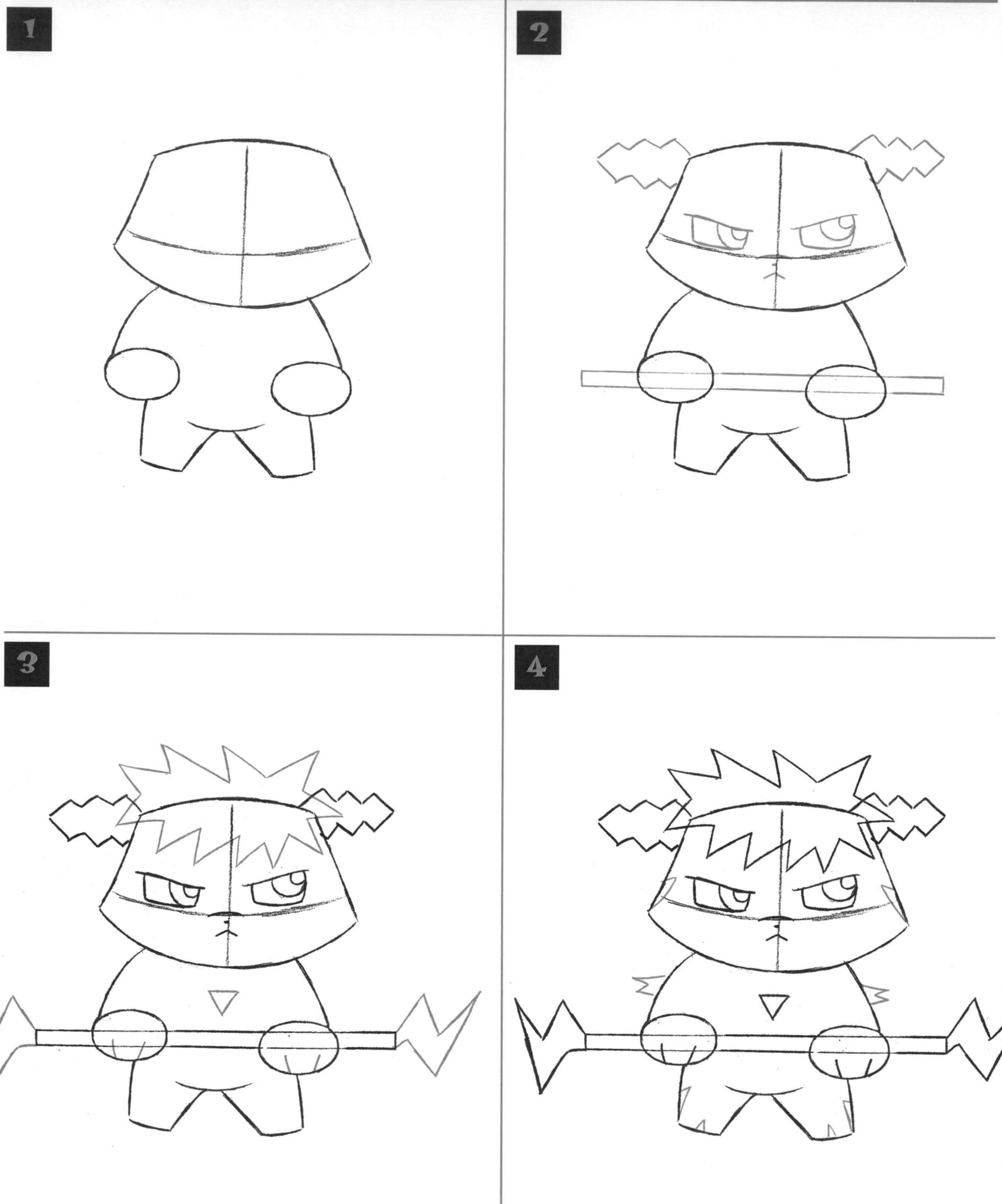

1
2
3
4

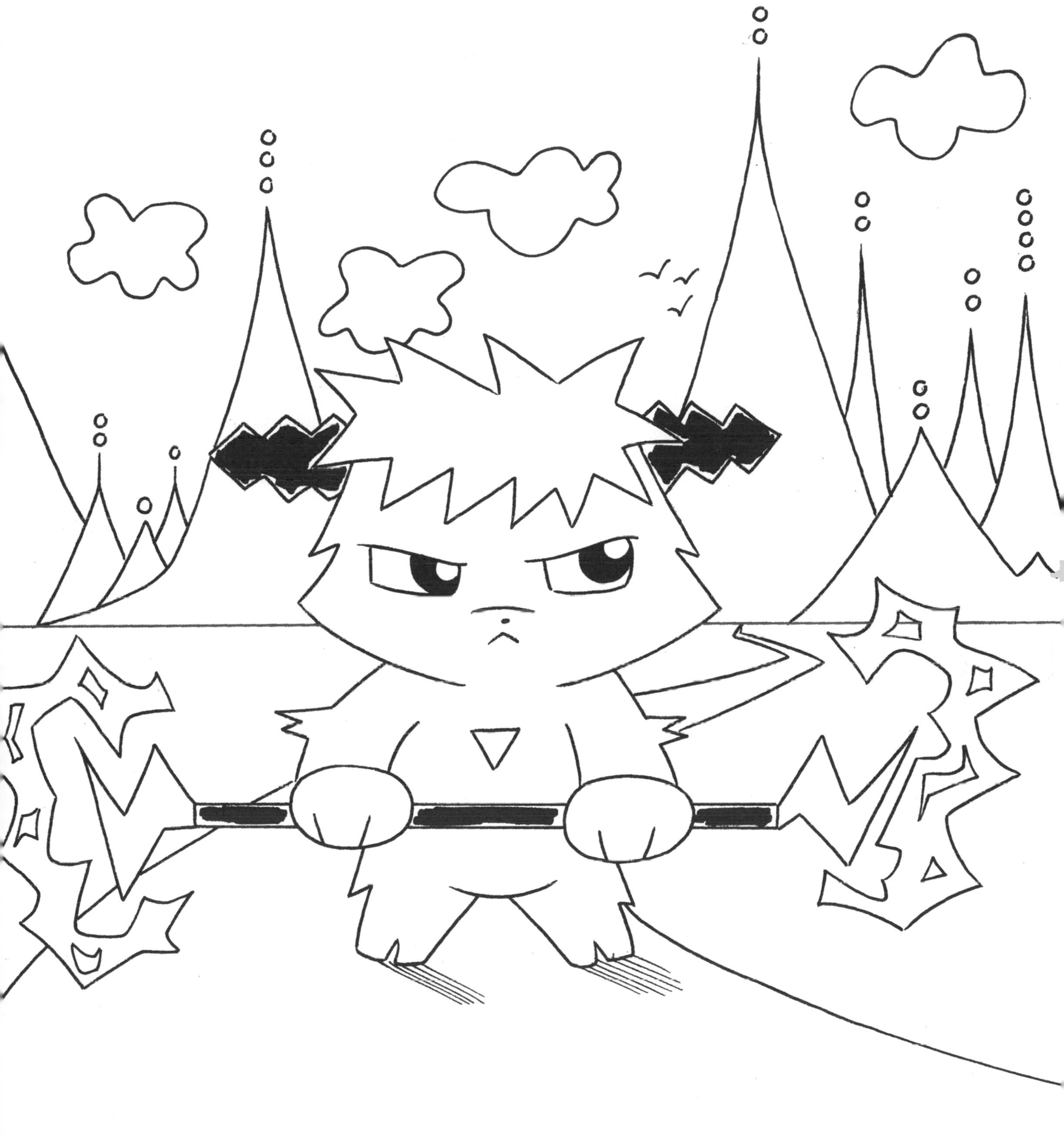

CHIMVEEK

1

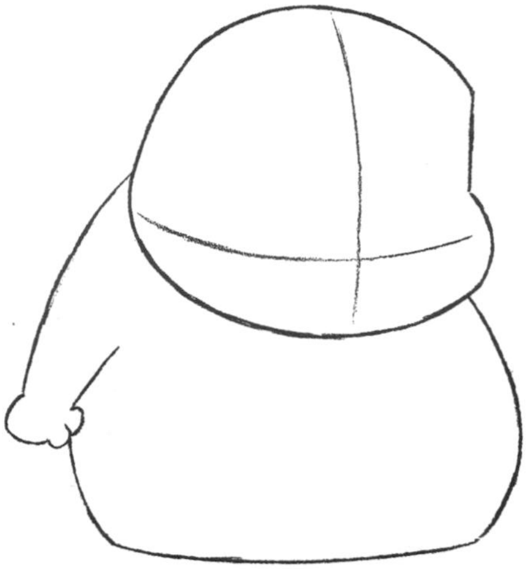

2

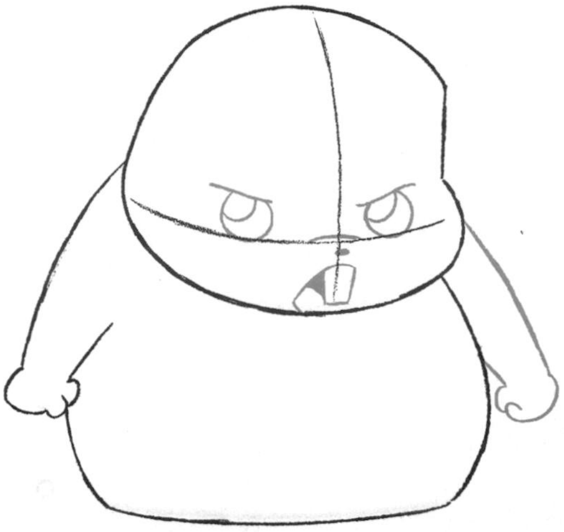

3

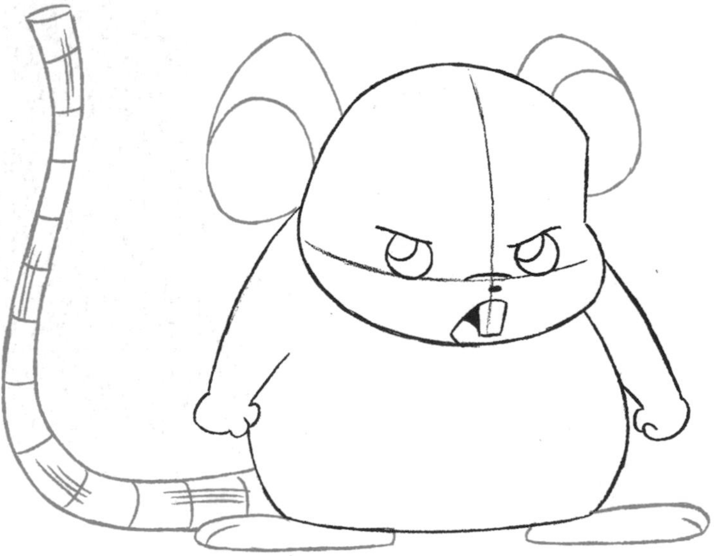

4

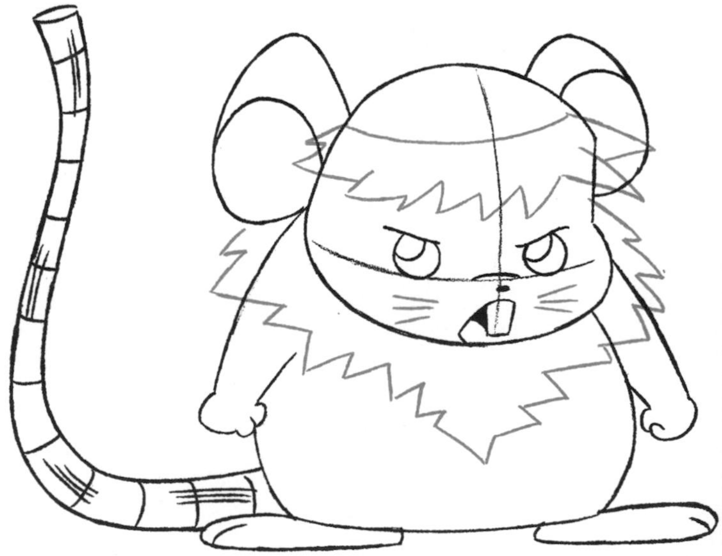

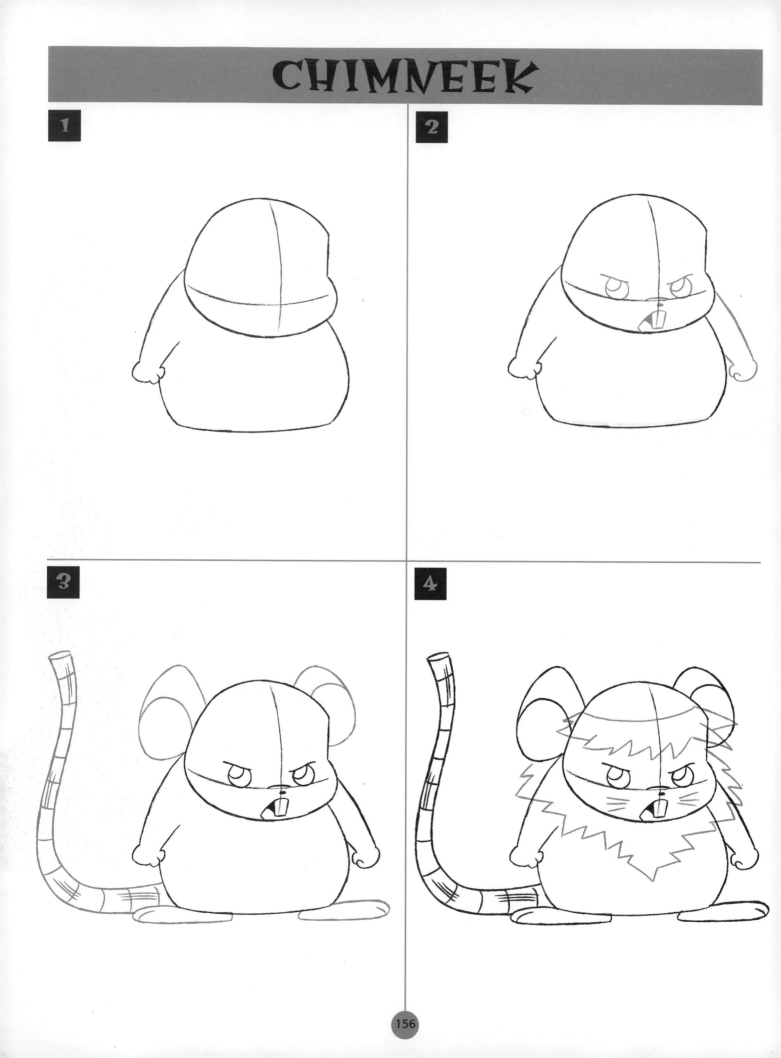

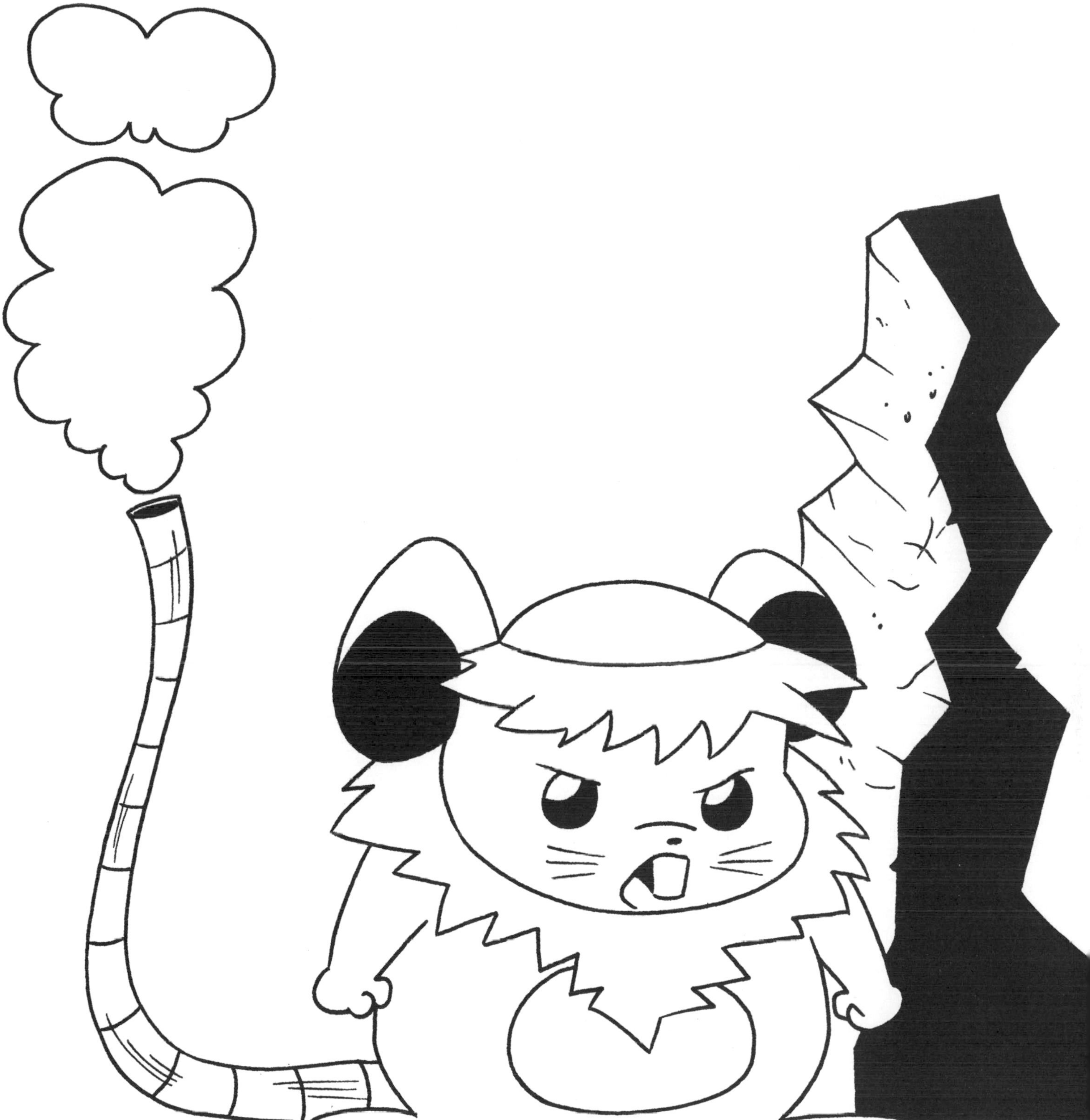

COOBOO

1

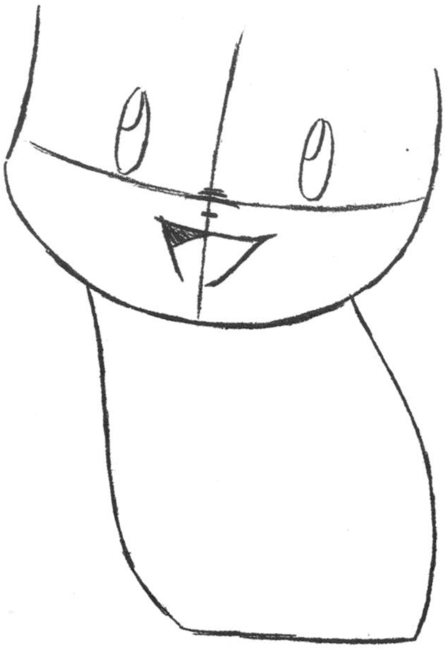

2

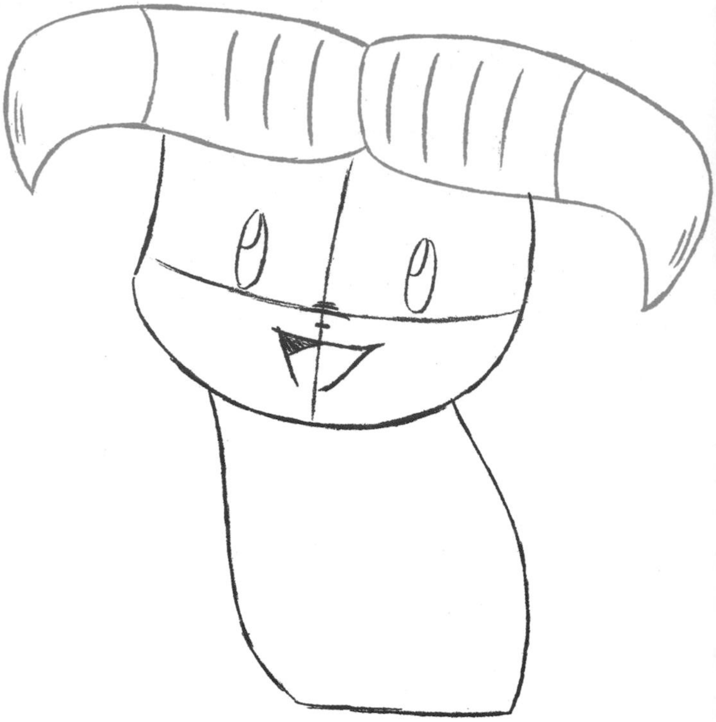

3

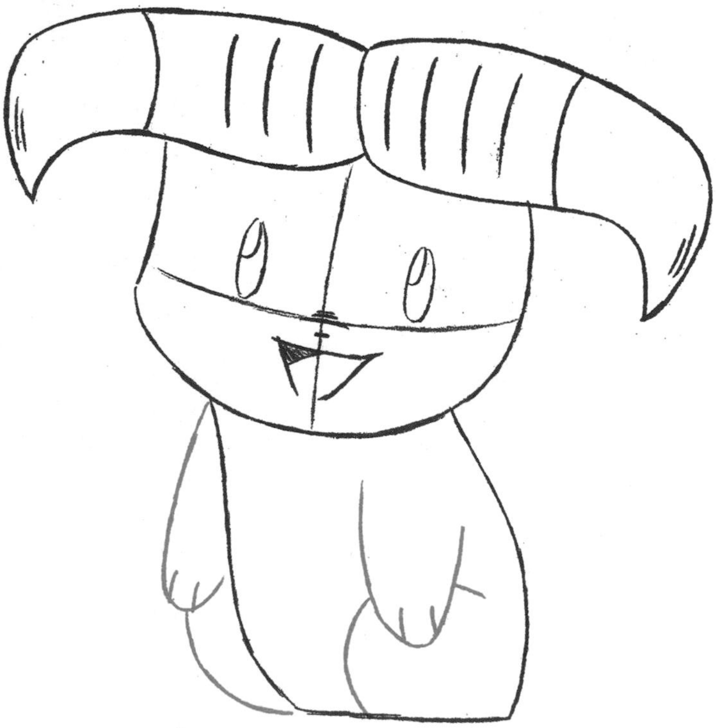

4

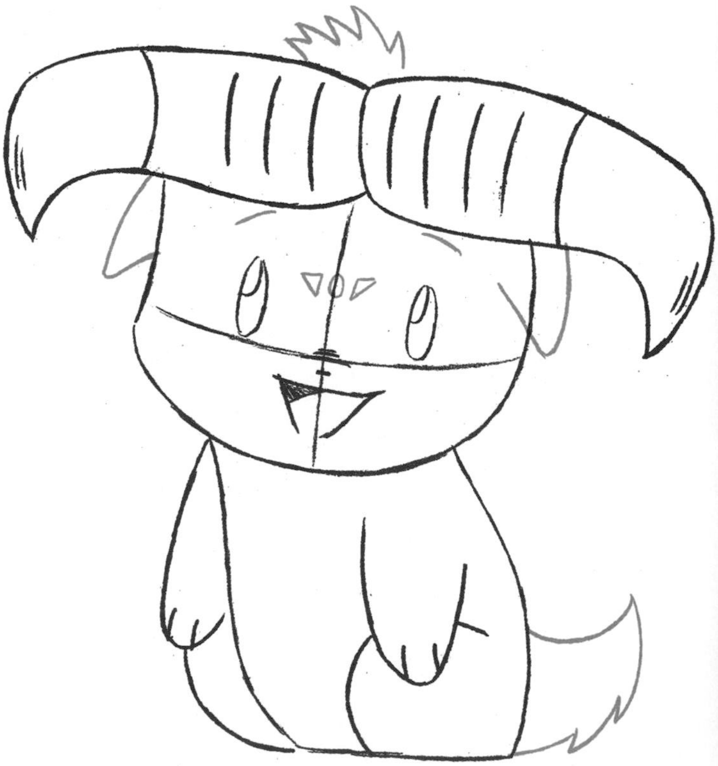

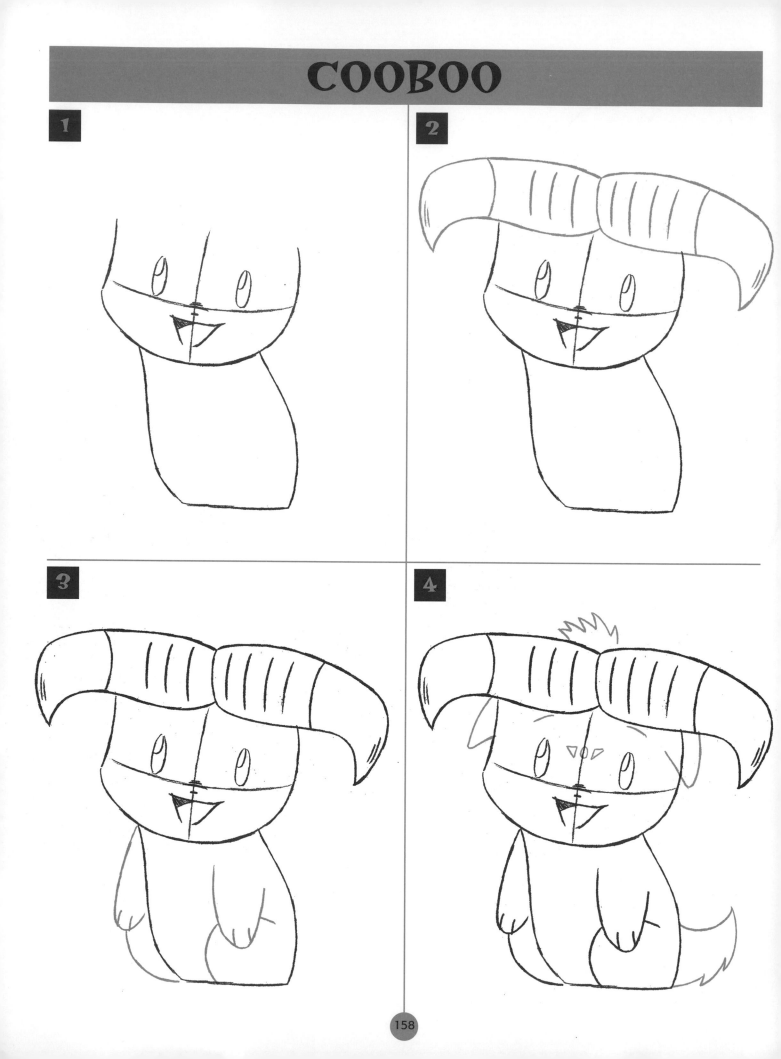

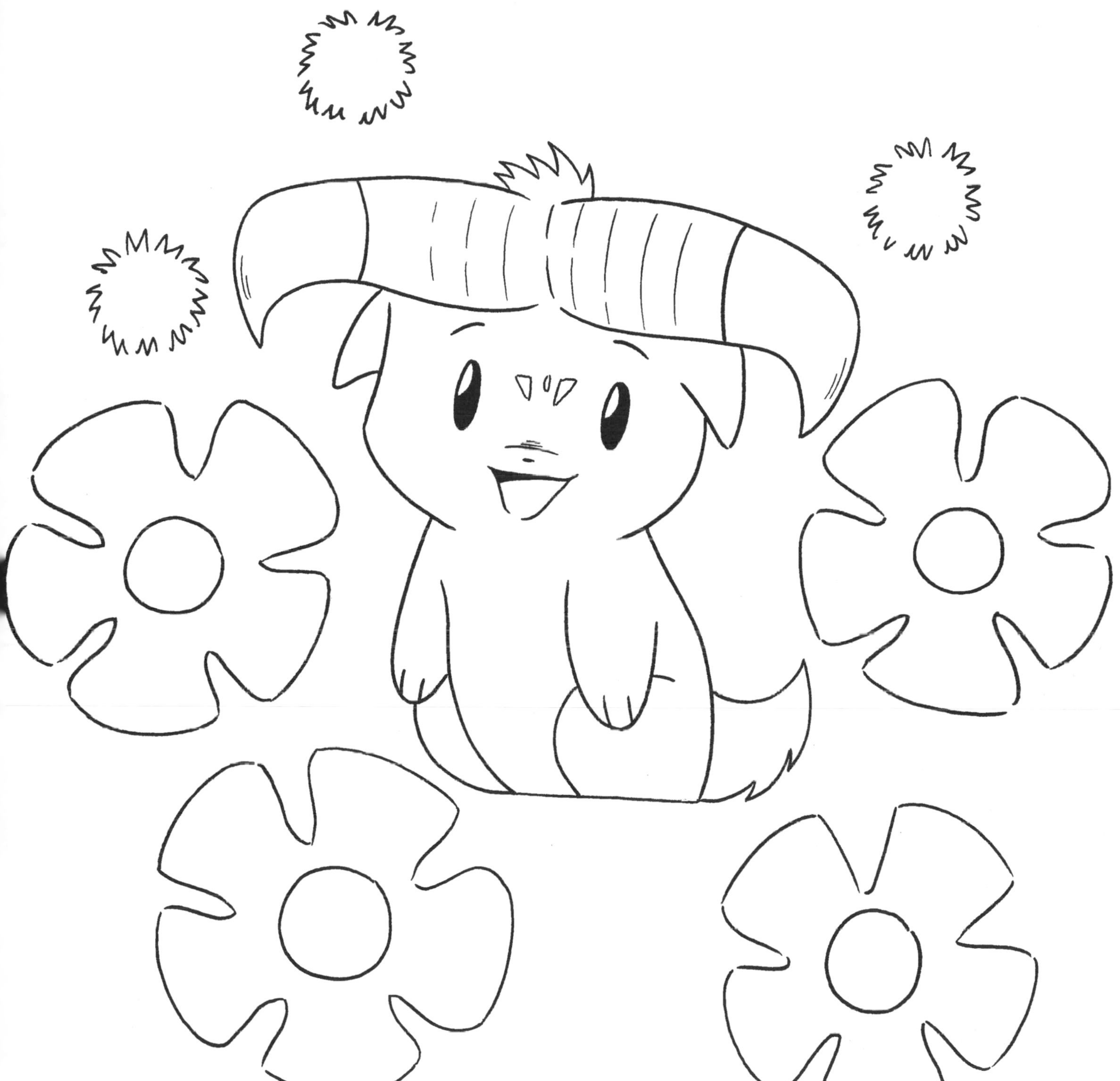

VOLTOX

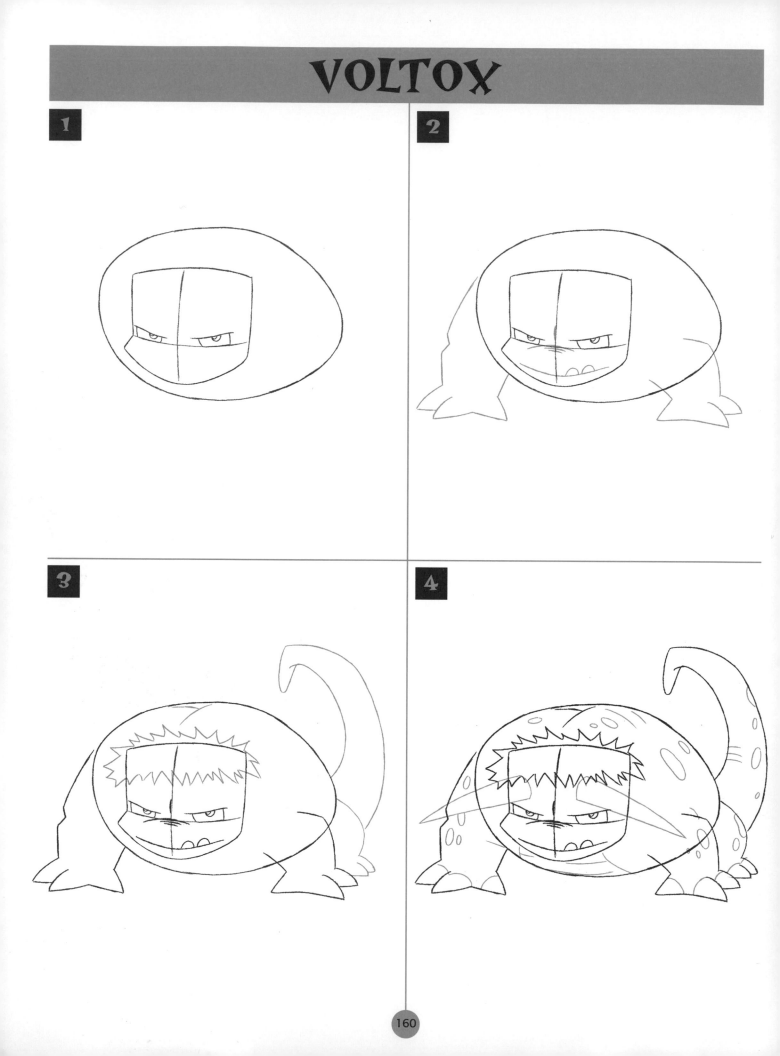

DEFENZAR

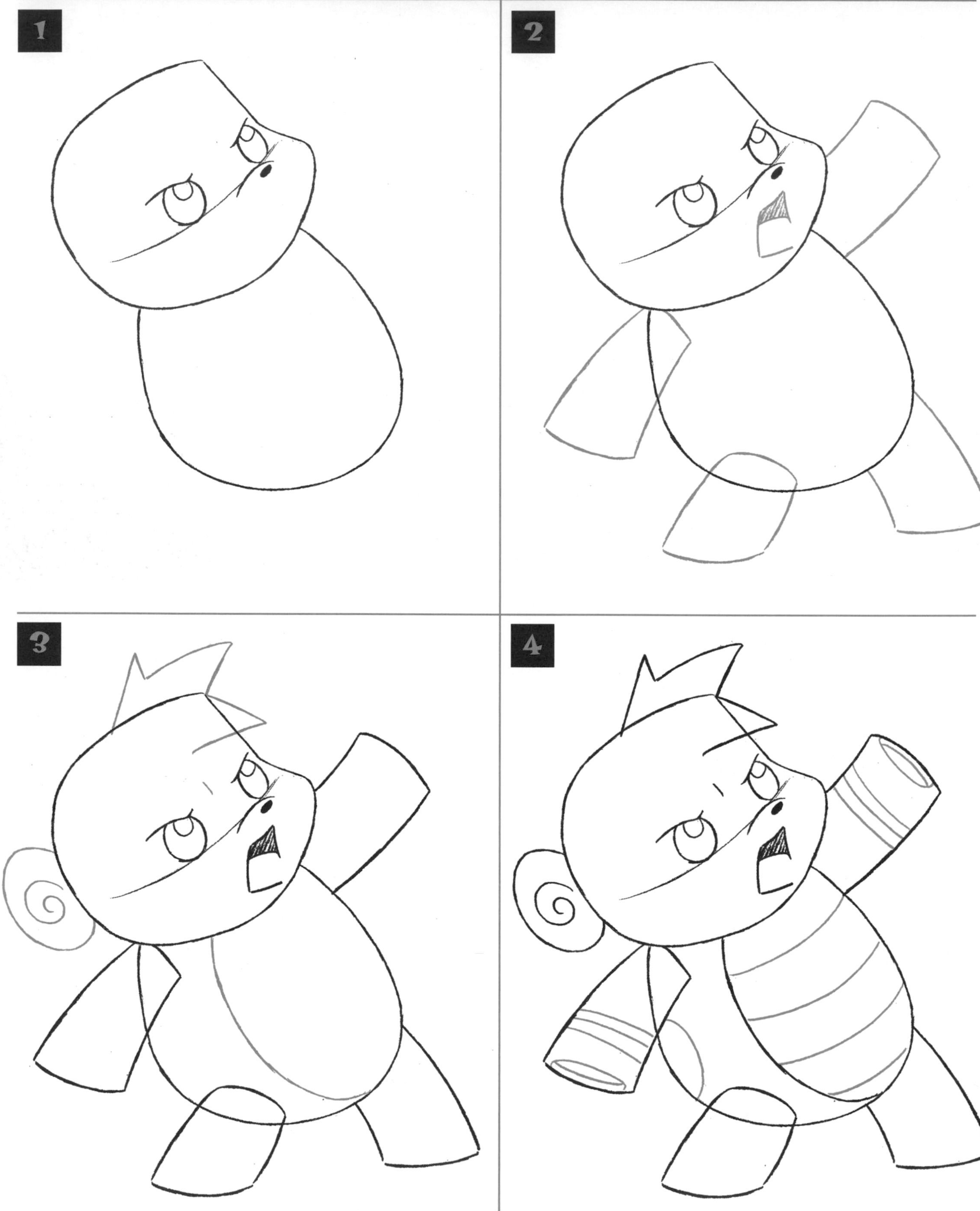
1
2
3
4

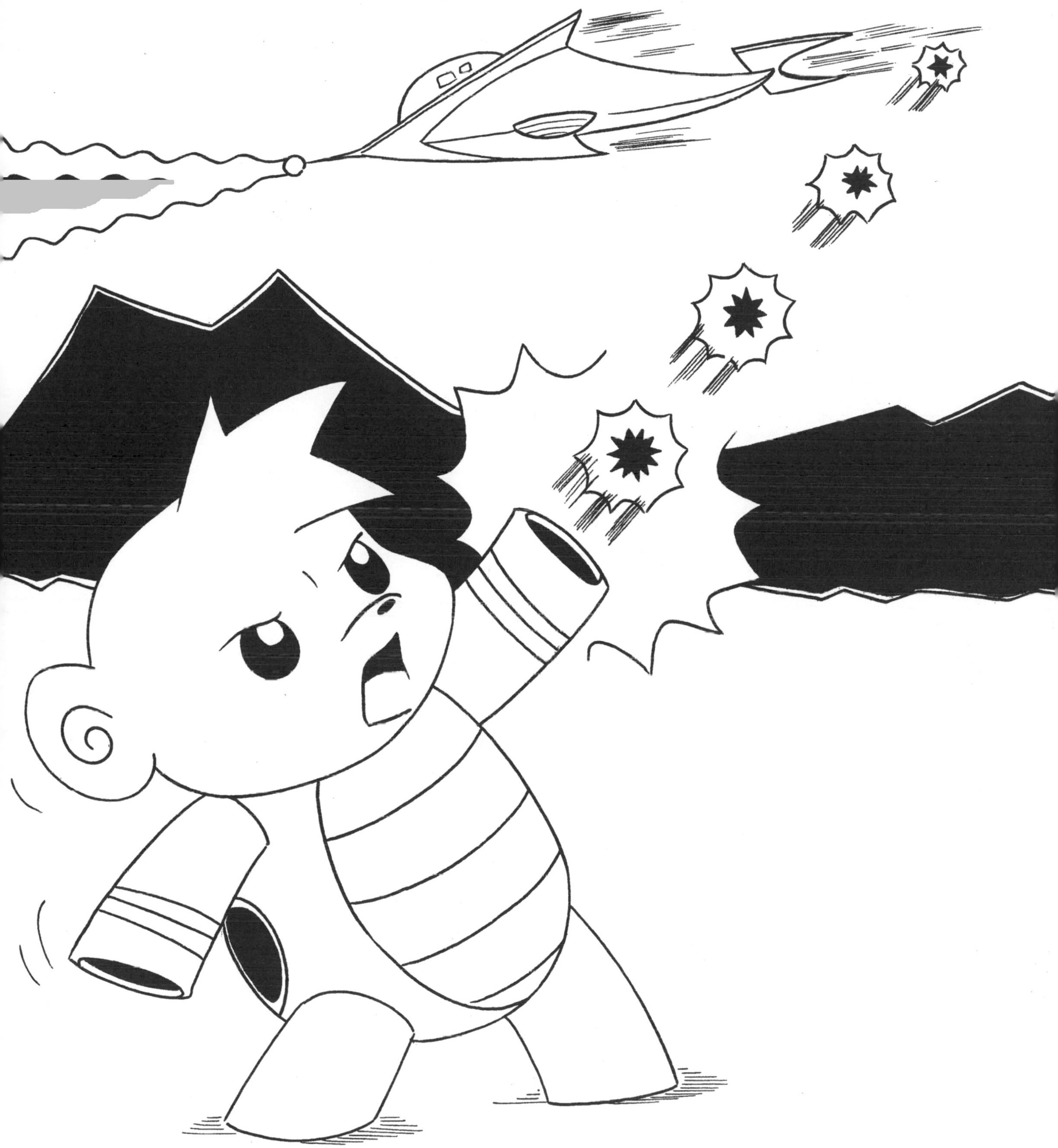

CHIPTAR

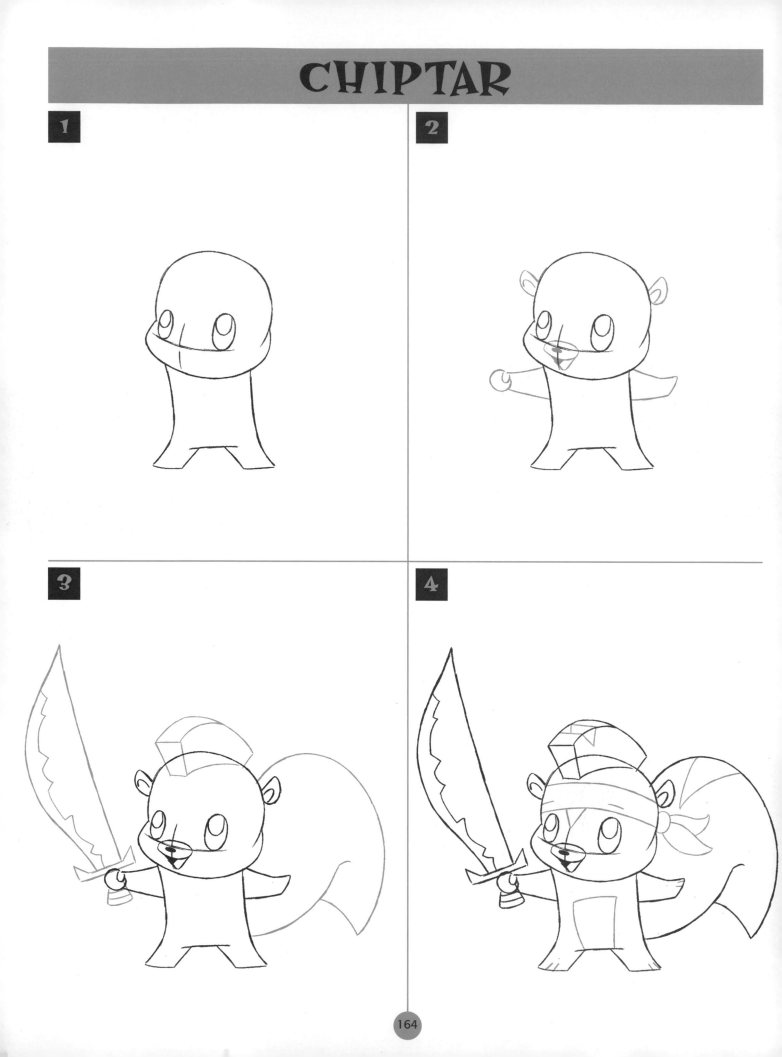

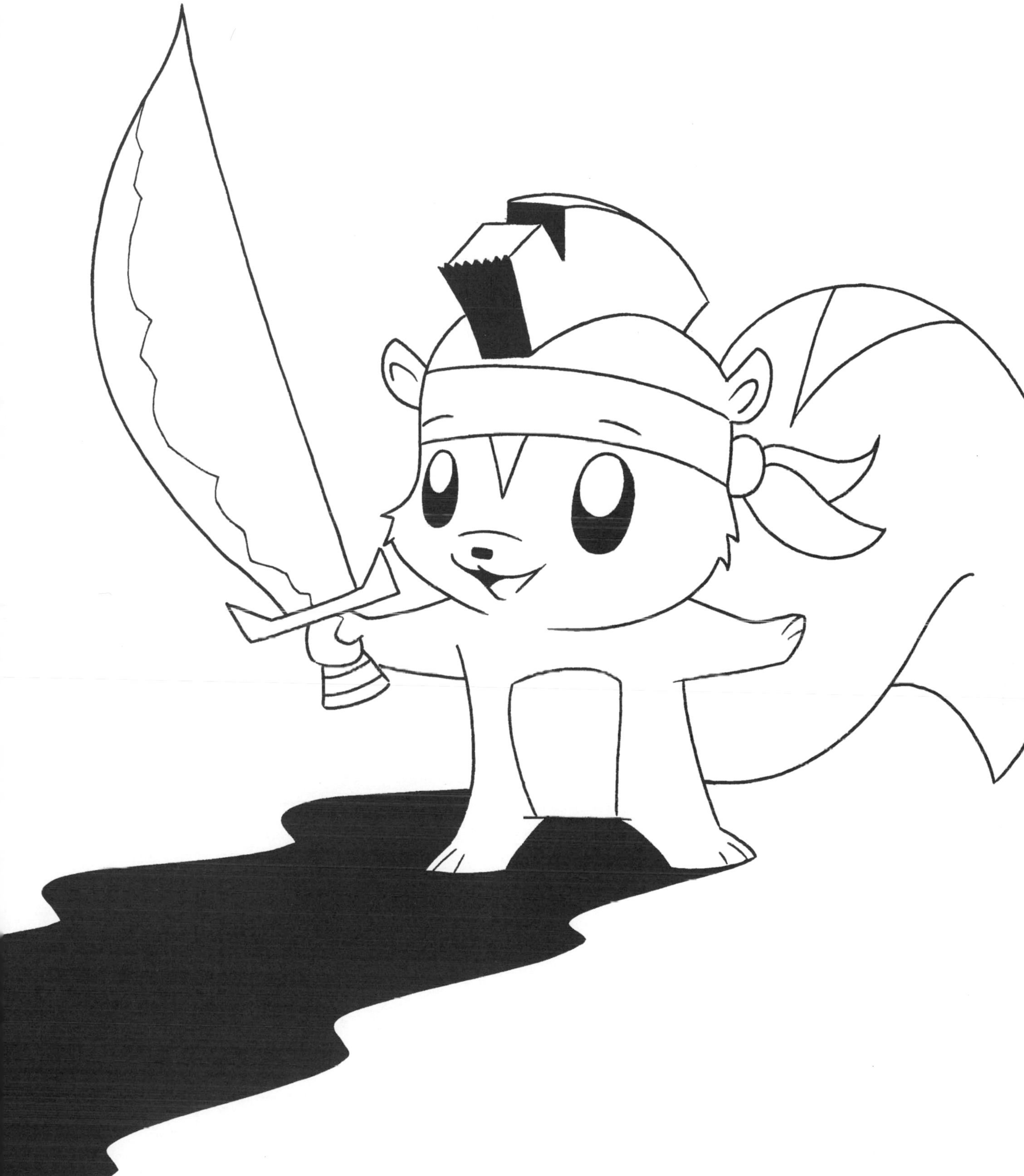

MEGASPIKE

1

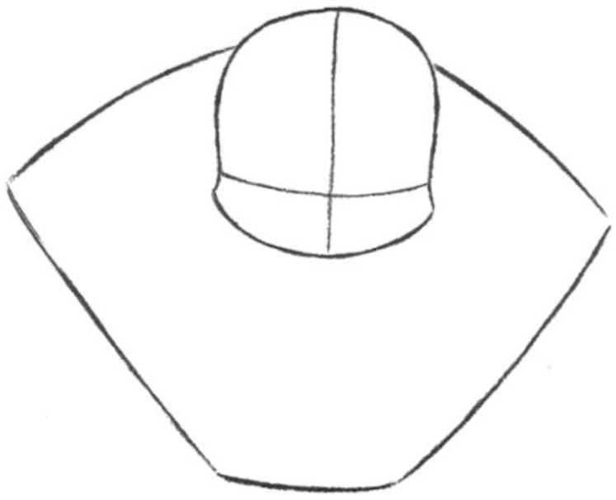

2

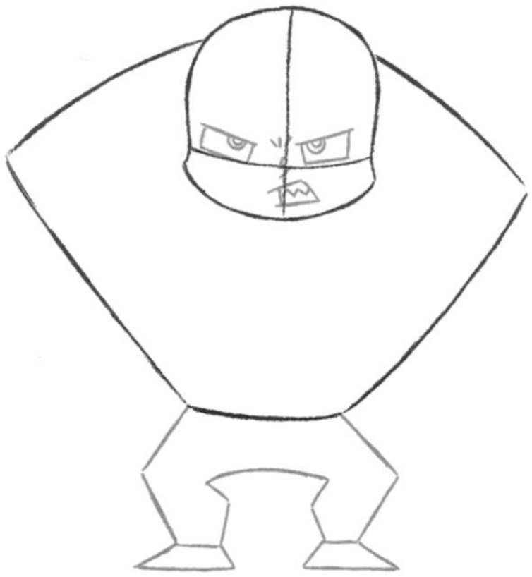

3

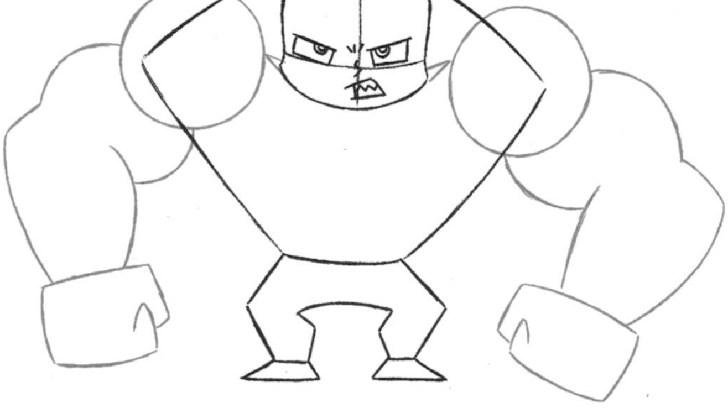

4

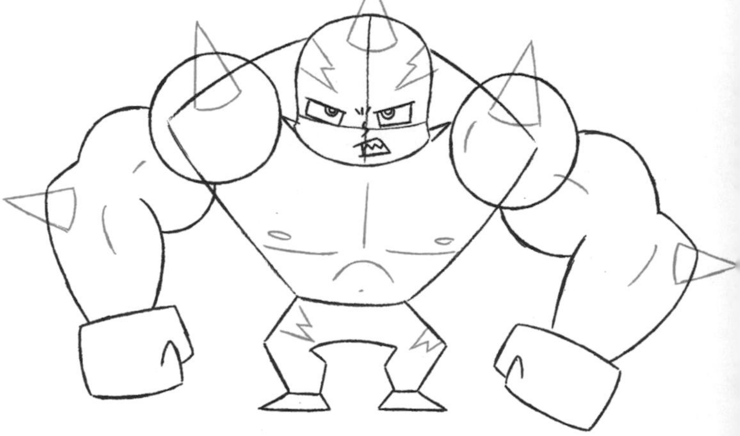

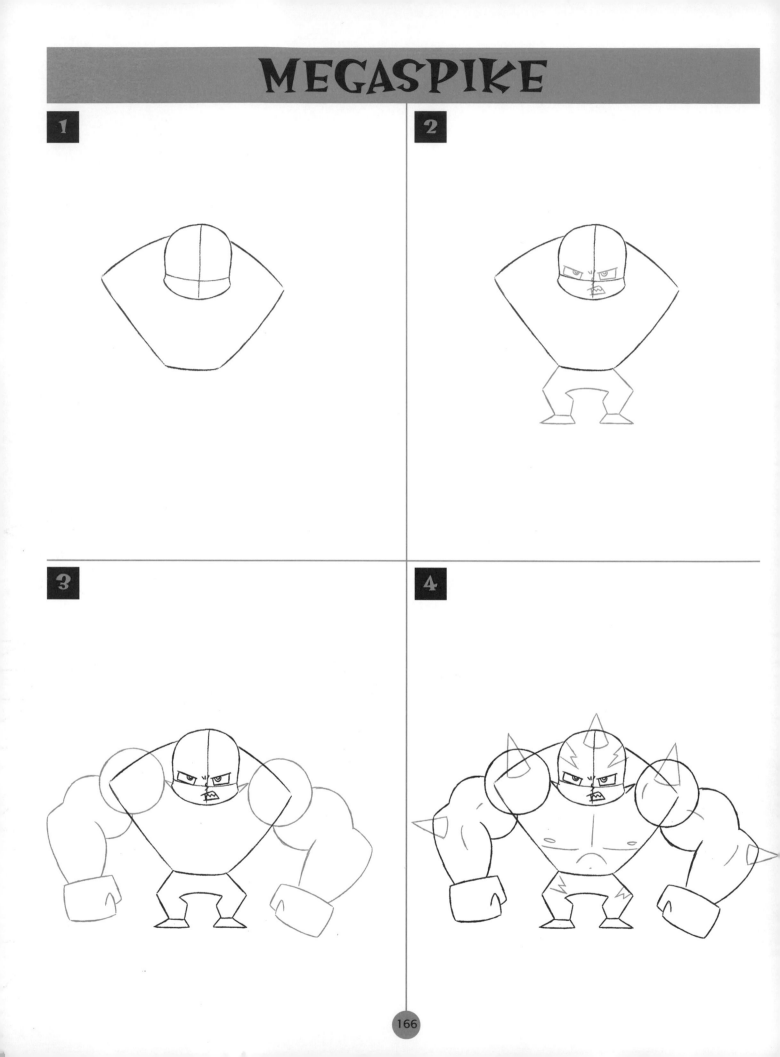

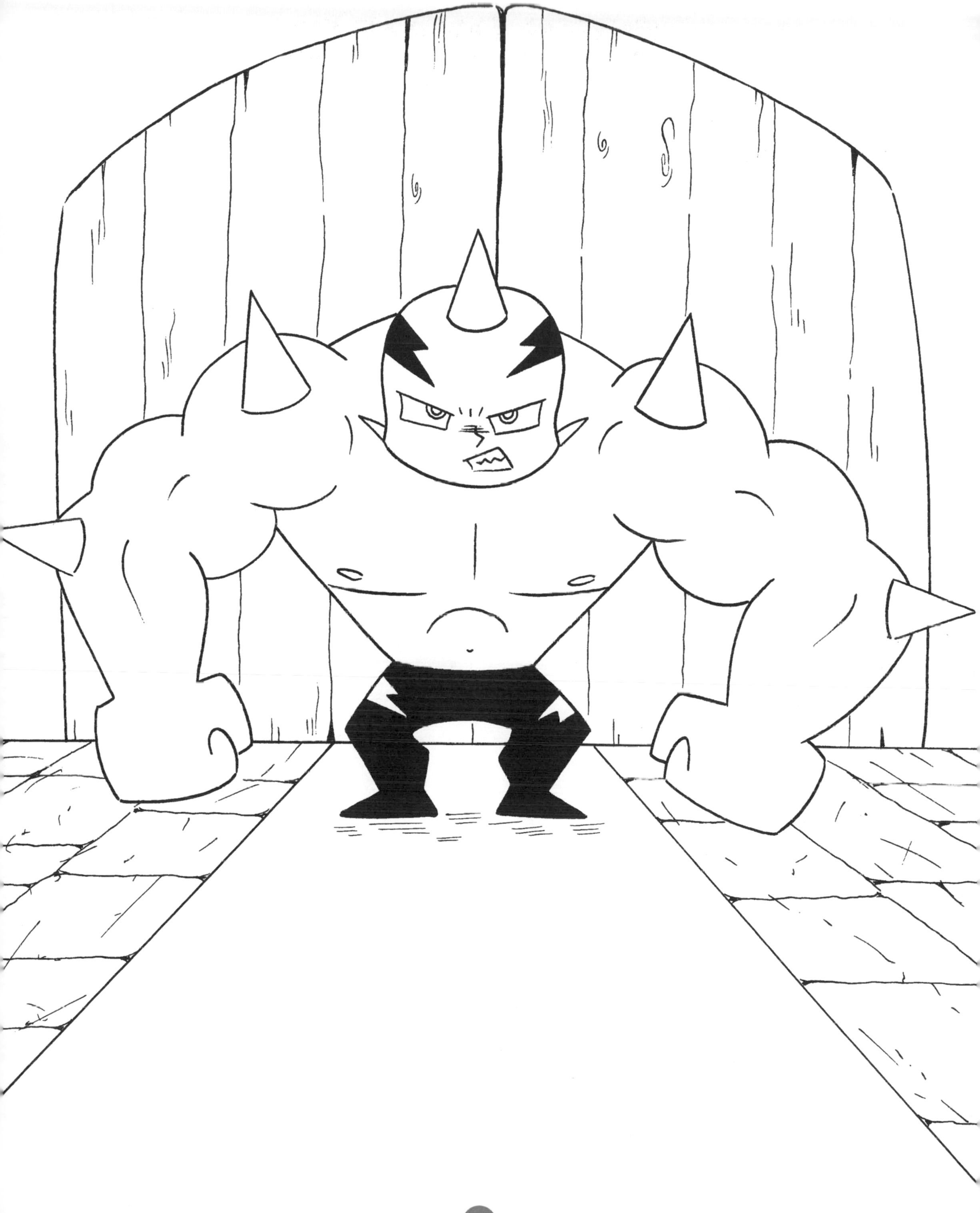

STOMPZILLA

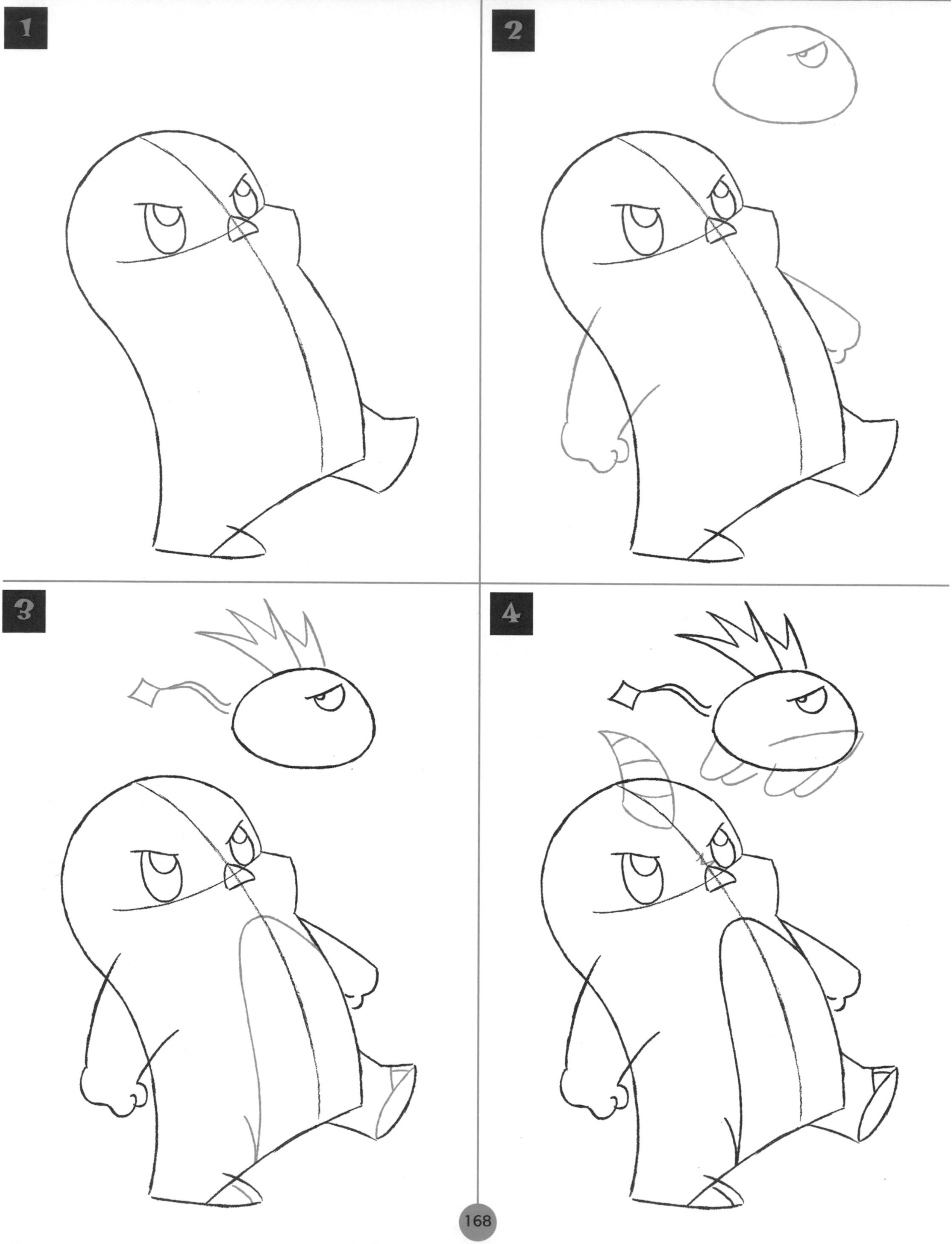
1
2
3
4

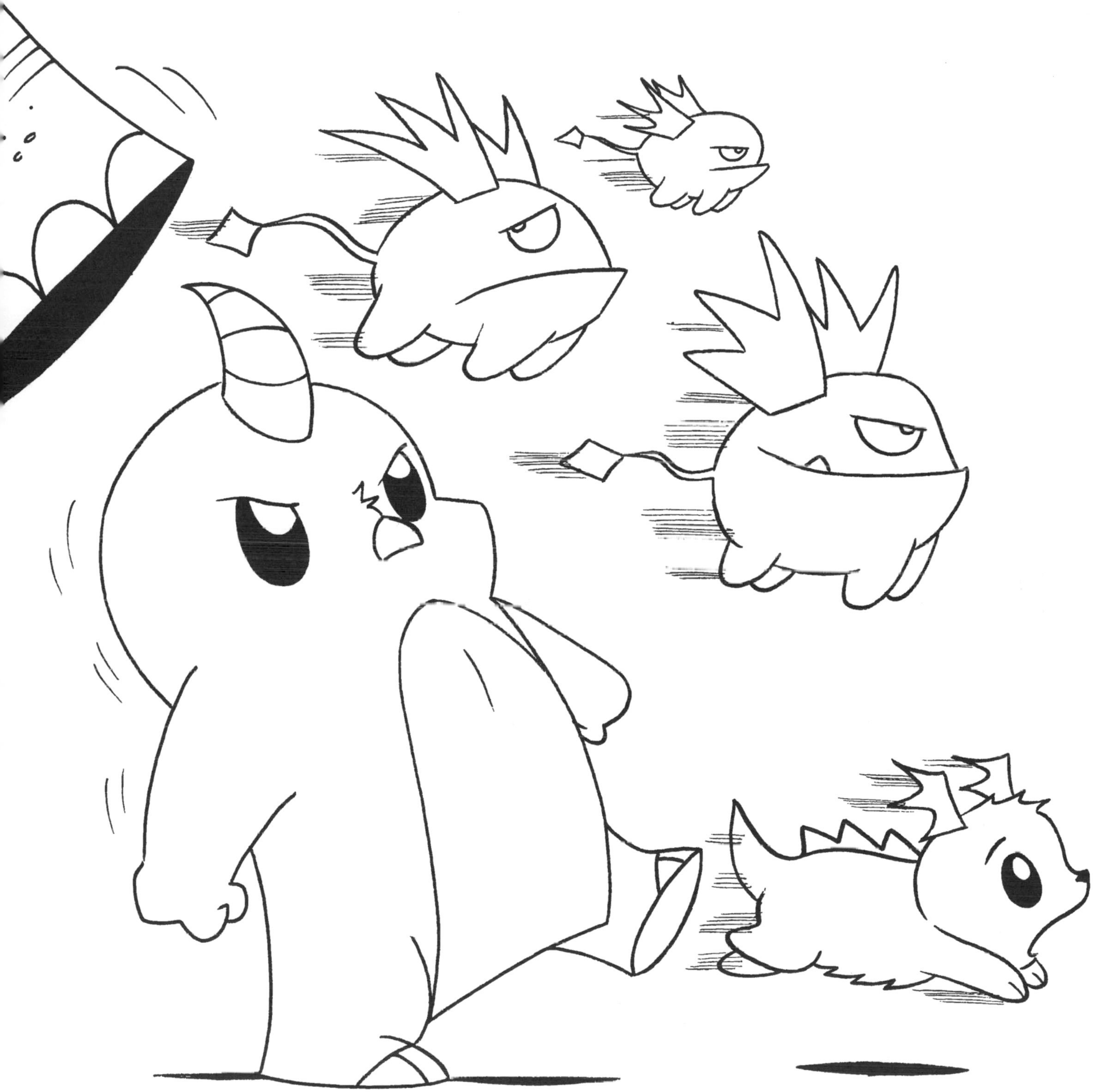

ZIGZAGGER

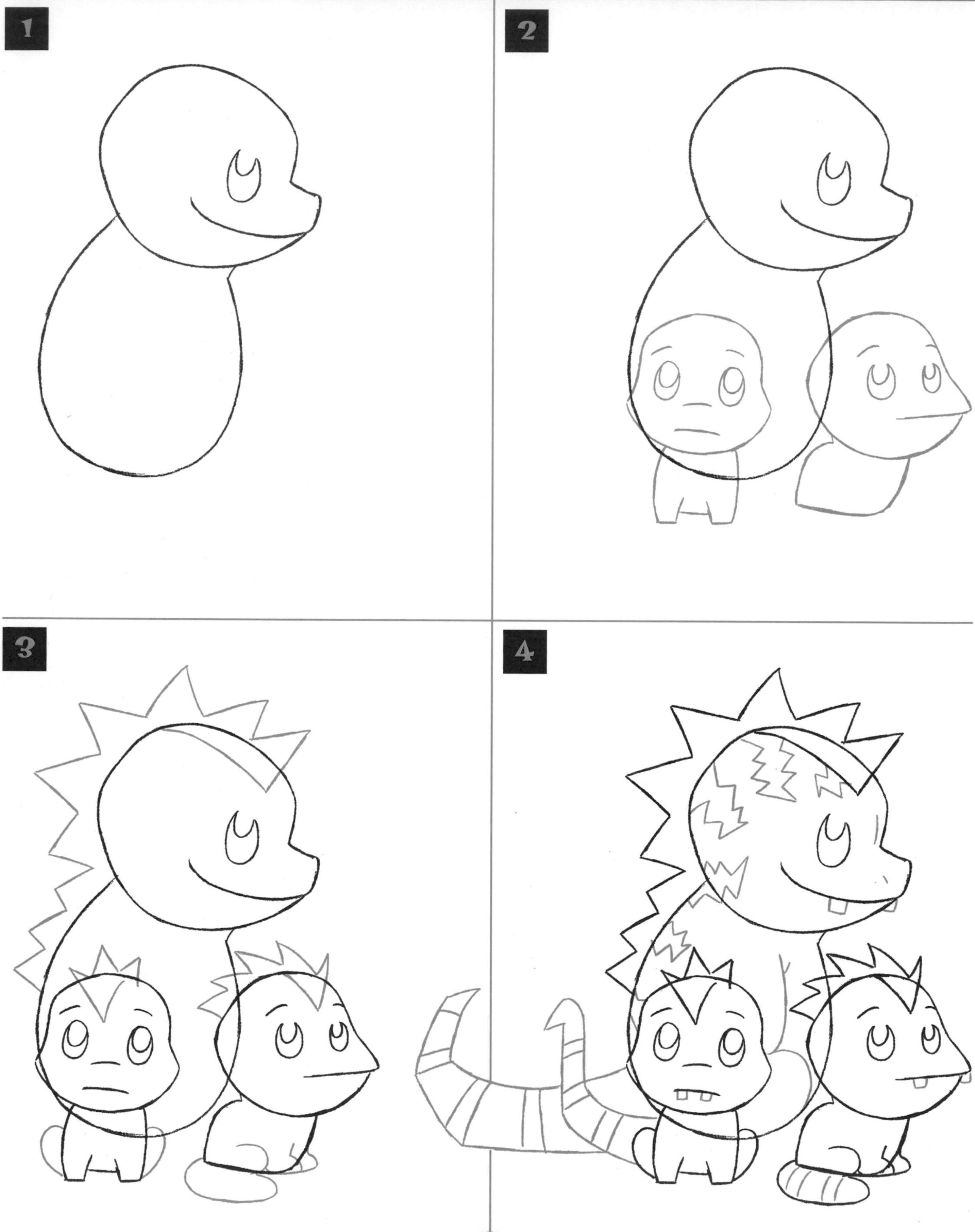
1
2
3
4

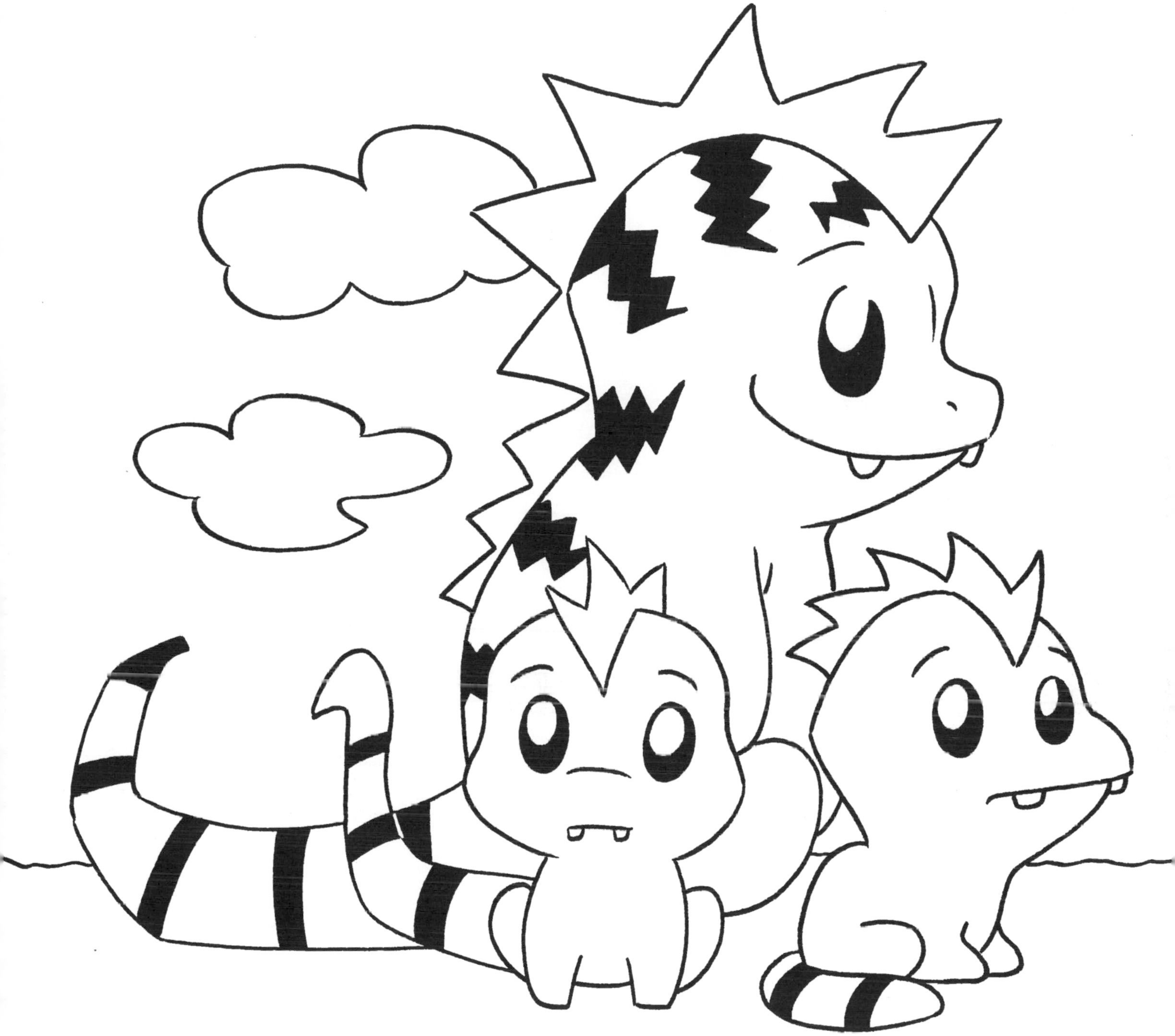

ZYRK

1

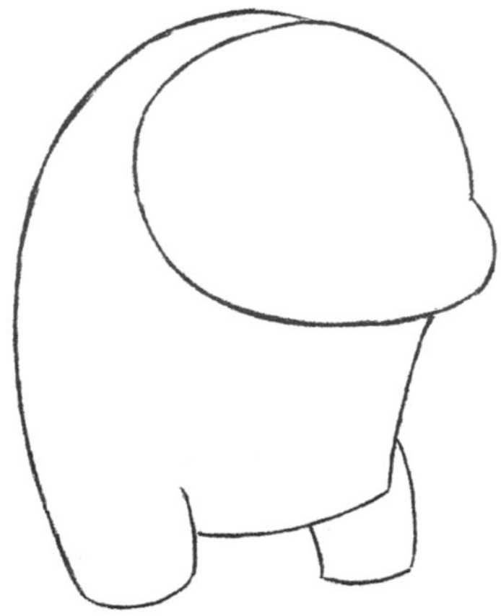

2

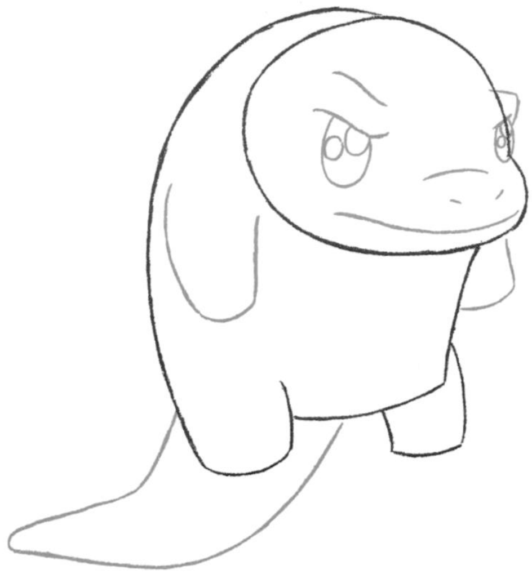

3

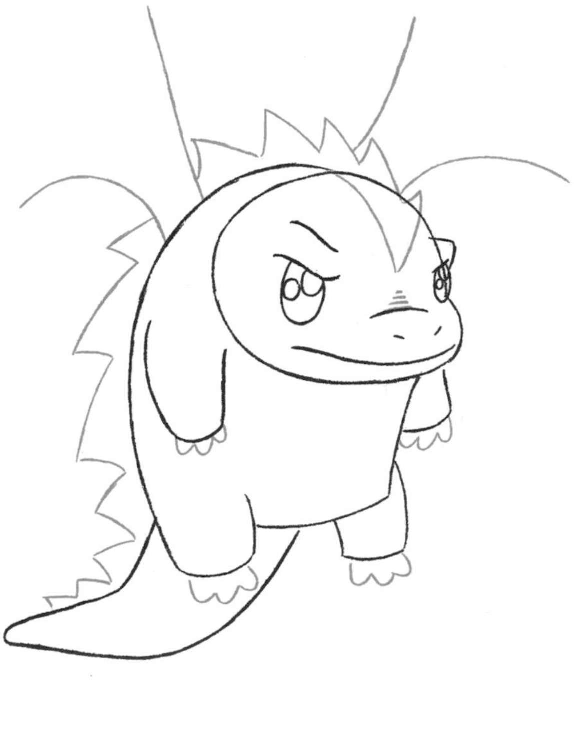

4

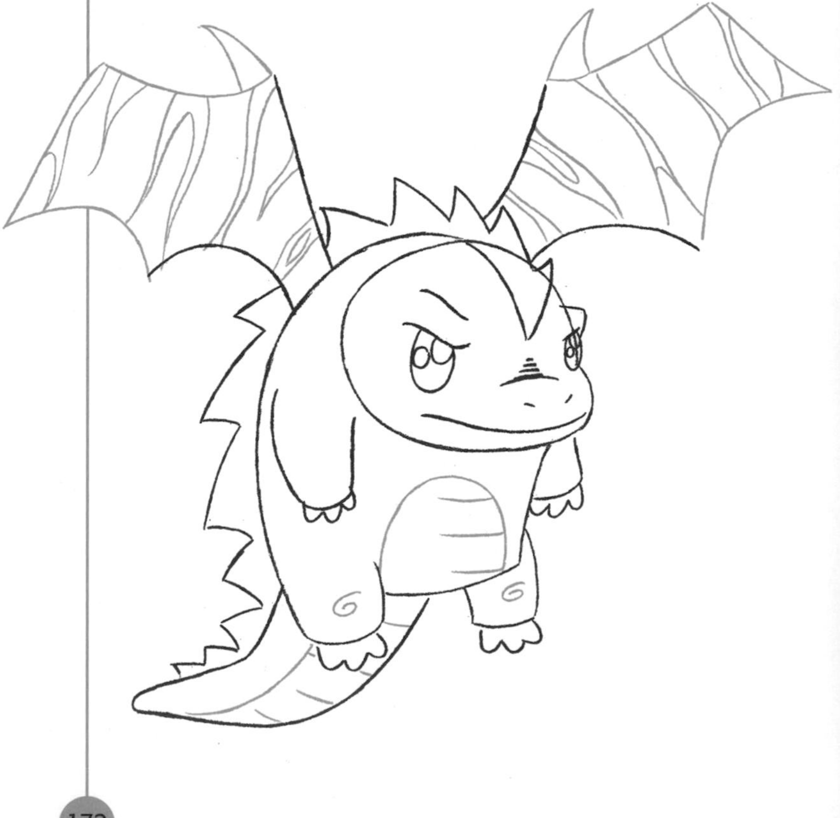

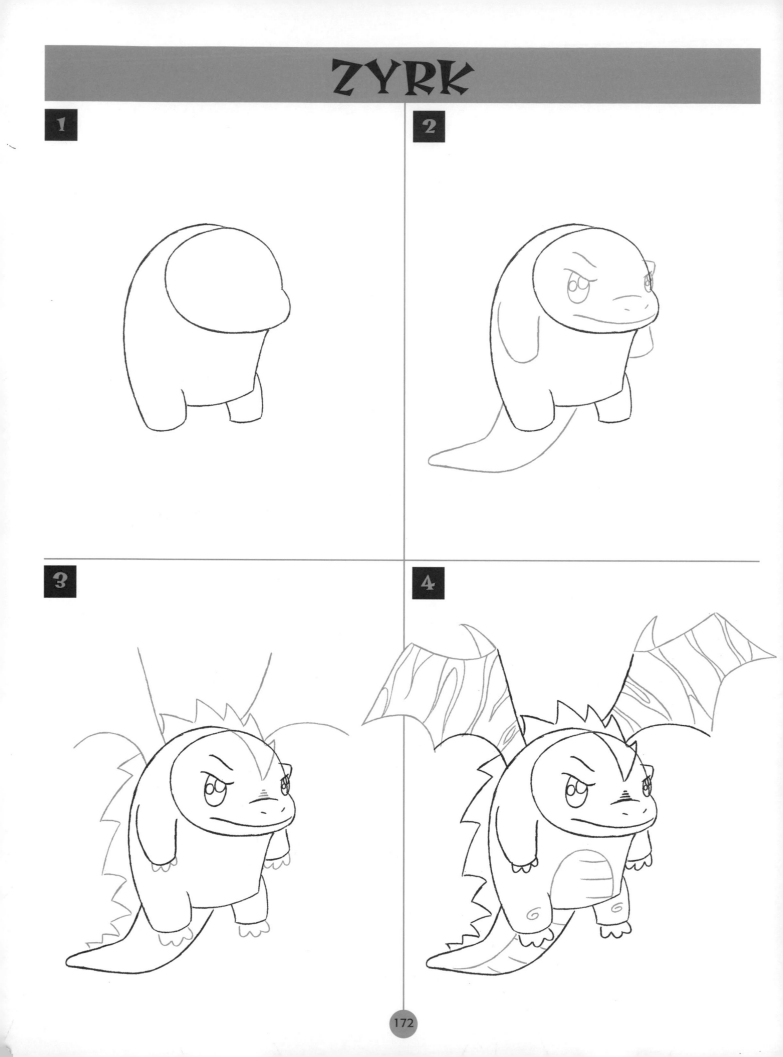

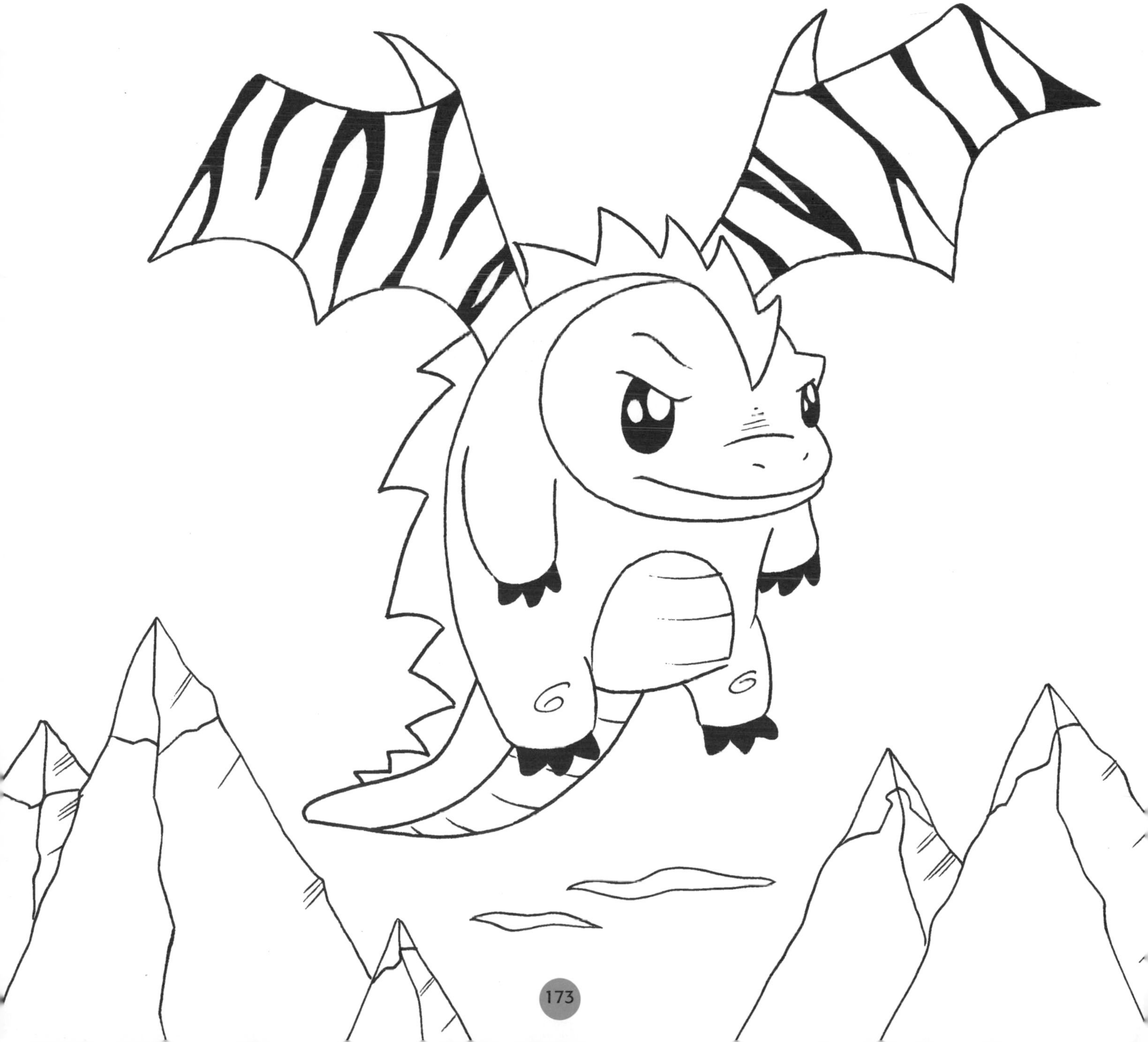

CRABULAR

1

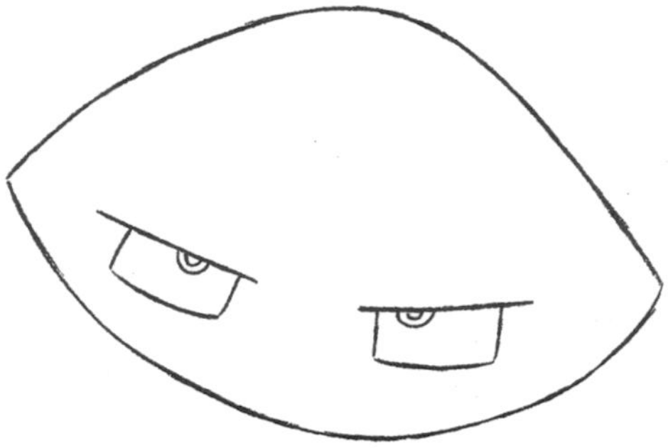

2

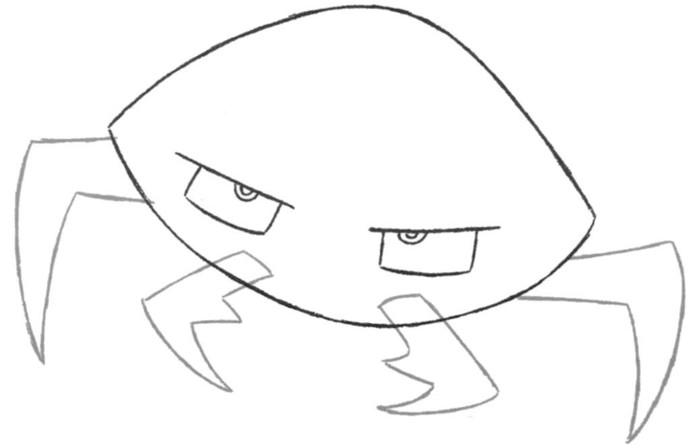

3

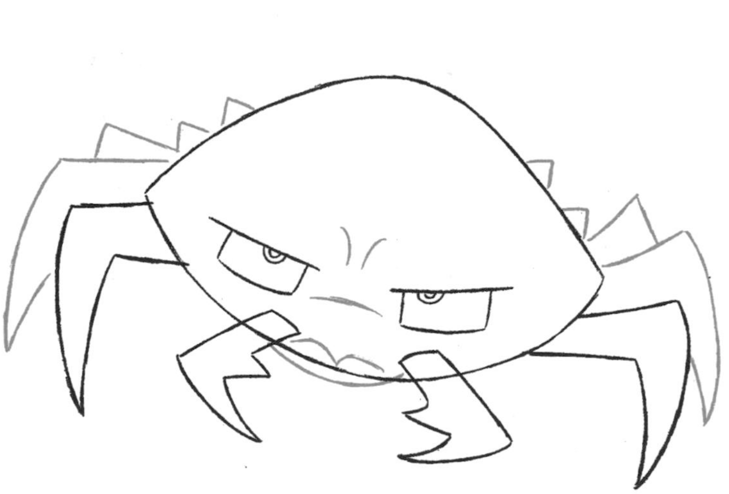

4

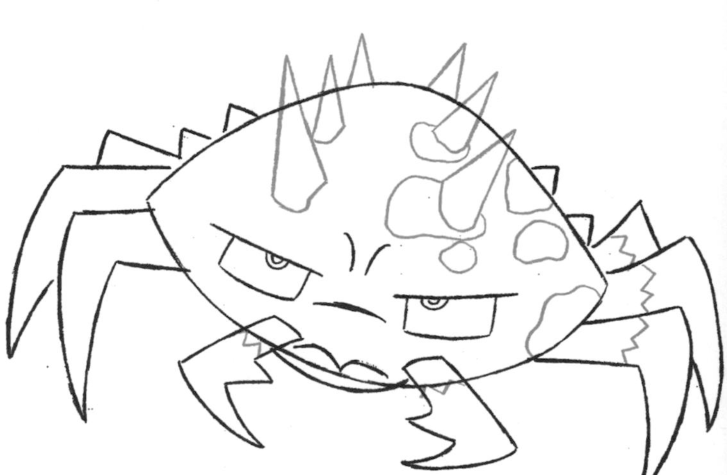

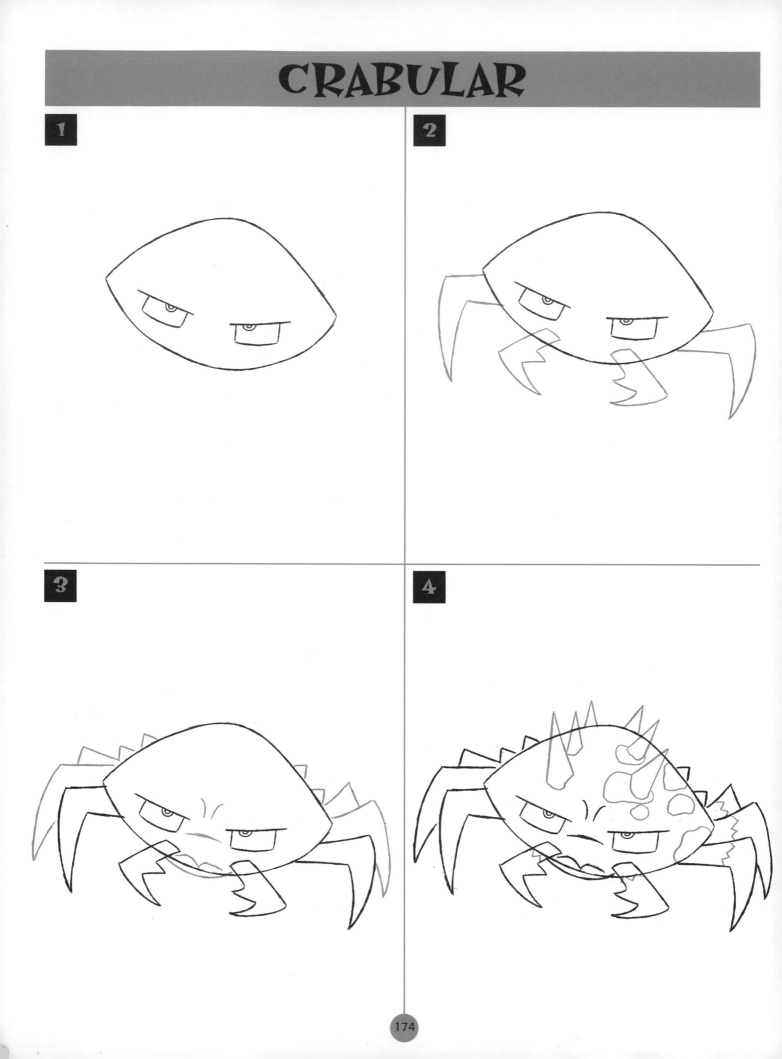

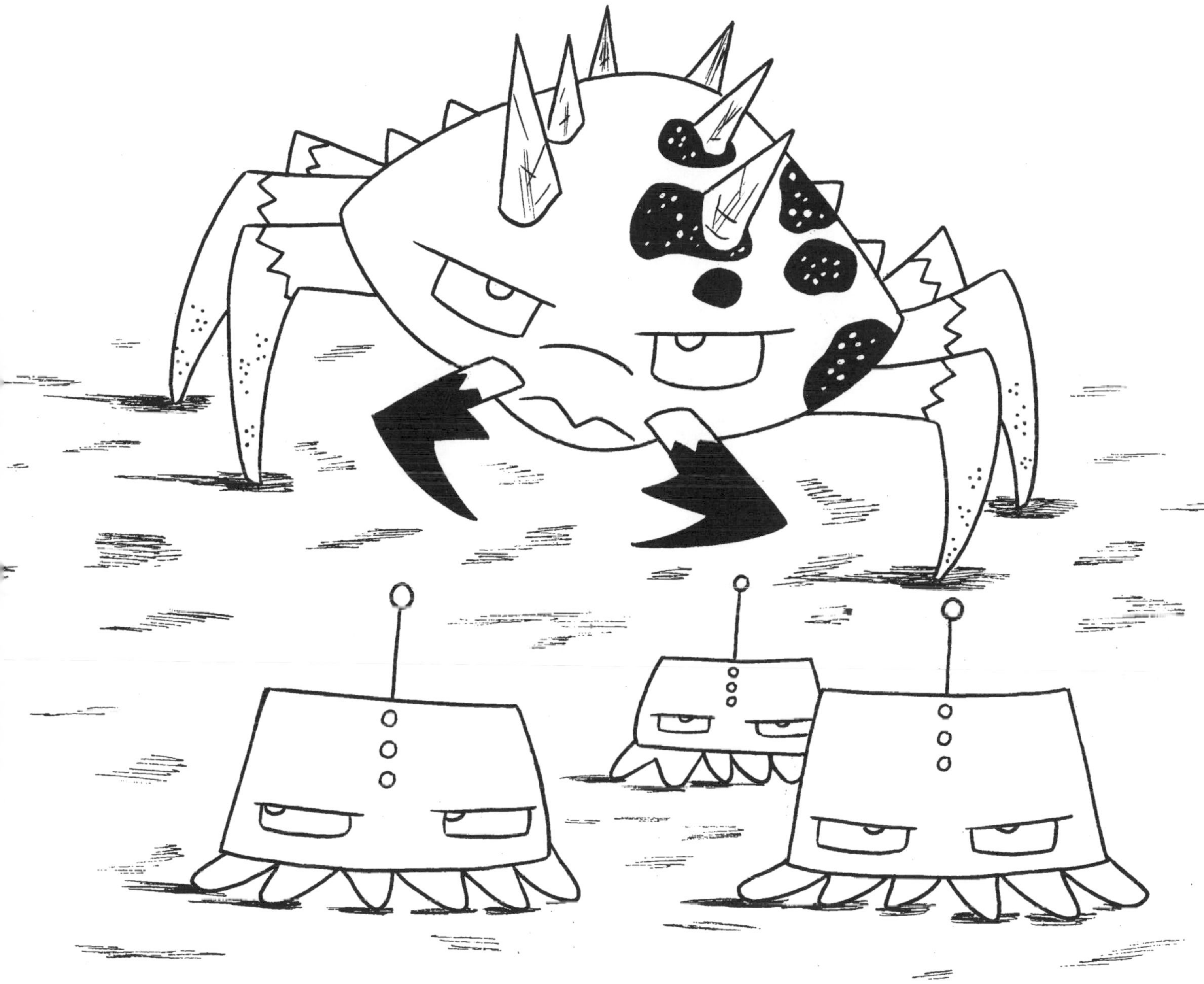

DOLPHNEENA

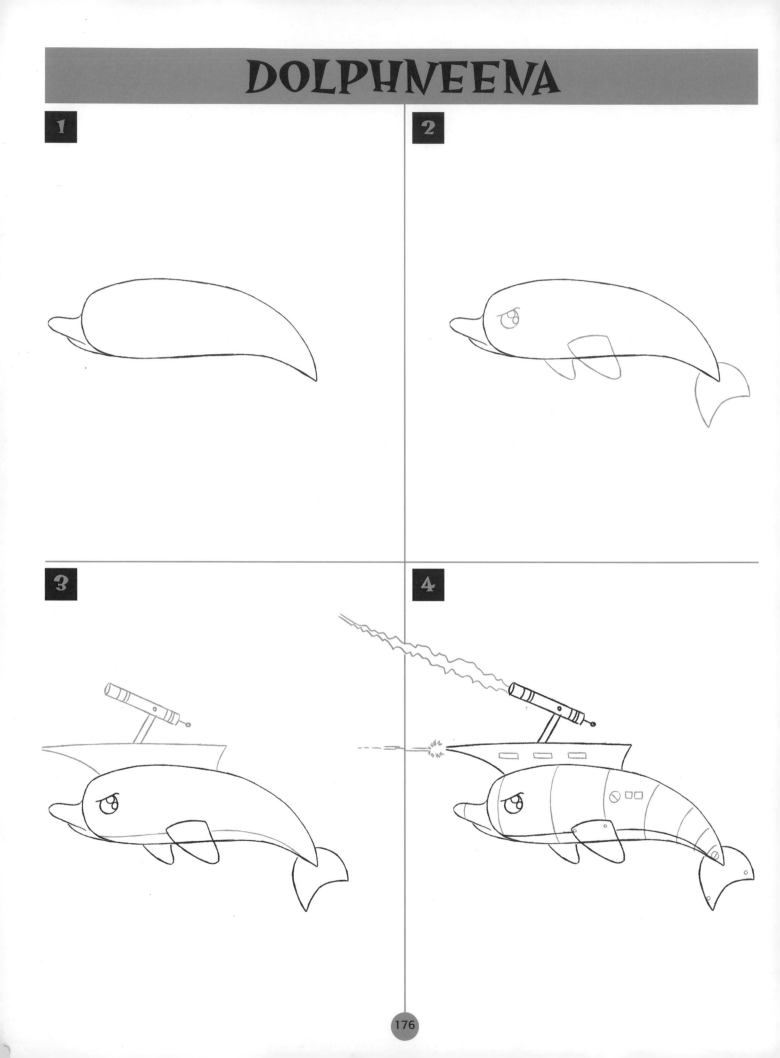

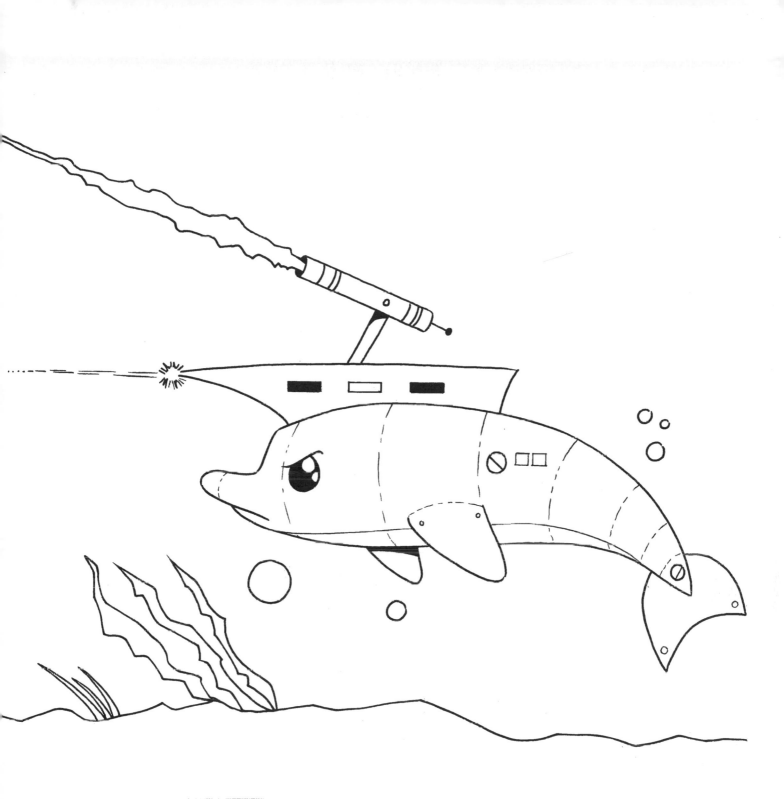

HI-FI

1

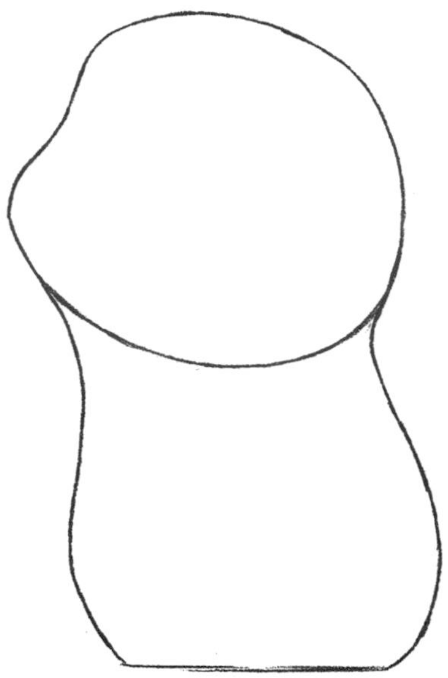

2

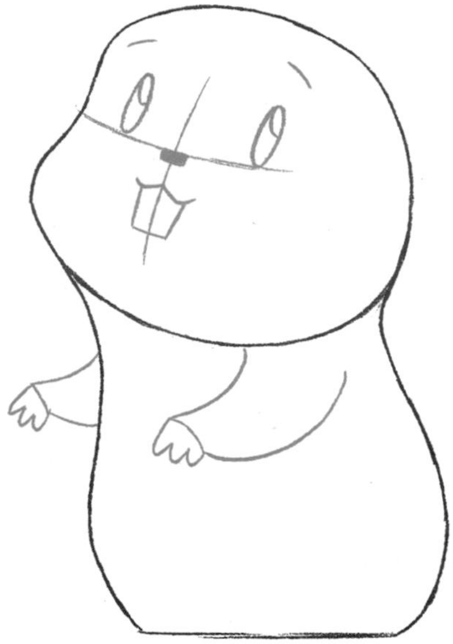

3

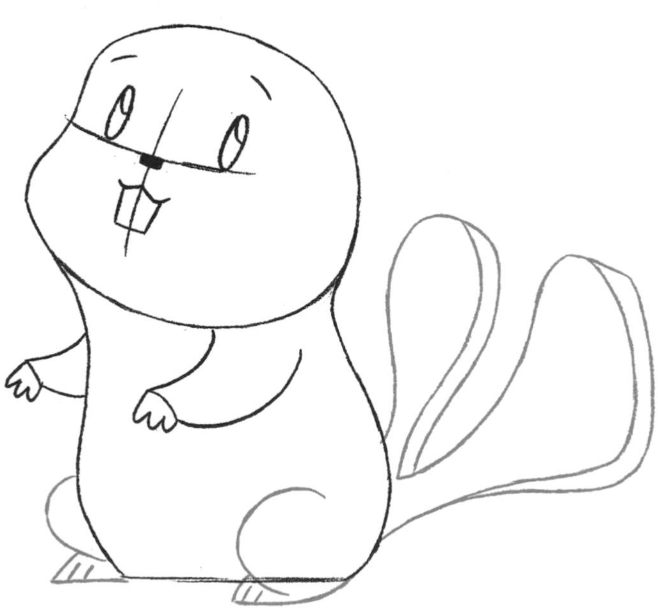

4

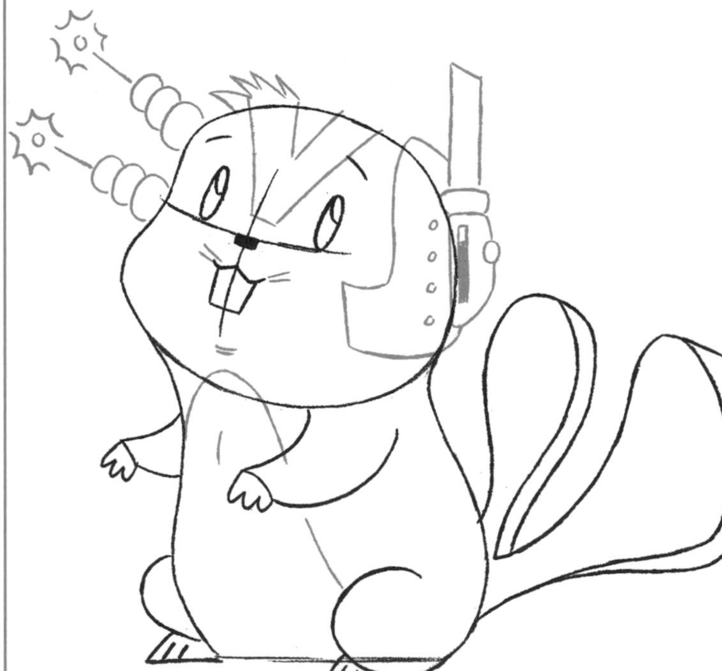

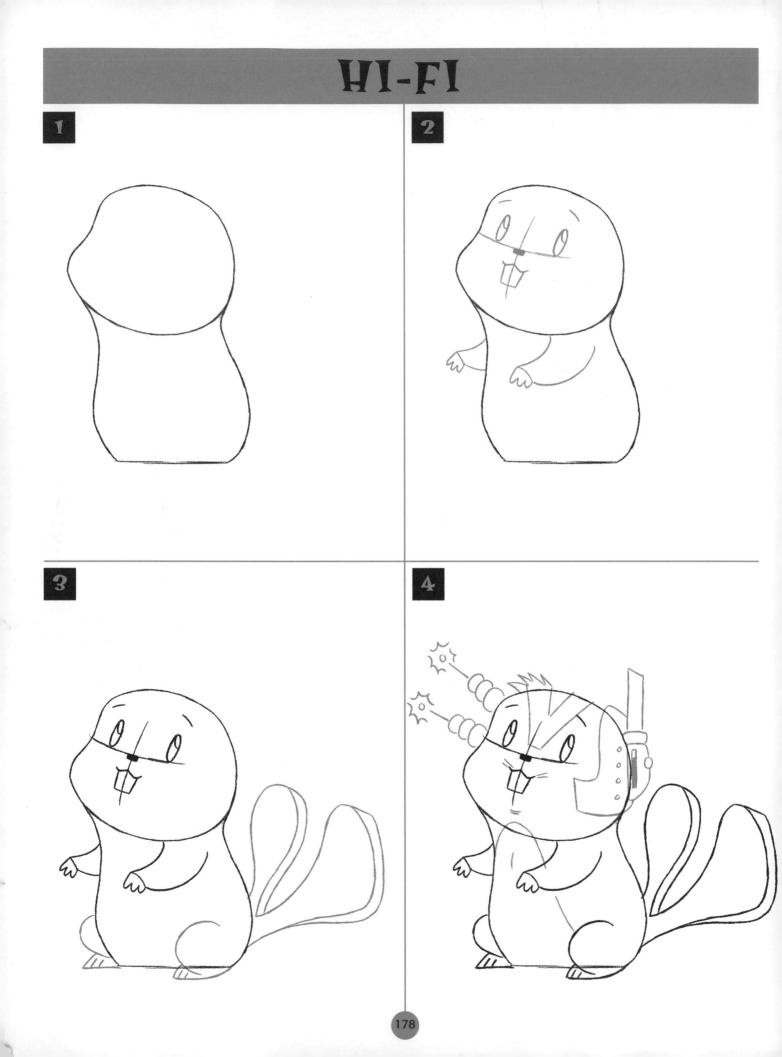

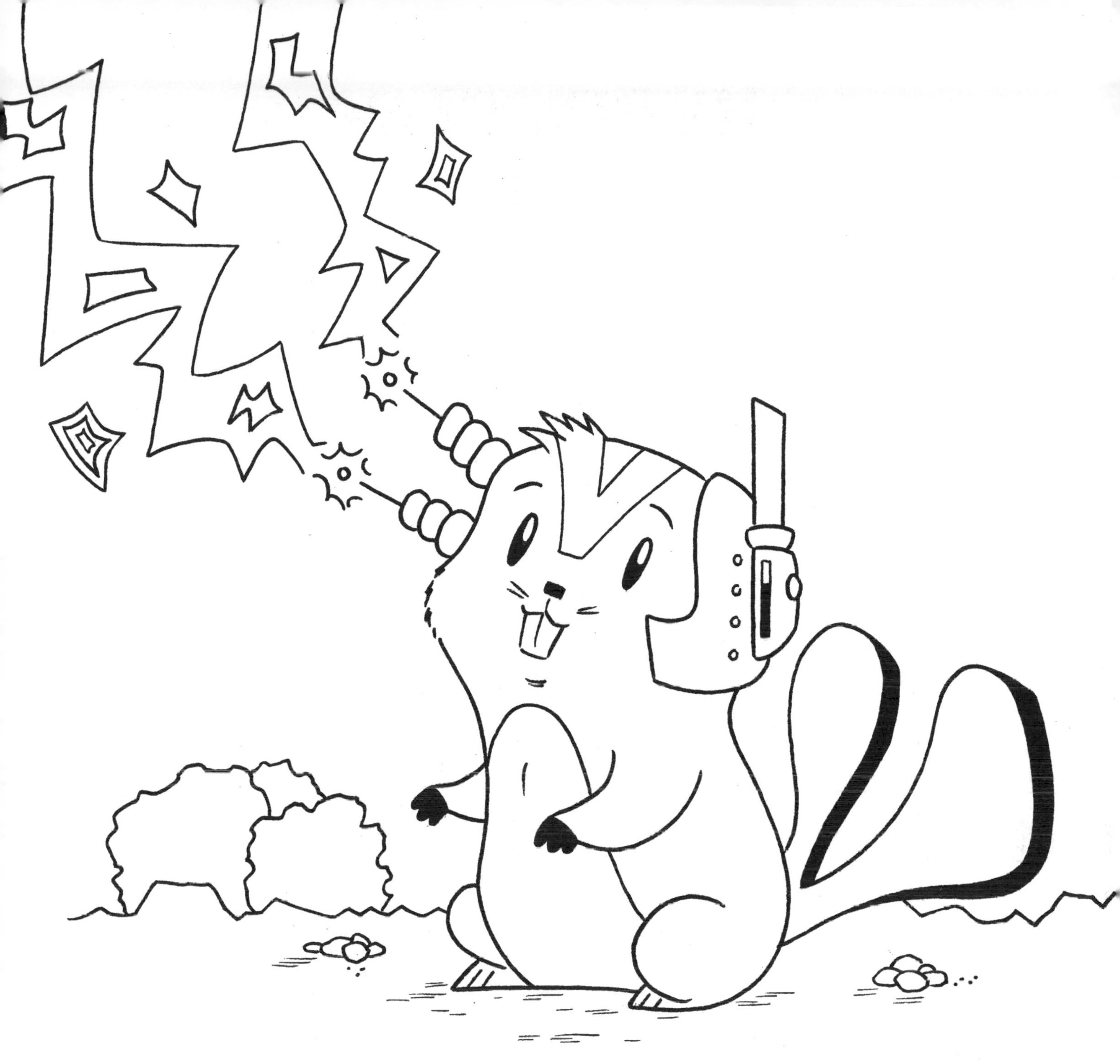

HERRA-CLAW

1

2

3

4

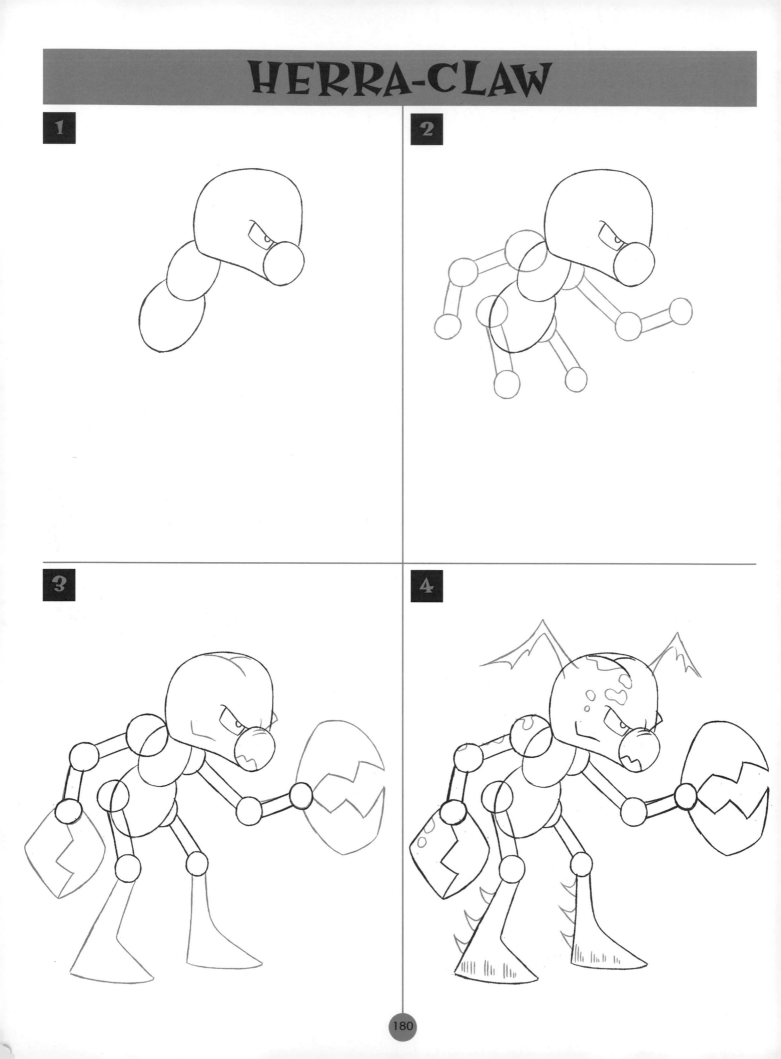

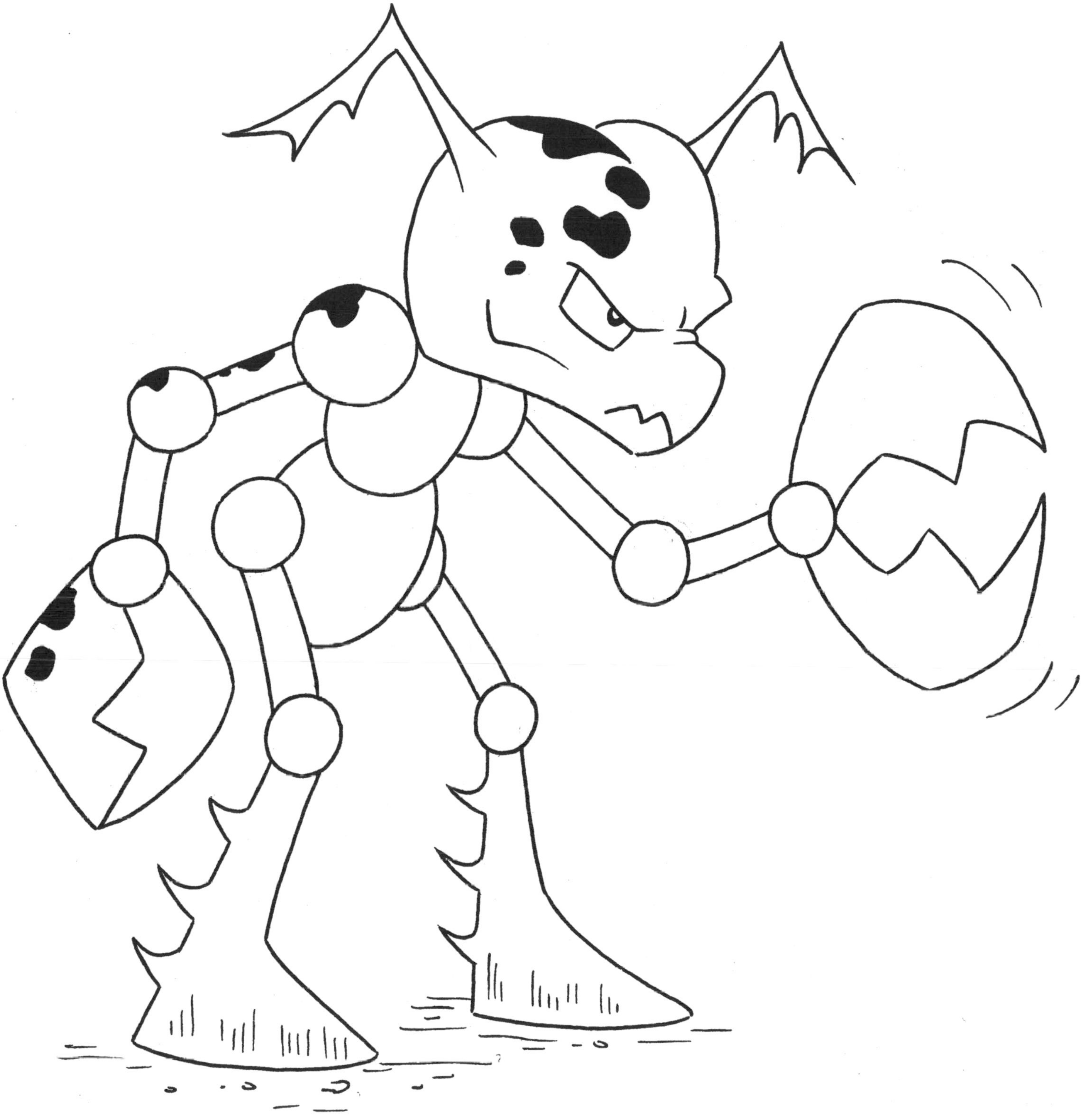

PUDGE AND TURTLOCK

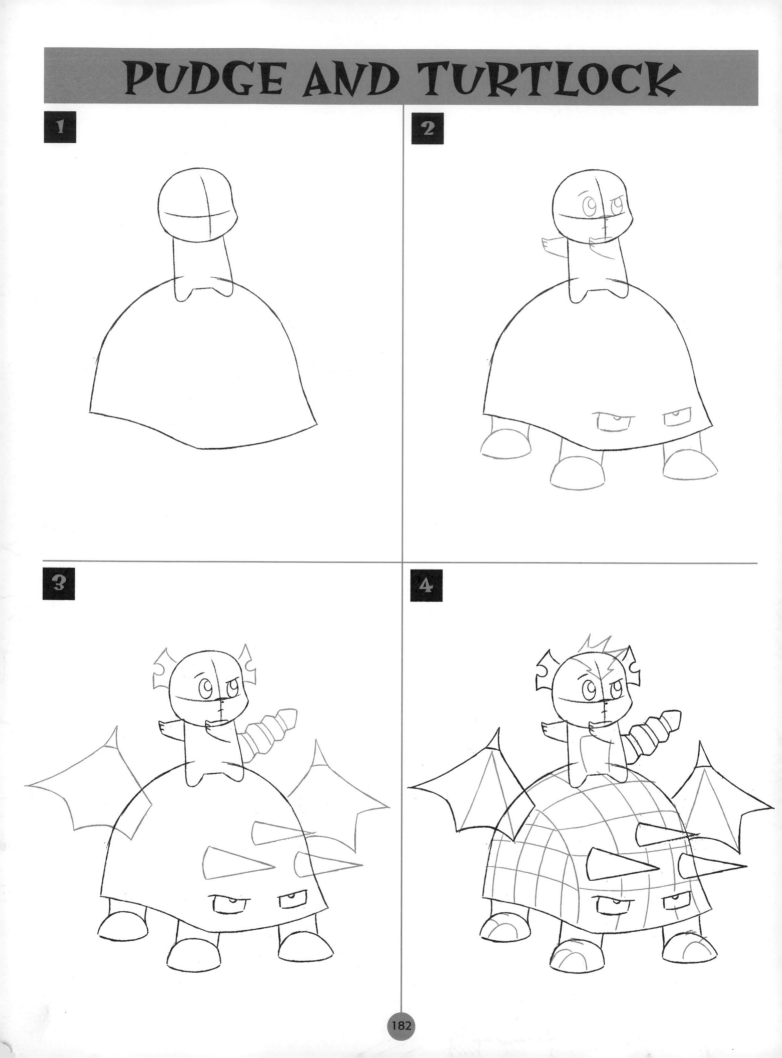

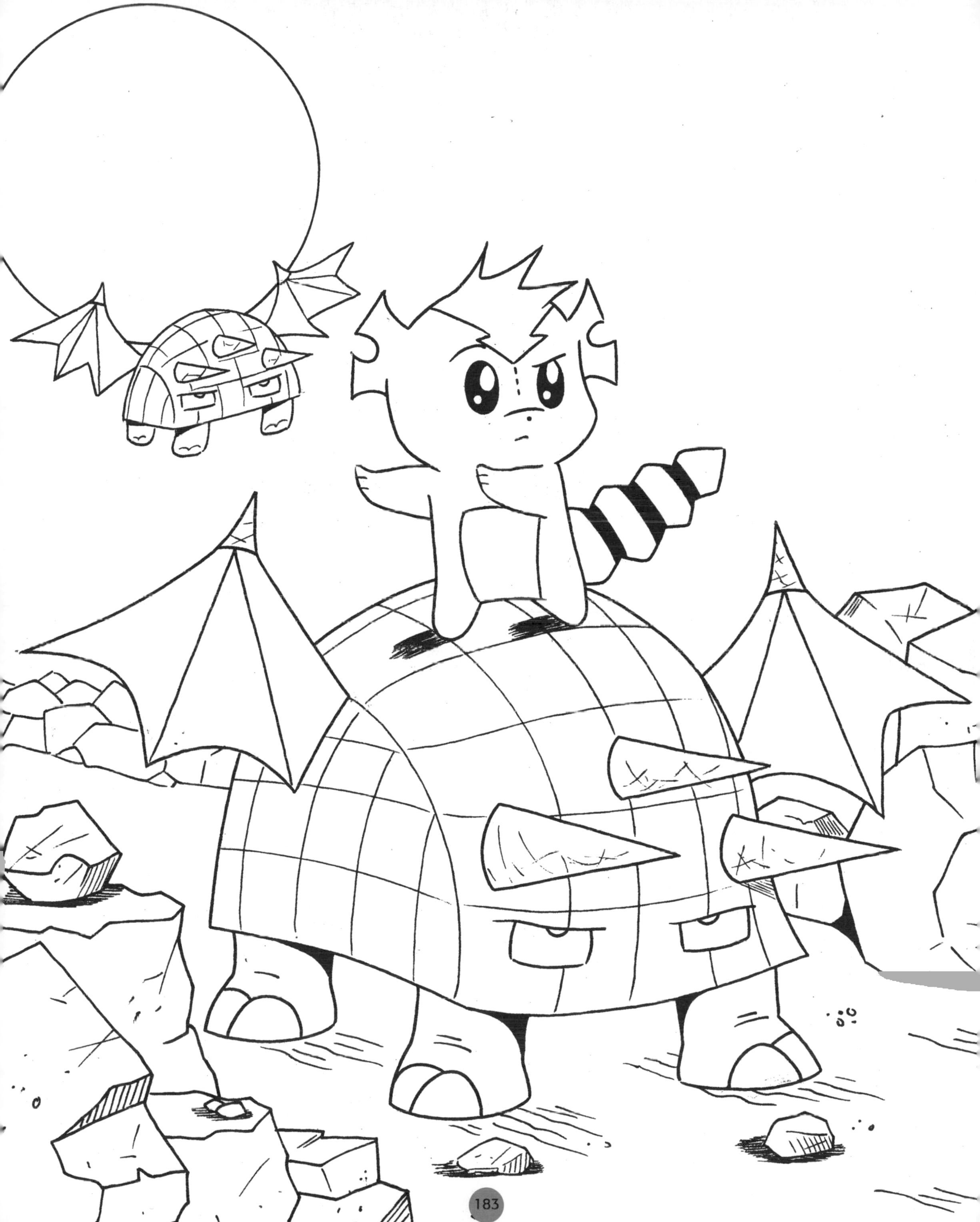

TIGAMECH

1

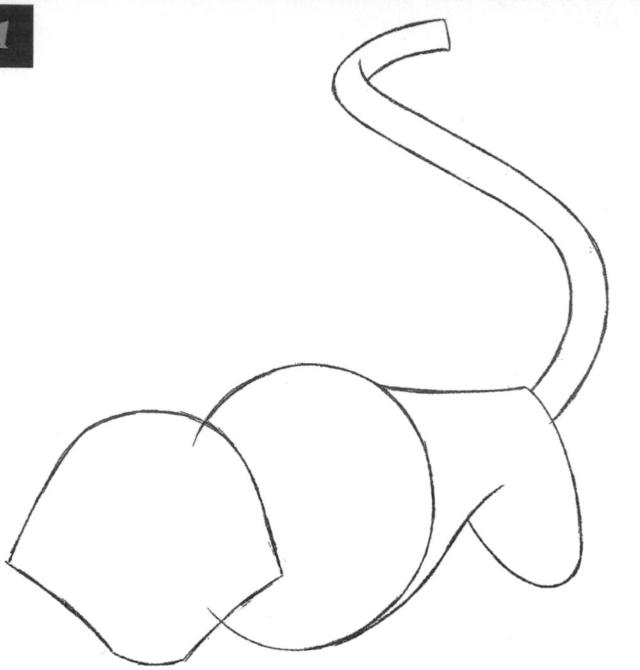

2

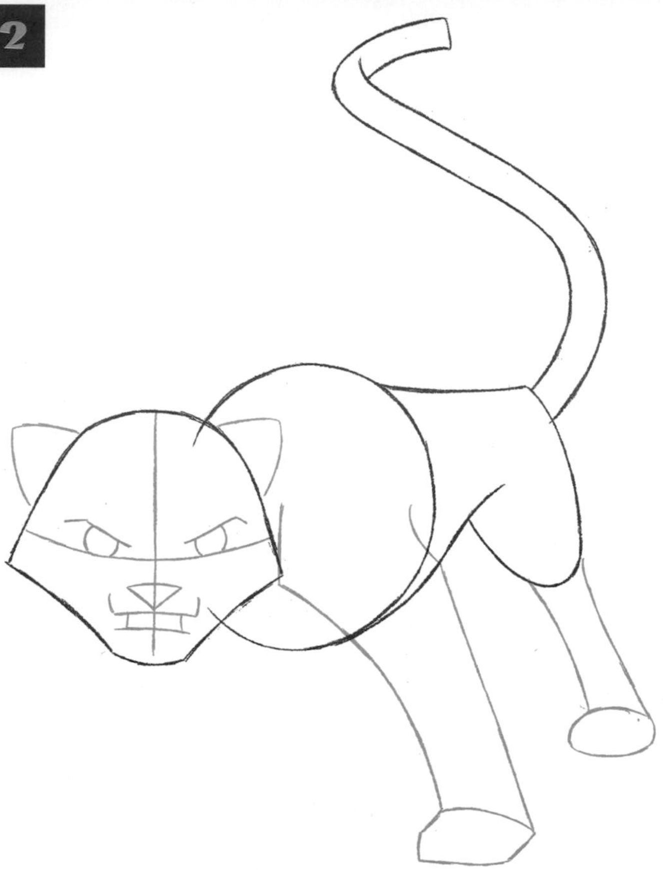

3

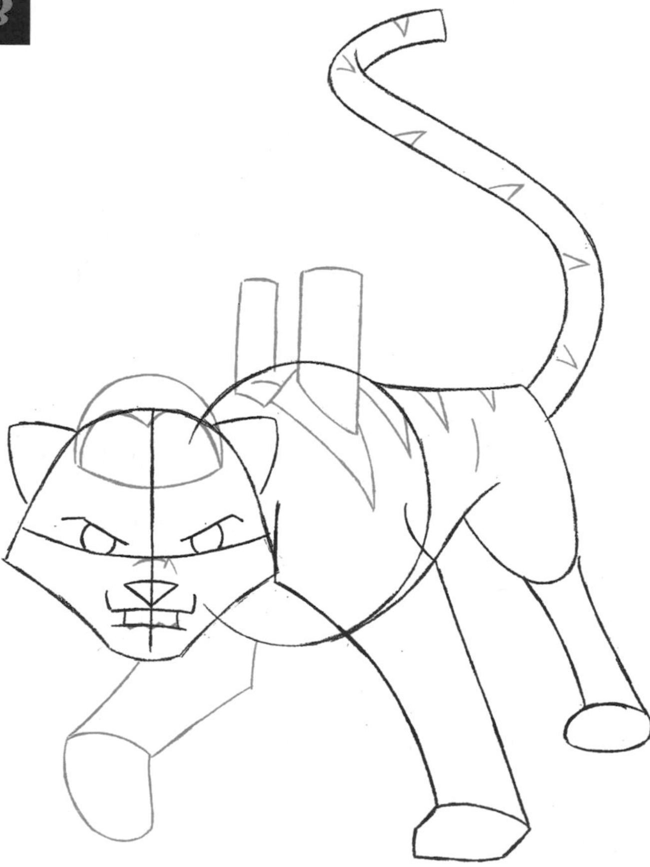

4

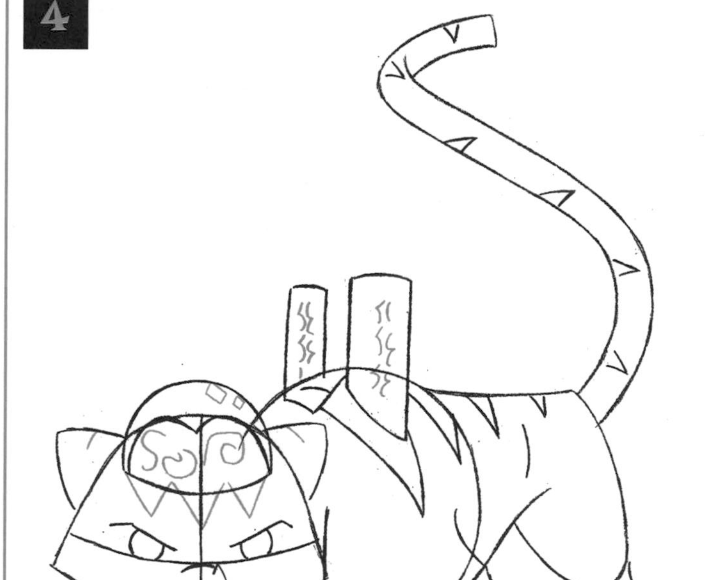

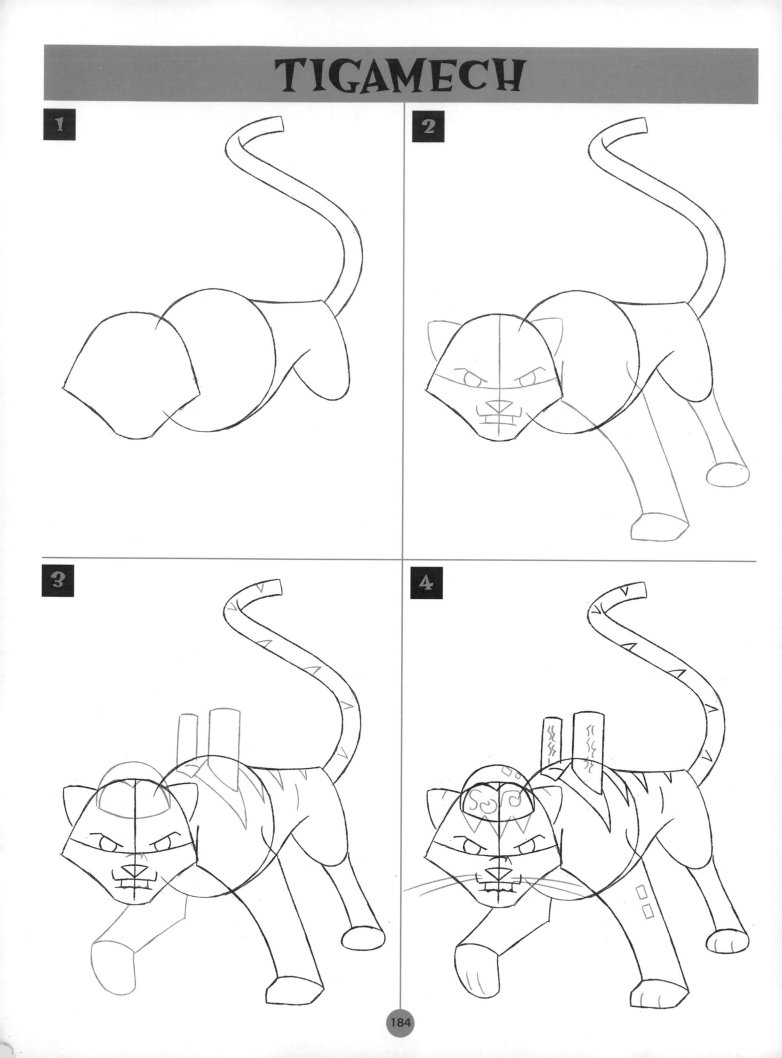

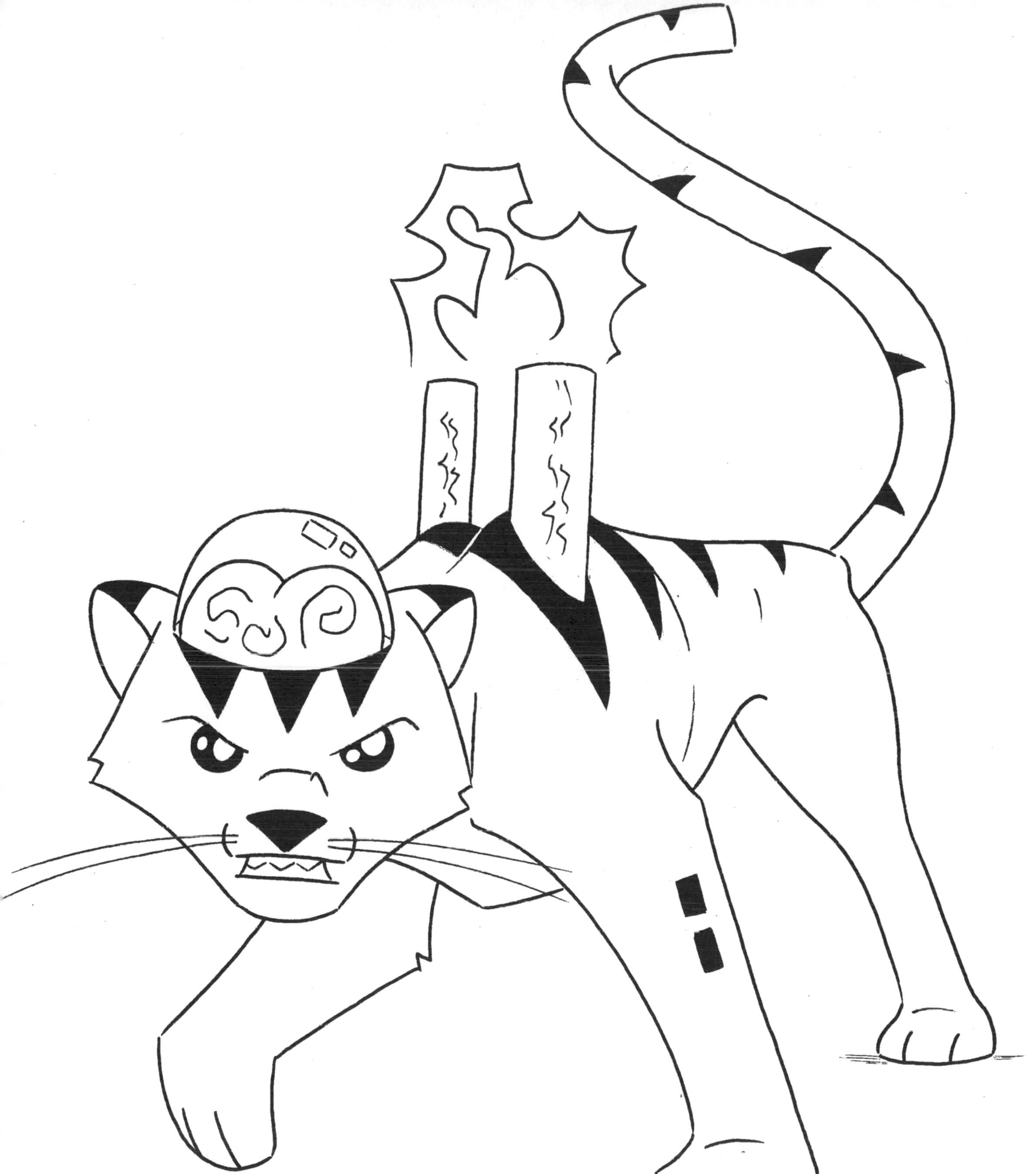

CORAFLAME

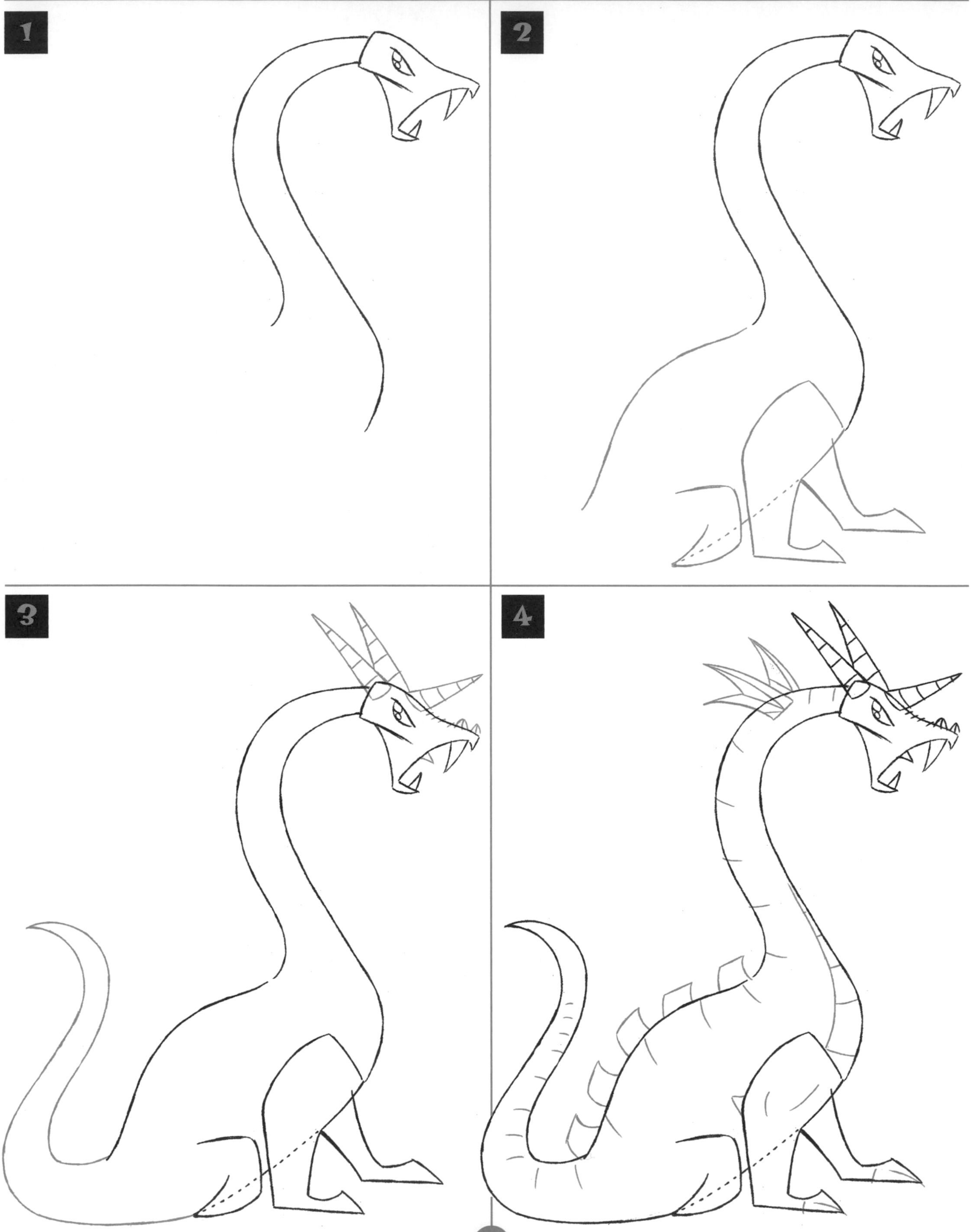
1
2
3
4

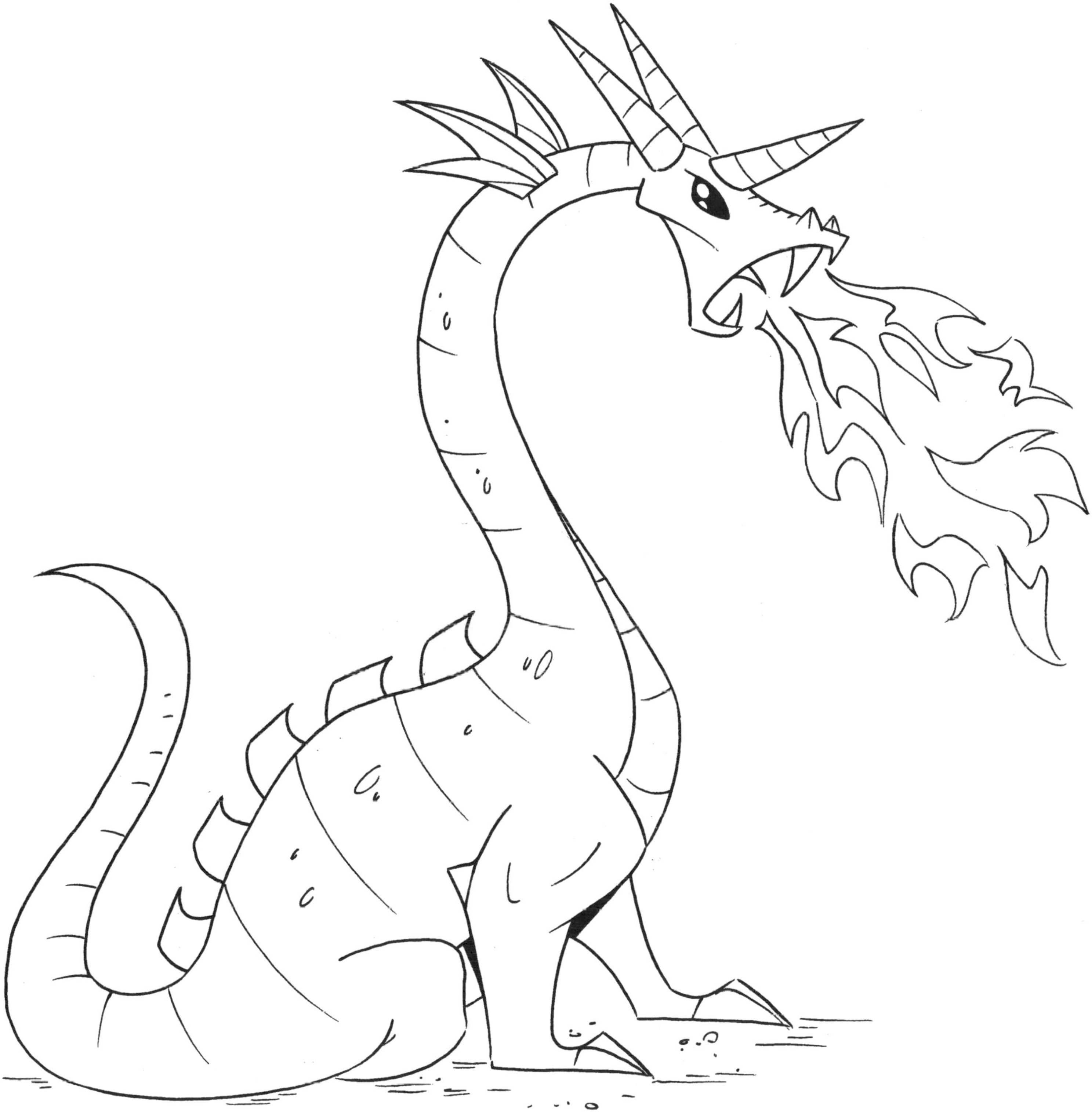

PUFF BUNNY

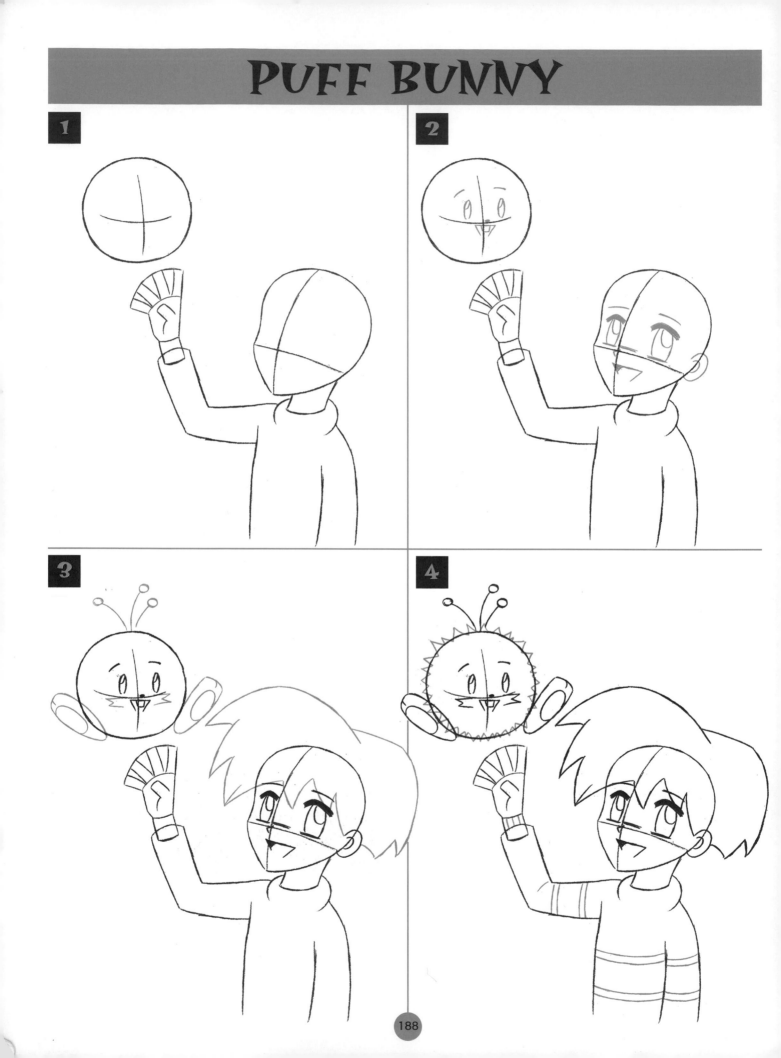

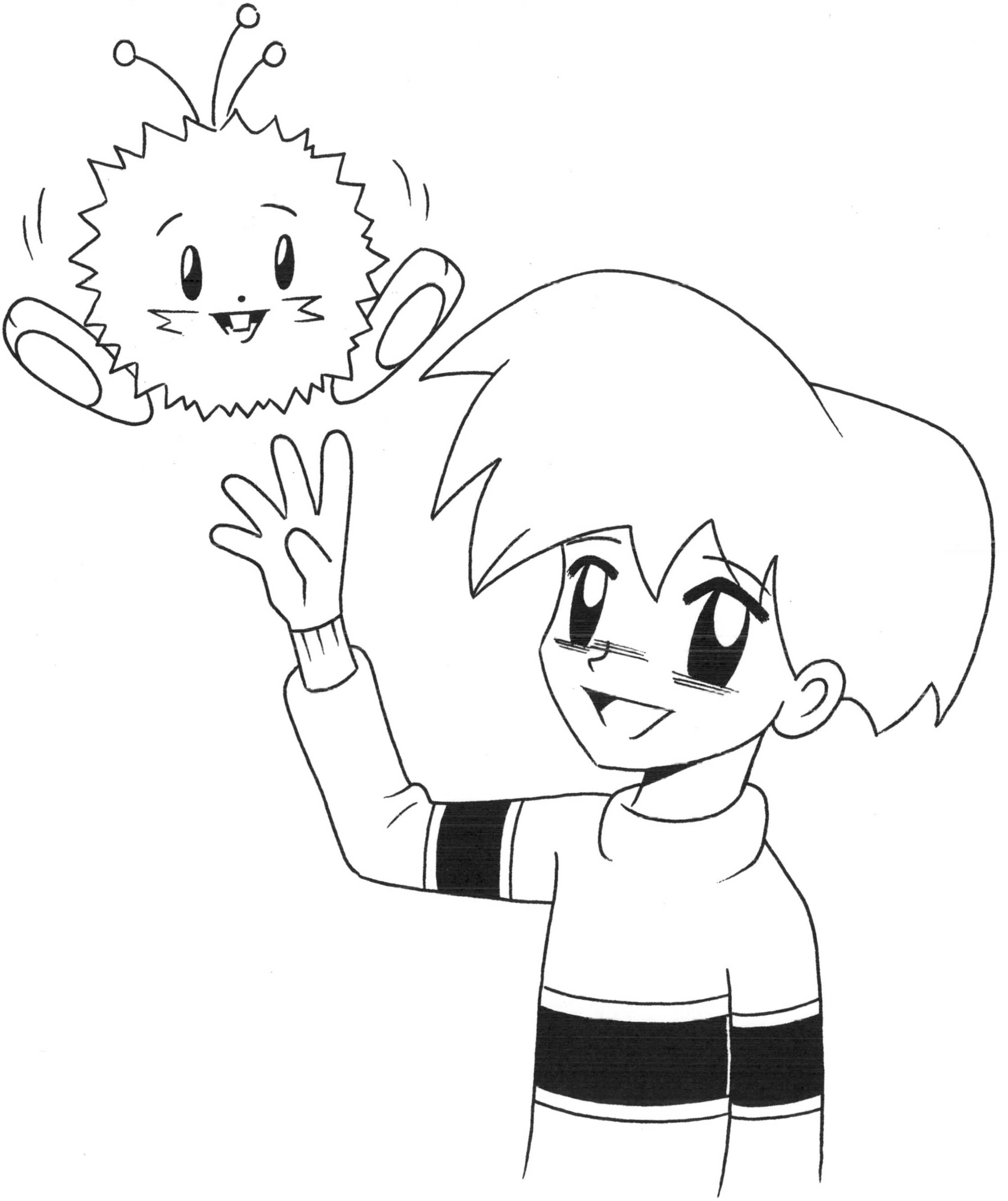

PIPTAR 1 AND PIPTAR 2

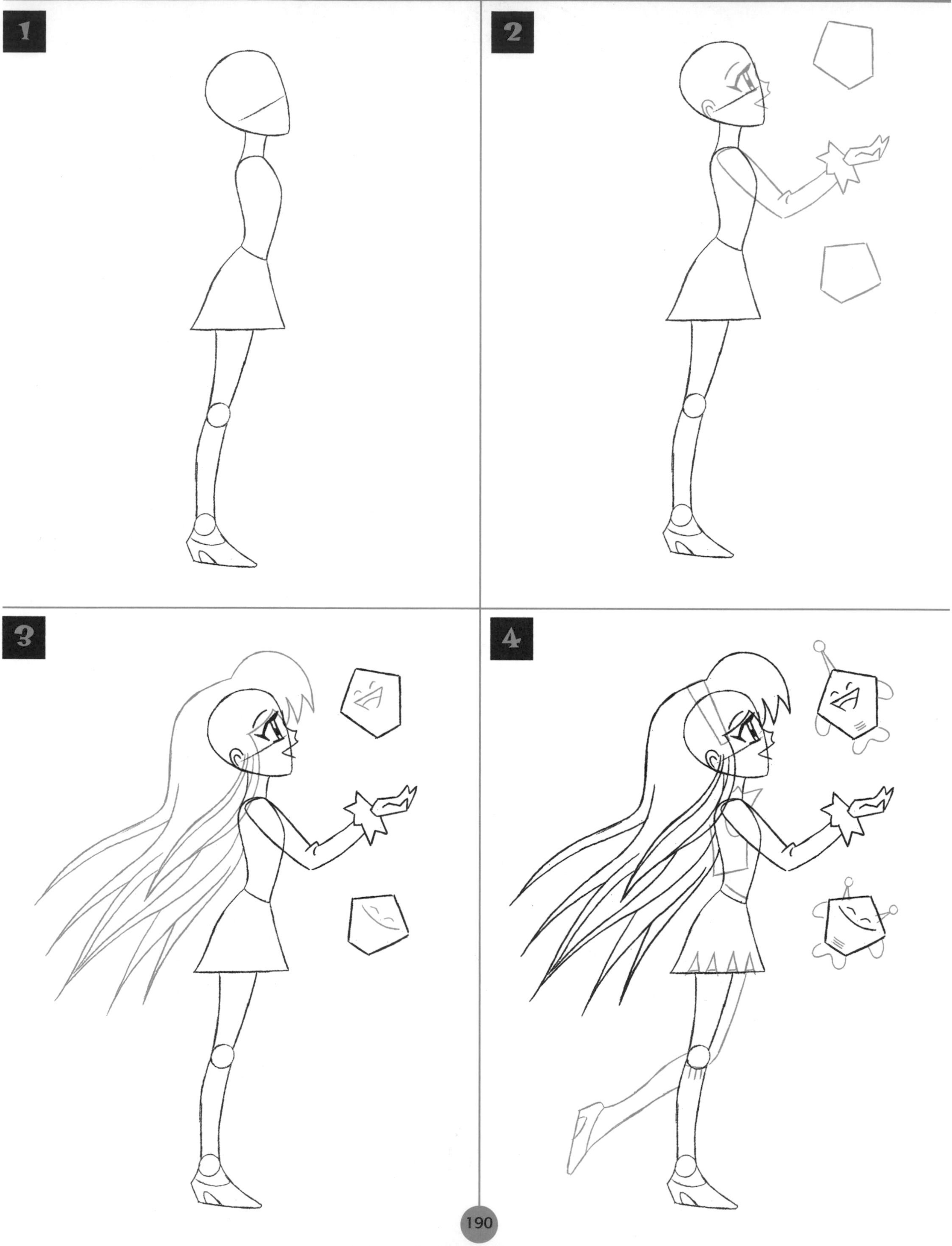
1
2
3
4

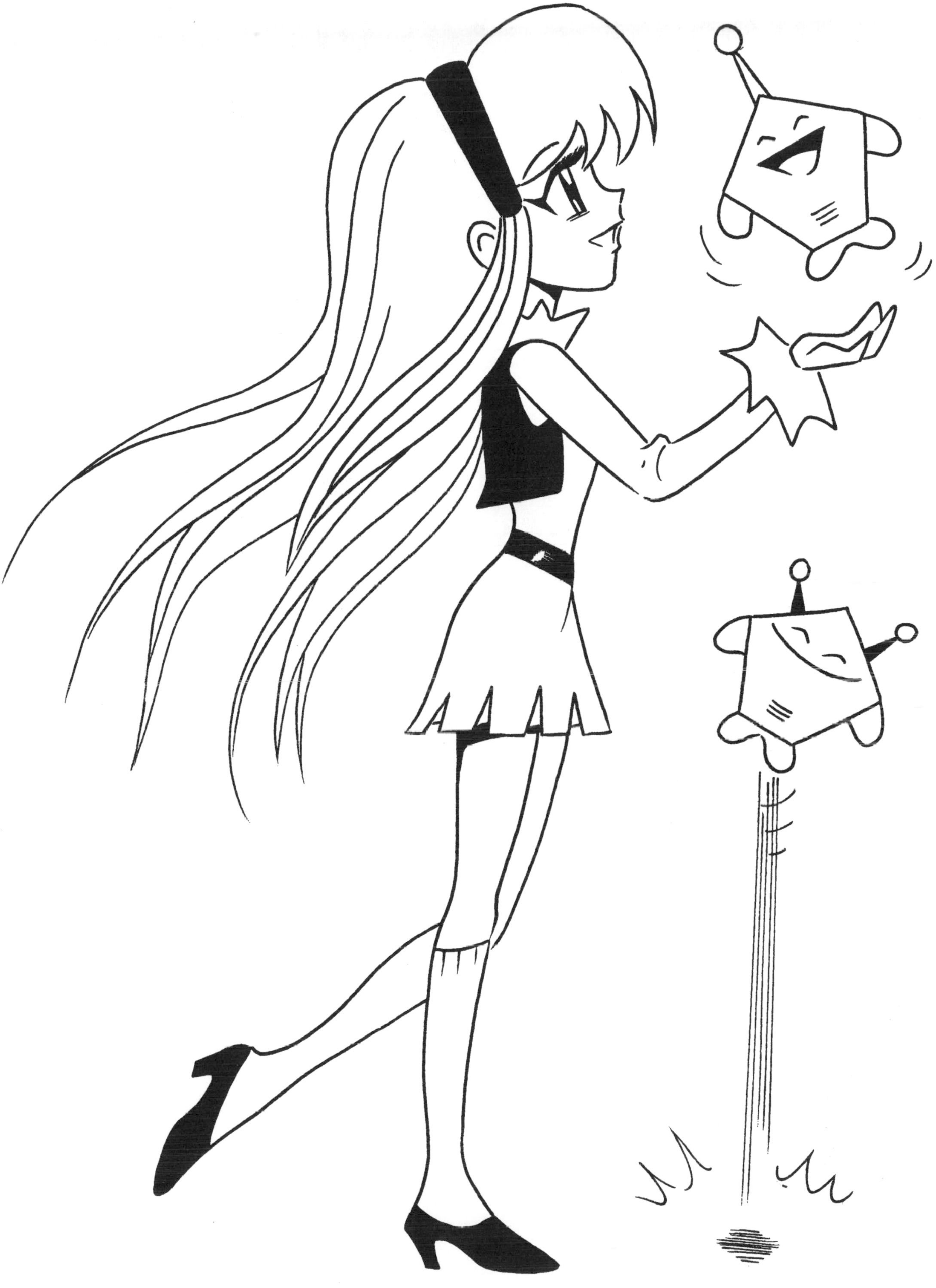

"Good-bye until . . ."